KILMICHAEL

Eve Morrison is an Irish historian specialising in the revolutionary period (1916–23) and its social and cultural memory. Both her doctoral research on the Bureau of Military History (Trinity College Dublin) and a postdoctoral fellowship on the Ernie O'Malley notebook interviews (University College Dublin) were funded by the Irish Research Council. From 2018 to 2021, she was Canon Murray Fellow in Irish History at St Catherine's College, University of Oxford.

KILMICHAEL

THE LIFE AND AFTERLIFE OF AN AMBUSH

Eve Morrison

IRISH ACADEMIC PRESS

First published in 2022 by
Irish Academic Press
10 George's Street
Newbridge
Co. Kildare
Ireland
www.iap.ie

© Eve Morrison, 2022

978 1 78855 145 8 (Paper)
978 1 78855 147 2 (Ebook)
978 1 78855 148 9 (PDF)

A CIP catalogue record for this book is
available from the British Library.

Typeset in Minion Pro 11/16 pt

Front cover image courtesy of the *Irish Examiner* Archive
Back cover image © Hemming Deposit, Box 19, ms CCC 536, QD.2.42,
Irish Papers. Reproduced by permission of the President and Fellows
of Corpus Christi College, Oxford
Cover design by riverdesignbooks.com

Irish Academic Press is a member of Publishing Ireland.

Contents

Acknowledgements

THIS BOOK TOOK A LONG time to research and write. Many individuals in Ireland, Britain, the USA and Canada have contributed their time, expertise, material and/or support.

Firstly, I am enormously grateful to Robin Whitaker, Peter Hart's executor. She went out of her way many times to help me source and access material, as did Peter's sister Susan and his late mother, Anne Hart. They were delightful company during my stay in St John's and, among other things, taught me how to pronounce 'Newfoundland' correctly.

Additionally, this book could not have been written without the exceptional generosity, in terms of knowledge and resources, of Fr John Chisholm, who died in 2014, and the family of Liam Deasy (the pre-Truce and Civil War West Cork IRA officer), especially his daughter, Kathleen McCaul, his nephew and namesake, the late Liam Deasy and his wife Norma. My friends Colum Cronin and Don Wood were inexhaustible wells of local knowledge and expertise about West Cork. I cannot thank them enough for their assistance and moral support over the years.

Other friends, relatives or associates of some of the people whose stories grace the pages of this book also contributed in one way or the other. I particularly thank James Baldwin, Alison Campbell, Liam Chambers, Helen Chisholm, Dave Crowley, Alan Guthrie, Brother John O'Driscoll, Marion O'Driscoll and Shelagh Putnam. Many others from or associated with County Cork were generous with their time and knowledge as well, especially Jim Barrett, Diarmuid Begley, Séan Crowley, Denis Coffey, the late Billy Good, J.J. Hurley, Jim Lane, Joe Lane, Tom Lyons, Mary Morgan, Jerry O'Callaghan and Gerry White.

I very much appreciate Charles Townshend, Clair Wills and Richard Grayson taking the time to read all or part of this manuscript. Many others also provided expertise and information: Joost Augusteijn, Andy Bielenberg, Bill Booth, Tim Bowman, Brigid Coady, Marie Coleman, Arlene Crampsie, Anne Dolan, John Dorney, Martin Dwan, John Fay, Mary Feehan, Orla Fitzpatrick, David Grant, Brian Hanley, Brian Hughes, Felix Larkin, Matt Lodder, Ian McBride, Conor McCabe, Anthony McIntyre, Ross McKibbin, David Monahan, Conor Mulvagh, John A. Murphy, Séan A. Murphy, Peter Murtagh, the late Donal Musgrave, Emmet O'Connor, the late Donncha Ó Dúlaing, Paul O'Higgins SC, John O'Beirne Ranelagh, Mary Staines, Carrie Twomey and Fr Stephen Verbest.

Much of this work was written during a three-year stint as Canon Murray Fellow of Irish History at the University of Oxford. I am very grateful to both the Faculty of History and to St Catherine's College.

Numerous archives and archivists helped to bring this book to fruition. Linda White and Paulette Noseworthy, from the Queen Elizabeth II Library in Memorial University of Newfoundland, could not have been more obliging. Lisa Dolan, Hugh Beckett, Noelle Grothier and the rest of the staff in the Military Archives, and Cecil Gordon (*née* Chemin), Senior Archivist/Director, Military Service (1916–23) Pensions Project were invariably helpful. So, too, were Kate Manning and her colleagues in the UCD Archives, who scanned material for me in exceptionally trying circumstances. I am also indebted to: Fr Pat Egan (Provincial Secretary and Archivist, Salesians of Don Bosco); Dan Breen and Dara McGrath (Cork Public Museum); Razib Chatterjee (RTÉ Television Archives); at the *Irish Examiner*, Anne Kearney (former Head of Library Services), Tim Ellard and Eddie Cassidy; Steven Skelton, Brian McGee and everyone at the Cork City & County Archives; Fr Brian O'Toole and Margaret Bluett (Kimmage Manor Archives); Clare Foley (Blackrock College Archives); Kevin Hughes, editor of *The Kerryman*; Shea Tomkins (*Ireland's Own*); Mike Lynch (Local History and Archives, Kerry Library) and Ferdia McCrann (Met Éireann). Pam McKenzie (Royal Aviation Museum of Western Canada) kindly sent me the Alexander Lewis letter.

In Britain, I am indebted to Cathryn Steele and Martin Maw (Oxford University Press), Debbie Ussher (Middle East Centre and Archive, St Antony's College), Jane Fish (Imperial War Museum (IWM) Sound and Video Archive), Jonathan Holt (Tank Museum), Peter Devitt (RAF Museum), Danielle Joyce and Katie Barrett (Cheltenham College Archives), and Ian Hook (Essex Regiment Museum, Chelmsford), as well as to the staff of the IWM, the British Library and The National Archives (Kew).

Conor Graham and, more recently, Wendy Logue, have each displayed remarkable patience and forbearance during this book's gestation. I am very grateful to them, and to Heidi Houlihan for her careful copy-editing of the text.

Finally, I am deeply indebted to my family, who have lived with me and this project for years. Juno Morrison Doyle, my daughter, translated Spanish and Italian newspaper reports for me and has been an excellent support generally. My heartfelt thanks also to Eunan O'Halpin, who has helped in too many ways to list. This book is dedicated to my mother, Barbara L. Morrison.

List of Abbreviations

1SD	1st Southern Division
AEPP	A.E. Percival Papers
ASC/QEII/MUN	Special Collections, Queen Elizabeth II Library, Memorial University
BEF	British Expeditionary Force
BICO	British and Irish Communist Organisation
BMH	Bureau of Military History
CAB	Cabinet Office
CC&CA	Cork City & County Archives
CEF	Cork Employers' Federation
CMC	Condensed Milk Company
CO	Colonial Office
CP	Chisholm Papers/Recordings
CPA	Cork Progressive Association
C/S	Chief of Staff
DAH	Disease of the action of the heart
DE	Dáil Éireann
deV	Éamon de Valera Papers
DIB	*Dictionary of Irish Biography*
DOIR	*Dead of the Irish Revolution*
DRI	Digital Repository of Ireland
EOMNbks	Ernie O'Malley Notebooks
FOD	Florence O'Donoghue papers

FMB	Frances Mary Blake
GAA	Gaelic Athletic Association
GHQ	General Headquarters
HC	House of Commons
HO	Home Office
HWP	Henry Wilson Papers
IEF	Indian Expeditionary Force
I/O	Intelligence Officer
IPP	Irish Parliamentary Party
IRACD	Irish Republican Army (from captured documents only)
ITGWU	Irish Transport and General Workers' Union
IWM	Imperial War Museum
JRWGP	JRW Goulden Papers
LD	Liam Deasy Papers
LNER	London and North Eastern Railway
MAI	Military Archives of Ireland
MEF	Mediterranean Expeditionary Force
MP	Mulcahy Papers
MSP	Military Service Pension
MSPC	Military Service Pensions Collection
NAI	National Archives of Ireland
NCO	Non-Commissioned Officer
NLI	National Library of Ireland
O/C	Officer Commanding
OIRA	Old IRA
OIRAMAC	Old IRA Men's Association (Cork County)
OTC	Officer Training Corps
PD	People's Democracy

PH	Peter Hart
PWIC	Peace with Ireland Council
RAF	Royal Air Force
RFC	Royal Flying Corps
RIC	Royal Irish Constabulary
RM	Richard Mulcahy Papers
RMA	Royal Military Academy
RORI	Record of the Rebellion in Ireland
RTO	Railway Transport Officer
SP	Strickland Papers
SR	Special Reserve
TBMJ	*The British Medical Journal*
TCDM	Trinity College Dublin Manuscripts & Archives
TF	Territorial Force
TLSAC	Thameside Local Studies and Archives Centre
TNAUK	The National Archives United Kingdom (Kew)
UCDA	University College Dublin Archives
UMacE	Uinseann MacEoin Interviews
WS	Witness Statement

Introduction

ON 28 NOVEMBER 1920, A few miles outside Macroom, County Cork, an Irish Republican Army (IRA) flying column attacked an eighteen-strong patrol of Auxiliary police, killing sixteen of them outright. One was wounded but survived. Another managed to escape but was later captured and executed. Three IRA Volunteers – Michael McCarthy, Jim O'Sullivan and Patrick Deasy – were also killed or mortally wounded.[1] At the July 1921 Truce ending the Irish War of Independence (1919–21), the Kilmichael ambush still represented the greatest loss of life inflicted by the IRA on Crown Forces in a single instance during the conflict, although Dromkeen in Limerick (3 February 1921), and the Headford Junction and Rathmore ambushes in Kerry (21 March and 4 May 1921) came close.

The ambush instantly became a rhetorical hook for wider polemics surrounding the Irish independence struggle. In its immediate aftermath, much of the commentary revolved around whether the attack was a legitimate act of war or an atrocity. Individuals and groupings on both sides, British and Irish, disputed the circumstances in which both the Auxiliaries and Volunteers had died. Dublin Castle issued graphic and overstated press releases alleging that the IRA had tricked the Auxiliaries and massacred wounded men. They maintained that the bodies were mutilated by insurgents kitted out in steel helmets and British military uniforms. Counter-assertions circulated that the Auxiliaries were put to death in retaliation for attempting some sort of feigned or 'false' surrender.

Several different accounts of what occurred emerged in the months and years after the ambush. What became the best-known version appeared in *Guerilla Days in Ireland*, the 1949 memoir of Tom Barry, the IRA commander who led the ambush.[2] The second Kilmichael controversy, which arose in the 1970s, was sparked by the publication of a rival account in Liam Deasy's *Towards Ireland Free*, a history of the 3rd Cork Brigade (West Cork).[3] This dispute also revolved around the events of the ambush, particularly the circumstances in which the three IRA dead were fatally wounded or killed. Deasy was Barry's one-time commanding officer and brother of one the Kilmichael fatalities. Barry's vituperative attack on Deasy's book exposed long-standing fault lines between West Cork IRA veterans.

The third rendition of the Kilmichael debate followed the publication of the late Peter Hart's *The IRA and Its Enemies: Violence and Community in Cork 1916–1923* in 1998.[4] He died in July 2010 at the age of just forty-six, but the 'Hart debate' remains one of the bitterest controversies in Irish history. He argued that Barry's *Guerilla Days* Kilmichael narrative was not an honest account of what had occurred, and that the April 1922 killings of thirteen Protestants in the Bandon valley – an even more contentious event – had been motivated by sectarianism. His conclusions unleashed a ferocious, unprecedented, conspiracy-laden deluge of vitriolic disputation that continues to this day. This round of the Kilmichael debate was informed by wider historical and political arguments over the status of traditional nationalist narratives in Irish history writing, especially that produced by academic historians.

The public dispute over Hart's work very quickly morphed into a clash over the rights and wrongs of the Irish independence struggle. Hart (and other academic historians) were accused of 'besmirching' Ireland's national heroes and of promoting false narratives of the revolutionary period (1916–23) in order to undermine contemporary republicanism and traditional Irish nationalism. This offered anti-republican iconoclasts an opportunity to attack their enemies, and they leapt to Hart's defence. Once his work became a foil for both sides in Ireland's ongoing culture war over 'revisionism', research into Kilmichael, the actual historical event, virtually stopped.

The arguments of Hart's detractors focused on discrediting both Hart himself and any evidence documenting other versions of the ambush that did not support Barry's version of events. Meda Ryan (Barry's first biographer), Brian P. Murphy and others argued that a captured IRA report on the ambush (hereafter 'the captured report') cited by Hart was forged. Because he anonymised his interviews, there were further accusations that Hart fabricated some of them in order to blacken Barry's reputation.[5] The most notorious allegation of all was that he claimed to have interviewed one ambush veteran, Ned Young, several days after he died.[6] This assertion is widely circulated to this day, despite the fact that Hart's main critics have been aware for more than a decade that his interview dates for Young predate the man's death by over a year.[7] Moreover, in 2012, I identified all but one of Hart's Kilmichael interviewees, and named the last one, Willie Chambers (the 'unarmed scout'), in 2017.[8] Predictably, Hart's detractors are now mine.[9] I have also identified and located all the recorded interviews Hart cited, although I was not given access to all of them.

Researching Kilmichael has been a bizarre experience. I met several exceptional people in Cork and elsewhere, and made some fast friends. I was also, on one occasion, threatened (verbally), actively misled more than once, shouted at in the street by strangers, and shadowed when visiting the ambush site. One individual I spoke to asked if I was 'wearing a wire'.

If the modern Kilmichael debate was really about the evidence, it would have ended long ago. An important part of the reason it remains so intractable is because too many people are either unwilling to come forward or seem to want the allegations against Hart to be true. Brendan O'Leary, the respected political scientist, evidently accepts them, as do Tim Pat Coogan and many others.[10] In 2015 the Fianna Fáil Senator Mark Daly denounced *The IRA and Its Enemies* in Seanad Éireann as a 'tissue of lies and a book of fraud' and called on Hart (who had died five years earlier) to 'apologise to the families of those involved in the Kilmichael ambush for making up what has now been revealed to have been an absolute falsehood'.[11]

METHODOLOGY

The release of new material relating to the independence struggle over the last two decades has greatly facilitated taking new approaches and asking different questions about Ireland's revolutionary decade. The subject of my

PhD, which I began in 2003, was the newly available Bureau of Military History (BMH) archive. I read all 1,773 witness statements and hundreds of administrative files relating to the project. The Department of Defence's ongoing, staggered release of Military Service Pension (MSP) records relating to radical nationalist veterans, which began in 2014, has added thousands of new participant accounts to the mix. The idea that a single, uncontested nationalist tradition exists to either uphold or dismantle is much less tenable today than it was when only a small selection of published memoirs, fighting stories and interviews with veterans were available.

The approach taken in this book has been influenced by a range of historiographical and methodological approaches and perspectives. In terms of Irish history, in addition to the archival rigour instilled in me by David Fitzpatrick, Louis Cullen and others, Gearóid Ó Tuathaigh's critique of the 'revisionist' debate provided the clearest route for moving beyond its narrow, overly insular parameters. Guy Beiner's innovative application of oral history methodology to folklore sources, and his explorations of social memory, provided another model.[12] Both Beiner and Ó Tuathaigh identified methodological conservatism rather than political ideology as the main issue to be tackled in Irish historiography.

Ó Tuathaigh argued that historians should try to actually pin down exactly what historical consciousness consisted of through studying mentalité, familiarising themselves with critical theory, and by paying 'careful attention to a wide range of sources and texts of a kind that many Irish historians were not accustomed to handling'.[13] He reprimanded both sides of the revisionist debate for dealing too much in unsupported generalisations about what precisely Irish people understood or wanted from their past: 'it is hard to know on what evidence [Brendan] Bradshaw (with relief) and [Roy] Foster (with resignation or regret) conclude that among the plain people of Ireland "the old pieties have it their own way" or that the temptation to taste the treacherous apple of revisionism is proudly scorned!'[14]

Almost all the contemporary evidence for Kilmichael was either generated by the British authorities or relates to the Auxiliaries. Much of what is known about the flying column's perspective on the ambush, by contrast, comes from popular histories and the memoirs and heavily mediated testimony of IRA participants collected many years later. Primary sources relating to the IRA's military campaign exist, but their chronological spread is uneven. Far more material survives for the last six months of the War of Independence, the Truce and the Civil War than for the pre-1921 period. The text of the captured report on Kilmichael survives because it was reproduced in the British military's internal assessments of the 1920–1 campaign.

The work of Guy Beiner, Cormac Ó Gráda, Alistair Thomson, Alessandro Portelli, Luisa Passerini and Paul Thompson all emphasises the 'orality' of much 'written' source material and the distinctive characteristics of oral history sources. Viewed through these lenses, there was more to analysing IRA veterans' testimonies than a straightforward extraction of detail.[15] Personal memories were not static imprints but narratives that were continually renegotiated throughout the lives of those remembering.[16] Participant accounts of Kilmichael were multi-layered, dynamic sources that could be interrogated from a number of different perspectives. They contained information about the past events under discussion, as well as the intervening years and the present in which the stories were told.

Alistair Thomson's classic oral history of the Australian experience of the Great War, *Anzac Memories: Living with the Legend*, published four years before *The IRA and Its Enemies*, provided a pertinent example of how complex war veterans' relationships to the past could be. He employed 'popular memory' theory to explore how 'personal identities are interwoven with national identities, individual memories intersect with public legends'.[17] The war memories of the Australian Great War veterans he interviewed were far less heroic or inspirational than the Anzac legend. Yet romantic narratives of the war could still provide them with a 'safe refuge'.[18] Uncomfortable memories were often silenced or repressed. Painful war stories and memories were discouraged at veterans' reunions in favour of yarns about solidarity and 'good times'.[19]

It was commonplace, in fact, for public or 'official' histories of wars and independence struggles to rely on simplistic 'good versus evil, right versus wrong, justice versus injustice' narratives, which were at odds with the more complex realities that live on in the memories of combatants.[20] From this perspective, it seemed perfectly plausible that the various, conflicting Kilmichael accounts might be an example of how unpalatable and incompatible the cold reality of war can become when put in the service of any nation's foundation myths. Clearly, it was necessary to bypass the polemic and focus on the ambush's 'vernacular historiography'.[21] Veterans' accounts of Kilmichael were shaped by the wider patterns of remembrance and the circumstances in which information about the revolutionary period was imparted. The various conflicting versions and disputes over what happened, and the wider arenas in which the ambush was remembered and commemorated, needed close attention.

Establishing what actually occurred during the ambush (as far as that is possible) is important too. Oral historians engaging with multiple accounts of violent conflict expect disparities, even across those given by the same person. Soldiers and veterans giving different versions of the same events, depending on the context, is not unusual.[22] I decided to contextualise and reassess all of the evidence relating to Kilmichael: primary sources, retrospective testimony, folklore and oral history.

Traditionalists still insist that before devious Dublin priests, duplicitous academics and anti-republican journalists involved themselves for their own nefarious purposes, Barry's 1949 account was almost universally accepted. In fact, the social memory of Kilmichael is diverse, rich and contradictory, and it always has been. Barry wrote or endorsed three different Kilmichael accounts between 1932 and 1941. The version in *Guerilla Days* was his fourth. Moreover, not only did Barry's story change over time, but a different version of Kilmichael penned by Flor Crowley, a respected local West Cork historian, had already been published when Barry's book appeared. Crowley's account, as we shall see, aligned more closely with the recollections of most of the Kilmichael veterans who went on record.

My first three chapters discuss the wider historical context and the aftermath of the ambush. They cover finding the bodies, criminal injuries awards, efforts by the authorities to identify those involved, the initial press coverage and the immediate political impact of the ambush. The revolutionary careers and post-revolutionary lives of Tom Barry and Liam Deasy are the subject of Chapter Four. The next chapter concentrates on ambush participation and participants, as well as various methodological issues which arise when analysing and using personal testimony and oral history sources. Chapter Six examines Kilmichael's *longue durée*, tracking the various popular historical accounts, memoirs, social memory and folklore relating to the ambush up to 1980, and discusses Barry's and Deasy's rival accounts of the 3rd Cork Brigade's activities during the War of Independence. Chapter Seven gives a detailed analysis of Kilmichael, which draws on all the sources but is derived mainly from the private or confidential accounts of ambush veterans. The reason this ambush reconstruction precedes the chapter discussing the modern debate is because an understanding of what most IRA participants actually said brings into clearer focus the sheer weight of distortion clogging virtually every aspect of the disputes over Peter Hart's work. Themes discussed in the final two chapters include the impact of the Northern 'Troubles' on the historiography, public history and commemoration of Kilmichael, the various manifestations of 'revisionism' and 'anti-revisionism' in the 1970s and 1980s, Hart's research and the contemporary debate generally.

The availability of new or previously inaccessible material has made writing this book easier. Fr John Chisholm entrusted to me his recorded interviews with West Cork veterans and other relevant material. These are now with Trinity College Dublin's Manuscript Department. After his death in July 2010, Hart's extensive papers were donated to the Queen Elizabeth II Library of the Memorial University of Newfoundland. They have been available for consultation since April 2016. MSP records also contain important new information about Kilmichael.

My ambition to assess *all* the relevant sources could not be realised. Some of Kilmichael veteran Jack O'Sullivan's recorded testimony is currently inaccessible. He was interviewed on at least five occasions over the course of his life. The interviews conducted by Fr Chisholm, Donncha Ó Dúlaing and Brendan Vaughan are in the public domain. Further interviews (by O'Sullivan's sons) are not, although Hart's notes from one of these are in his papers.[23] Meda Ryan declined my request to consult her interviews or to be interviewed herself. Her 2003 biography of Barry relies extensively on a cache of Barry's papers in the possession of David Willis, but he refused me access to them.[24] Dr Brian P. Murphy declined to be interviewed. This is unfortunate. All would add further nuance and complexity to historical understanding of Kilmichael. It is unlikely, however, that any evidence would make it easier to establish with absolute certainty what transpired on that lonely stretch of the Macroom to Dunmanway road.

Finally, a word about my own perspective seems appropriate, particularly as historians are often accused of either refusing to acknowledge their own biases or at least not being sufficiently aware of how their predispositions and interests influence what they write. So, before going any further, here are mine as I understand them. While the rights and wrongs of what happened at Kilmichael are worth debating, my primary interest is in what happened during the ambush, its political and military impact, who fought in it, what those who survived said about it later, and how Kilmichael was commemorated and remembered. I am old-fashioned enough to believe that historians should still be concerned with establishing, as far as it is possible, a factually accurate record of the past events they research. They should also aspire to be as fair-minded and even-handed as they can be to all the historical actors under discussion, even if total objectivity is an unrealisable goal. The point is, surely, to understand why individuals or groups came to their beliefs and actions. Furiously defending one side or the other in life is, at times, an absolute necessity. In history, it tends to obscure rather than clarify. Energy spent in acrimonious disputes over the past is more productively applied, to paraphrase Mother Jones, in fighting for the living.

That said, not all historical debates lend themselves easily to neutrality, and Kilmichael is one of them. Sometimes the evidence really does justify taking a firm line. If parts of this book come across to some readers as overly reflective of my frustration with aspects of the modern debate, others may be of the view that I have not been nearly critical enough. I do have several biases, which I not only freely admit to but also have no intention of giving up. I consider the revisionist/anti-revisionist binary to be a profoundly unhelpful and largely meaningless division. I am exceptionally biased against *ad hominem* attacks, unfounded conspiracy theories and individuals who seem primarily interested in discrediting people rather than in getting to the truth (as far as it is ascertainable). I see no point in engaging with those who hide behind pseudonyms and read political predispositions into every line of their opponents' work but keep schtum about or deny their own affiliations, or those who criticise other historians according to standards that they apply selectively and do not observe themselves.

Moral and political lessons can certainly be drawn about Ireland's various conflicts between 1916 and 1923. Assessing the extent to which Kilmichael's brutal *dénouement* can be justified or condemned according to the rules of war in operation at the time is a useful exercise. In my opinion, however – and this does reflect my world view – if blame is to be apportioned for the violence meted out by all sides it lies ultimately, as one military historian put it, with 'those who make wars, not with those who fight them'.[25]

1

Kilmichael in Context

THE RADICAL NATIONALIST REVOLT AGAINST British rule in Ireland, which commenced during the Great War and burgeoned into a full-blown insurgency after the Armistice, was rooted in a pre-war home rule crisis. The 'Irish Question' bedevilled British and Irish politics throughout the nineteenth century, and between 1912 and 1914 brought both islands to the brink of civil war. After the constitutional crisis over the 1909 'People's Budget' and the passing of the Parliament Act in 1911, the House of Lords no longer had the power to veto home rule legislation permanently. This engendered a wider crisis in Ireland. Ulster Unionists and their Conservative allies resorted to brinkmanship and extra-parliamentary agitation to prevent a measure which would make Irish Protestants a minority in an overwhelmingly Catholic polity and, they feared, weaken the very Empire.[1] Thousands of anti-home rule monster meetings and rallies, petitions and canvassing across Britain and Ireland culminated in the September 1912 mass signing of the Ulster Covenant and, in January 1913, the creation of the paramilitary Ulster Volunteer Force (UVF).[2] Radical nationalists responded by founding the Irish Volunteers on 25 November 1913, as a pro-home rule militia.

At the forefront of unionist resistance was Edward Carson, MP for Trinity College and leader of the Irish Unionists in parliament, and James Craig, a Unionist MP for East Down.[3] Although facing what was effectively a threatened *coup d'état*, Herbert Asquith, the prime minister, made no move against them. Even more ominously, when British officers stationed at the Curragh Camp in Kildare let it be known in March 1914 that they would resign rather than move against Ulster, the government backed down once more.[4] A month later, loyalists landed 25,000 German guns and three million rounds of ammunition at Larne, County Antrim.[5]

The probable slide into armed confrontation over Ulster was temporarily halted by the outbreak of the Great War in August 1914.[6] John Redmond, leader of the Irish Parliamentary Party (IPP), had secured control of the Irish Volunteers and retained the support of the overwhelming majority of them after his pledge to support the British war effort in exchange for home rule legislation fomented a split in September.[7] But the government's decision to suspend the final passage of home rule into law until the cessation of hostilities weakened the IPP's position, particularly as the war dragged on. In April 1916, a minority of the Irish Volunteers who had broken from Redmond staged the Easter Rising.[8] The executions and mass arrests that followed alienated nationalist Ireland. IPP morale suffered a further devastating blow in July when, despite their party's efforts in a new round of negotiations, it was announced that six Ulster counties were to be excluded from the home rule settlement.[9]

Meanwhile, all those interned after the Rising were released in December, and those imprisoned following courts martial were freed in June 1917, allowing Sinn Féin and the Irish Volunteers to commence reorganising almost immediately.[10] Éamon de Valera, the only surviving 1916 leader, was elected president of Sinn Féin in October, having already defeated his IPP opponent in the East Clare by-election in July.[11] Within months, events outside Ireland, once again, pushed an already tense political situation to breaking point and strengthened the hand of the radicals.

A massive German offensive in March 1918 broke through Allied lines on the Western Front, prompting the British government to decide to extend conscription to Ireland. All shades of nationalist opinion, the Catholic Church and the labour movement united behind Sinn Féin's campaign to oppose the move. A nationwide strike on 23 April 1918 was (and remains) one of the most widely supported industrial actions ever organised in Ireland. Trade unions and trades councils across Britain also condemned the government, as did the British Labour Party.[12] John French, the new lord lieutenant, used the 1887 Crimes Act to arrest seventy-three separatist leaders in May for supposedly conspiring with Germany, and in July, declared the Irish Volunteers, Cumann na mBan, Sinn Féin and the Gaelic League illegal organisations.

By the Armistice in November 1918, the limited home rule settlement legislated for in 1914 was an anachronism for a sizeable proportion of the Irish population.[13] Sinn Féin routed the IPP in the December general election. Their sixty-nine newly elected MPs (holding seventy-three seats between them) were pledged to form an Irish counter-government rather than take their seats in Westminster.[14] The generally accepted date for the start of the War of Independence is 21 January 1919. On that day, Dáil Éireann met for the first time and, by chance rather than design, a group of Irish Volunteers (rechristened the IRA that year) killed two Royal Irish Constabulary (RIC) men guarding a wagon of explosives at Soloheadbeg, Tipperary.

Press censorship imposed by wartime emergency legislation was formally lifted in Britain and Ireland in June and August 1919 respectively, but this was negated in Ireland within weeks. The 'Sinn Féin press' was driven underground and several newspapers were suppressed for advertising the National (Dáil) Loan.[15] As time went on, Ireland became an increasingly hazardous place for journalists and newspaper proprietors. In Cork, the names of journalists for *The Cork Examiner* and *The Southern Star* appeared on police intelligence suspect lists.[16] By February 1921, at least forty-six Irish newspapers had been suppressed for varying periods of time.[17] Both the IRA and Crown Forces responded to hostile coverage with raids, threats and sometimes the destruction of newspaper presses and premises. Of the two, Crown Forces were by far the most destructive, attacking or wrecking sixteen provincial newspapers between late 1920 and early 1921.[18] Chief Secretary Hamar Greenwood either denied such reprisals or characterised them as 'justifiable self-defence'.[19]

In response to censorship, the Dáil established its own news sheet, the *Irish Bulletin*, produced through the joint efforts of Desmond FitzGerald, Erskine Childers, Frank Gallagher and Kathleen McKenna Napoli. The first issue appeared in November 1919. Thereafter, it was published five days a week and forwarded to some 700 recipients.[20] As the Dublin Castle Press Bureau's attempts to garner public support and sympathy for Crown Forces became ever more counter-productive, Dáil Éireann's Publicity Department blossomed into one of the counter-state's standout successes.

The *Bulletin* was neither neutral nor always accurate, but it offered a much-needed counterpoint to blatant and persistent false accounting by Greenwood and Dublin Castle, and was regularly quoted in the international and British press.[21] Childers and FitzGerald worked with Art Ó Briain and the Irish Self-Determination League in London to cultivate good working relationships with journalists.[22] According to Larry Nugent, who supplied its premises, none of the visiting correspondents ever gave away their whereabouts to the authorities: 'I say every man of them was a credit to his profession, including the "man from *The Daily Mail*."'[23]

In April 1919, de Valera publicly denounced the RIC as 'spies in our midst'. He called on local populations to ostracise and boycott officers who refused to resign.[24] The RIC, established as an armed *gendarmerie* in the 1830s, was the most visible and reliable arm of central government at local level. By the turn of the century, almost 80 per cent of the rank and file were Catholic (though the majority of senior officers were Protestant), and relations between the force and the general population were generally good. This changed once the RIC was accorded primary responsibility for countering the radical nationalist threat after the Rising.[25] In September 1919, the Irish authorities declared Dáil Éireann illegal. Two months later, other radical nationalist organisations were banned.

The RIC was ordered to consolidate into large units in better-protected stations. Their abandonment of smaller and more isolated rural barracks allowed the insurgents to move freely across large tracts of the country. The Dáil and IRA GHQ both sanctioned attacks on police in January 1920. Police statistics attributed over 2,500 'incidents' against the RIC to 'Sinn Féin' between 1919 and 1921, with two-thirds occurring in just eleven counties, mostly in the south and west. The county with the highest number of recorded incidents was Cork.[26] Over 1,300 regular RIC men left the force between July and September 1920. They were neither trusted nor allowed to join the IRA, even if inclined to do so, except in exceptional circumstances.[27]

Due to the RIC's decline, in early 1920 the Irish Command of the British Army established military posts in the vicinity of police barracks and took over responsibility for what was designated 'political' criminality.[28] However, police raids, curfews and clampdowns on fairs and markets in 'Special Military Areas' (trouble spots) were largely counter-productive. A mass hunger strike by internees in April 1920 garnered so much public sympathy, including another two-day general strike, that the authorities released them. In May, Irish railwaymen and dockers began the munitions embargo, the most significant show of workers' support for Irish independence of the conflict. For seven months, they refused to carry armaments or armed police or military, forcing Crown Forces onto the roads, where they were more vulnerable to IRA attacks, and creating severe logistical problems for the military.[29]

The IRA's war against Crown Forces was accompanied by Dáil Éireann's takeover of civil government, described by one historian as a 'real, subversive attempt to create a counter-state'.[30] Although seldom mentioned, the revolutionary period also witnessed a great wave of strikes and industrial action.[31] Farm workers made up the majority of the Irish Transport and General Workers' Union (ITGWU) membership in 1920.[32] The *Skibbereen Eagle*'s report on Kilmichael appeared alongside another on Sinn Féin's unsuccessful efforts (due to the intransigence of local farmers) to mediate in an ongoing farm strike in Kilpatrick, outside Bandon.[33]

The fateful decision to shore up the faltering RIC with Great War veterans was taken in late 1919.[34] Recruiting commenced in January 1920, and the first 'Black and Tans', veterans from the ranks taken directly into the RIC, arrived in March. By the summer, Britain was in the midst of an acute unemployment crisis, with some 167,000 fit ex-servicemen without work.[35] Recruiting into the RIC was stepped up, and in June, the authorities also began enrolling into a newly formed Auxiliary Division, a force of elite, independent fighting units composed entirely of former officers. Numbering just under 1,000, these 'temporary cadets' were organised in eleven companies dispersed across Ireland, each comprising around eighty officers, drivers and cooks, etc.[36]

By the summer of 1920, British government in Ireland was in a state of collapse.[37] Virtually every countermeasure employed had increased antipathy towards the authorities, even among local rate payers, public officials and medical professionals, cohorts of Irish society which, in normal circumstances, could be counted on to support the status quo.[38] There was a significant measure of popular support for the insurgents, underpinned by widespread public acquiescence. The upsurge in violence over the autumn and winter of 1920 – including Kilmichael – was largely the result of the fact that Lloyd George chose to ignore the advice of his own experts.[39]

In May, Sir Warren Fisher, head of the British Civil Service and lifelong home ruler, advised the coalition leaders to recognise Sinn Féin and restore to Ireland 'elementary human rights as understood by Anglo-Saxondom'.[40] Sir John Anderson, whom Fisher sent to Ireland with a number of other civil servants to replace the incompetent unionist clique controlling the Dublin Castle administration, advised them to make an immediate offer of dominion home rule, but to no avail.[41] The Restoration of Order (Ireland) Act came into force in August 1920. It replaced coroners' inquests with military courts of inquiry, and Crown Forces were accorded widespread powers of arrest, internment and court martial. These coercive measures had the opposite effect to the one intended. IRA men who were forced to go on the run to avoid arrest formed themselves into flying columns. 'Serious outrages' rocketed up from just over 2,000 to nearly 5,300, an increase of 163 per cent. Crown Force casualties (killed and wounded) doubled, IRA raids on mails tripled and arms raids almost quadrupled.[42]

The Prime Minister's and the Secretary of State for War Winston Churchill's extraordinary alternative to either making peace or declaring war was what an appalled Field Marshal Sir Henry Wilson, Chief of the Imperial General Staff (CIGS), termed 'counter-murder'.[43] The police were encouraged to respond to IRA assassinations and ambushes with targeted killings and brutalisation of the civilian population.[44] Some commanders, such as Brigadier General C. Prescott Decie (RIC Divisional Commissioner for Munster), voiced misgivings about the efficacy of the policy of 'stamping out of terrorism by secret murder' from the beginning.[45] Nonetheless, in early June, Lloyd George assured Sir Henry Tudor (Police Adviser to the Irish administration since 15 May) that he had his full support.[46] The infamous euphemisms 'shot while trying to escape' and 'shot for failing to halt' were regularly employed by soldiers and police to explain away deliberate killings of prisoners or suspects. Ubiquitous 'armed and masked men' also carried out targeted assassinations, including those of three mayors.[47]

By October 1920, objections to the government's Irish policy were issuing from the hawks as well as the doves. Although not opposed to the policy of counter-terror in principle, Wilson was aghast at how it was being conducted: 'that windbag Hamar Greenwood seems to have made a speech yesterday in Dublin to the R.I.C. saying reprisals would not be tolerated while all the time he and Lloyd George and Bonar Law are conniving at them and telling Tudor they are the best and the only thing to do'.[48]

Public support in Britain was also wavering. Labour leader Arthur Henderson MP moved a vote of censure against the government: 'These reprisals,' he said, 'appear to us to be part of a deliberate and calculated effort to destroy the Irish political movement.'[49] In November, Labour formally adopted a manifesto recognising Ireland's right to self-determination and calling for a withdrawal of the 'British Army of Occupation'.[50] On 11 November, an IPP MP read out to the Commons over 100 reported instances of 'wrecking, looting, arson, and, in some cases, murder' by Crown Forces since the beginning of the year. By the end of the month, just before Kilmichael, 1,300 individuals had been arrested.[51] The IRA had killed 155 police and fifty-seven British military.[52]

COUNTY CORK

The area of responsibility of the 6th Division of the British Army's Irish Command, led by Major General E.P. Strickland, was much the same as the old Cork Military District and broadly coterminous with Munster, the most violent province during the War of Independence.[53] Over 40 per cent of the total incidents in the 6th Division's precis of 'important' confrontations with the IRA from April 1920 to 11 July 1921 occurred in Cork, Munster's most disturbed county. The precis listed almost seventy attacks on Crown Forces in the county between April and 27 November 1920, but the actual level of unrest was higher.[54] The Army exaggerated 'rebel' casualties and counted only ambushes, attacks, kidnappings, assaults and disarmings. Attacks on police barracks, most civilian deaths and all but a few of the illegal killings by Crown Forces were not included.

Cork County Council pledged allegiance to Dáil Éireann at its first meeting after the June 1920 local elections.[55] On 19 July, Strickland reported numerous attacks on Crown Forces, noted no improvement in the 'transport situation', observed that illegal Dáil courts were flourishing, and said relations between the military and the civil population were strained. Despite acquiring a good deal of local information on rebel activities, he concluded that it was 'doubtful whether it can possibly get any worse'.[56] He survived an assassination attempt that autumn.

The Manchester Regiment had arrived at Kilworth Camp, just outside of Fermoy, on 1 April 1920. In mid-July, detachments were sent to Ballincollig, Millstreet, Macroom in mid-Cork, and Ballyvourney and Inchigeelagh to the west. Their war diary also documented the steadily deteriorating situation.[57] The civilian population were nervous, rarely welcoming and often hostile. Shopkeepers were reluctant to serve them. Railwaymen refused to load military stores. Soldiers were held up and searched or disarmed by the IRA, and regularly approached to sell arms and ammunition. A lorry belonging to the Hampshire Regiment was burnt out. Roads were trenched. Mails were raided and official letters taken.

Crown Forces mounted patrols and checkpoints, and raided houses, confiscating separatist literature or communications, armaments and sometimes British Army uniforms and boots. By August, town fairs were banned and Macroom was under curfew. On 14 August, the IRA attacked a military party guarding a downed aeroplane outside Kanturk, killing one soldier. Two days later, a mixed patrol of army and police killed two IRA Volunteers during a house raid in Kanturk. A local priest later accused the soldiers of having 'stamped on their dead bodies and hacked them to pieces with their bayonets'.[58]

The first Auxiliaries arrived in Ireland at the end of July.[59] A detachment from D Company took over Macroom Castle on 12 September but were soon replaced by C Company. The population of the town were 'very nervous'.[60] C Company's 'diligent efforts to create a good impression' (noted by *The Southern Star* shortly after their arrival) did not last long. Houses were ransacked during night-time searches. Auxiliaries drove through Macroom brandishing a large republican flag captured in a raid. Young men were dragged out blindfolded, stripped of their clothes and forced to their knees as shots were fired over their heads.[61]

In Ballymakeera, a mixed patrol of army and police killed a local labourer named James Lehane on 15 October.[62] Raymond Cafferata, a member of C Company, later recalled that the man had been 'murdered in cold blood'.[63] Less than a month later, on 10 November, C Company shot dead Christopher Lucey, a young student, during a raid in Tooreenduff.[64] Police reports at the time stated that Lucey had fired on them. That was not how Bill Munro (another member of C Company) remembered it: 'It was just some young fellows who took fright on seeing us and ran for it. This incident depressed us, especially as it was a stupid and unnecessary death and it had, so to speak, opened war, which we had not wanted.'[65]

The situation became steadily more ominous. On 16 November, two C Company Auxiliaries, Bertram Agnew and Lionel Mitchell, disappeared while on leave in Cork City and were never seen again. Four days later, Captain Joseph Thompson, the Manchester Regiment's intelligence officer, disappeared. On 22 November, his body was discovered in a field. Three British officers were kidnapped from a train outside Cork City the same day, never to be found. Munro recalled that he and his comrades 'began to be uneasy and to think perhaps our luck was running out'.[66] He was right, but there is little indication that C Company felt any particular sense of foreboding. Auxiliary patrols continued their habit of following the same routes from week to week. The customary route of C Company's No. 2 section ran from Macroom to Dunmanway, then Bandon and back to Macroom.[67]

KILMICHAEL

Plans to attack the Auxiliaries were mooted by IRA GHQ at a meeting with officers from the Kerry, Limerick and Cork brigades in late July or early August 1920. Richard Mulcahy, IRA Chief of Staff (C/S), noted that two Auxiliary companies were in place, in Inistioge, County Kilkenny and Macroom, County Cork. They were likely to be more effective than ordinary British soldiers, he said. He and Cathal Brugha, minister for defence, encouraged the southern brigades to form armed units and commence attacks, with the proviso that 'in all cases the enemy would first be called on to surrender'.[68] Mulcahy also advised the local brigades to surround the villages and towns where the Auxiliaries were stationed in order to confine them to their bases. Cork officers Terence MacSwiney, Liam Lynch and Liam Deasy were sceptical about the tactics suggested. MacSwiney, O/C of Cork No. 1 Brigade and in charge of the Macroom area, argued forcefully that they had neither the arms nor the ammunition to implement Mulcahy's elaborate plan. Furthermore, expecting inexperienced IRA units to offer a surrender to experienced British war veterans in armoured cars robbed them of their most effective tactic – surprise – and was tantamount to suicide.[69]

MacSwiney was arrested in Cork on 12 August and died on 25 October after seventy-four days on hunger strike. By then preparations to attack the Auxiliaries were well under way. IRA companies across West Cork collected an arms levy imposed on the 'business and farming community', and seized cattle and other stock from those who refused to pay.[70] Kinsale Company seized goods and 'procured' ammunition from members of the Essex Regiment.[71] Arms Fund monies were pooled at a brigade council meeting in Glaun North on 21 November.[72] Local companies began selecting men for the flying column and sending it any arms they had. Members of Bantry IRA had secured ten revolvers, ten rifles and ammunition in a raid on a submarine chaser in November 1919.[73] Several rifles, captured in the attack on Schull Barracks in early October 1920, were also sent to the column.[74]

After several IRA actions failed over the summer, officers of the 3rd Cork Brigade had agreed to accept a local ex-soldier's offer to train them. They did not fully trust Tom Barry, a former Royal Field Artillery gunner (and son of an RIC man), but they needed him. According to one Cork veteran, Barry was 'watched day and night'.[75] Training camps were organised in October and November. On 21 October 1920, Barry, Charlie

Hurley (O/C 3rd Cork Brigade), Deasy and others ambushed an Essex Regiment detachment at Toureen.[76] Following this, in the days before the Kilmichael ambush, Barry, Michael McCarthy and Sonny Dave Crowley, both 3rd (Dunmanway) Battalion officers, looked for a suitable position in the area from which to attack an Auxiliary patrol. They eventually decided on a spot between Macroom and Gloun Cross.

2

Life and Death at a
Bend in the Road

AT 3.40 P.M. ON MONDAY 29 November 1920, Thomas Dolan, RIC District
Inspector in Macroom, sent a telegram to John Anderson in Dublin Castle.
The news was bad:

> Seventeen Aux[iliaries] force under dist-Inspr Crake went two lorries
> patrol 3½ pm yesterday were ambushed near Kilmichael by 70 or 100
> men fifteen auxs force killed one missing and one wounded & dying
> ammunition and arms taken lorries burned ambush supposed to have
> been about 10pm last night full details not to hand bodies are being
> [taken] into Macroom now other authorities informed.[1]

A later telegram from General Tudor to the Chief Secretary in London
claimed that eighty to 100 attackers in khaki and steel helmets had
disarmed and 'brutally murdered' the cadets, robbing their corpses.

It would subsequently transpire that the No. 2 Platoon, C Company,
Auxiliary patrol had, in fact, been eighteen strong. Arthur Frederick
Poole, the initially uncounted eighteenth man, was a Black and Tan who
had apparently joined the patrol as a respite from his regular duties as an
officer's batman. He should not have been there at all.[2]

The search patrol had found the remains of C Company a few hours
earlier, about nine miles south of Macroom in the parish of Kilmichael.
The distinctive S-shaped curving stretch of the Dunmanway road

where the ambush took place ran through Haremount, Cooleclevane Shanacashelkneeves and Shanacashel, four of the parish's forty-six townlands.[3] The search patrol entered the site from the Macroom end. The road arced to the left as they approached. Off to the right, a few yards up a 'boreen' (narrow country road), stood a farmhouse. As the patrol rounded the bend, a burnt-out 20/25 Crossley tender came into view, one rear wheel half submerged in the boggy wet of a ditch left of the road. William Thomas Barnes lay in a pool of blood a few yards from the tender. He had a 'gaping wound of axilla' (armpit), four other bullet wounds and a large gunshot wound in the chest inflicted after death. According to Alexander Lewis, a member of the search patrol, 'poor old Barnes' died smiling. This was mostly likely a 'rictus grin', a sign of rigor mortis.[4] Another body lay in the road a few yards distant, and as the search party continued along the curve, several more came into view. Then, about 170 yards further on, they saw a second wrecked tender near the entrance to Murray's Lane, another boreen running up to the left.

Many of the vehicles driven by Auxiliaries were refurbished Royal Air Force (RAF) vehicles manufactured by Crossley Motors Ltd. By the 1920s, producing military vehicles was the Crossley brothers' main source of income. During the Great War, the Manchester-based firm had supplied over 6,000 ambulances and general-purpose lorries to the Royal Flying Corps (RFC) and RAF.[5] Their 15-cwt open trucks could carry eight men in the back and up to three in the cab.[6] Fast and reliable though they were, they had offered the doomed patrol no protection from the flying column that had lain in wait for them from early Sunday morning.[7]

Further along the road, past the first tender, lay the remains of Albert George Jones and Henry Oliver Pearson. Jones's leg was broken and his body was riddled by seven gunshot wounds, one in the axilla. Pearson, shot in the head and leg, also had a jagged wound on one of his forearms. Midway between the two tenders lay Frederick Henry Forde. Remarkably, despite lying on the road all night severely wounded, he was alive. Air Ministry weather reports, compiled from information supplied by diligent local observers from the Irish Rainfall Association, record that southwest Ireland was wet and unsettled on 28 and 29 November.[8] The rain probably kept Forde's wounds clean and free of infection.[9] Off the road to the left, not far from Forde, on marshy ground near a small stream running between rocky outcrops, were Frank Taylor and William Pallister. Taylor had a perforated wound in the chest and had been shot five times, once with a shotgun at very close range. Pallister was shot in the chest and his head had been smashed open by 'an axe or some similar heavy weapon'.[10]

The stream ran under the road and re-emerged on the southern side at the other end of the ambush site. Several yards back from the road on the right lay William Hooper Jones, shot in the axilla and groin. The bodies of Frederick Hugo, Benjamin Webster and Ernest William Henry Lucas were lying around the furthest tender. Hugo and Webster were a few feet apart on the boggy ground to the north. Webster had a 'gaping wound on his shoulder', a broken arm, and had been shot three times in the back with a rifle. Hugo had 'extensive lacerated wounds of the lower extremities' and a fractured leg and skull. His wounds were thought to have been inflicted by some sort of bomb. Lucas had been shot in the head. He also had several other wounds on his body and a broken leg.

Christopher Wainwright and Poole (the Black and Tan) lay several yards to the north up Murray's Lane. Both had been shot four times, Wainwright twice in the back. Poole's head and face had been smashed in by a heavy, blunt instrument after death. The bodies of Francis William Crake (the platoon commander), Cyril Dunstan Wakefield Bayley, Philip Noel Graham, James Chubb Gleave and Leonard Douglas Bradshaw were piled in two heaps on the gorse-covered ground to the left of the lane. Crake had died from a single gunshot to the head. Graham, shot through the neck, also had a broken leg and several lacerated wounds on his body. Bayley had been shot through the back of the head and chest. Gleave and Bradshaw were farthest from the road. Gleave was shot in the chest and pelvis. Bradshaw, shot in the left axilla and the chest, also had a broken right arm and three other wounds 'in various parts of the body'. In both cases, some of the injuries had been inflicted by shotguns fired at close range. Cecil James Guthrie was missing.

According to Bill Munro, another member of the search party, the litter of corpses and debris told a grim tale:

Those with no empty cartridge cases behind them were obviously hit by the first volley, and, taking this as a criterion, we could envisage in what order they had died and what sort of a show they had put up. Some had been able to reload once or twice, but the number was soon reduced to three who must have put up a tremendous fight. There were literally hundreds of empty cases beside them … they had fought on even after being hit several times. They must have kept the enemy under cover for a comparatively long time and it took hand grenades thrown from this cover to silence them.[11]

The locations of the lorries and the bodies, as well as the positions taken by 'rebel troops', were mapped by platoon commander Lieutenant Edgar Fleming.[12] Dr Jeremiah Kelleher, a local doctor whose RIC inspector son Philip had been killed by the Longford IRA a few weeks earlier, examined the bodies. On the following day (Tuesday 30 November) he described their injuries to the Manchester Regiment officers conducting the court of inquiry.[13] Lieutenant H.G. Hampshire, also from the search party, testified that all the bodies had been badly mutilated. In his assessment 'as a soldier', he said, four of the patrol were killed instantly but the rest had been 'butchered'.

The news reached Westminster on 29 November, several hours after the bodies were found. Public business habitually ran late in the Commons and it was after 10 p.m. when Joe Devlin, an IPP MP representing the predominantly Catholic Belfast Falls constituency, accused Hamar Greenwood of ignoring the 'reign of terror' perpetrated by loyalists against nationalists and Catholics in the North of Ireland. Devlin was a brilliant orator and one of just six IPP MPs to retain their seats in the 1918 general election. He numbered among the small cohort of IPP, Labour Party, 'Wee Free' Liberal MPs and a smattering of other radicals who persistently criticised the government's Irish policy.[14]

Following this, Thomas Moles, another Belfast MP, became the first of many unionists to invoke Kilmichael when levelling accusations of hypocrisy at nationalist critics of loyalist and state violence: 'He talks about a reign of terror … I venture to say he was perfectly cognisant of what happened in Cork to-day, yet he skids away from it.'[15] Greenwood, too, dismissed Devlin's remarks and read out the two telegrams he had received about the ambush (from Dolan and Tudor), describing them as 'the most distressing' he had ever presented to the Commons.[16]

Kilmichael was the shocking culmination of what had already been a shocking week. On Sunday morning, 21 November, Dublin IRA squads carried out a series of targeted assassinations, killing thirteen suspected British intelligence officers as well as three civilians and two Auxiliaries. That afternoon, the police opened fire on a crowd watching a Gaelic football match in Croke Park, killing fourteen. Dick McKee, Peadar Clancy and Thomas Clune, IRA suspects who had been arrested the previous evening and brought to Dublin Castle, did not survive the night.[17] On the day following what became known as 'Bloody Sunday', Devlin was physically attacked in the Commons by an enraged Unionist MP after he asked Greenwood why he only read out the names of the dead British officers and not those of the civilians killed by the police. Jack Jones, a Tipperary-born Labour MP, came roaring to Devlin's side: 'If there is a fight I am in it!'[18]

Bloody Sunday and Kilmichael gave the lie to Lloyd George's and Greenwood's bumptious assurances that the IRA was on the verge of defeat. Before the end of November 1920, the British Cabinet thought they were winning.[19] Greenwood had assured the Commons that the IRA's 'murderous campaign' in Ireland would be over within months. Lloyd George had insisted that the IRA was a small, unrepresentative band of assassins best dealt with by the police. He dismissed Irish claims to nationhood as a 'sham and a fraud', refused to declare war on rebels, and famously bragged that the government had 'murder by the throat'.[20]

There were few reprisals in Macroom itself on 29 November; it seems that this was due to the combined efforts of Major Buxton Smith, C Company's commander, and Lady Ardilaun (Olive Charlotte Guinness), owner of Macroom Castle.[21] When a group of soldiers attempted to burn down the home of the parents of Charles Browne (a known IRA officer), several members of C Company helped to put out the fire.[22] Rail travel and telegraphic communications were largely suspended, although several journalists managed to locate and visit the ambush site. Businesses were closed. Groups of commercial travellers were prevented from leaving Macroom for several days. According to the Manchester Regiment's war diary, 'all wanted persons in the area are "on the run", and the entire population is in a highly nervous state'.[23] Many of those living in and around the ambush site either slept away from their homes at night or left altogether for several days. Patrick Dromey, from the nearby townland of Mamucky, then a small boy, remembered that his mother returned to the family farm twice daily to milk the cows. On her first visit back, she found 'six heifers dead', struck either by lightning or bullets. They were never sure which.[24]

The circumstances in which the Auxiliaries died were a magnet for controversy from the start. The British alleged that the IRA (dressed in khaki and steel helmets) had tricked them and then massacred wounded men. Several different versions of what was thought to have happened appeared in the first few days after the ambush. Lurid accusations of butchery and mutilation emanated from the House of Commons and Dublin Castle. The longest and most extreme official account appeared in newspapers across both islands and internationally on 2 December. C.J.C. Street (Information Officer in Dublin Castle) and General Nevil Macready (O/C of the Irish Command) each reproduced it in their memoirs.[25] According to this official version, the Auxiliaries encountered a group of what they took to be British soldiers sitting in a motor lorry pulled across the road. The attackers were all

clad in Khaki and Trench Coats and wore steel helmets, had drawn their motor lorry across the road and were mistaken by the first car of cadets for military. The first car halted, and the cadets, unsuspecting, got out and approached the motor lorry. The second car, which had been travelling 100 yards behind, now came up. Something aroused the suspicion of the cadets who had got out of the first car. Shooting began and three were killed instantaneously. Others began to run back to the first car. The cadets in the second car ran along the road to the help of their comrades.[26]

The Auxiliaries were then disarmed and brutally exterminated. The 'dead and wounded were hacked about the head with axes' and 'shot guns were fired into their bodies'. The IRA then robbed the 'savagely mutilated' bodies and drove away. The report characterised Kilmichael as an outrage committed by murderers, not a legitimate act of war carried out by recognised combatants.[27]

The response of Sinn Féin publicists was to focus on the Crown Forces' retaliatory reprisals, dismiss the mutilation accusations as war propaganda and explain (rather than deny) the condition of the bodies. The injuries were attributed to 'bomb fire'.[28] Dublin Castle press releases exaggerated the Auxiliaries' injuries. Dr Kelleher's findings did not support allegations of deliberate mutilation. Nevertheless, both private and published accounts by members of the Auxiliary search party suggest they genuinely believed the bodies had been mutilated. One unnamed Auxiliary told the journalists who visited the ambush site that 'It was the most ghastly thing I have ever seen … I went all through the war and never saw anything quite so horrible as the spectacle of the roadside. It was simply littered with bodies bashed and battered in a way that makes my flesh creep when I think of it.'[29]

The military and police, on edge and looking for opportunities to exact revenge, commenced a series of aggressively destructive raids and patrols.[30] On the day that the bodies were found, an agricultural labourer named Denis O'Sullivan was taken out of a pub in Coolderrihy, two miles from the ambush site, and shot dead. A few weeks later, Alexander Lewis confessed to his mother that before transporting the gruesome freight back to Macroom Castle 'every one of us went raving mad', trashing and burning houses and haystacks in the vicinity.[31] 'I don't care a hang what happens, things that a month ago would have shocked me have ceased to affect me in the same manner,' Lewis wrote. 'I can now kill a Sinn Feiner in quite a casual, conscientious way, to you, it may seem a horrid thing to say, but if you had only seen a quarter of what I had seen, you would quite understand.'[32] According to another former member of C Company, the 'gloves were pretty well off in most units' after Kilmichael.[33]

Two of the most notorious incidents of the conflict occurred within weeks: the shooting dead of a seventy-three-year-old priest, Canon Magner, near Dunmanway in Cork, by a K Company Auxiliary, and the burning of Cork City on 11/12 December. The infamous 'sweet revenge' letter written by one of the Auxiliaries involved in the burning was intercepted and published in December 1920.[34] 'In all my life,' he told his mother, 'I have never experienced such orgies of murder, arson and looting.'[35] Over the next six months, the number of insurgent and civilian deaths in Cork more than doubled. Conflict-related fatalities increased generally, as did the number of suspect Crown Force killings in the county. The 6th Division's precis recorded that 100 out of almost 300 incidents listed after 28 November 1920 occurred in Cork.[36] The conflict took its toll, even on senior figures in the army and administration. In January 1921, Strickland recorded in his diary: 'It's been one of the worst years I've known anywhere.'[37]

The Cork IRA were responsible for 200 further deaths.[38] In Cork City on 29 November 1920, the same day the bodies of the Auxiliaries were found, father and son Frederick and James Blemens were kidnapped by Cork No. 1 Brigade as alleged spies, never to be seen again. The execution of civilians suspected of informing increased significantly in the first half of 1921. The Rev. Daniel Cohalan, Bishop of Cork (and a Kilmichael native), famously issued a decree on 12 December 1920 condemning reprisals by Crown Forces and excommunicating IRA men who took part in ambush and kidnapping. 'Murder is murder,' he said. The bishop's pronouncement was swiftly contradicted by Fr Dominic O'Connor, chaplain to the Cork IRA, who marshalled the Old Testament books of Maccabees to argue that, in the circumstances, armed insurrection was 'not only not sinful' but 'good and meritorious'.[39]

Attempts to broker a peace deal by Archbishop Clune in early December failed, although the government knew that at some point it would have to negotiate with the insurgents. 'Official' reprisals were introduced in martial law areas, but unsanctioned ones continued, as did Hamar Greenwood's sustained campaign of public lying about them. On 1 December, K Company Auxiliaries ran amok in Fermoy. Nicholas de Sales

Prendergast, a forty-four-year-old ex-British military officer, was beaten up and then thrown into the Blackwater River, where he drowned.[40] There was a particularly dramatic spike in dubious killings of IRA Volunteers, which commenced on 2 December when Joseph Begley, James O'Donoghue and John Galvin were 'shot for failing to halt' at Laurel Walk in Bandon.[41] Many more Cork IRA men would die in suspicious circumstances over the next few months. The deaths of several of the twelve members of an East Cork IRA flying column killed at Clonmult in February 1921 were attributed by the Hampshire Regiment, pointedly, to a 'false surrender'.[42]

Rumours that the Auxiliaries at Kilmichael had tricked members of the column with some sort of 'false surrender' were also circulating. Lionel Curtis (Churchill's personal advisor during the Treaty negotiations) heard one of these stories when visiting Cork in the spring of 1921.[43] Although wary of the 'highly imaginative and emotional' Irish, he gave a public account of what he heard a few months later.[44] He described the Auxiliaries' bodies as having been 'shamefully mutilated' but said that, according to Sinn Féin, 'a white flag was put up by the police, and … when the attacking party approached to accept the surrender, fire was opened upon them'.[45] He did not say, however, that any of the Volunteers had been injured or killed in this attempted ruse.

However stridently the authorities characterised Kilmichael as an atrocity in public pronouncements, behind the scenes they were only too aware that one of their elite counter-insurgency units had been wiped out in a well-planned military action. Not only had C Company's habit of travelling the same routes at similar times in unarmoured vehicles made them easy targets, but the patrol seemed to have been lured into the ambush by a ruse that, as experienced war veterans, they should have seen through.[46] Steps were immediately taken to fit tenders and other vehicles with iron plates and netting. Internal British military assessments of the conflict emphasised the need for advanced guards and irregular movements of convoys when travelling by road. A guide for officers serving in Ireland compiled over the first six months of 1921 advised troops to avoid 'being led into traps by persons with plausible stories, even in British uniform'.[47]

INVESTIGATING KILMICHAEL 1920–2

British intelligence in Ireland during the War of Independence was comprised of an unwieldy combination of police and military organisations
who were supposed to liaise with each other and exchange information.
Their primary means of information gathering were raids and prisoner
interrogations. In practice, the system was not very efficient.[48] In Cork and
Limerick, however, the arrangements worked well, and this is reflected in
their investigations of Kilmichael.

Seized documents were the most valuable and reliable sources of
information available to British intelligence organisations in Ireland.[49]
Correspondence relating to GHQ's and the southern brigades' plans to
attack the Auxiliaries were among a cache of IRA C/S Richard Mulcahy's
papers seized in November 1920 (among the authorities' most fortuitous
captures of the entire conflict), which were later destroyed during the
Blitz.[50] The papers of Major General Charles Howard Foulkes, Director of
Irish Propaganda from January 1921, contain over 100 pages of epitomes
and indexes of seized documents, which he drew on in order to make his
propaganda leaflets and newspaper reports seem more authentic.[51] The
military used them to formulate strategy and tactics, compile IRA orders
of battle, map brigade areas and populate blacklists of suspects.[52]

Local Crown Forces identified some ambush participants within a
few weeks, but their most significant find was a captured report from the
O/C of the flying column, Tom Barry. It was reproduced in both military
analyses of the campaign, the 'Irish Republican Army from Captured
Documents' (June 1921) and the 'Record of the Rebellion in Ireland in
1920–21', a more substantial, five-volume campaign history compiled by
the Irish Command over the two months following the ratification of the
Treaty in January 1922.[53] The report briefly described the march to the
site, armaments and the positioning of the column into three sections, and
noted that the ambushers were actually in the process of leaving when they
realised the patrol was approaching their position:

> The action was carried out successfully, 16 of the enemy who were
> belonging to the Auxiliary Police from Macroom Castle being

killed, one wounded and is [*sic*] escaped and is now missing ... Our casualties were: – One killed, and two who have subsequently died of wounds ... I attribute our casualties to the fact that those three men (who were part of No. 2 section) were too anxious to get into close quarters with the enemy. They were our best men and did not know danger in this or any previous actions. They discarded their cover and it was not until the finish of the action that P. Deasy was killed by a revolver bullet from one of the enemy whom we thought dead.[54]

It is a testament to the ambush's impact that a transcription of the report was included in the military's internal assessments of their campaign. As it was standard for army intelligence to transcribe captured documents before forwarding them to the police, there is nothing particularly suspicious in the fact that it only survives as a transcription. It would have been more unusual if the original were still available.[55] This captured report is the only contemporary insurgent account of the ambush available and an essential starting point for any serious study of Kilmichael. As will be discussed in later chapters, several ambush veterans' accounts confirm the report's main details. There are no substantial grounds for viewing it as a forgery, although this has been argued.[56]

Unlike the 'sweet revenge' letter, the captured report had little propaganda value. Dublin Castle's allegations that axes were used on the bodies was an embellishment on the finding of the Court of Inquiry and Forde's information. Neither Dr Kelleher's assessment nor the captured report supported accusations of mutilation, which was why both the 'Irish Republic Army from Captured Documents' and the 'Record' supplemented their transcription of the latter with descriptions of what, in the Irish Command's view, had *really* happened. According to the former's commentary, which is less detailed, the patrol was

confronted in the dusk by a man in a steel helmet and a British uniform, who stated that he was a soldier, that his lorry had broken down and that he required assistance. The police at once went to assist and apparently [drove] straight into the ambush. A number of the attackers wore steel helmets and British uniforms. The Auxiliaries appear to have been practically annihilated in the first volleys but such as lay wounded on the ground were deliberately murdered. Only one of the sixteen escaped wounded. Their bodies bore evidence of having been hacked by axes. These details are not given in the account by the O.C. 'Flying Column'.[57]

The 'Record's' supporting commentary was much the same as the earlier assessment, but it was augmented with new intelligence.

After the Truce, the IRA made themselves visible. On the first anniversary of the ambush, masses for the repose of the souls of McCarthy, O'Sullivan and Deasy were offered up in at least eight churches in West Cork. Their families, along with contingents of IRA Volunteers from across the county, gathered at St Joseph's Catholic church in Castletown-Kinneigh. Wreaths were placed on the graves in the adjoining cemetery, and the rosary recited.[58] Rev. Patrick O'Connell, the priest who had heard the flying column's confessions the night before the ambush, celebrated the mass and paid 'stirring and touching tribute to the great military record of the I.R.A.'[59]

Reports on the masses and 'in Memoriam' notices for McCarthy, Deasy and O'Sullivan were marked and pasted into the Essex Regiment's newspaper cutting books.[60] By early 1922, when the 'Record' was compiled, the military had also learned the fate of Guthrie, and identified several IRA participants, including an ex-soldier: 'Of the whole of this party of 18, 16 were found lying on the spot; one had disappeared. It has since been ascertained from Thomas Bernard Barry, an ex-artillery man, and afterwards appointed liaison officer for the 6th Divisional area, who is believed to have taken part in the massacre, that this man also was butchered.'[61]

TOM BARRY

Gunner Thomas Bernadine Barry was demobilised from the Royal Field Artillery on 7 April 1919. His service records described him as a 'good hardworking man'. He was made a non-commissioned officer (NCO) (bombadier) in March 1916 but reverted to gunner at his own request two months later. Barry was disciplined on several occasions for minor offences including 'irregular conduct', 'stating a falsehood', 'improper reply to an NCO' and disobeying orders.[62] Newspaper reports in early 1916 stated that he was on the Western Front and was gassed at Ypres, but his service records indicate that this is untrue, stating that he was a veteran of the British campaigns in Mesopotamia and Egypt.[63]

During the war, Barry contracted malaria and 'disease of the action of the heart' (DAH), or 'soldier's heart'.[64] He experienced periodic bouts of illness throughout the revolutionary period and received a British disability pension until at least 1923, one of about 37,500 pensioned veterans living in the Irish Free State.[65] Symptoms of DAH included rapid heartbeat, chest pain, fatigue and shortness of breath. In the era of the Great War, soldiers with DAH believed they suffered from organic heart disease. By the 1940s, however, the condition had been redefined as a kind of psychoneurosis, a variant of what today would be referred to as PTSD.[66]

Barry arrived back in Bandon in the spring of 1919. He seems, at first, to have associated mostly with other veterans and the military. He joined, then left, the local branch of the National Federation of Discharged and Demobilised Sailors and Soldiers, one of the more radical British veteran organisations.[67] Barry enrolled in a college and sat but failed a British civil service exam. In early 1920, he applied for an 'Indian posting'.[68] At some point he also approached the local IRA, who were initially very mistrustful of him. Ted O'Sullivan, formerly brigade vice O/C, said Barry had been associated with the 'Anti-Sinn Féin Society'.[69] In Meda Ryan's first biography of Barry she cited still circulating rumours that he had been 'coached in intelligence' by British forces before joining the IRA.[70] If this is true, Barry went spectacularly rogue.

THE DUNMANWAY DIARY

An Auxiliary intelligence officer's diary found in Dunmanway Workhouse after it was vacated by K Company Auxiliaries in March 1921 indicates that

British intelligence officers had linked Barry to the ambush by the spring of 1921, although they do not seem to have realised he had commanded the column.[71] If this diary belonged to K Company's intelligence officer, then the owner was Chambre Baldwin, an Anglo-Irish officer with roots in Cork. In 1911, his uncle and namesake, a land agent, lived in Bandon.[72] Another possibility is that it was compiled by either Reginald Joseph Browning, I/O of O Company, or his company commander, Piers Fiott de Havilland. Both were stationed in Dunmanway from February 1921.[73]

The diary consists mainly of an alphabetical list of Cork IRA suspects. The provenance of the information is noted in many entries. Some intelligence was beaten out of two arrested local Volunteers.[74] More came from a captured IRA membership roll. A disgruntled Catholic farmer reported a Volunteer who collected £3 from him for the IRA's arms fund. Local Protestants supplied details relating to the killing of Alfred Cotter, a local baker and co-religionist who was executed on 25 February 1921 for defying the IRA's order to boycott Crown Forces.[75] Several names also appeared on earlier 'blacklists', which the 6th Division began compiling in January 1920. Well over half of all these suspects also featured on an Essex Regiment list dating from late summer or early autumn 1920, including several men who would later take part in Kilmichael.[76] Barry is not on the Essex Regiment list, which might suggest the authorities were not yet aware of his shifting allegiances.

'"Barney" Barry, Schull, ex-soldier … in Field Comp' was listed in the diary as one of the men suspected of having been involved in Kilmichael. It also noted that according to '17th Bge intelligence', he was treated in a Cork hospital in January 1921. Barry was not from Schull and most IRA accounts say he was in hospital a bit earlier, but the information about him was broadly accurate. The other suspected Kilmichael participants listed in the diary were: Sonny Dave Crowley, Cornelius Cornin [Cronin], James Donovan, Michael Dwire [Dwyer], Jack Hourihan, Jack Hennessy, Michael McCarthy, Tim McCarthy and 'Neill'. Local Crown Forces had identified Hennessy almost immediately, and they raided his family home within half an hour of his arrival there in early December, looking for the 'fellow that was wounded at Kilmichael'. He just managed to escape.[77]

There is not enough direct evidence to be certain, but given the nature of the intelligence, it is at least plausible that the information about Barry and Hennessy came from medical personnel. In February 1921, the military ordered hospitals to furnish 'daily particulars of wounded persons under their care', although many Irish doctors refused to comply.[78] Despite what Barry says in his memoir, hospital staff in Cork might have alerted the authorities that he was or had been there.[79] Another possibility is that one or both of the local doctors who treated Hennessy and other members of the column after the ambush passed on information. Both doctors are listed in the diary.[80] Eugene J. Fehily was a Sinn Féin suspect who worked as a GP in Ballineen for the rest of his working life.[81] Dr James Crowley, however, is listed in the diary as an intelligence contact. Then a dispensary medical officer in Murragh, he seems to have left Cork in March 1921.[82] According to a local IRA Volunteer, after Crowley refused to treat IRA wounded, he was arrested and handed over to Tom Barry: 'The doctor was ordered out of the country and he went.'[83] They also dismantled his car, and there is a car registration after Crowley's name in the diary.

Irrespective of how they found out about Barry's involvement in Kilmichael, his appointment as an IRA liaison officer during the Truce caused consternation.[84] General Strickland's diary recorded the news: 'Busy with C in C on telephone this evening re *Catholic Herald* & our "Liaison" (!!!) officer.'[85] Barry was already well known, and IRA GHQ was eager to give its famous flying-column commander more responsibility. In addition to becoming chief liaison officer for Munster, he was appointed divisional training officer and deputy commandant to Liam Lynch (O/C of the 1st Southern Division).[86] Strickland's comments might have been an expression of general dismay at having to liaise with the IRA, rather than a specific reference to Barry. Brigadier General Prescott-Decie knew who Barry was, however, and it was more than he could bear. He resigned in September 1921, refusing to work with 'murderers', specifically an ex-soldier who was 'known to have taken part in the murder and mutilation of temporary cadets of the Auxiliary Division in the Kilmichael Ambush.'[87]

The following month, indignant Unionist and Conservative MPs raised the issue of Barry's involvement in the ambush in the Commons.[88] The IRA's public response was defiant. Two weeks after Prescott-Decie's resignation, Barry appeared on the platform at a Skibbereen *Aeridheacht* (outdoor gathering) alongside several Sinn Féin TDs and IRA officers. Gearóid O'Sullivan, TD and IRA GHQ adjutant general, addressed the crowd in Irish and then English. He remarked that both the Boers and those who fought in the American War of Independence had been condemned by the British as 'murderers':

> Three years ago many people, even in this very field, sneered at the idea of an Irish Republic or an Irish Army ... Does any man say that Commandant Barry is a murderer? If he is, he is a very good one. Does anyone say that Commandant McKeown is a murderer? Does anyone say that Michael Collins is a murderer? These men are not murderers. They are soldiers of freedom ... We are proud of Crossbarry and proud of Kilmichael, and proud of Michael Collins.[89]

Relations between Barry and the British he was liaising with quickly soured. General Strickland described Cork Sinn Féin as 'truculent' and found Barry 'rude' and 'overbearing'.[90] British intelligence files also commented on Barry's 'swollen head'.[91] For officers who firmly believed that by the summer of 1921 the IRA was all but defeated, the Truce was an ignoble settlement foisted on them by treacherous 'frocks' (politicians).[92] Michael Collins (Dáil Éireann's minister for finance and director of IRA Intelligence), who was in Cork shortly after the Truce, described the British military there as 'arrogant and provocative', and doing their best to 'regard their position not as a truce but as a surrender on our part'.[93]

The animus Barry provoked among British officers reflected their intransigence and wounded pride as much as anything, but it was not only the British who found him difficult. By November he was no longer either a divisional or liaison officer, and both Lynch and IRA C/S Richard Mulcahy felt that appointing him had been a mistake.[94] The formidable Jennie Wyse Power, friend to Leslie Barry (*née* Price), Barry's wife since August, summed up the situation well: 'I think he was not good at it – his powers & capabilities lay one way only, & you understand what that way was.'[95] Barry was egotistical and unpredictable. He ignored or cancelled orders from Chief Liaison Officer Eamonn Duggan, and issued directives to civilians and IRA brigades over the heads of Lynch and IRA GHQ.[96] Then, rather than accede to his superiors' orders to moderate his behaviour, he quit. Barry resigned his divisional posts on 27 September 1921, with Lynch recommending his resignation be accepted.[97]

Despite this, Mulcahy convinced Barry to stay on as a training officer, but considered him to be 'very petulant and childish' and 'utterly undermined by his own vanity'.[98] Within days, Barry exacerbated an already tense situation by ordering Spike Island prisoners to commence a hunger strike.[99] 'This one time capable Officer has outstepped himself', Lynch remarked.[100] Three weeks later, Barry resigned as liaison officer and convinced other officers to do the same.[101] He sent his resignations directly to either the IRA GHQ or to the Dáil ministry, bypassing Lynch's authority. Lynch eventually requested that GHQ step in to deal with what he described as 'very grave indiscipline … We must have either Truce or War, and whoever, by any want of discipline, re-opens the War prematurely will have to be held strictly accountable for it.'[102] In early February 1922, Wyse Power described Barry as being 'in bad health & broken resources' and believed Leslie had behaved rashly: 'talk about marrying in haste. I am very sorry for her.'[103]

3

Ruse de Guerre or Atrocity? Early Press Coverage of the Ambush

THE FIRST, BRIEF REPORTS OF the Macroom ambush (as it was as often referred to initially) appeared in the final editions of several Irish and British evening dailies on 29 November. The shocking confrontation in Cork between '*sinnfeinistas*' and '*negrapardos*' [Black and Tans], the '*embuscade sinn-feiner à Kilmichael, près de Macroom*'[1] rocketed around the world via the vast web of overland and submarine telegraph cables, which, by 1920, criss-crossed the globe and linked Britain with its empire and dominions.[2] The ambush was a political and a media event on both islands, and dominated news and editorial commentary for most of that week. Dozens of journalists and press photographers, foreign and domestic, were already in Ireland covering the conflict.[3] Due to the time difference, press agency wires arrived in the United States and Canada in the morning and afternoon of 29 November. The news reached South America, Australia, New Zealand, China and India, was widely reported in France and was picked up by the Spanish, Italian and German press. To use today's terminology, Kilmichael went viral.

The emergence of global communications systems in the late nineteenth century was part of an unprecedented period of social, political and technological advance.[4] Significant increases in literacy and advances in printing enabled the advent of mass-circulation newspapers in Britain, much of Europe and the United States, which in turn fuelled the emergence of 'new journalism' and 'factual reporting'.[5] From the mid-nineteenth century, these advances facilitated the formation of press agencies to collect and distribute news, including international events, and newspapers soon began to play a central role in popular discourse.[6]

According to Mitchell's *Newspaper Press Directory*, in 1917 there were 2,366 newspapers in Britain and Ireland.[7] In 1920, Britain was still home to 169 local dailies (many towns had two), despite ongoing consolidation due to the development of large newspaper groups. The circulation of daily newspapers doubled in the interwar period.[8] Ireland experienced a similar explosion of print culture. There was a dramatic expansion of the regional press, with more than 150 new newspapers, mostly nationalist, established between 1885 and 1910.[9] Newspapers on both islands aligned themselves politically. They were either nationalist or unionist in Ireland. In Britain, although the descriptive 'independent', 'neutral' or 'non-political' was becoming more common, most newspapers were still various shades of conservative, unionist, liberal or labour. Most of the tabloid press ranged from mildly to virulently right-wing.[10]

Conservative and unionist newspapers across both islands were, and remained, scathingly critical of the Irish separatist campaign. From late 1920, however, the conduct of Crown Forces in Ireland, and particularly reprisals, prompted a 'profound shift' in how the war was covered by British correspondents and newspapers of all political hues.[11] Even *The Times* condemned reprisals. It was still considered by many to be the British elite's 'newspaper of record' and in 1915, Lord Northcliffe (Dublin-born Alfred Harmsworth), its proprietor, had been condemned by Sinn Féin as the 'Cromwell of journalese'. Yet shortly after Kilmichael, the paper was denounced in the unionist press for its 'viciously Separatist' turn on the Irish question.[12] It is not clear who was responsible, but during the War of Independence, Northcliffe and Wickham Steed (editor of *The Times*) were offered armed escorts after they received threats in the post.[13]

Liberal and left-leaning correspondents in Britain like Hugh Martin, H.W. Nevinson, J.L. Hammond, Alfred Powell Wandsworth and Donald Spendlove (dubbed the 'Sinn Féin Correspondent of the Press Association'), as well as C.P. Scott, *The Manchester Guardian*'s editor, played a crucial role in exposing the excesses of government policy.[14] Hugh Martin, a journalist with the liberal *The Daily News*, described the Croke Park shootings on Bloody Sunday as an 'Irish Amritsar'.[15] Philip Gibbs, one of the most well-known correspondents of the early twentieth century, resigned from the *Daily Chronicle* (owned by Lloyd George since 1918) over its support for sending Black and Tans to Ireland.[16]

By the eve of Kilmichael, much of the press on both islands had become reluctant to accept official statements at face value. Basil Clarke, in charge of Dublin Castle's Press Bureau, was dubbed the 'Black and Tan publicity man' by Irish reporters.[17] On the day before the ambush – two weeks after local Black and Tans carried out vicious reprisals against the local population in Tralee – the *Irish Independent* exposed bogus photographs and newsreel footage of Auxiliaries routing an IRA flying column in the Kerry town. In reality, they were clumsy fabrications produced by Dublin Castle's maladroit publicity officers, Hugh Pollard and William Darling. The *Illustrated London News*, which had dedicated its entire front page to one of the photographs, issued a formal apology.[18]

EARLY PRESS COVERAGE AND PUBLIC ACCOUNTS OF KILMICHAEL

Editorials and other public commentary on Kilmichael (and the situation generally) suggest that Irish events commanded both more interest and a greater diversity of responses in Britain than is often assumed. The prominence given to official versus independent reports varied from paper to paper. British newspapers and several unionist dailies in Ireland published Dublin Castle's 2 December atrocity account in full, but it was not, as is sometimes argued, 'uncritically accepted' by the contemporary media.[19] In fact, the press coverage and commentary after the ambush frequently reflected the growing mistrust of the authorities. While virtually all the newspapers used details from official statements about Kilmichael, with successive, often contradictory communiqués reproduced almost verbatim one after another down the page, this was generally done in conjunction with information sourced elsewhere. Newspapers and pressmen made independent efforts to verify what had taken place. A few even managed to visit and photograph the ambush site, source local information and interview eyewitnesses. Reporters also attended the Auxiliaries' funerals and the later court hearings where their families' compensation claims were adjudicated.

Briefer and generally less sensational summations appeared in Irish nationalist dailies and British labour papers like the *Daily Herald*. The tone and language used to describe Kilmichael varied, and, in some cases, doubts were also expressed about the veracity of 'official' accounts.[20] British, dominion and Irish unionist papers described Kilmichael as 'murder', a 'massacre', 'butchery', a 'Turkish' atrocity carried out by a 'hatchet fiend gang', 'savages', 'ghouls', 'republican thugs' and 'assassins in khaki and steel helmets'. Most Irish nationalist newspapers employed comparatively neutral headlines like 'Deadly Ambush', 'Sensational Ambush', 'Awful Death-Roll' or 'Awful Bloodshed'.[21] But the evidence indicates that the impact of even the most salacious headlines about Kilmichael on British and Irish opinion has been overstated.

Details about the ambush emerged in identifiable waves of press agency telegrams, official statements, press releases, interviews and correspondents' reports between 29 November and 2 December. As different reports employed slightly different place names, key phrases, and estimated combatant numbers and casualties, it is possible to track how the story developed over the week and, in some cases, to identify and to trace the information back to its likely origin.

At least three separate messages about the ambush were sent out by the Press Association on the evening of 29 November from 'official' sources. Clarke forwarded District Inspector Dolan's telegram and other details supplied by Pollard to the Irish Office in London.[22] A very brief official statement was issued in time for inclusion in the 'breaking news' columns of several papers followed by a second, longer one (both based on the initial Dolan and Tudor telegrams).[23] A third stated that fifteen Auxiliaries had been killed, one was wounded and another was missing (excluding Poole, the Black and Tan).[24] The final edition of Cork's *Evening Echo* that day published one of the earliest, if not the first, independent report. This stated that reprisals had taken place following a 'sensational ambush' in 'Johnstown, a village between Macroom and Dunmanway, and lying to the south of Inchigeela'. An unspecified number of 'military' had been killed.[25]

The next day, Tuesday 30 November, news of Kilmichael appeared in at least eighty newspapers across Britain and Ireland, as well as in the international press. Most of the early press reports, based on the Press Association wires, Dublin Castle official statements released to the press, and the Dolan and Tudor telegrams (read out by Hamar Greenwood in the Commons), were a mixture of accurate and erroneous details. Due to the confusion over Constable Poole, almost all of them understated the number of fatalities by one.[26] So did the *Irish Bulletin*.[27] A few papers reported that Forde was dead or dying.

Dublin Castle added to the confusion that afternoon by misidentifying Hugo as 'Hayes' and Poole as 'Pooley' in their first full list of the dead.[28] It then issued a corrected statement giving the names and Great War regiments of all eighteen members of the patrol accompanied by an exaggerated description of the Auxiliaries' injuries: 'Inspection reveals that they have nearly all as many as half a dozen bullet wounds and that they have been terribly mutilated, as though with hatchets.'[29]

The *Daily Dispatch*, *Daily Chronicle* and *Lancashire Daily Post* published both the official statements and reports from their own correspondents.[30] Although some of the details differed, their reports surmised that C Company had been completely outnumbered and subjected to a sudden and overwhelming attack. The *Dispatch* claimed, erroneously, that, in reprisal, Crown Forces had almost completely destroyed Macroom. A phrase from the *Chronicle*, that the Auxiliaries had been unable to fight back because the IRA's 'marksmanship was too true', was recycled by newspapers around the globe.[31]

Later that day, the *Evening Echo* published a more detailed account, stating that the two lorries of Auxiliaries from Macroom Castle were attacked on a secluded stretch of road 'covered by overhanging trees' in the townland of Shanacashel:

> It appears that a deep trench had been cut across the road ... The leading lorry ran into this, and was at once embedded whilst the

second, going at a fairly fast rate, ran into the wrecked car ... The firing was unceasingly maintained then from both sides of the road, and the Auxiliary police, taken completely by surprise, fell easy victim to the attack.[32]

This 'trench' account, originally sent out by the Press Association, was widely republished in British, Irish, North American and Australian newspapers.[33] The report also maintained that the Auxiliaries attempted to return fire, but all succumbed in the darkness and then the attackers came onto the road and burned the lorries.

Several British and Irish journalists made their way to Macroom on 30 November.[34] The local Auxiliaries did not make them welcome. *The Freeman's Journal* and *Irish Times* reporters said they were stopped continuously by hostile patrols. The *Irish Times* representative never reached the ambush site, but two British press photographers from the *Daily Sketch* and *Daily Dispatch*, as well as a *Freeman's Journal* journalist, did.[35] They photographed the lorries and interviewed Auxiliaries and locals.[36] Neither the *Sketch* nor the *Dispatch* mentioned the behaviour of the police, and instead claimed their representatives were threatened by the IRA. In a letter to *The Irish Times*, an unnamed British journalist described both its and *The Freeman's Journal*'s reports of the Auxiliaries' behaviour as exaggerated. He confirmed that the police stopped them several times, and that at one point they had been fearful for their lives, but said they eventually went for a drink with one of the Auxiliaries.

Further new accounts of Kilmichael appeared on Wednesday 1 December. Several dailies had sourced more accurate (though not error-free) details from Dr Kelleher's testimony to the confidential court of inquiry.[37] The London-based Central News Agency, widely considered to be the 'Conservative party's house organ', issued a telegram from a 'Skibbereen' correspondent stating that all the occupants in the first lorry had been killed when it hit a mine in the road.[38] The confusion over Constable Poole continued. Both the *Mirror* and *Sketch* initially published a photograph of a different (and very much alive) man named Thomas Poole. His wife was also sent a telegram enquiring about her husband's funeral arrangements.[39]

Other journalists had sourced reliable local information, and this was also in circulation. The *Daily Dispatch* and *The Freeman's Journal* published grim eyewitness descriptions of the site:

> A few burned and bloodstained Glengarry caps lie on the road itself. Beside the charred remains of the Crossley cars were strewn pieces of twisted iron, motor tools and spare parts … No living soul has passed along the road since Sunday's bloody struggle … At many points between the two cars are marks of blood and indications of the road being torn up.[40]

An 'eyewitness' account, reproduced in *The Manchester Guardian, The Cork Examiner* and other newspapers, dovetailed closely with later IRA veteran testimonies. Described as coming from someone who witnessed the ambush 'from a distance', it also appeared on Wednesday:

> The ambush took place at … Gneeves Cross, which is at the junction of three roads about half-way on the main road between Macroom and Dunmanway.
>
> The first intimation that any of the people in the district got of anything untoward being up was when large numbers of people going to Mass were ordered to avoid the cross and go circuitously to the church. Nothing unusual then happened until 4:40 in the evening, when apparently, as is their wont every Sunday, the two lorries full of Auxiliary cadets were seen approaching from the Macroom direction.
>
> When they reached the crossroads a terrific explosion was heard, and it would appear the road must have been mined at the place or else a bomb was thrown. The first lorry came to a sudden stop, and the occupants of the second, which was about 50 yards behind, when they heard the explosion, endeavoured to reverse the engine of the lorry, with the result that it backed down the incline. Shots now rang out from all directions, but the firing lasted only ten minutes in all, when there was a complete stillness. The two lorries were then seen to

be on fire, and the fires burned brightly in the silence of the evening on the lonely countryside.[41]

The Manchester Guardian contradicted the earlier 'Skibbereen' and 'trench' accounts, as well as this new eyewitness account, stating (correctly) that, according to 'people who have visited the spot', the road had been neither trenched nor mined.[42] The *Edinburgh Evening News* said that Guthrie, the missing cadet, had been shot down trying to escape.[43] Interestingly, one ambush participant who ran after Guthrie, Ned Young, did believe at the time that he had shot him.[44]

On the same day, Pollard interviewed Buxton Smith, the commander of C Company, about the ambush. The latter's information came from the search patrol's analysis of the ambush site and from Forde, the Auxiliary who survived.[45] Buxton Smith accused the local population of treachery for not sending word to the police and repeated the allegations that the bodies had been mutilated. Clarke sent a summary of this interview to the Irish Office, describing it as the story that 'supersedes all others'.[46] Dublin Castle's 'official' version appeared the following day.

Photographs were another important 'vehicle of mass communication'.[47] Images of the ambush site appeared on Friday 3 December. The *Daily Sketch's* striking oblong of a reporter standing near a burnt-out lorry took up most of the front page and became the most iconic photograph of the ambush.[48] The paper's signature style was the creation of Hannen Swaffer, a journalist and picture editor employed at different times by both the *Daily Sketch* and *The Daily Mirror*. According to James Jarché, one of the *Daily Sketch's* staff photographers, Swaffer did more for press photography than 'any man living'.[49]

FUNERALS

Most of the subsequent coverage of Kilmichael focused on the funerals. The bodies arrived in Britain on 3 December and were sent home for burial, escorted by Auxiliaries, military and veterans' organisations. Their return received far less official fanfare than there had been for the British officers killed on Bloody Sunday (who had been given a formal procession through

London and state funerals), but their obsequies were widely covered in the national and regional newspapers. Reports of the Auxiliaries' homecoming, often supplemented with details of their war service, family background and excerpts from the funeral orations, appeared throughout the week. Britain's most popular 'picture papers', *The Daily Mirror* and *Daily Sketch*, published photographs of the dead men, their families and the interments. *The Illustrated Chronicle* (Newcastle) published a giant photograph of Crake on the front page.[50]

Large crowds lined the streets and filled the churches in the localities to which the bodies were returned. Most of the funerals took place on Saturday 4 December, although Poole and Wainwright were buried on the following Monday. The clergymen presiding at the funerals of Pallister and Lucas attributed the ambush to the 'Devil himself'. At Crake's funeral, however, Rev. Cecil Gallopine Hall called for a 'spirit of forgiveness' towards 'men misguided', suggesting that England was also in need of prayers: 'She has not always understood. By misunderstanding and sometimes by oppression she has alienated the affections of a warm-hearted people. The many evil deeds of these days are the result of many centuries of misunderstanding and ignorance.'[51]

EDITORIALS AND PUBLIC COMMENTARY

Letters, editorials and public commentary after Kilmichael reflected how polarised British public opinion was over Ireland.[52] *The Morning Post*, predictably, insisted that the English were crying out for a return of the 'methods of Cromwell in Ireland'.[53] Other commentary reflected growing disillusionment with British conduct. A *Liverpool Courier* editorial suggested that the ambush was 'not quite so bad' as Greenwood had said, pointing out that Britain was in a weak position to take the moral high ground about it or Bloody Sunday: 'How can we complain that officers are dragged from their beds and butchered unarmed on the spot if Sinn Feiners are treated in precisely the same manner? How can we complain if Government and private property is wrecked by Sinn Fein if the agents of the Crown also destroy private property?'[54]

Some editorials did not accept that Kilmichael should even be classed as an atrocity.[55] A *Glasgow Evening News* editorial opined that the majority of people would be less horrified by Kilmichael than they had been by Bloody Sunday. 'There is an obvious though rough moral difference between killing men who are out on a patrol more or less prepared to defend themselves against attack and pulling men out of their beds to be shot without a chance to fight for their lives.'[56]

Evidence for more radical views, though less well-documented, also survives. As might be expected, *The Communist* was disinclined to take Hamar Greenwood's word for what had occurred, asking rhetorically: 'What is really happening in Ireland?'[57] Local parliaments, the popular debating clubs modelled on the Oxford Union (and run according to British parliamentary procedure) where young middle- and working-class men (and a few women) could hone their oratory skills, provided another venue for critics of government policy.[58] In December 1920, thanks to the efforts of Socialist, Labour and independent Liberal representatives in London – some of them Irish-born – the Southgate and Thornton Heath local parliaments each passed motions sympathetic to Irish independence.[59] The former voted in favour of negotiating with the insurgents and the latter called for the British government to 'fully and completely recognise' the 'de facto Government now in existence in Ireland'.[60]

The day the Auxiliaries' remains arrived in London, James H. Thomas, the patriotic union leader known as 'Empire Jack', addressed a labour rally in Wandsworth and blamed British 'military policy' for begetting crime in Ireland. Not even a million deaths would solve the Irish problem: 'Everything had been tried in Ireland – except Liberty!'[61] Lloyd George launched a vituperative attack on former prime minister and fellow Liberal Asquith at the Constitution Club the same evening for criticising reprisals.[62] By then Asquith was an irritant to both warring sides. He was heckled at a Peace with Ireland Council's (PWIC) mass protest meeting against reprisals, which packed out the Albert Hall in London on 4 December.[63] As prime minister he had sanctioned both executions and widespread arrests after the Easter Rising in 1916, and before the Great War he had failed to move against the Ulster Unionists and capitulated during the Curragh mutiny, thereby making partition a virtual certainty. His opposition to reprisals was laudable and even brave, but for sympathisers of radical nationalism in the audience it was too little, too late.

After the funerals, Kilmichael faded from British public consciousness, but the debate over the conduct of Crown Forces in Ireland continued, and informed other ongoing political debates and issues relating to the freedom of the press, home rule, humanitarianism, the rights of small nations and the future of the empire.[64] Even the most hair-raising declarations about the ambush seemed to harden resolve in favour of already decided opinions. Those who opposed British policy in Ireland continued to protest, and several anti-war meetings were held shortly after the ambush. Sir John Simon, MP, independent Liberal and member of the PWIC, publicly condemned reprisals after Bloody Sunday and Kilmichael.[65] In January 1921, he wrote to Erskine Childers: 'There is a spreading of the truth in this country which is gathering force and power.'[66] Labour's public inquiry into Irish conditions conducted in the weeks after the ambush was a 'damning indictment' of the authorities.[67] Its mass campaign against reprisals in January and February 1921 cemented public hostility towards government policy in Ireland.[68]

KILMICHAEL COMPENSATION

The compensation claims made in Irish courts by both the Auxiliaries' dependents and members of the local population injured by Crown Forces were also covered in the British and Irish press. Criminal or malicious damage cases were adjudicated by county courts within three months of the incidents in the locality where they had taken place. The West Cork Quarter sessions circuit, presided over by Judge John William Hynes, operated throughout the War of Independence. Claims from the families of the Auxiliaries who died at Kilmichael, represented by T.P. Grainger, were heard in Macroom in the Quarterly Assizes in mid-January 1921.[69] Major Buxton Smith and Dr Kelleher both testified on behalf of the families, with the former describing Kilmichael as having 'no parallel in warfare'.[70] Press reports reproduced Kelleher's description of the injuries, and an account of the ambush reputed to come from Forde was also released (about which more later).

The precedent for the Auxiliaries' awards was *O'Connell vs. the Tipperary County Council*, the claim lodged by the father of one of the RIC men killed at Soloheadbeg in January 1919. Claims were assessed according to the degree of injury and disablement sustained by the applicant or, in the case of the next of kin, the extent of pecuniary loss suffered as a result of the death.[71] Because the Auxiliaries were in temporary rather than permanent employment, Judge Hynes reduced all of the final awards.

Forde, as a survivor, received the highest award. He applied for £15,000 and, according to press reports, received £8,000–10,000. The families of Pallister, Wainwright, Webster and Crake applied for £12,000 and were all awarded £4,000. Relations of Barnes, Bradshaw and Jones applied for £5,000, but received £1,000. The relatives of Hooper-Jones, Gleave, Taylor, Graham, Poole, Jones and Bayley all claimed either £5,000 or £6,000. The first two received £1,500. The families of Taylor, Jones and Graham were awarded £1,000. Poole's and Bayley's families received £500. Hugo's relatives were awarded £2,000 and Pearson's, £1,500.[72] The original amount sought in their cases was not stated, but as they were both unmarried it was most likely around £5,000. Eileen Guthrie's claim came up in June 1921. She was still in Macroom with her baby daughter Dorothy, born two months after Guthrie's death, hoping for news.[73] She received £5,200 (having claimed £12,000). For several years, Guthrie's body remained buried in Annahala bog on the edge of the Gearagh, the alluvial woodlands just out Macroom, but it was eventually re-interred in Inchigeelagh churchyard.[74]

Several awards were also made to locals from in and around Macroom for damages caused by Crown Forces. Technically, this did not fall within the terms of criminal injuries and malicious damage legislation. Nonetheless – and another indication of the depth of alienation British policy was inspiring even among the most cautious and conservative sections of Irish society – a number of county court judges supported compensation claims against the army and police anyway. In January 1921, Charles Browne's parents successfully claimed for the damage caused to their Macroom home.[75]

The judge who caused the authorities the most trouble was M. McDonnell Bodkin in Clare. In January 1921, he served official notices on Greenwood and General Macready by telegram, and the following month sent Hamar Greenwood an official report stating that as Crown Forces were responsible for a significant number of the 356 criminal damage cases, more than £466,000 awarded in compensation should be met by the Treasury.[76]

At the Bandon Quarter Session in April, Judge Hynes made several further awards for criminal damages caused by the military or police after Kilmichael. Michael Crowley, a labourer from Mohana, Dunmanway, who was shot in the hip during a raid on his home in early January by a uniformed man looking for information about the ambush, was awarded £1,000. Timothy D. Kelly, whose farmhouse overlooking the ambush site had been destroyed by the search patrol who found the bodies, also made a claim. Judge Hynes was suspicious, remarking at one point that the local population must have helped the flying column, but seems ultimately to have supported Kelly's claim.[77] In February and March, the homes and furniture of John O'Brien, Grillagh, and Robert Hales, Knocknacurra, (respectively) were destroyed during raids by Crown Forces. O'Brien was shot in the face. He was awarded £190 for the burning and £300 for personal injuries. Hales received £1,405.[78] Both men's sons were leading Volunteers and O'Brien's son Patrick had taken part in Kilmichael. Eventually, in April 1921, General Macready forbade further claims against Crown Forces.

The War of Independence was ended by the Anglo-Irish Truce on 11 July 1921. There had been thousands of raids, arrests, internments and curfew orders. Five hundred and twenty-three policemen, 418 soldiers, 491 Irish insurgents and 919 civilians had died by the end of December 1921, and countless more were wounded. Recent research suggests that almost a third of fatalities attributed to Crown Forces in Ireland between 1919 and 11 July 1921 occurred in dubious circumstances.[79] British policy in Ireland was thoroughly discredited both at home and abroad. In Northern Ireland, however, well into the 1920s, unionists continued to characterise the 'Macroom Massacres' and 'Black Sunday' as atrocities when justifying partition, rebuffing charges of unionist sectarianism, rejecting the Boundary Commission and condemning republican political violence.[80] In the South, those who had fought or supported efforts against the insurgents (or were accused of doing so) either left or, if they stayed, remained silent, at least publicly.[81]

4

Barry versus Deasy: Two Roads Back from the Brink

THE CORK EXAMINER'S 28 NOVEMBER 1938 picture page ran with the headline 'Cork Honours the Manchester Martyrs/Rugby'. Reflecting the diversity of the county's post-independence political, sporting and cultural life, action shots of League of Ireland soccer and Gaelic Athletic Association (GAA) football matches, a rugby friendly between Dublin and Cork, and a team photograph of the Ulster side that defeated Munster in a recent Inter-Provincial rugby match were interspersed with images of a Manchester Martyrs procession, an *Aonach na Nodlag* [Nollaig] [Christmas fair] children's céilí, a history lecture, and a special West Cork IRA veterans' reunion held in conjunction with the annual Kilmichael commemoration. One of the reunion's attendees was Seán McCarthy, President of the GAA's Munster Council. The GAA's ban on members playing or attending 'foreign games' was still in place, and the Central Council would shortly remove Douglas Hyde – Ireland's first president, founder of the Gaelic League and the GAA's patron since 1902 – because he attended an international soccer match.[1]

The *Examiner* described the 1938 IRA reunion as 'unique' for bringing together 'men who had not only differed in their opinions but differed violently'. Seán Buckley and Ted Sullivan, both Fianna Fáil TDs, and several other prominent anti-Treaty republicans were there, as were representatives from the families of the three IRA Kilmichael dead, two of whom – the O'Sullivans and the McCarthys – had supported the Free State in the Civil War. In late December 1921, in the midst of the Treaty debates, Jim O'Sullivan's mother publicly challenged the fiercely anti-Treatyite Mary MacSwiney's entitlement to speak for all Irish women: 'As one who lost a son in the battle of Kilmichael, I claim the right to speak for myself.'[2] The following month, Cork District Council Cumann na mBan voted in favour of accepting the Treaty settlement.[3]

In the photograph, Liam Deasy, brother of Patrick (the third IRA Kilmichael fatality) stood beside Tom Barry. Both fought on the anti-Treaty side in the Civil War but had taken opposing sides in internal republican divisions. On the day, honouring the fallen took precedence over any underlying tensions. Barry and Deasy were actively involved in the associational and commemorative culture that developed among the revolutionary generation after independence. They were regularly called on to give orations at public events and to chair commemorative committees into the 1970s.[4] In the 1960s, both took part in the *Lorg na Laoch* (The Hero's Track) tours of famous West Cork ambush locations.[5]

The Kilmichael site had become a *lieu de mémoire* (site of memory) even before its first anniversary. Crowds of weekend sightseers were visiting the location as early as August 1921.[6] A few IRA veterans and local people gathered at the graves of the Kilmichael dead every November to pay their respects.[7] Poems and tributes to the IRA dead were published in the local press, and a memorial cross was erected at the site in 1926.[8] In the early 1920s, efforts were also made (by their former comrades) to commemorate the Auxiliaries. On the ambush's first anniversary, a small memorial service took place in Portobello Barracks church, Dublin, for the C Company Auxiliaries 'murdered by the rebels in Ireland'.[9] In 1924, former members of J and C Auxiliary Companies donated a memorial tablet dedicated to the RIC who died in 1920–21 to St Colman's Church of Ireland church in Macroom.[10]

More republican splits and new organisations had followed the Civil War. Éamon de Valera took significant cohorts of the IRA and Sinn Féin with him when he founded Fianna Fáil in 1926, although both organisations continued to exist. Fianna Fáil TDs took their Dáil seats the following year after the political crisis caused by the assassination of Kevin O'Higgins (the recently appointed minister for external affairs) by IRA men. The first Fianna Fáil government in March 1932 quickly initiated an 'economic war' with Britain, which sparked political upheavals in Ireland based mainly on Civil War divisions. There were violent clashes between the IRA and the 'potential para-fascist' National Centre Party and Army Comrades Association (the 'Blueshirts') in 1933 and 1934.[11] Cumann na nGaedheal amalgamated with the Blueshirts in September 1933 to form Fine Gael.[12]

By the mid-1930s two distinct political blocs had emerged: one anti-Treaty republican and left-wing (Fianna Fáil and Labour), the other conservative and 'pro-commonwealth' (Cumann na Gael/Fine Gael and the Farmers' Party). Between 1922 and 1938, there was a gradual increase in the combined total of the two main Civil War parties' share of the seats in elections (65 per cent to 88 per cent), although Anti-Treaty republicanism did not become electorally ascendant in Cork until the 1940s. Fianna Fáil's electoral foothold, especially in West Cork, was consistently lower – and pro-Treatyite parties' and Labour's higher – than their share of the national vote.[13] Labour clubs and farmers' unions were active and, in 1936, over 40,000 people attended a public meeting in support of the Spanish Fascist rebel Franco in Cork city.[14]

As time went on, relations between Fianna Fáil and the IRA, who had supported their former comrades' successful bids for power in 1932 and 1933, soured.[15] Significant cohorts of the IRA's membership and support base were gradually persuaded to soften their opposition to the new state in the years that followed. Fianna Fáil introduced a more inclusive MSP Act in September 1934 allowing neutral, anti-Treaty, Cumann na mBan and Fianna Éireann veterans to apply. A new constitution undoing key elements of the Treaty settlement was approved by the Dáil and confirmed by a plebiscite in 1937.[16]

Tom Barry became one of Ireland's most well-known and publicly lauded IRA veterans and 'Cork's own folk hero'.[17] He was a complicated individual. Fiery, charismatic and exceptionally brave, some of his friends and supporters guarded his reputation as jealously as he did. Even those who disliked him acknowledged the loyalty he could inspire.[18] Barry was never an easy person to deal with though, and he provoked equal measures of hostility, admiration and allegiance throughout his life. Bill Quirke, former 2nd Southern Division O/C, said Barry 'always wanted to do what he liked and resented orders from anybody'.[19] Unpredictable and as changeable as the weather, he remained much as Michael Hopkinson described him, 'a law unto himself'.[20] As we shall see, he also had a tendency to engage in public disputes and to make inaccurate statements about his revolutionary career.

Due to a combination of poor and/or naive use of source material and conscious attempts to present him in the best possible light, modern popular narratives of Barry's life have perpetuated many factual inaccuracies that, to this day, are disregarded or reiterated rather than challenged. Moreover, they overlook the fact that while no one denied Barry's martial abilities or his contribution to the independence struggle, he was very far from being considered a reliable narrator by many of his contemporaries. Liam Deasy's reputation and standing during the revolutionary period and later among the wider community of veterans, by contrast, has been obscured. The full resonance of the clash between Barry and Deasy in the 1970s only becomes apparent within the context of what preceded it. Despite the surface congeniality, differences between the two men were long-standing, reflected wider divisions between the irredentist and Fianna Fáil wings of anti-Treatyite republicanism, and predated their public dispute over Kilmichael by many decades. It is said locally that Deasy's youngest brother Pat's fatal wounding during the ambush was another tension.

TRUCE

In the months preceding the Civil War, while most of the 1st Southern Division leaders focused on efforts to avoid a resumption of conflict, Barry associated with the most uncompromising cohort of the anti-Treaty IRA (Ernie O'Malley, Rory O'Connor, Liam Mellows and Seán MacBride).[21] Deasy, one of a small number of local officers who had carefully and diligently built up the 3rd Cork Brigade after 1916, was also anti-Treaty, but supported the efforts being made by Liam Lynch to reunite the IRA through negotiations with the pro-Treaty side.[22] Barry advocated establishing a military dictatorship and then thwarted Lynch's efforts to put forward recently negotiated army unification proposals, which Deasy later said the 1st Southern Division would have accepted.[23] Had these been implemented, Lynch and Deasy would have become deputy chiefs of staff of a reunited IRA under Eoin O'Duffy.[24] Whether Barry's actions stemmed from resentment at not being selected for a position himself, as was suggested later, is difficult to ascertain.[25]

Deasy sat on the anti-Treaty IRA's executives from March 1922 until his arrest in January 1923. Barry, who was not involved in the April anti-Treaty takeover of the Four Courts, was co-opted onto the IRA Executive after fellow Corkmen Seán O'Hegarty, Florrie O'Donoghue and Tom Hales resigned in late April or early May in protest at the suggestion (by one wing of the anti-Treatyite leadership) that a general election be forcibly prevented.[26] Barry's proposal at the third Army Convention on 18 June – to reunite the IRA by renewing war with Britain – was narrowly defeated, but fomented a temporary split in anti-Treaty ranks. Later that day he, O'Malley and O'Connor disarmed a group of Civic Guards (the new police force) in Kildare, announcing that they had 'declared war on England'.[27]

Over the spring of 1922, the anti-Treaty leadership became more divided, and the new Provisional Government's efforts to consolidate its power by establishing an army and a police force were only partially successful. Local IRA brigades, many of whom were against the Treaty, took over evacuated British military barracks around the country.[28] As the South gradually but steadily descended into civil war, the six counties of Northern Ireland (granted a limited form of home rule) experienced an intense wave of inter-communal and overtly sectarian violence. Northern events were covered extensively in the southern press, ratcheting up an already volatile situation.[29] Then, in late April, a murky and highly controversial series of murderous attacks on Protestants in the Bandon Valley occurred, which were widely condemned by the southern revolutionary elite at the time, and by republicans and historians subsequently.[30]

On 26 April, an IRA officer was shot dead during an armed raid on a Protestant farm in Ballygroman in West Cork. The IRA later returned and killed and secretly buried three men who had fought them off a few hours earlier. Over the next four days, ten more Protestants were killed and twenty-six others (at least) were threatened or assaulted in Dunmanway, Clonakilty and (to a lesser extent) Bandon.[31] The attacks had not been sanctioned by the leadership, although they were almost certainly the work of members of IRA units. The situation was hastily brought under control by local IRA officers and Sinn Féin TDs.[32]

Southern Protestants 'reacted with horror' at what they viewed as a response to the violence meted out to Catholic communities in Northern Ireland and a sectarian reprisal attack on their community.[33] On 30 April, the Archbishop of Dublin, Rev. John Gregg, called on the government to protect them.[34] Five days later the *Church of Ireland Gazette* noted that 'For the past week all Ireland has been living under the shadow of the Cork murders. We have not ceased to protest just as strongly against the horrible crimes which have stained the reputation of West Cork for religious toleration.'[35] In mid-May, a Church of Ireland synod delegation asked Michael Collins 'whether the Government desired to retain them in Ireland, or wanted them to go'. He assured them that they would be protected.[36]

On 4 May, Erskine Childers (a Protestant, Sinn Féin's former Director of Publicity and trenchant anti-Treatyite) condemned the 'Cork Murders' as sectarian in a statement published in *Poblacht na h-Éireann*.[37] Two days later, the anti-Treaty IRA Executive in the Four Courts issued special orders that neither 'demobilised R.I.C.' nor 'other enemies' were to be harassed or attacked without authorisation, and that 'Land, Stock, Residences or property seized recently from Loyalists as reprisals for Northern Atrocities are to be handed back immediately.'[38]

IRA officers issued further warnings in May and June after Protestants in Skibbereen, as well as in parts of Kerry and Limerick, received anonymous threatening letters.[39] None of those responsible for the threats or the April 1922 attacks seem to have been disciplined. Police reports indicate that the situation remained precarious for some time. Protestant farmers in Clonakilty, Bandon and other parts of West Cork were targeted in robberies, cattle and sheep stealing well into 1924.[40] Nevertheless, the efforts made to stop the April 1922 attacks stand in considerable contrast to events in Northern Ireland, where unionist leaders took virtually no effective action against the loyalist gangs terrorising Catholic areas in Belfast.[41]

CIVIL WAR

The Civil War commenced on 28 June 1922. Barry was in Cork, having suffered another bout of illness, but was added as a signatory to the anti-Treaty IRA's first official statement.[42] Never one to miss a fight, he returned to Dublin and was arrested trying to enter the Four Courts. After his escape from prison in September, he was attached to First Southern Division's and then to the Southern Command's operations staff. [43] Liam Deasy was O/C of the Southern Command and deputy C/S to Liam Lynch. While Barry fought several successful actions in Cork, Tipperary and Kilkenny between October and December 1922, he was never, as is sometimes maintained, deputy C/S in this period, 'ipso facto' or otherwise. Nor at any point was he in 'charge of all anti-Treaty O/Cs'.[44]

Whatever initial advantage the anti-Treaty IRA had seemed to possess over the hastily assembled National Army[45] in terms of arms and trained fighting men, they had almost no popular support and their forces were dogged by poor planning, inadequate organisation and demoralisation.[46] Hopes that guerrilla tactics could secure a political victory and renegotiation of the Treaty proved to be delusional. The National Army quickly gained the initiative, with the government's unexpected strategy of moving troops by ship along the southern and western coasts contributing considerably to its eventual victory.

At the beginning of 1923, the anti-Treatyites began a sabotage campaign, but burning bridges and houses, attacking trains and destroying railway lines only served to further alienate local populations. Their forces were steadily depleted by defeats, deaths and arrests, and Deasy had already been discussing ways to end the conflict before he was captured near Fermoy in January.[47] Offered a stark choice between unconditional surrender or a martyr's death, he chose the former as the only realistic means of securing the Republic in the longer term.[48] He wrote to Lynch.

'I am prepared to bear any and all the "shame" that will follow.'[49] The government allowed him to issue an appeal to his comrades to surrender. 'From then on,' remembered Bill Quirke, things 'began to go to hell'.[50]

The anti-Treaty leadership rejected Deasy's appeal, but his actions had an unsettling effect and garnered considerable sympathy, particularly among groups of IRA prisoners under threat of execution.[51] By then, very few officers in Cork – Barry included – believed they were engaged in a war they could win.[52] Indeed, Barry seems to have embarked on the first of his own peace initiatives as early as August 1922, and his efforts gathered pace after Deasy's capture and subsequent appeal.[53] The diary of Florrie O'Donoghue, who remained neutral in the Civil War, as well as other correspondence and later interviews with IRA veterans, indicate that Barry and his wife, Leslie, worked closely on peace moves with Fr Thomas Duggan in the spring and early summer of 1923, although, periodically, Barry would deny this.[54]

Barry's attitude to Deasy's actions is difficult to determine. His peace moves were understood at the time as a 'continuation' of Deasy's efforts, and Barry defended Deasy at his court martial.[55] Deasy had also been best man at Barry's wedding in 1921. Yet, according to a January 1924 army intelligence report, Barry described Deasy's surrender as having 'put the Tin Hat on us'. He reportedly maintained that Deasy had 'wrecked the whole situation ... at our very highest level of success' and that Deasy had little support among the men (although this was clearly not the case).[56] Some of Ernie O'Malley's interviewees claimed that Barry had initially repudiated Deasy's actions and that he hated Deasy even then.[57]

So many contradictory assessments and rumours swirled around Barry from early 1923 onwards that no one was quite sure what to believe.[58] In May, police reports identified him and two other Kilmichael veterans (James 'Spud' Murphy and John 'Flyer' Nyhan) as the 'most prominent leaders of the forces of disorder in West Cork'.[59] Free State officers in Cork, however, later described Barry as 'neutral or semi-neutral'.[60] On 19 February, Fr Duggan was 'instructed after Div. meeting to convey' a 'statement from Barry' proposing a 'cessation of hostilities', 'temporary dumping of arms' and recognition of the government following the next election.[61] A wireless message sent two days later to Mulcahy, then the commander-in-chief of the Free State Army, stated that, pending a meeting with their Executive, the 1st Southern would accept the government's terms.[62] At a meeting between Division officers and Lynch on 26 February, Barry urged that prisoners (who wanted to follow Deasy's lead) be heard.[63] The IRA's position was hopeless, he said, and there was no value to be had in their best men being executed.[64]

Lynch, however, continued to insist that victory was at hand. Prisoners looking to discuss peace terms were warned to desist or be treated as traitors.[65] Despite this, O'Donoghue's diary recorded in March that 'Barry was making, through Fr. Duggan, proposals for a dump arms, to be published when a few signatures of prominent people had been got.'[66] Details of the 'Barry-Harty-Duggan' peace moves were published in the *Irish Independent* on 8 March.[67] Other signees included members of the Cork Employer's Federation (CEF) such as Frank Daly and T.P. Dowdall. On 9 April, the same newspaper published captured IRA Executive minutes from February, which documented Barry's remarks in relation to the weakness of the IRA's position and his proposal to end 'further armed resistance'. When put to the Executive, this had been defeated by one vote.[68]

Moss Twomey, then on Lynch's staff, later told Ernie O'Malley that the IRA in the south was 'going to bits' and that Barry and Tom Crofts had convinced most of the 1st Southern Division officers to support a surrender. He also said that the publication of the Executive minutes in April had caused 'great harm'.[69] Comments by Jim Moloney (formerly Lynch's director of communications) and Seán MacBride, though in different prisons, reflected the consternation Barry's efforts caused among some of the anti-Treaty leadership. MacBride called Barry a 'swell-headed' Corkman who was 'far worse than Decey [*sic*]'. Moloney reckoned that a 'very hot linseed poultice' applied to Barry's head might 'reduce the swelling a bit'.[70]

However, the overwhelming majority of the anti-Treaty leadership did not share Lynch's unshakable conviction that victory was likely. The IRA dumped arms and admitted defeat (but did not surrender) within weeks of his death on 10 April 1923. From then on, anti-Treaty forces were still on the run and being hunted by the National Army but were no longer at war. Barry clashed with de Valera and Frank Aiken (who had succeeded Lynch as C/S) over how to make their position less vulnerable.[71] Barry's June memo advocating the destruction of arms and an amnesty for anti-Treaty fighters is in Éamon de Valera's papers: 'I have reason to believe that the open destruction of Arms by us will stop all pursuit by F.S. Forces and automatically release men from jails.'[72]

Regardless of Barry's motivations and the manner in which he went about it, his continued efforts to secure peace and favourable terms for anti-Treaty fighters in the first six months of 1923 were, arguably, his finest hour, although they eventually caused him to break with the IRA Executive. The situation came to a head after Barry and two other officers threatened to appeal directly to the men (just as Barry had done when liaison officer during the Truce) in order to either secure an amnesty or restart the fighting. After Barry refused to back down, IRA C/S Aiken prevailed on him to resign in July 1923.[73] According to Aiken, Barry left the IRA entirely, and evidence suggests that he did not rejoin it until late 1932.[74] He continued to associate himself informally with the IRA in Cork and Tipperary. In 1925, when he was caught driving without either road tax or a licence, Barry refused as 'an IRA officer' to recognise the authority of (and reputedly tried to assault) the Garda who stopped him.[75]

In October and November 1923, Deasy, who was still in prison, took part in mass hunger strikes by IRA prisoners for their release.[76] Barry, on the run in Cork, re-established cordial relations with Frank Aiken, offering to help, but nothing seems to have come of this.[77] In mid-December, Barry walked into Cork Courthouse and was arrested, but thanks to Seán Prior (a local Cumann na nGeadheal TD) and Richard Mulcahy, he was released after a few hours.[78] Mary MacSwiney and Tom Crofts were both suspicious of these interventions by pro-Treatyite figures on Barry's behalf, and their relations with Barry became strained as a result. Crofts accused Prior of attempting to 'seduce Officers of the IRA from their allegiance to the Republic'.[79]

In the decades after independence, anti-Treaty veterans expressed a range of views on Barry, Deasy and the Civil War. Some blamed Lynch and Deasy for failing to develop a coherent military strategy in the crucial early stages of the conflict and disapproved of their continued attempts to make peace (particularly in Limerick in July 1922). Others acknowledged that the anti-Treaty IRA had very little popular support and believed that, with hindsight, they should have surrendered earlier.[80] It became *de rigueur* among some irredentists to say Deasy 'let the side down' in 1923.[81] By and large, however, he was well-liked and respected. Deasy's post-Civil War activities and political views were generally representative of the majority of anti-Treatyite veterans.

Barry was a more polarising figure. To some, he was the 'man who would do things', a 'good bloody man' and a 'great soldier'.[82] Others remembered an abrasive individual, respected but not particularly liked, who was notorious for wanting 'to be top dog in everything',[83] bragging about his military prowess and dramatic entrances: 'Do you know who I am?'[84] Barry's friends described him as both generous and vindictive.[85] 'Nudge' Callanan, a Cork veteran, summed up his contradictory character well: 'Barry was kind of a leader of men ... but then he'd do something queer'.[86]

AFTER THE CIVIL WAR

Deasy was released from prison in July 1924 and subsequently court-martialled and expelled from the IRA for issuing his January 1923 appeal.[87] Deasy told Máire MacSwiney he had no regrets and still believed he had done the right thing.[88] Both the IRA and demobilised National Army soldiers made parts of Leitrim, Tipperary, Mayo, Clare, Sligo and Cork largely ungovernable for most of 1924, but the Civil War was over.[89] In November, the government declared an amnesty for anti-Treaty fighters.

Deasy returned to West Cork after his release. He married in 1927 and immersed himself in the GAA. He was on the Southwest Cork Divisional Committee from 1926, elected chairperson the following year and was president of the GAA's Southwest County Board in 1933.[90] He became a successful businessman and, by the mid-1930s, was living in Dublin. His controversial appeal for peace in January 1923 did surprisingly little long-term damage to his reputation. Nudge Callanan said Deasy's surrender 'knocked the skittles' out of them but they 'never lost respect for Liam at all because we knew he was quite honest about it you see. Ah we knew ourselves, because we were beaten ourselves ... there was ... Tom Barry ... but all the rest now, all the West Cork men never took any notice of that.'[91] De Valera approached Deasy more than once to stand as a Fianna Fáil candidate in West Cork, but he always declined.[92] He applied for his MSP in 1935 and was awarded full service to the end of the 10th Period (1 April–30 September 1923) at Rank 'A' (the highest).[93]

Deasy also became a high-profile advocate for IRA veterans of the 1916–23 period, who were referred to collectively as the 'Old IRA' (OIRA) in order to distinguish them from those who remained in or joined the IRA in the 1920s and 1930s.[94] He was the first chairman of the Old IRA Men's Association (Cork County) (OIRAMAC) established in February 1934, and a founding member and first president of the All-Ireland Old IRA Men's Organisation established two years later.[95] Nudge Callanan described him as a careful, patient man who others went for help and advice: 'They all went with their complaint, they wouldn't go to Barry at all, to Deasy, not to anybody else ... and he'd listen to them, and he'd hear it out.'[96] Batt Murphy, another Cork veteran, said Deasy was the only 'top-ranking' man who took any interest in advocating on the OIRA's behalf.[97]

Around 1924, Barry secured a job as an inspection officer for the Condensed Milk Company (CMC) in Limerick and Tipperary.[98] According to Frank Daly, a member of both the Cork Progressive Association (CPA) and the CEF, who had been associated with Barry's March 1923 peace move, Barry gave 'every satisfaction' at the CMC.[99] In 1926, after he allegedly hired scab labour to break a strike in Knocklong, the *Voice of Labour* denounced Barry as a 'White Guard in the service of English capitalists and under the supervision of a Free State TD'.[100] This was a reference to Andrew O'Shaughnessy, the CMC's managing director and a CPA TD. These contacts served Barry well.[101] In December 1927, thanks largely to the combined efforts of republicans and CEF members on the Cork Harbour Board's management committee, Barry secured a temporary position as a 'general superintendent' of the outdoor works. He was made permanent the following year, despite objections from the board's Labour representatives.[102]

In late 1932, Barry also rejoined the IRA, and he played an important part in its resurgence in West Cork where no units had existed for years.[103] Impulsive as ever, he initially seems to have tried to convince the IRA to join forces with Fianna Fáil, who had taken office in March 1932. His allegiances and underlying sympathies shifted back and forth between the two bodies over the 1930s and 1940s.[104] Barry spent roughly six years in the IRA. The organisation went into a downward spiral after 1933, riven by factions and consistently outmanoeuvred by Fianna Fáil. Barry also engaged in a number of rancorous exchanges. He clashed with Timothy J. Murphy (the Dunmanway Labour TD) in December 1932, Frank Aiken in 1935, the MSP board, which adjudicated his pension, at the end of the 1930s, and with the OIRAMAC in 1941.

Relations between Barry and Deasy, and between the IRA and the OIRA generally, were tense during the 1930s. The IRA feared that the OIRA veterans' organisations – 'freakish combinations of Republican Free Staters' – would be used by the government to undermine their support base (and they were). In Cork, they were particularly concerned about the 'Crofts-[O']Donoghue-Deasy clique'.[105] The IRA's leadership eventually came to a more measured view of the OIRA, but the OIRA remained wary of them. In 1935, Florrie O'Donoghue, a member of the OIRAMAC, was formally admonished for accompanying Barry to a meeting with the latter's old friend T.P. Dowdall TD.[106]

Barry's row with Tim Murphy in late 1932 commenced after the local committee of the IRA's British Boycott Campaign (chaired by Barry) demanded that the West Cork Board of Assistance stop running adverts for British coal. While Barry and the West Cork IRA generally opposed the IRA's radical left wing, they shared its general disdain for the Labour party, trade unions, majoritarian democracy and the 'fog of constitutionalism'.[107] According to Donal O'Donoghue, who was in overall charge of the boycott campaign, Barry had the 'utmost contempt' for the masses.[108] Though largely forgotten now, Murphy was a former ITGWU organiser, lifelong Christian socialist and an exceptionally popular TD. He was friendly enough with the local OIRA, writing in support of Kilmichael veteran Ned Young's wound pension and for Michael McCarthy's father's dependents' allowance, but the hostility between him and the IRA was mutual and overt.[109] According to Moss Twomey, Murphy actively discriminated against local republicans.[110]

Murphy certainly made no secret of his views on Barry in 1932: 'when the people of this country are struggling hard in order to live, Mr. Barry is in a well-sheltered and well-paid position, which he got without any competitive examination or without any reference to the rights of any existing employee in that position'.[111] At a Bandon boycott meeting a few weeks later, Murphy and the board were denounced as 'despicable, slave-minded adherents of British Imperialism'.[112] Barry publicly accused Murphy of being a British agent, asserting that, during the War of Independence, the 3rd Cork Brigade had discussed taking 'preventative action against him'.[113] The accusations seem to have annoyed Liam Deasy (who had been, successively, adjutant and O/C of the brigade at the time), and Barry feared he might act as a witness for Murphy in any libel cases arising. He asked Twomey for copies of the 'official charges of his [Deasy's] courtmartial and the actual findings in detail'.[114]

These exchanges occurred shortly after the first large-scale Kilmichael commemoration. Thanks largely to Barry, it was held under the auspices of the IRA.[115] That year, 1932, was one of the most violent and politically volatile years since the Civil War, with running street battles between the Blueshirts, Fianna Fáil and the IRA.[116] For the commemoration, ambush veterans, accompanied by over 5,000 IRA Volunteers and members of Cumann na mBan and other republican organisations, assembled outside Dunmanway. Moss Twomey and Barry each gave orations.[117] Barry sent instructions to Twomey as to how his oration should be reported, then criticised coverage in *An Phoblacht*, arguing that he had been misquoted. The reporter stood over the account.[118] In the same letter Barry noted that Deasy had been 'kicking up rough since Kilmichael', and that 'they' (he did not specify who) had barred him from 'their' last meeting. Deasy might have objected to the political tenor of the commemoration, but it is difficult to be sure.

What seems to be the only explicitly pro-Treaty attempt to claim the Kilmichael legacy occurred a few weeks later, when W.T. Cosgrave and a large contingent of Blueshirts visited the site while electioneering in West Cork.[119] After that, although both pro- and anti-Treaty veterans attended, the Kilmichael commemoration became (and remains) an established public platform for republicans, with Béal na Bláth the annual pro-Treatyite counterpoint. Cork was home to around a quarter of the Blueshirts' nominal membership and at the epicentre of that organisation's violent confrontations with the IRA between 1932 and 1934.[120] Towards the end of 1933, Hugh O'Reilly and Cornelius Daly, two West Cork Blueshirts, were so viciously assaulted they died of their injuries.[121] According to Tim Pat Coogan, Barry was the main suspect in both cases.[122] Local Gardaí declined to question him about either incident, however, apparently in order to protect an informant. What, if any, involvement Barry actually had in the attacks is unknown, but a few months earlier, during the IRA's general army convention in March, he had requested the IRA's sanction to execute local Blueshirts, which he did not receive.[123]

In April 1934, Barry was arrested and eventually jailed on a separate charge of possession of a Thompson sub-machine gun. He was released in July but arrested again in March 1935. Barry and two others were brought before a military tribunal the following month. During the trial, Barry refused to recognise the court and objected to being tried alongside one of his co-defendants, who was a communist.[124] On 26 April 1935, he was sentenced to six months in prison for membership of an illegal organisation (the IRA), and for failing to answer police questions. The following month, Barry had a public row with Frank Aiken, then minister for defence.

BARRY–AIKEN DISPUTE

In mid-May, hecklers at a Fianna Fáil *ceidhe* in Dundalk interrupted Aiken's speech with shouts of: 'Up the Republic!', 'What about Tom Barry?' and 'Remember the 77!' Aiken responded, with some irritation, that the hecklers did not know much about the Civil War: 'When the I.R.A. were fighting and men were being executed,' he said, 'Barry was running around the country trying to make peace.'[125] His remarks sparked a series of acrimonious public exchanges with Barry which reflected the extent to which contemporary politics and more long-standing resentments dating from the Civil War could fuse in public discourse. Aiken was frustrated at the IRA's ongoing refusal to recognise the state.[126] Barry accused Aiken (and Fianna Fáil) of hypocrisy for jailing republicans for advocating the overthrow of Free State institutions and courts that they had once also condemned as illegitimate.

Peace moves were a touchy subject even then. Barry stated emphatically that 'at no time during the Civil War, or after it, did I seek to make peace'. On one single occasion, in March 1923, he said, he couriered Fr Duggan's and Archbishop of Cashel Rev. John Harty's proposed peace terms to the IRA Executive.[127] But Aiken did not back down. He said Barry's unsanctioned peace moves had greatly worried Liam Lynch. He maintained that Barry made a 'personal peace offer through the G.O.C. of the Cork Command' of the National Army (Colonel David Reynolds) on 19 February 1923, and circulated a memorandum urging the destruction of arms on 8 June. Barry flatly denied communicating with any 'Free State officer at any time', criticised Aiken's Civil War service, and accused him of deliberately misdating a communication from Lynch to bolster his false accusations. He challenged Aiken to produce the documents he had cited.[128]

Moss Twomey later confirmed to both Ernie O'Malley and Uinseann MacEoin that Aiken did have documents relating to Barry's 1923 peace moves. He surmised that Aiken did not release them for fear of compromising several of his associates in Fianna Fáil.[129] Twomey also told O'Malley that Barry refused to acknowledge his actions:

"'I never did that", said Barry.

"'You did", said I, "and Aiken has papers to prove it.'"[130]

Twomey was well placed to know the facts. As IRA C/S from 1927 to 1936 he had access to still-hidden Civil War correspondence. He was also from Cork and had been on Lynch's staff throughout the revolutionary period. He later told Florrie O'Donoghue that Aiken had also tried to use papers in his possession to 'influence him in a certain direction' in 1932.[131] Aiken's comments in relation to Barry's peace moves were ill-judged, but the latter's subsequent public denials made everything worse and put his defenders in a very awkward situation.

Several individuals and veterans' organisations came to Barry's defence, including Fr Duggan and Tom Crofts (former O/C of the 1st Southern Division). Unsurprisingly, as both were aware that Aiken's remarks regarding Barry's peace efforts were substantively correct, they chose their words carefully.[132] Duggan ignored Barry's denials, instead admonishing Aiken for criticising Barry's peace efforts because the anti-Treatyites were clearly beaten by January 1923. Crofts fudged, confirming that he, Barry, Duggan and others had met a deputation of prisoners from Cork Gaol on 19 February, and that Duggan met Colonel Reynolds in hopes of preventing their execution, but he also said that Barry had not authorised the meeting.[133] Tom Kelleher also publicly challenged Aiken's comments about Barry's peace moves, despite the fact that Kelleher had been a member of the prisoners' delegation who had advocated following Liam Deasy's lead.[134]

Riven by internal divisions over policies, the IRA's position became more precarious as the 1930s progressed. Radicals within the IRA split from the organisation in 1934 to found the short-lived Republican Congress. The government then banned the IRA after the killing of retired Vice Admiral Henry Boyle Sommerville in June 1936 (an attack which Barry ordered). Barry took over as IRA CS in 1937, overseeing a rapprochement between the Congress and the IRA. It was an indication of how weak both organisations had become.[135] He courted both Irish communists and Nazis in hopes of securing funds to attack Northern Ireland but was thwarted by the Dublin leadership.[136] According to one West Cork IRA veteran, Barry's plans to attack a barracks in Armagh fell through not because of a security breach (as was said at the time) but because Dublin refused to release the necessary funds.[137] Eventually, in April 1938, Barry, Seán MacBride and several others resigned from the IRA after Seán Russell regained control of the Army Council. They (quite sensibly) objected to Russell's scheme to attack Britain. The IRA's British bombing campaign, which began in January 1939, was disastrous.

Barry announced his support for Fianna Fáil in the upcoming elections in June 1938.[138] This also strained relations with his former comrades in the IRA. Staunch Kerry republican Mai Dálaigh described Barry as 'foreign legion', a man who would fight for any side. According to her, Barry left her brother Tom's funeral in August 1939 before it started because Moss Twomey, Paddy McLogan and other IRA men refused to speak to him.[139] In December 1938, Barry applied for an MSP. He informed the board that he would 'take no other rank' than an 'A', and vociferously disputed his initial award of 'B'.[140] He made several claims about his revolutionary career that are difficult to reconcile with the evidence.

In January 1939, he told the pension board that he joined the IRA in July 1919, and that between April and June 1921 he had been in 'complete and absolute control of all the Active Service Units in Cork, Kerry, Waterford and West-Limerick'. He further maintained that, as 'Deputy Divisional O/C', he 'ranked co-jointly' with Lynch.[141] Ted O'Sullivan later told O'Malley that 'Barry brought up before the Board 3 men who had held no rank at the time to prove that he Barry [sic] had been training men before he joined the IVs ... C[ivil]/W[ar]: Barry had resigned officially. He had no rank. He said he was deputy C/S.'[142]

Barry also claimed that O'Malley, Rory O'Connor, Dinny Lacey and Seámus Robinson had all been under his command during the Limerick stand-off in April (actually March) 1922. He stated on several occasions that after his escape from prison, he was appointed 'Director of Operations' by Liam Lynch and held the position until July 1923.[143] O'Malley, Deasy and other veterans contradicted or qualified much of this testimony, and Barry backed down somewhat when he was shown a copy of his July 1923 letter resigning from the IRA. However, others who testified on Barry's behalf defended him and made strong arguments that he deserved special consideration in light of his exceptional services. In the end, at de Valera's personal prompting, the MSP board declined to increase Barry's period of recognised service but raised his rank to 'A'.

Barry was far from being the only veteran to make dubious claims or to receive special treatment. Three years earlier, Aiken promised O'Malley a pension within a couple of weeks if he returned to Ireland, and made roundabout but suggestive observations about how, if O'Malley had fought in the 1916 Rising, he would qualify for a higher rate.[144] O'Malley's MSP application later duly made such a claim although, in reality, he does not seem to have joined the Irish Volunteers until after the Rising.[145]

Barry then fell out with the OIRAMAC. Joining forces with Tom Hales, in June 1941 they jointly complained to the pensions board that the Cork veterans' organisation (which referred MSP claimants to the pensions referee) had 'no status whosoever' and was not qualified to adjudicate Cork claims.[146] This move was counterproductive and created much bad feeling.[147] Flor Begley, writing to the pensions board in response, dismissed both men: 'Persons such as Mr. Barry & Mr. Hales do not cut much ice down here either with genuine claimants or the general public I can assure you.'[148]

Fianna Fáil's and the OIRA's integration into the mainstream of Irish political life continued in the 1940s. Negotiating this transition proved difficult for Barry. Deasy and many other former anti-Treaty officers served in the army during the Emergency (Second World War). Barry was invited for officer training in July 1940 but according to his army intelligence file, he arrived drunk, failed to turn up to parade the next day and was discharged within a week.[149] Letters quoted by Meda Ryan suggest he felt hard done by, but as the evidence is in his inaccessible papers, this is impossible to verify. Barry ran as an independent in a 1946 Cork by-election but alienated most of his potential support base (according to the republican and communist Mick O'Riordan), and lost his deposit.[150] In late 1949, during a speaking tour of the United States for de Valera's ill-fated Anti-Partition League, he caused a minor political scandal (according to press reports) by declaring that Northern Ireland would have to be taken by force, that 'guns may bark again' and that the Irish government had set aside millions of pounds to purchase arms.[151] Not for the first time, Barry then denied ever saying such a thing.[152]

For many, however, and particularly among republicans, Barry remained a much-admired folk hero. Several of MacEoin's interviewees were proud to refer to themselves as 'Barry's men'.[153] Dublin veteran Tony Woods had 'immense admiration' for him: 'None of the controversies about him could ever wipe out for me the memories of Toureen, Kilmichael and Crossbarry. To me he was one of the big generals of the struggle against the British.'[154] Understanding the underlying dynamics and differences between Barry and Deasy, and attitudes towards both men generally, is made more difficult by the fact that many of the public accounts of the revolutionary period often glossed over the internal tensions within the leadership at the time. Florrie O'Donoghue's meticulous profile of Liam Lynch, for instance, carefully skirted around several controversies, omitting any mention of Lynch's troubles with Barry, and contradicted O'Donoghue's own diary's notes about Barry's peace moves during the Civil War.[155]

Protecting Deasy's reputation was another priority. In correspondence relating to the Lynch biography, Moss Twomey commented:

> Nobody wants to put anybody in the pillory, and least of all Liam Deasey [*sic*]. His case and the action which he took in 1923 appears more reasonable to-day than it did then, and chiefly because a vast majority who denounced him then, have themselves since swallowed much more than Deasey [*sic*] then proposed. He recommended just a military surrender, by a beaten Army. They gulped down the Treaty and the whole outfit arising out of it *voluntarily* a few years later. This goes for deV and all the big chiefs.[156]

Barry's unpredictability, his tendency to exaggerate (or deny) his role in events, his quarrels with Murphy and Aiken in the 1930s and, later, with the pensions board are important contexts for his various Kilmichael accounts. In many respects, Barry was his own worst enemy. His obvious intelligence, combat prowess and exceptional courage coexisted with – and were often overshadowed and undermined by – narcissism and an aggressive, unpredictable hubris. 'Mercurial' hardly does him justice. In relation to what happened at Kilmichael, it would have been more surprising if what Barry said had remained unchanged. The reality is more in keeping with the man that he was. Barry's accounts changed more than anyone else's.

5

Issues and Participants

ENGAGING WITH HISTORICAL MEMORY IS unavoidable when researching and writing about the Irish revolution. This chapter addresses evidential and methodological issues that arise when employing individual testimony and oral history accounts as evidence. The maxim that Ireland's revolutionary generation rarely spoke about their experiences is often repeated, but true only to an extent. A significant cohort of them talked about it all the time. For many decades, IRA participants were the main source of information for their activities. For some veterans, writing, speaking and commemorating their war was a central preoccupation of their lives. Their 'retellings' could be found in fighting stories, memoirs, newspapers, interviews, public orations, testimony before pension and compensation boards, and private conversations.[1] Veterans penned memoirs and histories that were serialised in the popular press. Shorter accounts of actions and ambushes were published as fighting stories in *The Capuchin Annual* and by Anvil Press.[2] Veterans also addressed local history societies and gave orations at public events and annual commemorations. They spoke to their fellow veterans, local librarians, local historians and family members, and were interviewed for public history projects.

Participant accounts of the IRA campaign were shaped by the precise circumstances of the telling, the personal world view and experience of the tellers, and the broader political context. The main political cleavages in independent Ireland derived from the Civil War, and the polemical nature of Irish politics and public remembrance left little space for the confusing, contradictory and often brutal realities of war that veterans often remembered. Most of them, pro- and anti-Treaty, at one time or another, proffered, facilitated or acquiesced in dubious or carefully sanitised public accounts of the past. Some were unwilling to speak badly of former comrades, others made a point of doing so or dismissed the contributions of anybody save themselves and their friends. The facts imparted by some individuals altered very little over the years, while the narrative content of other accounts and recollections shifted and changed like the sands.

Public narratives of the revolutionary period were influenced by both wider circumstances and individual experience. Commentary on controversial or disputed events was often filtered through coded narratives in both published accounts and retrospective personal testimony. Points of contention were addressed indirectly, by analogy or in counter-narratives full of deliberate and meaningful divergences from other accounts, but without drawing explicit attention to the fact that they were contradicting what others said. The implications were often lost on those unfamiliar with the underlying controversies, but those in the know could read between the lines.

The natural and inevitable decline in remembered detail over time and minor reconstructive errors – normal characteristics of autobiographical memory – were often less of a factor in determining accuracy than how much the tellers were prepared to say.[3] If outright fabrication was relatively rare, oblique references, ambiguous language and the omission of crucial detail was quite common. Not everyone was willing to lay themselves bare to the judgement of others. Some veterans refiltered and reinterpreted conflicted and contradictory actions. Others were never very good at the truth from the start. High-profile public narratives linked to personal reputations or wider political positions were particularly prone to distortion. Public disputes and rival accounts of ambushes, frequently quite bitter, were common. Challenges, disagreements, claims and counterclaims (and the occasional legal action) by individuals or groups who felt slighted or misrepresented were not unknown.

While idealised public accounts of the 1916–23 period had a certain authority, the reminiscences of the revolutionary generation as recounted to families, neighbours, colleagues and friends over cups of tea also became part of the fabric of Irish life, despite the fact that younger generations did not always fully appreciate the significance of their elders' recollections until later. What veterans told others informally was often more explicit and infused with attitudes and emotions too complex to fit neatly into the heroic mould of 'official' narratives. The vibrant folklore and social memory of the War of Independence and Civil War was frequently suffused with what Gearóid Ó Tuathaigh describes as a 'much more complicated sense of historical process and historical narrative' that was 'easily, uncontroversially and pervasively present in everyday views and attitudes to the [then] recent past.'[4]

Veterans' personal memories were in constant dialogue with these public and private contexts. The circumstances of their lives and who they were speaking to impacted on how readily the messy, exhilarating, painful, terrifying and sometimes terrible realities of the revolutionary period were acknowledged. Some felt obligated to support exculpating versions of the past that were at odds with their own memories. The exchanges between Max Caulfield, author of a vivid 1963 history of the Easter Rising, and Simon Donnelly, one of his interviewees, are a good example of how personal remembrances could compromise or threaten public reputations.

Caulfield's book came under fire after publication because it made reference to Éamon de Valera's 'nervous state' while in command of the Boland's Mills garrison.[5] Donnelly, de Valera's second in command and the source for Caulfield's remarks, publicly denied either meeting or being interviewed by the author, even after Caulfield confirmed that he still had a recording of their exchange.[6] Despite this, Donnelly seemed more convincing to many at the time. His intercession was an important factor in preserving de Valera's reputation and the president was grateful for it.[7] In reality, however, Caulfield was the one telling the truth about the interviews.[8] Donnelly was clearly conflicted. His two BMH accounts of Easter Week were released in 2003. One defended de Valera. The other confirmed most of what Caulfield had written.[9] While Caulfield's tribulations are all but forgotten now, the trouble over Kilmichael has never really ended.

From the early 1920s to the end of the 1950s, thousands of testimonies, interviews and documents about the 1916–23 period were collected from all sides in various contexts, although few were available for consultation until decades later. The Irish Grants Committee and James Richard Weekes Goulden (a teacher of Irish, a Protestant and RIC sergeant's son) collected material from southern loyalists and former RIC men.[10] From 1923 onwards, the Department of Defence acquired a vast archive of information about the Irish Volunteers/IRA and associated organisations through adjudicating claims for military service and disability pensions and dependents' allowances.[11]

The introduction of pensions made certifying actions and identifying participants a priority for veterans' organisations and pension boards, but it could be tricky. The pensioning process was built almost entirely around remembered evidence. Certification generally depended on endorsement by other veterans and local OIRA committees. Legitimate participants were sometimes forgotten. Veterans emigrated or became otherwise hard to trace. Irredentists refused to recognise the state and would not support pension claims or endorse participant lists. Veterans gave written and sometimes oral evidence in respect of applicants' claims, which were then assessed by the pensions referee and his advisors, most of whom were also veterans.

Former officers on local brigade committees vouched for an applicant's service (or sometimes declined to do so). Scores of OIRA and other veterans' associations (Old Cumann na mBan, Old Citizen Army Comrades' Association, etc.) were formed in the decades following the Truce of July 1921, and especially in the wake of the 1934 MSP Act. For some years after 1935, local OIRA veterans' committees compiled nominal rolls of members and activity reports.[12] An added layer of difficulty was the controversial 'notional grades of rank' stipulating that only former officers of units over a certain size would qualify for the largest pensions available. This provision of the pension legislation was not only unpopular but also virtually an invitation to inflate the rolls.[13]

THE BUREAU OF MILITARY HISTORY

The BMH was a government-funded public history project. Between 1947 and 1957 it collected 1,773 witness statements and over 300 document collections from members of the revolutionary generation. Witnesses were given personal copies of their testimony to use however they wished, but the collection as a whole was confidential and the statements and documents were not released until 2003.[14] Investigators doing fieldwork were advised (quite correctly) not to reconcile conflicting or contradictory accounts of events. Tom Barry initially agreed to help but, alarmed at having no access to or control over what might be said by other veterans, then changed his mind.[15] In a letter to Michael McDunphy, BMH director, he expressed particular concern about 'malicious' IRA members who had 'developed a mental kink about other men and matters which had no foundation in fact'. He refused to submit a statement himself. Any material that was not 'authenticated or confirmed by immediate investigation', he argued, should be destroyed.[16]

Barry made regular public attacks on the project over the years, although there is no evidence that the BMH administrators or staff harboured any animosity or doubts about him.[17] If anything, the opposite was the case. McDunphy had welcomed Barry's initial willingness to help.[18] The source for the BMH chronology's Kilmichael entry (compiled to aid investigators and witnesses when drafting statements) was *Guerilla Days*: 'RIC feign surrender, re-open fire and kill M. McCarthy, Jim O'Sullivan and Pat Deasy. IRA re-attack. Entire party of 18 RIC killed.'[19]

Barry's worries about what might be said in confidential statements were not unfounded. In May 1949, when *Guerilla Days* was being serialised in *The Irish Press*, Seán Collins informed McDunphy that a group of Cork veterans had met and decided not to submit their BMH witness statements until after Barry's memoir was published because they wanted to 'examine it critically'.[20] Six Kilmichael ambush participants gave statements: Ned Young, Paddy O'Brien, Jack Hennessy, Timothy Keohane, Michael O'Driscoll and Spud Murphy.[21] All were either recommended by or associated with Liam Deasy.[22] Their accounts, which Chapter Seven discusses in more detail, do not support Barry's 1949 Kilmichael narrative. According to a BMH investigator, O'Brien took several months to 'study the period from notes he possessed and to make sure he was giving all the data correct' before drafting his testimony. O'Brien later requested that

Deasy check over a draft.[23] Over thirty other BMH witnesses who did not take part directly in the ambush discuss it, including one man who had tried unsuccessfully to deliver a dispatch to the column.[24]

The BMH's consultation with Deasy about potential interviewees was not unusual, particularly as Barry had refused to cooperate with the project. BMH investigators made extensive use of the network of OIRA veterans' organisations established to assist the Department of Defence in administering the 1934 MSP legislation. It was standard practice for investigators conducting fieldwork to consult prominent local veterans or OIRA veterans' organisations both about potential witnesses and about which key events to discuss. The BMH was also given full access to the MSP archive, which became the project's main source for identifying potential witnesses, and issues and events to be investigated. Ernie O'Malley carried out his own interviewing project in a broadly coterminous period.[25]

Attitudes among BMH witnesses towards Barry overall were mixed, though they were generally less critical of him than O'Malley's interviewees. Dónal Hales described Barry's book as 'unreliable in details'.[26] Seán O'Driscoll (a veteran of Barry's column) endorsed it, and included page references to *Guerilla Days* in his statement's list of IRA actions.[27] Eamon Broy, likewise, recounted Barry's version of the false surrender at Kilmichael as 'what really happened', although, as a Dublin policeman in 1920, he had no direct knowledge.[28] Deasy drafted two witness statements for the BMH in the 1950s, but in the end decided not to sign and return the more 'lengthy and important' of the two.[29] He told Florrie O'Donoghue that he did not trust the BMH's promises of confidentiality, and feared that the testimony given would still 'be at [the] disposal of undesirables' (writers).[30] Instead, he embarked on a project of his own.

The BMH and MSP collections, both released over the last two decades, have had a transformative impact on scholarship relating to the revolutionary period. In addition to the six substantial BMH accounts of Kilmichael, the MSP records contain biographical details about participants and small nuggets of interesting information about the ambush itself.[31] There are over thirty MSP claim files, for instance, from individuals whose names have rarely, if ever, appeared on official participant lists.

The majority, mostly women, were involved in pre- and post-ambush supporting activities.[32] These claims make a substantial contribution to understanding of the IRA's wider support networks. Some undermine previously held assumptions and include new details relating to important issues and controversies. Numerous MSP claimants (and one BMH witness) for instance, acted as dispatch carriers. Kattie O'Driscoll conveyed a communication by Barry relating to two captured British deserters the day after Kilmichael.[33] This presents serious difficulties for those who reject the captured report as a forgery on the grounds that Barry did not issue any written communications.[34]

PARTICIPANT TESTIMONY

Further interviews and testimony were collected from the 1960s to the 1990s by RTÉ, Thames Television, the British Library and the Clogher Historical Society, as well as individual researchers and historians such as Max Caulfield, Nollaig Ó Gadhra, Meda Ryan, Fr John Chisholm, Kenneth Griffith, Fr Louis O'Kane, John O'Beirne Ranelagh, Ulick O'Connor, David Fitzpatrick, Peter Hart, Joost Augusteijn and Uinseann MacEoin. Several lengthy recorded interviews with Kilmichael veterans survive. Some were conducted for broadcast (radio, television or film), others privately for research. Barry was interviewed by Seámus Kelly (1966), Ó Gadhra (1969), Ó Dúlaing (1970), Griffith (c. 1973) and Thames Television (1979). Fr Chisholm spoke to him informally. Ó Dúlaing also interviewed Jack O'Sullivan and Ned Young, as well as several locals who were in the vicinity of the action.[35]

Liam Deasy and Chisholm collected testimony from and/or interviewed O'Brien, O'Sullivan, Young and Jack Aherne in the 1960s.[36] O'Sullivan was also interviewed by his son Dan and by Brendan Vaughan in the early 1980s.[37] Peter Hart (taking notes) spoke to Ned Young twice, in April and June 1988.[38] There is no direct commentary about Kilmichael in Hart's notes, although Young mentioned Flor Crowley's review of *Towards Ireland Free* as a source for the 'Barry–Deasy' conflict (discussed in the next chapter).[39] Hart also asked one of his Protestant interviewees what they knew about Kilmichael. Only what Ned Young told them, they said – that he and Barry had walked down the road to meet the first lorry, and that most of the Auxiliaries had been killed with revolvers.[40]

Hart interviewed Willie Chambers and Dan Cahalane (not a Kilmichael veteran) together on 19 November 1989. Both were members of the Kilmichael and Crossbarry Commemoration Committee, and Chambers was a very good friend of Ned Young's.[41] According to Chambers' son, Liam, the interview took place in their home, with his mother present. Chambers also gave Hart a tour of the Kilmichael ambush site, and told him he witnessed some part of the action. Confusingly, he told his son that he was posted some distance away, at either the Manch or Enniskeane bridges.[42] Chambers' case is discussed further in the section to follow, which looks at who took part in the attack, an issue that has become much more fraught than it needs to be.

BMH witness statements, MSP records and the Chisholm, Ó Dúlaing and other recorded interviews all have strengths and weaknesses. They were gathered in different contexts over extended periods of time, and disparities are to be expected. Both the circumstances in which information was imparted and the perspective of the interviewers and the tellers impacted on what was written and said. BMH statements contain the most structured operational narratives. MSP claims brim with useful information but include little narrative detail about the fight. Chisholm talked too much and tended to interrupt his interviewees. Nevertheless, his recordings contain the most explicit descriptions of how and when the Auxiliaries were killed. Ó Dúlaing was a far more polished interviewer, but both his questions and his interviewees' responses were elliptical and cautious, probably because his Kilmichael interviews were for a radio broadcast and, moreover, he had been advised that the 'false surrender' was controversial and that he should tread carefully.[43] An abundance of local folklore, family memories and ground-level stories also survive. This material does not qualify as reliable evidence in the strictly positivist sense. Nevertheless, much can be gained from being aware of mentalities and local memory. Sometimes, when they can be verified, folkloric accounts also turn out to be surprisingly accurate.[44]

Eyewitness and retrospective testimonies are not always easy to use as evidence, but they can be triangulated, analysed and assessed against both primary and secondary sources. Cross-referencing them can identify commonalities and inconsistencies. Familiarity with allegiances and animosities amongst different groups of veterans makes it easier to identify meaningful discrepancies. Sometimes errors are just errors. Indirect or offhand remarks might have no deeper significance, but minor divergences or mistakes, once contextualised, often turn out to be purposeful interventions with significant implications rather than faulty remembering.

How different veterans described the number of sections into which the flying column at Kilmichael was divided is a case in point. The captured report and several veterans agree that the column was divided into three (or more) sections.[45] The same basic positioning of the various subsets of men is given in all accounts, but how they were described also reflected differences of opinion over the rank and status of Michael McCarthy. Young and O'Brien (and Flor Crowley in 1947, as discussed in the next chapter) said he had been second in command at Kilmichael and that he and Barry were each in charge of one of two sections. According to Barry and Stephen O'Neill, however, there were three sections and McCarthy was only a section commander. In other words, they demoted McCarthy. Young and O'Brien were both members of the 3rd (Dunmanway) Battalion. McCarthy was their vice O/C and he was a great friend of Young's. It might be significant that, although O'Neill is generally described as the other section commander, in his pension application he said *he* was second in command, and Barry backed this up.[46]

PARTICIPANTS

Defining 'participation' and compiling uncontested lists of those who took part in IRA actions is not a straightforward exercise. Insurgencies and guerrilla wars by their nature blur divides between civilians and combatants. *The Wild Heather Glen*, the Ballineen/Enniskean Area Heritage group's profile of forty-six Kilmichael veterans, remains the most extensive and detailed list of IRA participants available, but it is not definitive.[47] Much more information survives for Barry than for the others. According to *The Wild Heather Glen*, the majority of Kilmichael veterans were later neutral or anti-Treaty in the Civil War, although several fought for the Free State or joined the new Civic Guard (re-named the Garda Síochána in July 1923).[48] Jeremiah O'Mahony had been killed before the truce, in March 1921. Jack Hennessy, Spud Murphy and Flyer Nyhan fought with Barry in Tipperary during the Civil War. Jack Hourihan and Paddy 'Kilmallock' McCarthy would die fighting on opposite sides in that conflict.[49]

More than twenty of the Kilmichael veterans emigrated after the Civil War.[50] Before Sonny Carey left for the USA in August 1923, the Skibbereen Young Men's Society presented him with a 'purse of sovereigns'.[51] In New York City, Carey met up with fellow Kilmichael veterans Timothy Crowley and Sonny Dave Crowley. In a letter home a few years later, Sonny Dave's wife, Babie, described meeting Carey: 'He is so changed that I hardly knew him,' she wrote, 'only for his smile.'[52] Sadly, Babie herself was in poor health and died in December 1926, a few months after joining her husband. 'Well she is gone,' Sonny Dave wrote afterwards, 'and left me to mourn her loss alone with poor little Joe motherless ...'[53] He and several other veterans later returned to Ireland. Others did not.

Establishing who took part in the ambush was controversial from the start. In 1938, *The Cork Examiner* supplemented its short report on the annual commemoration and IRA reunion with a list of Kilmichael 'survivors' (as they were often called).[54] Within days, it acknowledged the inadvertent omission of John 'Denny' Sullivan (Baurgorm, Bantry).[55] A couple of weeks later, after publishing the same list, *The Southern Star* noted that Dan O'Brien, a former captain of Lisheen Company, 7th (Skibbereen) Battalion, should also have been included.[56] Over the years, in various contexts, further individuals were named. In 1948, Flor Crowley acknowledged overlooking O'Brien and, the following year, John J. McCarthy.[57] O'Brien was finally added to the Kilmichael and Crossbarry Memorial Committee's list in 1965, only to be omitted again in 1971. Two years later, Crowley noted that O'Brien, Denis O'Neill, Tom McCarthy and Tim Keohane had been added to the committee's list after 'considerable debate.'[58]

Kilmichael survivors were accorded both status and admiration in independent Ireland, and not all participant claims need to be taken seriously. Ned Cronin, for instance, was not wounded at Kilmichael despite what his obituary asserts.[59] Other cases are much less straightforward, and the possibility of false claims should not be overstated. Both inadvertent and deliberate exclusions from honour rolls, public accounts of actions and memoirs relating to the revolutionary period occurred for all sorts of reasons.[60]

Some ambush participants with whom Barry quarrelled went unmentioned in *Guerilla Days*. One of these was Sonny Dave Crowley. According to his grandson, he fell out with Barry during the 'mopping up' after the ambush (about which more later).[61] Crowley was a well-known, popular figure, and both Ned Young and Paddy O'Brien made a point of saying he fought beside Barry, as did Flor Crowley in 1947.[62] A strong but less definitive case can be made for Thomas O'Driscoll, quartermaster of C (Dunmanus) Company, Schull Battalion, who always said he took part in the ambush.[63] In 1985, in his *Ireland's Own* 'The Irish Abroad' column, Dónall Mac Amhlaigh published an account of O'Driscoll's participation written by his son, Brother John O'Driscoll, a Cork-born Cistercian monk based in Utah.[64] Brother O'Driscoll maintained that his father had a row with Barry in early December 1920 over the death of Michael McLean at Gaggin (6 December 1920). He thought that his father's intense dislike of Barry stemmed from Barry's subsequent failure to acknowledge his part in Kilmichael.

Brother John's letter provoked several angry replies, including missives from Meda Ryan and the Kilmichael and Crossbarry Memorial Committee denying that O'Driscoll had taken part.[65] Others were more sympathetic. Bill Allen, who seemed to know both Ned Young and Barry, contacted Brother John after the furore:

Without a doubt, your late Dad's opinion and sizing up of the late T.B.'s character is in keeping with everyone with whom I discussed him. He was certainly a very brave man, and a competent ambush planner; but to my knowledge he frequently lied, and was absolutely

ruthless … Deasy's book … made no mention of the 'false surrender'
… Several of the survivors stated in conversation about the conflict
that they were sorry that they had anything to do with it; so we can
all draw our own conclusions … Now that T.B. is gone, I feel that
Ned [Young] could tell me more than on a previous chat I had with
him.[66]

Ryan maintained that Thomas O'Driscoll was one of the men who arrived
late in a sidecar, an incident discussed in later chapters.[67] According
to Brother John, however, his father was already at the site when the
sidecar (which he said was a 'tub trap') arrived. Several other details in
the O'Driscoll narrative recounted by his son are unique to that account.
Hopefully the release of O'Driscoll's and the sidecar occupants' MSP files
will provide more information.

Another previously unknown participant is John Condon, a Bandon
Volunteer. His recently released MSP claim says he suffered a nervous
breakdown after taking part in the ambush.[68] Mick O'Dwyer, named as a
Kilmichael participant in both the Auxiliary diary and by Barry in 1974,
might have been overlooked on the same grounds. According to one West
Cork IRA veteran, the nerves of several 3rd (Dunmanway) Battalion
officers were so badly affected after the ambush that they were eventually
replaced. He did not mention names, but O'Dwyer (quartermaster) was
'removed' in March 1921.[69]

Willie Chambers, who was interviewed by Peter Hart (the 'unarmed
scout'), was posted at either the Manch or Enniskeane bridges during the
ambush. Another Dunmanway Volunteer, he is not included on any known
ambush participant lists. Those engaged in logistical support rarely were,
so this is not as significant as it might seem. Chambers and his brother Con
were members of Ballineen Company.[70] MSP Brigade Activity lists regularly
cite him as guarding arms dumps and prisoners, and engaging in scouting
and sentry duty.[71] He was also listed as an IRA suspect in the Auxiliary
diary.[72] If Chambers was on foot, the fact that he was posted several miles
away during the fight (as he told his son) is difficult to reconcile with his
witnessing some of the action (as he told Hart). The activity reports for his

company, however, say Chambers and other Volunteers commandeered bicycles and horses and carts 'from hostile people in the Coy area … almost daily'.[73] Conceivably, if Chambers was using one of those modes of transport, he could have been sent to check the bridges earlier in the day and returned at some point during the ambush.

Chambers also told his son that the original plan was for the column to return to Belrose (a nearby townland), but after scouting the bridges he had suggested to Barry that crossing over the Bandon River was a safer option. So, after the fight, the column marched to Granure, Ballinacarriga instead. If this turns out to be true, then Chambers and Barry could have been in contact during or in the direct aftermath of the attack. Without more concrete information, however, it is impossible to verify Chambers's testimony one way or another. His MSP file (not yet available) may clarify matters.

Finally, there is Curlus Cronin, another suspected Kilmichael participant in the Auxiliary diary. As he left the area in the 1930s with his first cousin (whom he later wed) and one of his family's cows, never to be heard from again, he is likely to remain a mystery.[74] A former lieutenant in Coppeen Company, the local OIRA's nominal rolls (which gave members' addresses as well) listed Cronin but stated that his whereabouts were unknown.[75] More evidence is needed, but neither his nor Mick O'Dwyer's participation was questioned by Flor Crowley in his published six-part transcription and analysis of the K Company Auxiliary diary.[76]

The participation of Sonny Dave Crowley, Tim Keohane and Dan O'Brien can be verified across multiple sources.[77] Evidence for the others is less definitive, but they should not be rejected out of hand. MSP files relating to over fifty people who participated in one way or another are available at present. This figure will likely increase with further releases. Compiling a definitive participant list is probably impossible. As it stands, erring on the side of inclusiveness, at least 100 individuals took some part in Kilmichael, either directly or by providing logistical support.[78]

Although a certain amount of material is still beyond reach, at the time of writing over forty separate accounts from twenty-four ambush participants are available. These vary greatly in terms of their quality and level of detail, ranging from a sentence or two confirming involvement to lengthy interviews and detailed testimony. Half come from just four veterans: Tom Barry (11), Jack O'Sullivan (5), Ned Young (5), Paddy O'Brien (3) and Stephen O'Neill (2).[79] As will be discussed, the same or similar divergences from *Guerilla Days* crop up repeatedly in the other veterans' accounts in relation to who was on the road and when, the number of sections, the fighting at the first and second lorries, the circumstances in which the three IRA fatalities occurred and why surrendered Auxiliaries were put to death. They also often hinted at or recounted a much grimmer reality than any of the public narratives.

AMBUSH SITE ANALYSIS

The ambush site itself is another important source of information. Efforts by local commemoration committees to 'preserve and enhance' the site in 2013 led archaeologist Damien Shiels to conclude that it was now impossible to 'accurately assess the 1920 terrain'.[80] The changes have certainly made it more difficult, but preserving the physical integrity of the site was never much of a priority. Alterations to it commenced many decades ago, and much had already changed by 2013. The road, which ran through the townland of Shanacashelkneeves, was widened and paved in the 1950s. Cork County Council's 'Special Roads Committee' established a group of IRA veterans, including Barry, to advise on how to proceed when works reached the area.[81] In 1966, some of the rocks north of the road at the western end (where the three IRA fatalities occurred) were removed to accommodate a new Kilmichael monument. A forestry track with an entrance on the north side was installed about halfway between the memorial and the now disused entrance to Murray's Lane.

The contemporary evidence has limitations as well. Lieutenant Edgar Fleming's map described the terrain, marked where the Auxiliaries' bodies lay and identified the positions of the flying column and the two lorries. Contemporary evidence suggests that these should be considered approximations. A photograph of the first lorry published in the *Daily Dispatch*, for instance, matches Flor Crowley's contention that it 'lodged in the southern ditch 10 yards from Barry's position in the Lane', rather than where it is marked on Fleming's map.[82]

Nor does his map detail the condition of the then unpaved road. Newspaper accounts published in the direct aftermath of the ambush described debris being left on and around the road (see Chapter Three), and not all of it was removed. In July 1953, a 'steel helmet of the British type' was found in a drain at the ambush site which, according to a press report, had belonged to one of the IRA men involved.[83] Was debris concentrated in specific areas? Were there drag marks? Without this information it is impossible to establish the positions of the three Auxiliaries who fought on even after being wounded and whose remains were, according to Bill Munro, surrounded by hundreds of empty shell casings. As some Kilmichael participants describe Auxiliaries downing their rifles and walking down the road with their hands in the air, it cannot be assumed that where the bodies were found correspond to their position during the fight. They could also have been moved by the Volunteers during or after the ambush. An archaeological investigation might have established with more certainty the positions of the Auxiliaries before they were killed.

Although much has been irretrievably lost (or was never collected in the first place), maps, photographs and newspaper reports survive.[84] Establishing the position and line of sight for each individual who gave an account of the ambush is essential for analysing what was said and this can still be gleaned from the landscape. To that end, local historian and photographer Colum Cronin and I conducted a thorough survey of the ground, identifying and photographing the vantage points from all the IRA positions. Reaching points south of the road involved climbing under fences and wading through thorny furze, whereas the terrain was almost barren into the 1970s. Attendees at annual commemorations could sit on the rocky outcrops where Volunteers had been positioned during the ambush.[85] We took a further set of photographs moving up and down the road from the position occupied by Section One (including the Command Post) to that of Section Two, and then from there to Kelly's Cross, where a farmhouse still overlooks the site. I also measured the full length of the road from the Command Post to the Cross with a surveyor's wheel and consulted other maps and photographs.

Colum also kindly allowed me to use a large aerial photograph of the site he took some years before the renovations. I marked it up with the measurements of the road, the positions of the two lorries, where the Auxiliaries' bodies were found and where those Volunteers who gave ambush accounts were situated. The perspective of the men who were either on the road or in any of the positions north of it (Tom Barry, Spud Murphy, Paddy O'Brien, Jack Hennessy, Tim Keohane, Michael O'Driscoll) was limited. None of the men in Section One (eastern end) could see what occurred in Section Two (western end) and vice versa. Jack O'Sullivan and Ned Young, both situated on the rocks to the south, would have had a clearer line of sight to the fighting at both lorries. What all of these veterans said occurred, and how their testimony compares to public narratives of Kilmichael, is the subject of the next two chapters.

6

Tellings and Retellings 1921–80

THIS CHAPTER TRACES THE VARIOUS public accounts of Kilmichael through newspapers, memoirs and popular histories as they appeared from 1921 to 1980. Contextualising and tracking narrative differences is not as pedantic as it might seem. That Barry's *Guerilla Days in Ireland* rendition of Kilmichael was 'universally and uncritically' accepted before the publication of Peter Hart's *The IRA and Its Enemies* in 1998 is a matter of faith for some traditionalists, but it is also at odds with reality.[1] Despite what is often claimed, conflicting accounts of the ambush had already been in the public domain for decades when Hart's book was published. Barry himself wrote or endorsed three versions of the ambush over the 1930s and 1940s. The one in his 1949 memoir was his second extended published account. A very different version of events had appeared two years earlier, in a Kilmichael account penned by Flor Crowley, a local historian from West Cork.

RUMOURS AND ACCUSATIONS 1921–32

The earliest documented public reference to the Auxiliaries' attempting to surrender and then reopening fire appeared in an article by Lionel Curtis in June 1921 (see Chapter 2). He did not attribute any IRA fatalities to the incident but, in 1924, rumours as to how Michael McCarthy and Jim O'Sullivan had been killed were relayed by army officers attached to the Cork Command writing in support of their families' dependents' claims. McCarthy, it was said, had been shot in the head after standing up to accept the Auxiliaries' surrender. The cause of O'Sullivan's death was less clear cut. Some said he was killed in action, others that he was accidentally shot by his own side while wearing a steel helmet.[2] Piaras Béaslaí's commentary on Kilmichael, published in 1926, was similar to that of Curtis in not attributing the IRA fatalities to the Auxiliaries' trickery, although he dismissed allegations of mutilation and the wearing of British uniforms by the IRA.[3] A *Cork Examiner* report, published the same year, however, noted ambiguous rumours about a 'hand-to-hand struggle' after the Auxiliaries 'shot three of the ambushing party'.[4]

It is worth noting that in the 1920s, Barry had no compunction about acknowledging that the IRA shot unarmed soldiers during the War of Independence. He strongly rebuked Cork Sinn Féin for saying otherwise in 1924: 'Everyone will realise that Volunteers had to resort to every means in their power,' he said; denying it could make many of those 'who carried out those orders ... feel they are being stigmatised'.[5]

The 1932 memoir of General F.P. Crozier, in overall charge of the Auxiliary Division from July 1920 until he resigned in February 1921 (after his efforts to discipline the force were countermanded), also mentioned Kilmichael. Crozier's version was similar to Barry's captured report (1920), which described Pat Deasy's fatal wounding:

> Arms were supposed to have been surrendered, but a wounded Auxiliary whipped out a revolver while lying on the ground and shot a 'Shinner' with the result that all his comrades were put to death with him, the rebels 'seeing red', a condition akin to 'going mad' – as often given in defence of the Black and Tans by Mr. Churchill and others.[6]

Barry's first public account of the ambush appeared in November of the same year. It was published in both *The Irish Press* and *The Southern Star*, and reproduced later in a 1934 Kilmichael commemoration souvenir programme.[7] He sent a newspaper clipping of it to the pensions board in 1935 when writing in support of Pat Deasy's mother's dependents' claim. His handwritten and signed letter stated that he was the author and mentioned that it had been 'published two years ago in the *Irish Press*'. The piece would, he said, give the 'full particulars' of Deasy's death:

The first lorry rounded the bend, passed the I.R.A. section detailed to attack the second lorry, [and] came abreast of the section awaiting it. Simultaneously, the second enemy lorry came abreast of the second section. A whistle blew, a volley rang out and a Mills bomb exploded; I.R.A. and Auxiliaries were engaged in a death struggle. After eight or ten minutes of terrific fighting the first lorry was overcome and a party of three men from the then disengaged section of the I.R.A. advanced up the road to help their second section. They were firing as they advanced to the relief of their sorely pressed comrades, three of whom had already fallen. The end was at hand and in a short time the remainder of the Auxiliaries fighting the second section were dead. They, like the I.R.A., had fought to a finish.[8]

Barry also said in his letter that Deasy was 'killed' in action 'towards the end of the fight', just as he had in the captured report. At some point after 1935, however, Barry's Kilmichael account changed. He wrote or endorsed two further versions of the ambush before his 1949 memoir appeared. He sanctioned a short account by Kilmichael veteran Stephen O'Neill, and then wrote a lengthier one himself published a few years later. There are key points of difference between them but both attributed the IRA fatalities to Auxiliaries who pretended to surrender.

O'Neill's account was one of three articles on actions of the West Cork flying column (Kilmichael, Crossbarry and Rosscarbery) to appear in *The Kerryman*'s annual 'Xmas number' in 1937.[9] According to the newspaper, Barry approved them before publication. Various details in O'Neill's account were inconsistent both with what Barry would later state and with testimony given by other ambush participants subsequently. While later versions by others said O'Neill was at the other end of the ambush site across from Barry, for instance, O'Neill's 1937 account implied that he was positioned with the section fighting the Auxiliaries from the second lorry. O'Neill stated that Section Two 'failed to dislodge' the Auxiliaries and that the 'O/C [Barry], with three of the Section responsible for the destruction of the first lorry, came to our assistance'. He said they approached from behind, at which point Barry ordered the Volunteers to stop firing and

called on the Auxiliaries to surrender. The latter indicated they would,
but then fired on the Volunteers who stood up to take the surrender,
killing two. It was only at that point that the column 'renewed the attack
vigorously and never desisted until the enemy were annihilated'. O'Neill
named the three IRA fatalities towards the end of the article but did not
explicitly identify who stood up or which two were fatally wounded by the
feigned surrender.[10]

Barry's Kilmichael account was published under the pseudonym
'eyewitness' in *An Cosantóir* in 1941. In this version, crucially, instead of
the 'Column Commander' (Barry) calling on the Auxiliaries to surrender
(as per O'Neill) the Auxiliaries offered to do so of their own volition.[11]
They grounded their rifles but then reopened fire with handguns and
were wiped out. In this instance, Barry was also very specific about the
IRA fatalities. McCarthy was killed in the initial exchanges of fire with
the second lorry and was not among the four Volunteers who stood up in
response to the false surrender. Only Deasy and O'Sullivan, he said, were
mortally wounded or killed when the Auxiliaries reopened fire. An editor's
note in the article stated that some paragraphs had been omitted. Meda
Ryan, the only historian (as far as is known) to have consulted the proofs
and associated correspondence in Barry's private papers, says that the false
surrender passage 'was not censored'.[12]

Traditionalists like Ryan have gone to extensive lengths to gloss over,
ignore or otherwise discredit evidence that Barry's story changed. She
argues that the 1932 *Irish Press* account – which said that the three IRA
Volunteers had 'fallen' before Barry reached Section Two – was altered
without Barry's permission. Her main piece of evidence for disputing his
authorship of the final version is a carbon copy of a November 1932 letter
from Barry to the newspaper's editor in which he protested at the omission
of the false surrender.[13] Unfortunately, the carbon copy is in Barry's papers,
so analysis of it was not possible. The fact that Barry himself sent a clipping
of the 1932 *Irish Press* account to the pension board in 1935 and endorsed
it in an accompanying letter handwritten and signed by him complicates
Ryan's argument. There are several issues to consider. For a start, the carbon
copy could be misdated. According to Ryan's citations, Barry's papers

contain at least two separate runs of correspondence between him and *The Irish Press*, one from 1932 and another from the mid-1940s when *Guerilla Days* was being serialised. Conceivably, the letter could date from the later run. This would make more sense. Even if Barry did protest the omission of the false surrender in 1932, however, he still publicly acquiesced to the published version of events. Barry's 1932 account was reproduced on other occasions under republican auspices for events at which Barry was one of the main speakers. This suggests that the 'false surrender' account was not the generally accepted version of events in the mid-1930s. Nor does the letter in Barry's papers alter the fact that he had endorsed or written three different Kilmichael accounts by 1949, four altogether if the captured report is included. It also begs the question as to why *The Irish Press* would feel the need to revise what he wrote in the first place, particularly given that a very different account of the ambush had been published in December 1947.

THE FIGHT THAT ROUSED A NATION

Flor Crowley's 1947 account, entitled 'Kilmichael – the Fight that Roused a Nation', is still one of the most laudatory reimaginings of the ambush ever written.[14] Although several of its core details aligned broadly with what appeared in Barry's 1932 piece, and Crowley's narrative included a 'false surrender' by the Auxiliaries, it was entirely at odds with both O'Neill's (1937) and Barry's post-1935 versions. Contrary to what is often said, the main proponents of the alternate Kilmichael narratives were either ambush veterans or dedicated republicans. Crowley served on the Kilmichael Commemoration Committee from its inception in the 1960s and wrote numerous articles about the War of Independence in West Cork. A national teacher and respected local historian from Dunmanway, he was also a sportswriter, avid bowls player, founding member of *Ból-Chumann na hÉireann*, a competitive 'sharp shooter' with *Foras Cosanta Áituil* (FCA) and a member of the Gun Club Federation.[15]

According to Crowley's account, the flying column was divided into two main sections, each of them split into smaller units of men positioned at various points north and south of the road. Barry, in overall command, took charge of Section One, north of the road at the eastern end of the position. He personally commanded five men in the 'Command Post' at the entrance to Murray's Lane. Michael McCarthy, second in command, was in charge of Section Two, also north of the road but at the western end of the site. He and several others positioned themselves on a rocky outcrop across from O'Donoghue's Lane.

Barry's section was to deal with the first lorry, McCarthy's the second. Just before 4 p.m., 'two traploads' of men from the Kealkil and Bantry Companies arrived. Barry moved onto the road to speak to them just as scouts signalled the approach of the Auxiliary patrol. The men were ordered to 'retreat at full speed back the old road from Kelly's Cross to Johnstown'. They were barely out of sight when the first lorry drove into position, past Section Two. When it was within 30 yards of the Command Post, men in Section One, on the rocks behind and to the left of Barry's unit, opened fire, killing the driver: 'Out of control, the lorry zig-zagged from side to side and lodged in the southern ditch 10 yards from Barry's position in the Lane.'

Most of the Auxiliaries from the first lorry were wiped out by a combination of 'Barry's grenades', volleys from the rocks and 'sniper fire'. Crowley paid tribute to them: 'let it not be forgotten that they fought a daring fight, that they were not easily overcome'. At this point, however, according to Crowley, five of those remaining – hoping to trick their attackers into discarding their cover – feigned a surrender and then resumed firing. Their ruse was unsuccessful. Barry ordered the men in the various subsections of Section One onto the road: 'From the north, from the Lane, from the scattered rocks to the south, the boys began to close in, and the first lorry and its occupants were no more.'

The Auxiliaries in the second lorry could hear but not see the attack as they approached: 'Strictly speaking,' Crowley wrote, 'they were not ambushed at all.' When the lorry was straight across from McCarthy's section, but before it had quite rounded the bend, Section Two opened fire. The Auxiliaries leapt out and took positions among the same rocks where the column men were situated, and 'fought doggedly back'. The driver tried to reverse the lorry, nearly reaching Kelly's Cross before he was shot. The Auxiliaries were now so close it was difficult for McCarthy's section to fire without exposing themselves and it was at this point that the three IRA men were fatally wounded. O'Sullivan was killed instantly by a bullet that 'hit his left hand, blew the bolt off his rifle, and passed through his lower jaw' in the 'first blast of retaliatory fire from the second lorry'. McCarthy was shot in the head and survived for about an hour. The bullet that mortally wounded Deasy entered his left hip, passed 'through his stomach and out at the groin'.

Barry and 'four of his section' ran up the road with 'complete disregard for their own safety', catching the Auxiliaries 'upon the exposed flank' as they rounded the bend. They then, as Crowley put it delicately, 'finished the fight'. The IRA fatalities – one dead and two mortally wounded – were taken to Gortroe by Tim O'Connell (the source for much of Crowley's information) and a few others.[16] McCarthy died on the way. Deasy died at the farmhouse at around 10 p.m.

Crowley wove fragments of the rich local lore about the ambush (which survives in one form or another to this day) into his narrative, reflecting his enduring fascination with the habits and traditions of his native place.[17] He mentioned McCarthy's premonition of his death, various theories then circulating about what happened to Cadet Forde, and the story of Paddy Fly, a tramp who wandered into the ambush before it began, which was probably based on a real incident. Kept under guard by scouts John Kelly and Neilus Cotter throughout the attack for fear he would alert the authorities to the column's presence, Fly's hat was shot off his head.[18] For all its flowery and idealised prose, Crowley still recounted a well-executed, pitiless surprise attack with an unlikely and not fully explained outcome: 'The fight was fought at point-blank range, and how it was that Craig [sic] and his men, experienced fighters that they were, did not take a heavier toll of Barry's men, is one of the mysteries of Kilmichael.'

GUERILLA DAYS IN IRELAND

In his introduction to *Guerilla Days in Ireland*, Barry's memoir published in 1949, General Michael Joseph Costello (a Tipperary pro-Treaty IRA veteran, career army officer and close friend) noted carefully how Barry 'says in his preface' that only his wife and solicitor read the memoir before it was sent to the publisher.[19] This was not true. Several individuals helped Barry gather information, and at least three people read drafts of his book before publication.[20] Barry commenced writing in 1947.[21] In September, after reading the manuscript, Costello was so worried that, without telling Barry, he brought it to Florrie O'Donoghue and asked for help. Costello said the memoir was 'unworthy of him [Barry] as it stood'. He had already persuaded Barry to destroy the last three chapters, 'which were even worse than the rest'. O'Donoghue sent Costello 'seven long pages of comment'.[22] Barry himself asked O'Donoghue to look over the manuscript in April 1948 (less than two weeks before it was serialised in *The Irish Press*), apparently still unaware that O'Donoghue had read an earlier draft. According to Liam Deasy, O'Donoghue did a 'bit of pruning and shaping' at the end.[23] As O'Donoghue's own renditions of Kilmichael followed the one in *Guerilla Days*, it is reasonable to assume that he did not question (or decided not to challenge) Barry's 1949 version of events.[24]

Whatever O'Donoghue did in relation to Barry's manuscript, he was not especially impressed even with the revised version, which he described as 'somewhat informed'. He nevertheless thought that it would 'pass muster with the public … only those of us who know something of the organisation at the time will see the holes in it. On the whole not a bad book at all now'.[25] Seán O'Hegarty, the former O/C of Cork No.1 Brigade to whom O'Donoghue also gave the text to read, was similarly underwhelmed and of the view that Barry should have been left to make an 'imbecile of himself'.[26]

Barry's new Kilmichael account differed from Crowley's on several key points.[27] Contrary to Crowley's version, Barry said the column was divided into three sections rather than two, and Michael McCarthy was a section commander in charge of Section Two rather than second in command. Crowley said Stephen O'Neill was in Section One. According to Barry, he was in charge of Section Three which was south of the road and directly across from the 'Command Post'. Barry said three men (rather than five as per Crowley) were with him at the entrance to Murray's Lane: Michael

Herlihy, Flyer Nyhan and Spud Murphy. He omitted any mention of Sonny Dave Crowley, who had also been beside him at the Command Post.[28]

Barry also made a point of rebutting the idea that any kind of surrender had occurred at the first lorry: 'Once I got a side glimpse of Flyer's bayonet being driven through an Auxiliary, whom I had thought dead as I passed him, but who had risen to fire and miss me at four yards' range. There was no surrender called by those Auxiliaries.' While Crowley said all of Section One moved onto the road to fight the first lorry (on Barry's orders), Barry's later accounts (1941 and 1949) credited the Command Post men as being largely responsible for wiping out almost the entire enemy patrol. In 1974, Barry stated even more emphatically that only the 'Command Post Party' ever 'set foot on the road' before all of the Auxiliaries were dead.[29]

Barry's and Flor Crowley's accounts of the fighting at the second lorry were entirely at odds. Crowley said the second lorry reversed towards Kelly's Cross. Barry said it 'stopped thirty yards at our side of No. 2 Section' (the reason why this is important is discussed in Chapter Seven). According to Barry, after the fighting at the first lorry was over, he, Herlihy, Murphy and Nyhan then 'ran crouched up the side of the road':

> We had gone about fifty yards when we heard the Auxiliaries shout 'We surrender.' We kept running along the grass edge of the road as they repeated the surrender cry, and actually saw some Auxiliaries throw away their rifles. Firing stopped, but we continued, still unobserved, to jog towards them. Then we saw three of our comrades on No. 2 Section stand up, one crouched and two upright. Suddenly the Auxiliaries were firing again with revolvers. One of our three men spun around before he fell, and Pat Deasy staggered before he, too, went down ... I ran the short distance to where I had seen our men fall and scrambled up the rocky height. Michael McCarthy, Dunmanway, and Jim Sullivan, Knockawaddra, Rossmore, lay dead and, a few yards away, Pat Deasy was dying.[30]

In 1932, Barry said that the Auxiliaries 'fought to the finish' and that the three Volunteers had 'already fallen' by the time he and his unit came up behind the second lorry 'firing as they advanced'. In *Guerilla Days*, even more explicitly than in 1941, Barry and his three men were silent witnesses to the Auxiliaries' treachery. His description of who fell victim to it in 1949 was, however, more ambiguous than in 1941. In the earlier account he said that Deasy and O'Sullivan were shot in a false surrender, but that McCarthy was already dead. In *Guerilla Days*, Barry said that three men stood up (rather than four as in 1941) and that two were killed in a false surrender. Deasy was the only one of the three mentioned by name. O'Sullivan was not identified as the other Volunteer who was killed, nor was there any mention of McCarthy having been shot earlier. Barry must have known that he was departing from other widely accepted accounts of how the three IRA fatalities occurred, particularly as he had written one of them himself (for *The Irish Press*).

Barry's subsequent retellings of the false surrender were similarly vague and contradictory.[31] In 1966, he told Seámus Kelly that 'one man' was already dead when 'three of this section stood up' and that 'Auxies opened fire immediately ... they killed the two of them after surrendering'.[32] When interviewed by Nollaig Ó Gadhra in 1969, he stated that two of the three who rose to take the surrender were killed 'standing up'.[33] According to Meda Ryan, that same year, in a lecture at University College Galway, Barry said that all three IRA fatalities stood up to take the surrender because they were 'green'.[34] Pat Deasy was the only victim of the false surrender he identified by name after 1941 apart from on one occasion: in 1970, he told Donncha Ó Dúlaing that he was not sure whether it was O'Sullivan or McCarthy who was shot alongside Deasy.[35] Yet in 1974, Barry berated Paddy O'Brien for saying that Deasy had been killed rather than wounded during the action, which ruled Deasy out as being one of the two who, according to Barry, were 'killed standing up'.[36]

Barry's various renderings of the false surrender could not all be true, but they were ambiguous enough for disparities to go unnoticed or be overlooked, and so they were. The equivocal description of the consequences of the false surrender in *Guerilla Days* was widely interpreted in the way Barry obviously intended it to be – that McCarthy, O'Sullivan and Deasy were all killed or fatally wounded by the false surrender.[37] So, what would become the most well-known public version of Kilmichael, the one most people knew and, more importantly, the one they wanted to be true, was accepted, despite Barry's conflicting versions of what happened.

What added to the confusion was a public habit of recounting whichever version of the ambush was most suited to a particular situation. Flor Crowley was always careful to respect the 'false surrender' versions of the ambush. When the occasion demanded it, he described the Kilmichael most appropriate for the circumstances rather than the one he actually believed in himself. In December 1949, for instance, just weeks after *Guerilla Days* appeared in the shops, *The Kerryman* published Crowley's tribute to ambush veteran 'Flyer' Nyhan, one of the men who fought beside Barry during the ambush:

> They saw the bogus surrender. They watched three valued comrades accept that surrender as genuine, only to be shot down when they exposed themselves. They saw all this in the minute or two that it took them to cover those 150 yards of road, and they exacted ample penalty for the treachery that had killed Michael McCarthy, Jim Sullivan and young Pat Deasy.[38]

Nyhan had been Barry's great friend. It would have been immensely disrespectful for Crowley to have said anything else, and his actual views were already a matter of public record. The Nyhan piece was republished in *The Southern Star* a decade later, slightly revised: 'They saw two of the comrades shot down when they exposed themselves to accept the surrender.'[39] This subtle change implies that objections to the suggestion that McCarthy, in particular, was tricked by Auxiliaries were made early on. As we shall see, ambush veterans made similar remarks to both Fr Chisholm and Peter Hart.

Guerilla Days was avidly read, published and republished. There were even plans at one point to translate it into braille.[40] No one seems to have publicly contradicted Barry's memoir at the time, but there were private rumblings of dissatisfaction. In May 1948, a few days after Barry's new Kilmichael account appeared in *The Irish Press*, Flor Begley wrote to Liam

Deasy. As far as he was concerned, Barry had undervalued and ignored the contribution of other Volunteers:

> His tribute to the type of men I have mentioned was most grudgingly given if given at all. I have not seen any tribute in the real sense so far. TBB's courage and initiative appears to have overshadowed all other men and things. Poor devil he is not over-modest mind you. Modesty does not seem to be a virtue with him when it comes to writing stuff in connection with the Tan war.[41]

Begley suggested that another book was needed to be read in conjunction with *Guerilla Days* in order to facilitate a more 'accurate picture of the organisation generally'. Meda Ryan cites several letters Barry received while *Guerilla Days* was being serialised in *The Irish Press*. These would be very useful for contextualising the Begley–Deasy correspondence, but they are in Barry's inaccessible papers.[42]

TOWARDS IRELAND FREE

In 1961, Liam Deasy met his former Civil War nemesis, General Richard Mulcahy, for the first time since that conflict at a funeral in Dublin. Deasy told him he was working on a history of the War of Independence in West Cork. He sent Mulcahy an early outline plan and notes for what would become *Towards Ireland Free*, and consulted him about the meeting with Cork officers in the summer of 1920 at which GHQ had mooted the idea of ambushing the Auxiliaries.[43] Mulcahy described Deasy as combining a 'very good pictorial recollection of things that happened' with a 'very detached approach'.[44]

In the decades after the Civil War, Deasy was regularly consulted by IRA veterans gathering information and writing histories about the revolutionary period. Ernie O'Malley and Florrie O'Donoghue both asked him to recommend Cork interviewees in the 1940s.[45] Later, Deasy, Moss Twomey and George Power worked with O'Donoghue when he was drafting *No Other Law*, his 1954 biography of Liam Lynch.[46] In 1955, Deasy gave a lecture on the War of Independence to the National University of Ireland Club in London.[47] He corresponded with de Valera about Beál na Blath, and published two articles about the War of Independence in Cork in *Éire-Ireland* in 1966.[48] Deasy also gathered information from West Cork veterans about various incidents during the 1916–23 period in the 1960s, working closely with O'Donoghue and (separately) with two priests.[49]

Fr Timothy Lyne (1900–77), a Salesian originally from Killarney and an old friend, was an uncredited co-author of both Deasy' *Éire-Ireland* articles. Lyne also actively encouraged him to write *Towards Ireland Free* and assisted Deasy throughout the research and writing of the book, including helping to draft some chapters.[50] Fr John Chisholm (1922–2014), whom Deasy met around 1968, agreed to assist in the researching, drafting and editing the following year.[51] A philosophy lecturer in University College Dublin and the holder of three doctorates, Chisholm was also a biblical scholar, choirmaster and teacher at the Holy Ghost Father's (Spiritan) Missionary College in Kimmage Manor in Dublin.[52] Doctrinally, he was an unabashed conservative, not unlike Archbishop John Charles McQuaid (who encouraged his academic career). Chisholm was also a trenchant critic of Israel. He visited the Middle East a number of times in the 1970s and 1980s, touring Iraq with Charlie Haughey in 1976.[53]

The Deasys lived just down the road from Kimmage Manor, and trainee priests from West Cork were regular visitors to the family home in the 1950s. Deasy's daughter Ena was also friendly with Chisholm's sister.[54] In an early planning meeting, Chisholm asked Deasy if he would object to his conducting recorded interviews with some of his contemporaries.[55] Deasy agreed to this, and supplied Chisholm with a list of individuals to approach. In the spring and summer of 1969, Chisholm interviewed over thirty people.[56] He also seems to have made contact with Flor Crowley, whose doubts about the false surrender sparked Chisholm's own interest in the issue. Deasy's nephew and namesake took it in turns with Flor Begley to drive his uncle around West Cork while he conducted his research. According to Deasy (nephew), he was there himself when his uncle collected Paddy O'Brien's account of Kilmichael.[57]

O'Brien's original account in Deasy's papers is much longer and more reflective of ordinary vernacular speech patterns than the published version. Deasy (nephew) told me that what O'Brien actually said was even more explicit than what his uncle recorded.[58] The days of the week are precisely noted in the original written account, suggesting that he consulted a diary (or perhaps the notes he had used when preparing his BMH statement) while drafting it. It details the ambush preparations, the action and subsequent events up to 1 January 1921. Chisholm's later attempts to coax more out of him about the false surrender were unsuccessful. He said O'Brien just smiled, shook his head, and would neither confirm nor deny it.[59] O'Brien had been positioned across from the Command Post with Stephen O'Neill, at the opposite end of the site from where McCarthy and the others were. The fact that he had been too far away to witness the fight at the second lorry might provide a partial explanation for his reluctance to say one way or the other.

The bulk of Chisholm's interview with O'Brien was taped over, though Chisholm would allude to some of the things O'Brien had told him when interviewing Ned Young.[60] Most of the graphic details in O'Brien's original written version were omitted from what appeared in *Towards Ireland Free*, quoted below:

> The opening fusillade killed the driver instantaneously, and the tender came to a halt. Barry appeared on the road and threw a hand grenade into the back of the tender, and all was over so far as that one was concerned. When Stephen O'Neill and I came out onto the road from the opposite side, we found 'Flyer' and 'Spud' were at the first tender; all the occupants had been killed.
>
> Meanwhile, the second tender was about one hundred and fifty yards behind, and had become stuck at the side of the road where the driver had tried unsuccessfully to turn it. The Auxiliaries had jumped out, threw themselves on the road and were firing from the cover of the tender. We then opened fire from their rear and when they realised that they were caught between two fires, they knew they were doomed.

It was then realised that three of our men had been killed in Michael McCarthy's section; he himself had been shot through the head, Jim O'Sullivan through the jaw, and Pat Deasy had two bullet wounds through the body. Two others had been wounded, Jack Hennessy and John Lordan, but though they had lost a great deal of blood, their wounds were not serious. It had been a short but grim fight.[61]

The original account did not contain the paragraph discussing the second tender. It also stated (correctly) that Deasy was wounded rather than killed outright.[62] Nevertheless, both the original and the published versions were in keeping with O'Brien's witness statement, taken fifteen years earlier, and Crowley's (1947) and Barry's earlier (1932) account. Neither were compatible with the false surrender and other key issues recounted in *Guerilla Days*. The retellings of several other incidents in Deasy's book also differed from Barry's, including the execution of two British deserters, the killing of Joseph Begley (Flor's brother) and two others by Crown Forces outside Bandon on 2 December 1920, the Gaggin Ambush of 6 December 1920 and the celebrated action at Crossbarry (19 March 1921). Some of the information sourced by Deasy and Chisholm (available in Deasy's papers) was not used in *Towards Ireland Free* at all.

Maureen Deasy, Liam's eldest daughter, helped type the manuscript.[63] A draft of Deasy's book, provisionally entitled 'Irish Guerillas versus British Might' was finished by August 1971. It was sent to Dan Nolan, editor of Anvil Press, and Robert Dudley Edwards, the UCD historian.[64] Nolan was initially enthusiastic, describing it as a 'monumental work of the greatest importance … I know what you meant when you said that it was controversial in parts.'[65] His attitude changed, however, after receiving notes on the text from journalist Pat Lynch, his 'staff man in Cork', who said the book was potentially libellous because it implied that Barry's memoir was unreliable.[66] According to Lynch, Deasy should have consulted Barry himself before conferring with Florrie O'Donoghue who, he said, considered Barry's book to have been 'exaggerated'.[67]

Lynch sided with Barry from the outset, and was particularly concerned that the Kilmichael account differed 'considerably' from *Guerilla Days* which, he maintained, had never been questioned by other survivors.[68] This was rather odd coming from Lynch. He had joined *The Kerryman*'s staff in 1946, the year prior to its publication of Crowley's Kilmichael account, and had worked closely with Nolan on the newspaper's historical content, and later on Nolan's Anvil Press *Fighting Story* series.[69] He had also written or revised several of the articles in the second edition of *Rebel Cork's Fighting Story*, published in 1961.[70] The first edition (1947) had used Stephen O'Neill's Kilmichael account, but this was replaced in the revised edition with excerpts from *Guerilla Days*. Nolan described O'Neill's version as 'very sketchy'.[71]

When made aware of Lynch's criticisms, Deasy responded that he was surprised at his tone. O'Brien's Kilmichael account, he said, had been confirmed by two other ambush participants: 'Perhaps if Pat enquired more closely into the full details of the fight he might come to appreciate that I have been more discreet than he would seem to credit me.'[72] In the end, Nolan decided not to publish Deasy's book, citing, as his reason, an argument between *Kerryman* staff and Deasy's son-in-law over the whereabouts of the manuscript.[73]

The real difficulty was that Deasy refused to change what he had written or consult Barry. Diarmuid Brennan, an Irish journalist and IRA veteran (from a later period) living in England, who had already withdrawn his own manuscript from Anvil Press after differences had arisen with Nolan, sent Deasy excerpts from a letter he received from Nolan in April 1972: 'For some strange reason, Deasy has not contacted Barry … I cannot publish a book which flatly contradicts Barry, unless Barry is consulted as a source.'[74]

Exchanges between Barry, Nolan and Frances Mary Blake a few years later, while she was editing *The Singing Flame* (Ernie O'Malley's Civil War memoir) for Anvil Press, give a good indication of why Deasy refused to let Barry read *Towards Ireland Free* before publication. In 1977, Nolan sent Barry (at Barry's request) all passages mentioning him, and received the following reply:

> Those excerpts relating to me in O'Malley's manuscript are the most fantastic imaginations of a disturbed mind and are completely untrue. I think you are correct in assuming they were written when he was

living as an Indian in a wigwam in Mexico about 50 years ago …
O'Malley was accepted by all who knew him as an oddball with a
mixture of pretentiousness.[75]

Nolan himself described Barry as 'both proud and vain' and 'jealous of
his reputation'. He was also aware that many of Barry's criticisms of what
O'Malley had written were inaccurate. Nevertheless, the offending passages
were revised to accommodate him.[76]

Deasy stuck to his guns and eventually Mercier Press agreed to publish
Towards Ireland Free. He was very pleased with the final draft, which was
completed by November 1972. Deasy thanked Fr Chisholm warmly: 'I just
want to convey to you in very simple language the great appreciation and
deep gratitude for [what] you have done so capably and so unselfishly.'[77]
Deasy's history was launched by Taoiseach Liam Cosgrave (whose father
had led the pro-Treaty government from August 1922 to March 1932) in
September 1973.[78] Barry, who was not invited, launched a blistering public
attack within days, describing the book as a 'travesty of history'. When
approached for comment, Deasy stated emphatically that he would not
change a single line.[79]

The Southern Star published a three-part review of *Towards Ireland Free*
by Flor Crowley in October and November 1973.[80] Crowley's comments
were circumspect, but meaningful. In the first instalment, he distanced
himself from the Barry/Deasy dispute: 'That they do not, apparently, see
certain things from the same viewpoint doesn't make either of them a
dishonest man or an unreliable historian.'[81] In the second he remarked
enigmatically that not enough detail had been given relating to the 'actual
fire and fury that was the bloody Battle of Kilmichael'. The 'final words'
about the ambush, he wrote, 'have not yet been written'.[82] In the last
instalment, Crowley described the Clonmult Ambush (20 Feb. 1921) in
passing as 'Kilmichael in reverse'.[83] For those familiar with the events of the
War of Independence, his remarks could hardly have been more pointed.
Several of the twelve East Cork flying column members killed by Crown
Forces at Clonmult – the IRA's single greatest defeat during the conflict –
were shot unarmed after surrendering.[84]

Deasy did not agree with all of what Crowley said in his review, but he took his comments seriously. He made notes on proposed revisions of his book in light of Crowley's analysis and Barry's attacks. On Kilmichael, he remarked that Barry had given various 'different versions' of the ambush and that he had decided to replace O'Brien's account with one from Barry, but not the *Guerilla Days* version:

> I was not present and, therefore avoided getting involved and felt the version of one who played a very important part there was sufficient. I refer to Paddy O'Brien's contribution. On reflection now: if I were to re-write the story of Kilmichael I would publish in toto Tom Barry's first 'public' report which appeared in the *Irish Press* 6/11/1932 [*sic*].[85]

Deasy died in August 1974. Barry's apoplectic *The Reality of the Anglo-Irish War: Refutations, Corrections, and Comments on Liam Deasy's Towards Ireland Free*, was published by Anvil Press a few months later.[86] In November, Fr Lyne reported to Fr Chisholm that Charlie O'Donoghue (a Cork IRA veteran and Deasy's brother-in-law) was organising several former 3rd Cork Brigade officers to issue a letter disassociating themselves 'in toto' from Barry's pamphlet:

> I expect you have read Barry's diatribe and will naturally be feeling very resentful. The whole production is despicable; while normally one would feel some pity for a man so bitter and so utterly unscrupulous. It reeks of a psychopat[h] whose ego has been exploded; the utter disregard for truth is surely something amazing ...[87]

The public letter, signed by Paddy O'Brien and thirteen other OIRA veterans representing all seven battalions in the West Cork Brigade, appeared in December 1974. All the signatories had contributed to *Towards Ireland Free* in one way or another. Ten were Chisholm interviewees.[88] *The Southern Star* serialised Barry's pamphlet in January 1975, but also published the letter defending Deasy.[89] Mercier Press decided to ignore Barry and inserted the

OIRA statement as an appendix in the 1977 paperback edition of *Towards Ireland Free*.[90]

In his much shorter review of Barry's pamphlet, Crowley (writing as 'JS') described the Deasy–Barry controversy as an 'unseemly wrangle'. Barry's latest broadside would 'convince nobody as to which general won the War,' he said. 'I know my vote goes to the silent young men who shouldered their guns – when they had them – and trudged the narrow bye-ways of West Cork and looked an Empire in the eye.'[91] Crowley also wrote an article about the aftermath of Kilmichael in 1978, in which he described the deaths of McCarthy, O'Sullivan and Deasy just as he had in 1947.[92] A reader's letter noted the deviation from what had become the standard version, that the 'Auxiliaries raised the white flag and then the three Volunteers got up to take the surrender and were machine gunned.'[93] No one seems to have responded.

After his dispute with fellow West Cork veterans, Barry stopped attending the official commemoration, though he laid a wreath at the Kilmichael monument every year. He died in July 1980. His passing and funeral were widely covered in the Irish press. Charlie Haughey, the Taoiseach, Garret FitzGerald, Jack Lynch and Tim Pat Coogan were among those who paid public tribute to him.[94] Flor Crowley died a month later. Tributes appeared for him in the local Cork newspapers and *The Southern Star* noted that he had 'contributed more articles about Kilmichael than any other single engagement'.[95]

This chapter has tracked the various public Kilmichael accounts as they emerged in the decades after the independence struggle. Ambush participants also gave private interviews and confidential statements to the BMH, pension boards, media personalities, family members and historians. Most of these supported Flor Crowley's rather than Barry's version of events, but until relatively recently they were difficult to access. The next chapter draws on all the available evidence – British and Irish, contemporary and retrospective – to analyse and reconstruct the ambush in detail.

7

28 November 1920

The stories that were worth telling produced grim silence or whispered curses: they had blood on them.

Séan O'Faolain[1]

BY 4 P.M. IT SEEMED that the Auxiliaries were not coming. Ned Young and Jack O'Sullivan said that when the scouts signalled their approach, the column was in the process of pulling out or changing position. Barry himself said he had 'more or less decided to withdraw'.[2] Josie Coughlan, who had brought tea to the men in McCarthy's section, was unable to get away in time. She spent the ambush lying concealed, facing up at the IRA men: 'I remember thinking when I was lying by the fence, I'd never again see Johnstown'.[3] Another woman is also thought to have been beside Coughlan.[4] According to Young, Barry was on the road at Section Two at this point and met a horse and trap (a jaunting car or 'sidecar') carrying armed Volunteers as he ran back towards Section One. Barry ordered them to drive on. Accounts differ as to which direction the sidecar came from and which road they took to get away. Why this was important is not entirely clear, but they obviously mattered to those veterans who mentioned the incident as they tend to be very specific about the details.

Most say that it entered the site from Dunmanway, which meant it would have driven past Section One.[5] Barry said the opposite, that it came from the direction of Macroom, drove around the 'entrance bend' (at the western end, Section Two's position) and then up a 'ditchless lane leading to the house'.[6] This could refer to Murray's or O'Donoghue's Lane, or Kelly's

Cross. Other veterans (and Flor Crowley) said that the sidecar drove up a laneway at the Macroom end. Young said it was 'going towards Johnstown', which suggests Kelly's Cross.[7] O'Brien's original account to Deasy, like most of the others, said the sidecar drove in from the Dunmanway direction and that the occupants were ordered to drive on rather than reverse.[8] For whatever reason, Chisholm and Liam Deasy came to a different conclusion, or perhaps O'Brien changed his mind. *Towards Ireland Free* said the sidecar drove into 'Murray's Yard'. Flor Crowley noted in his review of Deasy's book that this answered a 'question that has been asked more than once in the last fifty-three years'.[9]

Most accounts agree that the vehicle was only just out of sight when the first lorry arrived.[10] Interestingly though, Thomas O'Driscoll told his son that the Auxiliaries in the first lorry slowed down because they *saw* the sidecar. No other participant account released so far supports this, but if it is true this might explain the origins of the overly elaborate ruse described in the Dublin Castle account (released to the press in December 1920). In that version, the Auxiliaries encountered a lorry drawn across the road carrying men dressed in khaki and wearing steel helmets. That said, according to both the 'Irish Republican Army (from captured documents only)' and 'Record of the Rebellion' (the British authorities' two analyses, see Chapter Two), the patrol met what they thought was a lone British soldier who told them his lorry had broken down.

Barry himself said that he was alone on the road when the first lorry came around the bend. Murphy's account does not support this, but those of Young and the British suggest he was. Whomever the Auxiliaries encountered, and it was probably Barry, the start of the action was confused and chaotic. His decision to let himself be seen and perhaps even exchange a few words with the Auxiliaries showed considerable quick thinking and nerve. Barry never explained whether his being on the road had been planned or not, although in one interview he remarked that the Auxiliaries 'may have thought for a minute that I was one of their own' because he was wearing a Volunteer uniform kitted out with a Sam Browne belt and other 'accoutrements' of a British officer.[11]

Although accusations that the flying column disguised themselves as British military were rejected out of hand by Sinn Féin publicists at the time and by others since, evidence suggests that the allegations were exaggerated rather than being entirely untrue.[12] An early description of Jim O'Sullivan's death said he was wearing a steel helmet, and one was found at the site in the 1950s (see Chapter 5). Jack Hennessy said he was wearing a 'tin hat'. According to a recently released MSP file, a local Cumann na mBan member had given him a trench helmet and bayonet she pinched in Ballineen from a soldier home on leave.[13]

Paddy O'Brien recalled that the IRA had acquired British uniforms in raids not long before the ambush.[14] There is plenty of evidence that the IRA did sometimes impersonate Crown Forces by wearing Sam Browne belts outside their trench coats, generally to trick suspected spies into thinking they were giving information to the British military. According to Spud Murphy, Thomas Bradfield, a Protestant farmer, was 'identified' as a spy using just such a ruse.[15] One of Hart's Protestant interviewees told him that

> Tommy Barry was very active there [Kilmurray]. He was one of the bad lads in the troubled time. He and a few more came into Cotter, and they were dressed up in British uniform. Barry was in the British Army as you know. They got a lot of information that way and there were a lot of people shot.[16]

Wearing military kit was devious but clever. As Bill Kautt has pointed out, it was intentional subterfuge but it did not contravene the rules of war.[17]

THE FIRST LORRY

In *Guerilla Days*, Barry said he stopped the first lorry by throwing a Mills bomb a distance of thirty-five yards into the cab, killing the driver (quite an extraordinary feat).[18] This differs from both British (see Chapter Two) and other IRA accounts. According to Spud Murphy, who was beside Barry in the Command Post, the grenade was thrown from five yards. He and several others also said Barry threw it into the *back* of the lorry rather than the cab.[19] Barry also maintained that he and his unit were the only Volunteers on the road during the entire fight. Most participants, in keeping with Crowley's version, said that several others fought the first lorry, and that it was a volley from Section One, not the Mills bomb, which killed the driver. Jack O'Sullivan held, in two separate accounts, that nearly all the Auxiliaries in the first lorry were killed by this initial blast of rifle fire: 'I think the whole then, tumbled, toppled over like that ... I'd say they were all dead after the first volley':[20]

Ó Dúlaing: And ah, what was it like as a fight?

O'Sullivan: Well, the fight was nothing. The fight was over before it started nearly. It was only just a case of one volley nearly, and they were wiped out.[21]

Dr Kelleher, who examined the bodies, said James Gleave, Philip Graham, Frederick Hugo, Ernest Lucas, Henry Pearson and Frank Taylor suffered extensive lacerating wounds. All but the last two men were found in the vicinity of the first lorry. Séan A. Murphy, a former Irish Army ballistics expert, has argued, convincingly, that their injuries could have been caused by either high or low velocity weaponry (rather than 'explosive bullets') but did not rule out a grenade.[22] Several early newspaper reports (see Chapter Three) described an explosion of some sort. Young's account of what he witnessed also suggests the Auxiliaries were panicking and confused, which is consistent with the percussion effects of a blast:[23]

I saw the first lorry coming on and the fire opened and the lorry went to the left (Chisholm: yes), down to the left. So when the lorry went to the left, they were coming out of the lorry, here and there, and they were running from, they were running, the driver was shot, and the others they were running to the left and to the right. (Chisholm: yes) Some of them went up, there is a boreen just at the (Chisholm: Murray's field) at Murray's Lane ... there were some of them went up that lane and they were shot when they went up.[24]

In view of the damage to be expected from a Mills bomb at close quarters, if Young's account is accurate, it seems more likely that it landed in the vicinity of the lorry or, as Séan A. Murphy has suggested, that some of the Auxiliaries had already exited the vehicle (as stated in British accounts) when it exploded.[25]

O'Brien, Young and Flor Crowley, like Barry, said several Auxiliaries survived the initial attack. According to Young, they were 'taken care of by Paddy O'Brien and the party … who had been placed in position south of the road'.[26] He said they 'didn't last five minutes, ten minutes':

> Chisholm: Yes, now, what else did you see there?
>
> Young: Well, then, you see, everything was over. I saw the first lorry now below … when the first lorry went down I saw the Tans running, you know, to the left and to the right (Chisholm: to the right yes). I saw the fellows that were on the left, Paddy O'Brien and a couple more of them, coming down towards them, and [whispers] shooting them at the bottom of the … well, I suppose I shouldn't be saying things like that too, but coming down …[27]

O'Brien likewise confirmed in three separate accounts that he and others had been on the road at this point: 'we three jumped out on the road immediately and rushed the first tender. As well as the driver, two Auxiliaries in the back were killed, four others had taken cover underneath, two more were lying wounded on the road …'[28]

O'Brien's more graphic remarks to Liam Deasy described pulling the bodies from the lorry:

> After taking down the driver, who was dead, and placing him on the southern bank, Flyer got on the lorry, but there was no stir. There were two dead in the lorry so we decided to put them on the bank south [sic] also; I went into the lorry; Spud and Stephen took the bodies and laid them down. I can say definitely they were killed by the hand grenade.[29]

His published *Towards Ireland Free* account said that 'all the occupants had been killed' when he reached the first lorry, but that is not what O'Brien seems to have told Fr Chisholm.[30] Unfortunately, most of this interview was taped over, but Chisholm did question Ned Young about some of what O'Brien said:

> Chisholm: ... Paddy O'Brien was telling me about one of the Auxiliaries in the first lorry when they were lifting him down and putting them on the bank he said, 'I'm a Catholic, don't shoot me,' did he ever tell you that?
>
> Young: He did.[31]

Young's brief comments to Ó Dúlaing about the fight at the first lorry, for public consumption, were more equivocal and less challenging of Barry's account. They provide an interesting contrast to what he said elsewhere:

> Ó Dúlaing: There was some fierce hand-to-hand fighting went on, I think, in Kilmichael was there?
>
> Young: There was. A good, a good few men ... the hand-to-hand fighting.[32]

Overall, most of the veterans' testimonies relating to the first lorry suggest that the 'hand-to-hand fighting' described in public accounts consisted mainly of finishing off wounded or disorientated Auxiliaries, at least one of whom was reportedly begging for his life. According to Dave Crowley, his grandfather, Sonny Dave, wanted to fetch a priest for a mortally wounded Auxiliary who said he was a Catholic, perhaps the same man described by O'Brien, but Barry refused to allow it.[33]

FALSE SURRENDER AT THE FIRST LORRY?

Although Flor Crowley's 1947 version of the ambush generally aligns with what most participants said happened, there is one important exception.

None spoke of a false surrender by five Auxiliaries at the first lorry. According to Crowley, no Volunteers were hurt by the ruse but he implies that it decided the Auxiliaries' fate. An intriguing piece of evidence in Hart's papers suggests there might be something to the story. In December 2004, Mealy's Auctioneers in Castlecomer, Kilkenny, put up a small collection of documents for sale: 'Three manuscript documents on leaves from a copy book, containing statements from O.C. Flying Column III Cork Brigade relating to Kilmichael and Crossbarry.'[34]

An Phoblacht, Sinn Féin's weekly newssheet, ran an article about them.[35] Hart's notes indicate he attended the auction and actually consulted the documents. He also mentioned a 'recently discovered account' in a 2004 seminar.[36] What appear to be Hart's notes from the documents read: 'Kilmichael. No mutilation – in one case, man out of bullets, attack up close by Auxie (rigor mortis – broke arms to fit in caskets) false surrender – by 5 – "treachery". K 3 – then – no details. "On patrol" with 25 men then decided to attack.'[37]

According to Mealy's description, the documents were addressed to the IRA 'Director of Propaganda'. Another envelope in the same hand was addressed to the O/C of the 6th Division, Victoria Barracks, Cork. Mealy's suggested the documents might be copies of IRA correspondence sent to the authorities by an informer. If this is true, then perhaps the Irish Command were aware of but ignored rumours that some of the Auxiliaries had attempted a ruse. Or this could be an early IRA effort to justify taking no prisoners. The handwriting might identify the individual, but unfortunately the actual documents have disappeared without a trace. Until or unless whoever purchased them comes forward, no firm conclusions can be drawn.

Overall, of the four main public accounts (O'Neill's, Crowley's, Barry's and O'Brien's), Barry's is the least supported by other veterans' testimony. The discrepancies between *Guerilla Days* and what most of the others said in relation to the second lorry are even starker.

THE SECOND LORRY

Barry's descriptions of where the second lorry stopped on the road and how he and his unit approached and attacked it, as well as when and how the three IRA fatalities occurred, differ radically from other veterans' accounts (and Flor Crowley's). Almost none of the available evidence supports Barry's version of events, and maps based on the *Guerilla Days* account do not match either contemporary or retrospective sources.[38] According to Barry, the second lorry drove into the ambush and 'stopped thirty yards at our side of No. 2 Section'.[39] In other words, it was between Sections One and Two and was in Barry's line of sight as he moved up the road.

Flor Crowley and other veterans said that the second lorry stopped when it was directly across from McCarthy's section at or just *before* the bend, and that the driver then reversed, running into a ditch.[40] Nell Kelly, who was laying on the floor inside the farmhouse at Kelly's Cross throughout the ambush, described the positions of both lorries to Donncha Ó Dúlaing:

Ó Dúlaing: You were very close to it weren't you there?

Nell Kelly: Sure we were inside in the house, just, the lorry was there just south of the [Kelly's] Cross, the other one was between Donoghue's Lane and Murray's Lane, and this one was half way between the Cross and Donoghue's Lane, so t'was very near us you know.[41]

Her description is confirmed by photographs of the second lorry taken the day after the ambush. The distinctive curves of O'Donoghue's Lane are clearly visible some distance behind the burnt-out second lorry.[42] The memorial cross marking the spot where Jim O'Sullivan died (erected by his family in 1956) is also high up on the rocks overlooking where the second lorry reversed into a ditch.[43] The position of the second lorry is important because, if it was halfway between Kelly's Cross and O'Donoghue's Lane (as virtually all the evidence indicates it was), the Auxiliaries who were fighting in and around it could not have seen Barry, and he could not have seen them, until he rounded the bend. Barry also maintained that he and his men crept silently up the road, unbeknownst to the Auxiliaries who, after pretending to surrender, killed or fatally wounded Volunteers who stood up in response. Most other accounts, including the one Barry wrote in 1932, say he ran up the road signalling and calling on other Volunteers to come down onto the road to fight the second lorry, and that the three IRA casualties had already occurred when Barry reached it.[44] According to Ned Young, Barry and his section 'advanced along the road towards the second lorry shooting as they came'.[45] Spud Murphy, in Barry's unit, said: 'We were ordered out on the road – Tom Barry first – and we followed. We got down on our knees and we opened fire on the men that got out of the lorry at the other end (west) of the position.'[46] Even Stephen O'Neill's 1937 account, which Barry initially endorsed, said Barry called on the Auxiliaries at the second lorry to surrender and ordered the column to cease fire.[47]

THREE FATALITIES

As discussed earlier, in all, including his report captured in 1920, Barry wrote or endorsed five successive versions of Kilmichael. In 1932, he maintained that the three IRA fatalities had already occurred when he and his unit wiped out the Auxiliaries at the second lorry. After 1935, however, Barry and Stephen O'Neill accorded at least two, and sometimes all three, of the deaths to a false surrender by some of the Auxiliaries. Flor Crowley's 1947 account contradicted these later versions of events root and branch. Some of the details vary, as we shall see, but Crowley's is the account that is confirmed by almost every ambush participant who went on the record. They either said explicitly that the Volunteer fatalities were shot *before* Barry reached Section Two, or that they did not realise there were IRA casualties until the end of the fight.[48]

Michael O'Driscoll was beside Jim O'Sullivan. According to his witness statement, O'Sullivan, McCarthy and Deasy were hit around the same time in the initial confrontation with the second lorry. He also described how O'Sullivan was killed: 'As far as I could judge, a bullet struck his rifle and part of the bolt was driven into his face.'[49] Jack O'Sullivan was across the road. He was not close enough to witness what O'Driscoll described, but he could have seen Jim O'Sullivan standing up. That is not what he said happened:

Ó Dúlaing: It must have been a terrible thing to see your comrades falling.

O'Sullivan: Well, I didn't see them falling. They just happened to be in the section, in the Number Two section across from us. We didn't see them falling, but the sad part of it was that, I'd say that there wasn't, there wasn't much cover. They hadn't too much cover, especially Jim Sullivan. He was up kinda high and I know very well in his position he was only after pulling old heath and putting it in front of him. He could be laying there all day long and nobody would see him but when you got up, you had to get up on your elbows and show, expose your shoulders and your head to fire, to fire a rifle.[50]

The implications of Jack O'Sullivan's comments were clear enough. If Jim O'Sullivan was shot after getting 'up on his elbows' and exposing his shoulders, he had been lying flat. He could not be one of the two Volunteers Barry claimed had been killed standing up.[51]

Hennessy and Tim Keohane, who were both in Section Two, also each said that the man shot beside them (McCarthy and Deasy, respectively) had already been hit when Barry came around the bend. In common with other available participant accounts (and what Barry said in 1932), Keohane states explicitly that O'Sullivan, McCarthy and Deasy had all been shot before Barry reached the second lorry. Chisholm also questioned Young about the three Volunteer fatalities:

Chisholm: … did you see Michael McCarthy standing up?

Young: No, I didn't.

Chisholm: So he just fell, and he was shot.

Young: That's all.

Chisholm: And the same with Pat Deasy and Jim O'Sullivan?

Young: That's right.[52]

At another point in the interview, Young described what happened to Deasy in more detail:

JC: ... I don't know how Pat Deasy was killed.

NY: Pat Deasy was killed above, he was lying down when as far as I could ascertain about the situation he was lying down on the, above the, where they were in the hole, you know like, (JC: Yes) up that way (JC: Yes) and that he was more exposed than the fellows inside in the hole.[53]

The captured report, Barry's first account, stated that Deasy was 'killed' at the end of the fight by an Auxiliary whom the IRA had thought was dead. In reality, he lived for several hours before succumbing to his wounds.

VETERANS' TESTIMONY AND THE CAPTURED REPORT

The report's description of Deasy as 'killed' (rather than wounded), as well as the fact that it gives the casualties at the end of the fight as 'one dead and two wounded' are two of the main grounds on which it has been dismissed as a forgery. In fact, other accounts tend to broadly confirm most of the captured report's details relating to when and how the three IRA fatalities occurred. There are several instances, for instance, in which Kilmichael veterans used 'killed' as shorthand for fatally wounded and subsequently dying. In 1935, Barry himself described Deasy as having been 'killed' towards the end of the fight', just as he had in the captured report. Tim O'Connell and Paddy O'Brien alternated between describing McCarthy as 'killed' and 'wounded' at the end of the ambush.[54] Flor Crowley said Jim O'Sullivan was killed instantly, McCarthy lived for about an hour and Deasy died that night. O'Brien said the same in his witness statement.[55] Ned Young's states that at the end of the fight, there were two dead and one wounded (Deasy) but when he described to Fr Chisholm coming upon McCarthy after he was hit, Young said McCarthy 'wasn't dead, but he was finished anyway'.[56]

The captured report also said that the column had 'started the return journey' when scouts signalled the Auxiliaries' approach. Young and Jack O'Sullivan both say that the column was in the process of either changing position or leaving. Their testimony belies the argument that 'all other accounts' apart from the captured report said the men remained 'in situ'.[57] The report also said that O'Sullivan and McCarthy were shot because they were so close to the enemy and 'discarded their cover', as do other IRA participants.

Before going any further, it is also worth pointing out that almost all of the evidence Meda Ryan marshals in support of Barry's false surrender is either second-hand or otherwise problematic. According to her, Paddy O'Brien, Pat O'Donovan (her uncle), Dan Hourihane, Tim O'Connell, James O'Mahony, Jack O'Sullivan and Ned Young all 'confirmed' the false surrender to her.[58] Yet O'Connell, one of the veterans on whose information Flor Crowley based his 1947 account, was not beside Deasy in Section Two as she says.[59] He was in Section One, on the rocks near the Command Post at the other end of the ambush site, and could not have seen what occurred at the second lorry.[60] Paddy O'Brien, also in Section One, is described by Ryan as having 'heard' rather than seen the false surrender.[61] As will be discussed further below, evidence suggests that there were several surrenders and a great deal of confusion. Moreover, hearing Auxiliaries surrendering is not evidence for Volunteers being killed or fatally wounded as Barry described. O'Brien also said that he did not realise they had lost any men until after the fighting was over.

In addition, Ryan quotes Dan Hourihan's description of Jim O'Sullivan being shot in the false surrender, but according to his recently released MSP claim, Hourihan left under orders *before* the fight to prepare billets for the column.[62] Some later secondary accounts say Hourihan left *after* rather than before the ambush, but that is not what he said himself in his earliest known account.[63] One member of the pension board even noted that his 'fighting service' began in 1921.

Ryan's analysis of Jack Hennessy's, Young's and Jack O'Sullivan's accounts are also problematic. Nowhere is Hennessy on record as saying he 'almost' stood up with McCarthy, who was then shot by Auxiliaries, as Ryan maintains, apparently relying on her interview with Hourihan.[64] Nor is it clear from what Ryan writes in relation to Young and O'Sullivan that either man told her they saw the false surrender. Unfortunately, what they said cannot be confirmed either way because on that occasion she 'took no notes'.[65]

Some veterans obviously tailored what they said according to their audience. Various members of the Kilmichael commemoration committee and relatives of Kilmichael veterans told Ryan that they heard the men talk about the false surrender.[66] There is no reason to doubt this. She also correctly points to public occasions when veterans did not contradict Barry directly. Young's curiously equivocal comments to Ó Dúlaing are a good example: 'They [the Auxiliaries] probably asked, as Tommy Barry said, I suppose probably when they said "we surrender", I suppose the lads jumped up and, probably, some of them came out and they, well, they finished it off.'[67] Yet he told Chisholm that he did not hear or see a false surrender, or witness any of the IRA fatalities standing up.[68]

FINISHING THE FIGHT

According to both Hennessy and Keohane, the men in Section Two were under orders to break their cover and move onto the road when they heard a prearranged signal from Barry. Hennessy said: 'Our orders were to keep under cover until the Column O/C blew one blast on his whistle or fired a shot.' Both their statements contradict Barry's contention that he and his unit moved silently up behind the Auxiliaries. According to Keohane:

> Tom Barry blew a blast on his whistle as a signal that all men should get on to the road. At the same time he moved with his section along the road from the east to take the survivors in the rear. Tom Barry then called on the enemy to surrender and some of them put up their hands, but when our party were moving onto the road they

again opened fire. Two of our men (John Lordan and Jack Hennessy, I think) were wounded by this fire. Pat Deasy had been wounded, while Jim Sullivan and Mick McCarthy (V/C Dunmanway Battn) had been killed prior to this happening.[69]

Hennessy recalled the same incident although his account does not entirely confirm Keohane's. According to Hennessy, he was already wounded when he shot dead the Auxiliary who threw down his rifle and took out his revolver:

> I continued to load and fire but the blood dripping from my forehead fouled the breech of my rifle. I dropped my rifle and took Ml. McCarthy's. Many of the Auxies lay on the road dead or dying. Our orders were to fix bayonets and charge on to the road when we heard three blasts of the O/C's whistle. I heard the three blasts and got up from my position, shouting 'hands up'. At the same time one of the Auxies about five yards from me drew his revolver. He had thrown down his rifle. I pulled on him and shot him dead. I got back to cover, where I remained for a few minutes firing at living and dead Auxies on the road.[70]

So both Hennessy and Keohane say no one was killed or fatally wounded when the Auxiliaries resumed firing. Neither statement supports Barry's false surrender.

Those who argue that Hennessy thought the fight was over when he heard Barry's whistle are on very shaky ground.[71] Bayonets are weapons intended for close-quarter combat.[72] Ned Young said: 'Barry told us before we went into the fight that it was a fight to a finish (Chisholm: yes) and if we were to fight it to a finish we were to fix bayonets and come out on the road and fight them. I put on the bayonet, on the rifle, and came down the road.'[73] Most importantly, both Hennessy and Keohane said that Volunteers stood up *in response to Barry's orders*, not because they saw the Auxiliaries surrendering. It is also worth noting that O'Neill's 1937 account also stated that Barry called on the enemy to surrender as he came around the bend.

Barry could easily have seen Hennessy and Lordan standing up, but the three Volunteers who died had already been hit. Still, the Auxiliary did throw down his rifle, perhaps in a gesture of surrender, and pull out his revolver: was it an attempted ruse? Maybe. Then again, it could just as easily have been a moment of confusion, or the Auxiliary's rifle might simply have been out of ammunition. Another possibility is that, with most of the Auxiliaries lying dead or dying on the road, and Barry shooting as he rounded the bend, Hennessy's Auxiliary did not heed Barry's call to surrender or Hennessy's shouts to put up his hands. He might have decided to fight on regardless. Whatever happened, and whatever his motives, Hennessy's Auxiliary paid the ultimate price.

According to Hennessy, he and other members of Section Two then killed other wounded Auxiliaries on the road:

> The Column O/C sounded his whistle again. Nearly all the Auxies had been wiped out. When I reached the road a wounded Auxie moved his hand towards his revolver. I put my bayonet through him under the ribs. Another Auxie tried to pull on John Lordan, who was too near to use his bayonet and he struck the Auxie with the butt of his rifle. The butt broke on the Auxie's skull.[74]

What Hennessy described matches the injuries of William Pallister and Frank Taylor. In addition to several other injuries, Pallister's head had been split open 'with an axe or some similar heavy weapon', while Taylor had a perforating wound in his chest.

Interestingly, the January 1921 account attributed to the wounded Cadet Forde, the lone Auxiliary survivor, is not unlike what Hennessy described:

> After knocking us about, they called on us all to stand up and hold our hands up ... There was no response for a time, but after about two minutes two of the party were able to stagger to their feet, and were immediately shot down again at very close range by the Shinners. Then one of the cadets quite near me, who had been lying on his

back, groaned heavily and turned over. One of the civilians, who had a rifle and bayonet, immediately walked up to him and plunged the bayonet into his back as near as I could see between the shoulder blades.[75]

Forde had been shot in the head and body, so there is no guarantee his recollections were entirely accurate. His position on the road suggests he could have been one of the Auxiliaries who tried to surrender. He might not have told his superiors everything. His account was also released to coincide with his compensation claim. It is, for all of these reasons, less reliable than the captured report. Despite these caveats, enough details in the Forde account match subsequent IRA testimony to indicate that he, the lone survivor, witnessed the incident described by Hennessy. Pallister and Taylor were found lying off the road between the two sections rather than on the road, but their bodies could easily have been moved from their original position.

SURRENDERING

Barry's earliest accounts, as well as Flor Crowley's and Paddy O'Brien's published narratives and some witness statements, say Barry and his unit came up behind the Auxiliaries at the second lorry and wiped them out, but they do not give details. Other veterans' accounts do, but the implications of some of even the briefest and most oblique descriptions are impossible to ignore. In his MSP claim, Tim O'Connell wrote: 'we marched to Kilmichael on Sunday morning, lay in wait for the enemy until late that evening, finally they arrived, and after a hard & bloody fight, the few that remained surrendered. When all was over we were all grief stricken to find two of our comrades dead and one mortally wounded.'[76] According to Michael O'Driscoll's statement: 'Tom Barry had dealt with the first lorry and he led a party along the grass verge of the road to come up behind the Auxies fighting us. Soon the fighting was over. We were ordered out on the road.'[77] Young, in his, said similarly that the 'survivors' from the second lorry fought on 'but in a few minutes all firing had ceased.'[78]

Young and Jack O'Sullivan were more explicit when speaking to
Chisholm. Both described disarmed Auxiliaries being shot or clubbed
down with their hands in the air:

Young: … I saw one Tan under the lorry and I said to him to come
out and put up his hands. I fired at him first and he jumped and he
turned back and he could have shot me as well as I could have shot
him. But he jumped, and he came out from under the lorry when I
asked.

Chisholm: With his rifle?

Young: With his rifle.

Chisholm: He didn't drop the rifle?

Young: He did. He put his hands.

Chisholm: And put up his hands?

Young: And put up his hands. He asked me 'What would he do?' and
I said go down the road and they'll tell you. (Chisholm: yes). When
he went down about five or six yards, or ten yards, or something to
that effect, I saw him falling on the road.

Chisholm: And he was shot?

Young: He was shot.

Chisholm: Did he go down with his hands up?

Young: With his hands up.

Chisholm: And they shot him.

Young: They shot him.[79]

The body closest to the second lorry was William Barnes, the first Auxiliary found by members of the search patrol (see Chapter Two). He could easily be the man Young described. He most likely encountered Barry and his men firing shots as they rounded the bend. Chisholm also asked Young about the death of another surrendered Auxiliary:

NY: … I saw Lordan coming out. When I was going down the road I saw Lordan coming out and hitting this (JC: this fellow) Tan.

JC: Had he surrendered?

NY: He had.

JC: Surrendered?

NY: Surrendered.

JC: Was there another man who surrendered too? Another Auxiliary?

NY: Except in the first lorry, I don't know.

JC: No, but there were only two who surrendered from the second lorry so far as you know?

NY: That is all.

JC: The man who surrendered to you (NY: Yes.) and then the man that surrendered there when Lordan hit him with the …

NY: Yes, but they told me afterwards that they said that the Tans said, 'We surrender' and then started to fire again, but I didn't hear that portion of it.

JC: No. You didn't hear any cry of surrender?

NY: I didn't.

JC: No. That was what you heard afterwards.

NY: That was what I heard afterwards.

JC: Can you remember who told you that? Did Lordan tell you?

NY: No, he didn't. I don't know who said it.

JC: You don't remember who said it?

NY: I don't remember who said it.[80]

Young was running up the road after Guthrie, the Auxiliary who escaped, when Hennessy and the others stood up in response to Barry's orders. He witnessed Lordan killing the Auxiliary lying on the ground as he came back down the road. His comment that the two men from the second lorry were the only Auxiliaries who attempted some sort of surrender 'except for the first lorry' might also mean that he witnessed Auxiliaries from the first lorry being shot after surrendering.

In all of Jack O'Sullivan's accounts, he attributed the IRA fatalities to two Auxiliaries who had, as he said to Ó Dúlaing, 'done the damage'.[81] He said both Jim O'Sullivan and McCarthy were shot by Auxiliaries fighting from a prone position in the road. When speaking to Chisholm he also said that it had been the 'wrong thing to say, that McCarthy got up out of his position and got shot':

Chisholm: … The men then, that jumped out, the Auxiliaries who jumped out on the road, they lay down on the road?

O'Sullivan: They did and any of them that were able to lay down and were able to fire.

Chisholm: Able to fire, they got down on the road. Now they were of course, eh, shot at by the Volunteers?

O'Sullivan: Yeah.

Chisholm: Yes. Now you would say that McCarthy was then shot by one of them from the road, one of the (O'Sullivan: I would) Auxiliaries from the road.

O'Sullivan: I would, I would, I would.

Chisholm: And the same would hold for Jim O'Sullivan?

O'Sullivan: I would, because they continued, they, no matter how we tried, they were able to continue (Chisholm: firing?) firing, because like now, you're laying there, you are, you are, you are laying, laying there, and McCarthy and his section are there, and they were, there was a lit ... there were, at that time there was a little dyke in the road, a little dyke, and they were laying in that little dyke, and even now, eh, it would be hard to pick a man laying down like that.[82]

Ned Young, likewise, said that the Auxiliaries 'laid down onto the road' and 'fought until the last man'.[83]

According to Hart's notes made while listening to a recording of the interview Jack O'Sullivan's son conducted with his father, Jack O'Sullivan said that the Volunteers in Section Two were incensed at the death of their comrades, and that these two Auxiliaries were killed, not because of any trickery on their part, but in revenge:

No, there was no such thing as a surrender ... The stories that were told afterward that they were screaming & cursing. Where we were, there weren't ... a murmur. They died without saying a word & asked for no mercy ... & got no mercy ... they died, to my mind, a cruel death, becos [sic] the men that were in with Mick McCarthy, where he was shot, they knew their 2 men were shot, & they came out & they shot 'em & I think a bayonet was used on one, or maybe two of them … [They] Put up their hands & went up the road & went back the road … The firing was stopped. I dunno who gave the signal … We knew it was all over when we saw our men getting out on the road.[84]

O'Sullivan also described these two Auxiliaries to Fr Chisholm:

Chisholm: So you then saw that the Volunteers were, or as is to say the Auxiliaries were being shot and killed on the road but the two of them were left.

O'Sullivan: Two of them were left, and I don't believe that they were ever wounded while they were laying in the road. (Chisholm: no) I seen them getting up perfect, everybody putting up their hands, going back up the road towards …

Chisholm: You saw them and they left their guns down?

O'Sullivan: Left their guns.[85]

This might refer to Pallister and Taylor, who were most likely killed by Lordan and Hennessy. Pallister could be the Auxiliary whom Young was told afterwards had surrendered and reopened fire. He could not be the Auxiliary whom Hennessy described as having thrown down his rifle before pulling out his revolver because Hennessy shot him dead before moving onto the road.

Whoever the two Auxiliaries were, O'Sullivan did not say that they ever pretended to surrender. He says they eventually just surrendered. According to O'Sullivan, they fought so hard and skilfully that the Volunteers in Section Two were unable to dislodge them. Barry and his unit did that. If, as O'Sullivan maintained, these two Auxiliaries were responsible for the IRA fatalities (which most accounts say occurred during the initial exchanges between Section Two and the second lorry) and were then killed by Volunteers enraged at the death of their comrades, this is not a surprising outcome. Surrendering, as military historians have noted, is always a 'distinctly risky practice given the propensity of soldiers to kill rather than take prisoners'.[86]

Veterans also say, either explicitly or by implication, that wounded Auxiliaries were finished off at both the first and second lorries, and that some were killed after genuinely trying to surrender. Barnes, Leonard Bradshaw, Alfred Jones and William Hooper-Jones were all wounded in the axilla (armpit). Séan A. Murphy came to the same conclusion that I did in 2012, that these men were most likely shot with their arms in the air. Barnes and Jones were found between the second lorry and the rocks where McCarthy and Hennessy were positioned in Section Two. Bradshaw and Hooper-Jones were in the vicinity of Section One.[87]

Jack O'Sullivan also said that, after the ambush, he shot a wounded Auxiliary lying on the road in the head, on Barry's orders:

Chisholm: You saw one wounded, and then you reported this to Tom Barry?

O'Sullivan: He was just caught and becrying after me.

Chisholm: Was he, was he trying to kill you?

O'Sullivan: Oh no (Chisholm: no) not at all.

Chisholm: But you saw him wounded?

O'Sullivan: I seen him wounded … I said to Tom, this fellow's still alive and he says 'finish him'.

Chisholm: Finish him. So you just used a revolver on him, did you?

O'Sullivan: Yeah.[88]

It is possible that no firm decision had been made in relation to taking prisoners before the ambush. If Flor Crowley's account of a false surrender at the first lorry is correct, then perhaps it was this that determined the outcome. Young's and O'Brien's accounts of the fighting, however, suggest that Barry did not have to order or bully Volunteers at the first lorry into finishing off the wounded and dying.

Liam Deasy (nephew) and Fr Chisholm said some Kilmichael veterans were haunted by what occurred during the ambush.[89] This is well known locally. According to local folklore, one ambush participant was so distraught after Kilmichael that his hair turned white overnight. One West Cork man interviewed in 2013 told a television crew:

> The boys of Kilmichael – I knew three or four of those men very well. I often tried to discuss it with them. None of them were very keen to talk about it, you know. They'd all go quiet. They'd say to you, 'I wish I wasn't there that night.' So they were very reluctant to talk about it. You felt you were prying.[90]

Some of the women who tended column members after the ambush described them as being in shock, in a 'state of collapse', 'worn out and nerve wrecked' or 'fatigued and afraid'.[91] Jack O'Sullivan remembered that 'one man got sick on the road & he had to be taken away'.[92] Another Volunteer, Denis Cronin, 'got sick' on the march to Granure, where most of the column retired after the ambush.[93] Barry said he had to drill his men to calm them, and he himself suffered another bout of DAH within a few days of the ambush.

While there is little evidence for deliberate mutilation, several bodies had four to six separate injuries (Barnes, Bradshaw, Graham, Hugo, Lucas, Poole, Taylor, Wainwright, Webster) and one had more than six (Jones). At least two Volunteers were armed with shotguns which, particularly at close range, can inflict terrible damage.[94] Barry also said that after the column ran out of ammunition, some of the Auxiliaries were killed with rifle and revolver butts.[95] Four Auxiliaries were shot at close range by shotguns (Barnes, Bradshaw, Gleave, Taylor). Some injuries were inflicted

DAILY SKETCH.

No. 3,658. Telephones { London—Holborn 6512. / Manchester—City 6501.   LONDON, FRIDAY, DECEMBER 3, 1920.   [Registered as a Newspaper.]   ONE PENNY.

THE DAILY SKETCH AND MACROOM ASSASSINS

The burnt-out second lorry with the distinctive curves of O'Donoghue's Lane in the background, behind the journalist who is surveying the wreckage.
(© British Library Board. All Rights Reserved / Bridgeman Images).

MACROOM AMBUSCADE: FIRST PICTURES.

It was a well-chosen spot for a murder—unfrequented and desolate. The wall to the left concealed the Sinn Feiners, who fired point-blank at the cadets on the open tender.—*Daily Dispatch* photographs.

The spot where the Sinn Fein assassins lay in wait for their victims near Macroom. Stone walls such as this are common in Ireland, and, crouching behind it with firearms pointing through the "loopholes" formed by the unevenness of the boulders, the murderers had the patrol at their mercy as they rounded the corner.

No warning came from a dwelling near by, whose occupants must have known, so it was burned.

The first patrol tender was pushed into the bog by the roadside, where it lay disabled and forlorn-looking, a memento of a shameful tragedy, carried out brutally and without mercy.—*Daily Dispatch* photograph.

More contemporary photographs of the ambush site, showing the location of some of the IRA men, the burnt-out farmhouse at Kelly's Cross and the lorries destroyed in the attack. These are from the *Daily Dispatch* of 3 December 1920.
(© British Library Board. All Rights Reserved / Bridgeman Images)

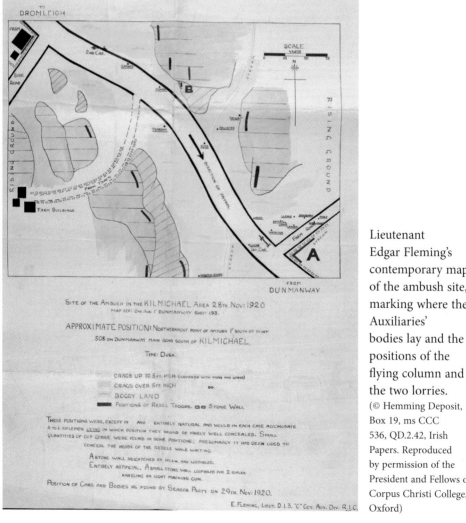

Lieutenant Edgar Fleming's contemporary map of the ambush site, marking where the Auxiliaries' bodies lay and the positions of the flying column and the two lorries.
(© Hemming Deposit, Box 19, ms CCC 536, QD.2.42, Irish Papers. Reproduced by permission of the President and Fellows of Corpus Christi College, Oxford)

An amalgamation of photos of the full ambush site *c.* 1940s. On the far left is the farmhouse at Kelly's Cross, which was burnt out by the Auxiliary search patrol.
(Courtesy of Michael Collins House, Clonakilty)

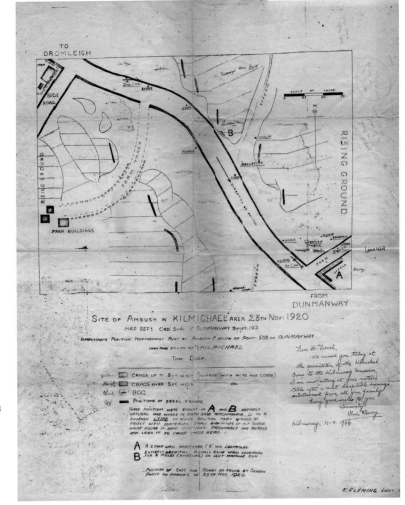

A copy of the Fleming map, annotated and signed by Tom Barry.
(Courtesy of Coppeen Archaeological, Historical & Cultural Society)

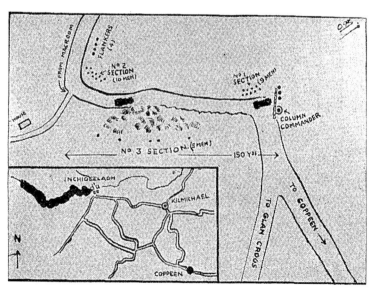

Map of The Scene of Action

A= SPOT WHERE MICHAEL M^cCARTHY WAS KILLED.
B= " " PATRICK DEASY WAS KILLED.
C= " " JAMES O'SULLIVAN WAS KILLED.
X= " " FIRST LORRY WAS ENGAGED & DESTROYED.
Y= " " SECOND " " " "

TO JOHNSTOWN
TO MACROOM (9 MILES)
RANGE OF LOW HILLS
MARSH
BOG
KELLY'S CROSS
KELLY'S FARMHOUSE
(BURNED AS REPRISAL)
SAND PIT
MONUMENT
MARSH
MARSH
HILLOCK HELD BY 6 MEN
MURRAY'S LANE
POSITION OCCUPIED BY
TOM BARRY + SONNY CROWLEY
TO DUNMANWAY (9 MILES)
SCATTERED HILLOCKS
(USED BY SNIPERS)
DONOGHUES FARMHOUSE
(ALSO BURNED)

SCALE IN YARDS
50 100

The map accompanying Flor Crowley's account of the Kilmichael Ambush published in *The Kerryman*, 13 December 1947. The second lorry is halfway between Kelly's Cross and the rocky outcrop where Section Two was positioned.
(Courtesy of Independent News & Media)

FROM MACROOM
FLANKERS (4)
N° 2 SECTION (10 MEN)
HOUSE
N° 1 SECTION (9 MEN)
COLUMN COMMANDER
N° 3 SECTION (6 MEN)
150 YDS
TO GLAN CROSS
TO COPPEEN
INCHIGEELAGH
KILMICHAEL
COPPEEN
N

The map accompanying Tom Barry's *Guerilla Days* Kilmichael account published in *The Irish Press*, 18 May 1948. The second lorry in this map is between Section Two and the Command Post.
(Courtesy of the National Library of Ireland)

Liam Deasy (probably), Tom Barry and Dan Breen *c.* 1922.
(Courtesy of Louise O'Donovan)

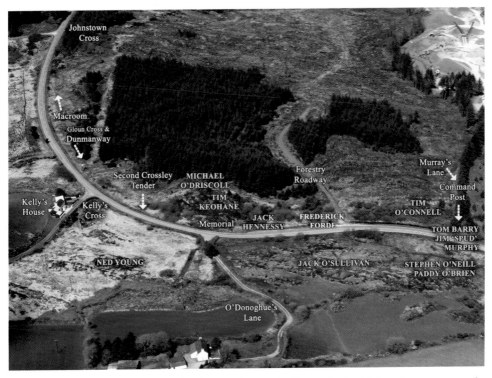

An aerial photograph of the ambush site taken in 2008, marked with location names and the positions of those who gave accounts of the action. (Courtesy of Colum Cronin)

The West Cork IRA veterans who attended the 1938 Kilmichael commemoration. Tom Barry and Liam Deasy are standing in the middle immediately behind the row of men kneeling in the foreground. (Courtesy of the *Irish Examiner* Archive)

Members of the Executive of the Kilmichael and Crossbarry Memorial Committee. Tom Barry (president) and Flor Crowley (secretary) are in the front row, standing on either side of Rev. C. O'Brien (chairman). (Courtesy of the *Irish Examiner* Archive)

Kilmichael veterans at the commemoration marking the fiftieth anniversary of the ambush, which took place on Sunday, 9 August 1970. (Courtesy of the *Irish Examiner* Archive)

Two black and white photographs of Ned Young taken at the 1987 Kilmichael commemoration. In the image on the left, John Young, his son, is beside Ned as he lays a wreath in honour of his comrades. The small colour inset of Ned was taken the following year at the 1988 commemoration. (Courtesy of the *Irish Examiner* Archive)

The statement by former members of the 3rd West Cork Brigade dissociating themselves from Barry's *The Reality of the Anglo-Irish War* in *The Cork Examiner* of 12 December 1974. (Courtesy of the *Irish Examiner* Archive)

Flying Column men reject Barry's claims

COLLEAGUES of Comdt. General-Tom Barry who fought with him during 1920-21 in the West Cork Flying Column have dissociated themselves from his account of those years, published recently in booklet form as a refutation of an earlier book by the late Comdt. Liam Deasy.

Barry's refutation of the Deasy account was the subject of some controversy when published last week. The book, entitled, "The Reality of the Anglo Irish War in West Cork, Refutations, Corrections and Comments on Liam Deasy's 'Towards Ireland Free'," caustically attacked Deasy's version of details and events prior to the ambush at Kilmichael and Crossbarry, and challenged Deasy's editor, Rev. Professor Chisolm, to state why the false surrender of the British Auxiliaries at Kilmichael was not referred to in the book.

STATEMENT

Yesterday's statement by 14 former members of the Flying Column was as follows: "We, the undersigned, former mem-

bers of the 3rd West Cork Brigade, 1920/21, wish to dissociate ourselves from the contents of a booklet entitled 'The Reality of the Anglo Irish War 1920-21 in West Cork, Refutations, Corrections and Comments on Liam Deasy's 'Towards Ireland Free', by Tom Barry and published by Anvil Books Ltd., Tralee. Liam Deasy's book is, in our opinion, a very fair and complete account of the organisation and activities of the 3rd West Cork Brigade 1920-21".

In his refutation, General Barry said: "As one who regards himself, and who is regarded by surviving officers, as the principal target for Deasy's misinformed and misinforming **TURN TO BACK PAGE Col. 4**

Attendees at the Gortroe unveiling of a plaque dedicated to the memory of the IRA's Kilmichael dead in August 2007. *Left to right:* Sean Crowley (guest speaker), Kitty O'Donoghue (niece of Jim O'Sullivan), Margaret Foley, Ann Bradley, John Noel Murphy, Pat Dromey, Seamus Harrington, Joan Dineen (niece of Jim O'Sullivan), Patsy Collins (niece of Jim O'Sullivan) and Liam Deasy (nephew of Pat Deasy). Michael McCarthy's nephew Donal McCarthy, Jim O'Sullivan's nephew Michael Collins, and Jim Deasy, another nephew of Pat Deasy, also attended. (Courtesy of Colum Cronin)

after death (Barnes, Pallister, Poole). The femurs (thighs) of four men had been fractured (Graham, Hugo, Jones, Lucas). Two others had fractured shoulders (Bradshaw and Webster). Another's face had been smashed in with a 'heavy blunt instrument' (Poole).[96]

In contrast to Hennessy and O'Sullivan, Young was adamant that he had not killed any wounded Auxiliaries. One possible reading of this is that he had refused to do so. This might be the real story underpinning another folkloric account, that Young ended the ambush with the same number of bullets with which he began. Young himself was clear that not shooting the Auxiliary he disarmed was the right thing to do: 'He could have shot me and I could have shot him, but I thought it was the bravest thing I could do, maybe, at the time.'[97] Perhaps the reason that Barry singled out Murphy, Nyhan and Mick Herlihy for praise was that they, like Barry, did not hesitate to finish the fight (as Flor Crowley put it), even when faced with men who had downed their weapons and raised their hands in the air – men who could have shot them but did not, or disorientated men staggering up Murray's Lane, their ears ringing from a Mills bomb, or wounded men begging for their lives. Young and Sonny Dave Crowley, who wanted to fetch a priest for a wounded Auxiliary, and perhaps some of the others, might have either refused to shoot the surrendered Auxiliaries or at least challenged the decision to finish them off in such a brutal manner.

It is impossible to know exactly what happened at Kilmichael. Nevertheless, there is very little evidence to support key elements in the *Guerilla Days* version of events. Ambush veterans were careful not to contradict Barry directly in public accounts, but they did so by inference and implication. What distinguishes the multiple accounts of O'Brien, O'Sullivan and Young and the other BMH witness statements is the consistency with which they broadly confirm each other and deviate from O'Neill's and especially Barry's accounts. That a group of ambush veterans did not agree with the version that appeared in *Guerilla Days* was well known. The disparities between the versions of the ambush Barry gave in the 1940s and what he said originally, and the divergences of other participant accounts from Barry's, cannot be explained away by Chisholm's interview technique or the BMH's faulty methodology. A counter-narrative can be traced as early as the 1930s. It was never a secret history. The alternative version of Kilmichael was given by Barry himself in 1932, in Crowley's 1947 account, in BMH statements and by O'Brien in *Towards Ireland Free*. Barry's post-1935 accounts are the ones that do not fit.

Some veterans obviously said and believed a false surrender had taken place that led to the deaths of the three Volunteers, but few of these had been in a position to see whatever happened at the second lorry. In some cases, loyalty to Barry seems to have been an important factor influencing what was said. The fact that no veterans publicly contradicted him explicitly is not nearly as significant as some have suggested. They did not need to do so. Any account of Kilmichael which did not include a false surrender mortally killing or wounding some or all of the slain Volunteers *was* contradicting Barry. The false surrender was also what most people wanted, not the chaotic, merciless event that much of the veterans' testimony describes.

There is no evidence that those who gave alternative accounts of Kilmichael were intent on compromising either Barry's reputation or that of other ambush veterans who did support the *Guerilla Days* account. If anything, their testimony suggests that this is exactly what they were trying to avoid, although they still felt their version of events needed to be told. It is a shame that Barry felt unable to accept this compromise. None of the veterans' accounts, apart from Barry's and O'Neill's, say anything negative about the conduct of the Kilmichael Auxiliaries either. Perhaps the sentiments expressed by Flor Crowley in 1978 reflected what many ambush veterans felt themselves:

'Killed in action!' That was how the British Army and the British Press described their own men who fell at Kilmichael and Crossbarry and elsewhere. Let us not quarrel with them for it has ever been the way of Armies, even the way of every National Press the world over. A foe overcome and slain in a fair fight ceases to be a foe, and should be remembered more with respect than rancour.[98]

Hard copies of newspapers have been available in libraries for decades, and the Irish Newspaper Archive has been online since 2006.[99] For the last fifteen years, finding Flor Crowley's 1947 account of the ambush involved no more effort than typing 'Kilmichael' into the search bar and having the patience to read through the results. Liam Deasy's papers, released in 1999, document his refusal to change or remove O'Brien's Kilmichael account before the publication of *Towards Ireland Free* and, in the face of Barry's attacks, to challenge the latter's 1949 account more overtly. Similarly, the witness statements from Kilmichael veterans in the BMH archive, opened in March 2003, considerably weakened the case for Barry's uncontested Kilmichael account. Yet almost all of this evidence has either been distorted or ignored by those who insist on privileging Barry's later account over all others, including his own earlier ones. The most important question to be answered at this point is why.

8

They Were All Revisionists Then

ON SUNDAY 20 NOVEMBER 1983, in the tiny village of Darkley, South Armagh, about two miles from the Monaghan border, gunmen opened fire on the Pentecostal Mountain Lodge Church during a religious service. They circled the wooden building, firing indiscriminately through the walls. One of the three church elders mortally wounded at the door while welcoming latecomers and handing out hymn sheets survived long enough to warn the congregation. Nine of the sixty people inside were wounded.[1] An anonymous phone call to a journalist from the 'Catholic Reaction Force' said that the killings were in retaliation for the 'murderous sectarian campaign carried out by the Protestant Action Force'. Unless they stopped killing innocent Catholics, said the caller, 'we will make the Darkley killings look like a picnic'.[2]

Darkley was universally condemned. Dominic McGlinchey, leader of the Irish National Liberation Army (INLA), confirmed to the *Sunday Tribune* that he had given one of the weapons used in the attack to an INLA member whose brother had been recently killed by loyalists. The man in question must have been 'unbalanced', he said, as there was no justification for Darkley.[3] After the attack, the local community in South Armagh, almost 90 per cent Catholic, 'wrapped itself around the church congregation in sympathy'.[4] Three days after the incident, the Bishop of Cork and Ross called on his parishioners to boycott the annual Kilmichael commemoration because Gerry Adams, leader of Sinn Féin, was to give the oration. Darkley was an 'added reason why people should not go', he said.[5]

Several local Fianna Fáil members complied.[6] Two members of the Kilmichael Commemoration Committee resigned.[7] Defence Minister Paddy Cooney ordered the army not to supply arms for the traditional volley over the graves. *An Phoblacht* said the decision reflected the 'Free State's' contradictory attitude towards the national question. The following week it published a Kilmichael account (the false surrender version), comparing the current 'hysteria' over the Adams invitation to the 'media and establishment' reaction to the ambush in 1920.[8]

All sides involved in the public debate over the commemoration laid claim to Tom Barry's or Kilmichael's legacy. John Dennehy, the Fianna Fáil mayor of Cork, maintained that Barry would not have condoned the 'planting of a bomb in a public place on an indiscriminate basis'.[9] John A. Murphy, the historian and senator, said Kilmichael represented a 'much longer story of resistance by a sturdy people to the oppressors of their class and nation'. He described Adams's presence at the commemoration as an 'obscenity' that would besmirch the ambush's memory.[10]

The fact that Barry had expressed a range of attitudes towards the conflict in the 1970s made it easier for the different sides to claim him. He was certainly more sympathetic to the IRA than Liam Deasy. In Barry's oration at the fiftieth annual Kilmichael commemoration, celebrated in August 1970 with marching bands and an open-air mass at the site, he took issue with 'utterances from certain people' who seemed to be suggesting that Kilmichael veterans should apologise for the men 'who died with guns in their hands'. He extended his sympathies to the 'victims of British imperialism ... in the Six Counties'. The ending of partition was a matter for the entire island, he said, and 're-establishing' the Republic was still the objective.[11] By contrast, in 1973, when Liam Deasy was asked for his views on the use of violence in the 'current Northern situation' by a reviewer who maintained that the 'glamour attached' to books about the War of Independence had faded, he declined to comment.[12]

Overall though, Barry's views mirrored wider public opinion in the South, where sympathy for the IRA peaked in the first years of the Troubles before going into fairly rapid decline once the bombing campaign began in late 1970.[13] Barry praised the IRA after Bloody Sunday (January

1972) but condemned the Birmingham pub bombings (November 1974) and distanced himself from the hunger strikes in Portlaoise in 1977. The organisation was losing support, he said, and they 'had only themselves to blame'.[14]

At least 1,200 people attended the 1983 commemoration. Two weeks earlier, Adams had replaced Ruairí Ó Brádaigh as Sinn Féin president.[15] It marked his and other northern republicans' ascendency within the party. Adams had been elected MP for West Belfast in June and gave the annual Wolfe Tone commemoration address at Bodenstown a few days later.[16] Speaking from the platform, Adams condemned Darkley but described Kilmichael as a 'necessary and morally correct' action in 1920. The contemporary IRA were freedom fighters at war with the same enemy for the same cause and the police and the army were the terrorists. The men who fought at Kilmichael had also been vilified and misrepresented by the 'British and Irish establishments': 'Could it be that my presence here brings the reality of Kilmichael into perspective – not as a glorious and historic episode from the past in a long-gone struggle … but as an historic and ruthlessly fought part of the unfinished and continuing struggle for independence?'[17]

Another speaker told the crowd that, shortly before his death, Barry said he agreed fully 'with the freedom fighters in the North'.[18] That evening, a dinner was held in honour of Kilmichael veterans Ned Young and Jack O'Sullivan.

A letter published shortly after the commemoration from Meda Ryan also compared the prevailing situation with 1920: 'Contrary to the helpful attitude now purported to have existed at the time, relatives of "The Boys of Kilmichael" were subjected to local rebuff and antagonism during the period following this ambush – an ambush now regarded as the most decisive and a "turning point" in the War of Independence … Are there echoes of history being repeated?'[19]

Public commentary on the commemoration continued for several weeks. Rev. Ian Paisley, MP for Antrim North, raised the issue of Adams's presence at the commemoration in the House of Commons, where Kilmichael had not been mentioned for eighty years: 'There will be no coming together of the people I represent and Mr. Adams,' he said.[20] At the end of December, Cork county councillors condemned the IRA and the INLA. The Kilmichael ambush had been, they said, 'a just fight [fought] in an honourable way, unlike the London bombers and the [Don] Tidey kidnappers'.[21]

With the outbreak of the Northern Irish conflict in 1969, the legacy of the Irish independence struggle, including Kilmichael, became associated with highly charged and polemical debates relating to the legitimacy of the armed campaign being waged by contemporary republicans who laid exclusive claim to past struggles. Numbers of still living members of the revolutionary generation were dwindling in the 1970s, but older disputes among them relating to their long-standing disagreements continued in parallel with these modern debates. As time went on, arguments old and new relating to Kilmichael and other events of the 1916–23 period fused. From the 1970s to the present, the tenor of public discourse relating to the revolutionary period and the status of traditional nationalism in academic history (and in Irish society more generally) has shifted and changed in response to the ongoing political situation. The full resonance of the dispute over Peter Hart's work following the publication of *The IRA and Its Enemies* in 1998 is only really comprehensible within the context of these broader circumstances.

***

From the 1940s to the 1960s, the annual Kilmichael commemoration had been a relatively low-key affair. There was a mass, a decade of the Rosary, an oration, and a volley fired over the graves. Kilmichael veterans and other OIRA men, their families and associates always played some role.[22] Orations were given variously by ambush veterans, Fianna Fáil TDs, republicans and local personalities. Cork units of the FCA re-enacted the ambush at the site, often with Barry supervising.[23] In the 1950s and 1960s, the IRA and Sinn Féin in Cork held what seem to have been separate commemorations at the ambush site.[24] In 1965, a committee established to raise funds for a new memorial was chaired by Rev. Fr Cornelius O'Brien, a parish priest. Barry was elected president. The *Southern Star's* report of the first meeting included a Kilmichael account that followed Barry's *Guerilla Days* version to the letter.[25]

The monument's unveiling in July 1966 was very much a community celebration. Veterans, local schoolchildren, FCA units and pipe bands marched to the monument. A *Cork Examiner* editorial described the names of Kilmichael veterans as 'synonymous with valour'. The story of the ambush was a 'legend which will be recalled around the firesides of West Cork when other actions have faded into obscurity'.[26] In his oration, Fr O'Brien prayed both for the souls of the Kilmichael dead and also for '300 years of peace between Ireland and England; that these two islands might in future live in peace and harmony, in mutual understanding and co-operation'.[27] His prayers went unanswered. When he died in December 1975, a six-day gun battle was raging between the Metropolitan Police and an IRA ASU besieged on Balcombe Street in London.[28]

In December 1969, the IRA split into rival 'Provisional' and 'Official' factions. Both laid claim to the legacy of the revolutionary era. The latter ended their armed campaign in 1972. The 'Provos' continued into the 1990s. Most commemorations associated with the 1916 to 1923 period began to reflect the more volatile political atmosphere one way or another. The Official and Provisional wings of the IRA, the Defence Forces and Fianna Fáil all held separate events at Bodenstown. The UVF twice set bombs at or near the Wolfe Tone monument.[29] Ireland's main political parties all scornfully rejected the IRA's assertions that they were 'fighting the same fight' and, despite political differences, began to close ranks against republicans.[30] Jerry Cronin, the minister for defence, became the first ever Fianna Fáil minister to give the oration at Béal na Bláth (a Fine Gael commemoration).[31] Republicans organised separated commemorative events or disrupted those organised by mainstream nationalists.[32] In 1976, in Northern Ireland, thirty separate marches commemorated the Easter Rising, and over 10,000 people defied the Fine Gael–Labour coalition's ban on the Provisional IRA's march in Dublin.[33]

Kilmichael commemorations became venues for speakers to comment on current events, much as in the 1930s. Not everyone approved. In 1979, Commandant Éamonn Young, Ned Young's nephew, objected to how Neil

Blaney used the event to promote his political views: 'Give us back the Kilmichael we had,' he said, 'where honour was true, bright and never lashed to the wheel of party politics.'[34] The decision to invite Blaney (and Adams in 1983) reflected the political views of several members of the Kilmichael and Crossbarry Memorial Committee. They, as well as some surviving ambush veterans, were openly sympathetic to Sinn Féin and the IRA. Donal MacGiolla Phóil (Donnie Powell) and ambush veteran Jack O'Sullivan took part in West Cork 'H' Block Committee support group events during the 1980–1 hunger strikes, as did IRA veterans Tom Kelleher and Dan Cahalane.[35]

Because media interviews with the IRA were banned under the Broadcasting Act in 1971 (Section 31), both Kilmichael and Bodenstown became important venues for Sinn Féin to air its views in the 1970s and 1980s, and also afforded rest and recreation to republican activists.[36] In the 1990s, the Kilmichael commemoration provided a platform for Sinn Féin to comment on the Northern Peace Process.[37] Martin McGuinness, during his oration at the 1995 commemoration (the ambush's seventy-fifth anniversary) said he would have 'crawled from Derry to West Cork' to speak at Kilmichael.[38] Two years later, Gerry Adams discussed his meetings with Tony Blair and, noting that he spoke at the commemoration fourteen years earlier, commended the Kilmichael and Crossbarry Committee for 'keeping the faith'.[39]

THEY WERE ALL REVISIONISTS THEN

For many, Kilmichael remained a much-romanticised event from the past, though the political situation was beginning to undermine this comfortable distance. In July 1969, when the Cork showband Art Supple & The Victors' rendition of 'The Boys of Kilmichael' reached number fourteen in the Irish charts, riots were raging in Derry, Belfast and Dungiven.[40] The Provisional IRA laid exclusive claim to the revolutionary period and regularly referenced it to justify their armed campaign:

So what mandate did Pearse, Connolly and their men have? Certainly they had none … they were far more rejected than the present IRA

... The men of 1916 had the same mandate as have the IRA today –
the mandate of justice, of nationality and of history. To deny this is
to say that they – and the present IRA – were wrong. But one cannot
condemn one and condone the other.[41]

'Revisionism' became a 'catch-all phrase' to describe a new and often more
critical re-assessment of traditional narratives of the revolutionary period
engendered by the Northern conflict.[42] It became commonplace to link the
valorisation of IRA gunmen and War of Independence ambushes to the
'Troubles'.[43] Conor Cruise O'Brien and Ruth Dudley Edwards produced
trenchantly critical studies of Irish nationalism and nationalist heroes, but
their 'revisionist' challenge was just one facet of a much broader and more
complex societal phenomenon.[44] Both revisionists and their critics came
in all stripes.

From the mid-1970s onwards, journalists and media figures like
Kevin Myers, John Waters and Eoghan Harris made concerted efforts to
undermine the IRA's claim to legitimacy.[45] Myers in particular used his
weekly 'An Irishman's Diary' column to comment on current events and
historiographical debates. He criticised, at various junctures, both David
Fitzpatrick and Brendan Bradshaw, and frequently sparked rounds of
angry letters from other historians and public commentators.[46] The regular
columns by Con Houlihan for *The Kerryman* and John Healy in the
Western People were also bitterly critical of the IRA and blamed them for
the ongoing violence.[47]

Some of Peter Hart's most vociferous critics in recent decades
were scarcely recognisable in the 1970s. Members of the British &
Irish Communist Organisation (BICO) promoted the Two Nations
Theory recognising the 'democratic legitimacy' of Ulster Protestants.
They argued that the IRA had no right to force them into a 'state run
by gombeen men and priests'.[48] Some of them described the Belfast
IRA (in the 1920s and 1930s) as a 'Roman Catholic sectarian militia'.[49]
Then, in 1985, BICO members Brendan Clifford and Jack Lane founded
the Aubane Historical Society in Cork, reincarnating themselves as
traditional nationalists.

Dan Nolan, at Anvil Press, remarked on the negative impact that the Northern conflict was having on the market for books dealing with 'violence in Ireland since 1913'.[50] In April 1977, after watching an RTÉ television programme about the 'cult of 1916', he described 'revisionism' as the 'in' subject for debate. He felt that historians and commentators such as Ruth Dudley Edwards, Conor Cruise O'Brien and John A. Murphy were misconstruing the motivations of men like Barry and Ernie O'Malley.[51] According to *An Phoblacht*, O'Brien and Murphy represented different variants of revisionism, unionist and nationalist respectively.

A diverse array of cultural critics, political activists and historians accused 'revisionist' historians of conspiring to promote, through their work, a 'political programme, masquerading under the cloak of scholarly objectivity'.[52] Some characterised the new 'revisionist' history as a 'neo-unionist' attempt to 'rehabilitate' Britain's role in Ireland.[53] The early modern historian Brendan Bradshaw and public commentator Desmond Fennell argued that traditional nationalist narratives should be preserved because Irish people needed them. In Bradshaw's now famous 1989 intervention, 'Nationalism and Historical Scholarship in Modern Ireland', he challenged the 'interpretative principle of value free history', which he argued was being promoted by the 'revisionist enterprise'. In his view, historians should engage in 'purposeful unhistoricity' and promote the traditionalist nationalist narrative, 'its wrongness notwithstanding'.[54] His intervention had been prompted by the hostile reception afforded to his paper (making a similar argument) at a conference of Irish historians in Britain the year before.[55]

Seámus Deane, the well-respected literary scholar who died in May 2021, was a northern Catholic from a working-class Derry background. He raged (quite understandably) at southern indifference to the plight of northern nationalists, arguing that scholarship should be geared towards effecting political change. Students and staff in Dublin universities, he said, knew very little about the realities of life in Northern Ireland. They adopted a 'one-side's-as-bad-as-the-other' attitude towards the Troubles in order to insulate themselves from any requirement to engage more actively with what was happening.[56] As we shall see, Deane's argument that 'revisionist' historians had 'switched sides' to become defenders of 'Ulster or British nationalism' would later become a central tenet of Hart's main critics.[57]

Some historians were angry as well. Work promoting the value of archival research and challenging orthodoxies was sometimes peppered with asides like 'By then, the results of simplistic historical hero-cults had become obvious in the carnage of Northern Ireland' and references to 'ancient and atavistic attitudes'.[58] Other historians used quite aggressive imagery in describing their role as repudiators of myth and legend.[59] It became quite common to portray history as an antidote to what F.S.L. Lyons referred to as the 'dire present' and a natural enemy of popular traditions and beliefs, particularly historical memory, and to promote the idea that the latter was hopelessly atavistic, mired in imaginings and virtually impenetrable to historical revelation and research.[60] History was a 'mental war of liberation from servitude'.[61] Statistics were hammers for 'shattering Irish self-deception'.[62] The language employed, particularly quoted out of context, could seem very patronising.

Nevertheless, blanket characterisations of historians as 'unionist' hinged on ignoring the considerable diversity of views, as well as much of what was actually being said. The arguments made were generally nuanced and intended to promote debate.[63] It was not at all clear that Theo Moody, the TCD historian, and Robert Dudley Edwards (UCD), generally considered the two founders of modern Irish revisionism, had ever advocated 'value-free' history.[64] Moreover, a commitment to academic standards did not dictate individual responses to events. Moody was more opposed to the media censorship of republicans than many in Fianna Fáil. He was a member of the RTÉ Authority sacked by the government in November 1972 after it broadcast an interview with Seán Mac Stíofáin (then C/S of the Provisional IRA).[65] Other historians acknowledged that Brendan Bradshaw had a point or, not without justification, argued that the attacks on the historical profession were relentless character assassinations rather than meaningful critiques of their work.[66]

Outside of academia, traditionalists and republicans were making accusations not unlike Deane's. In a 1973 oration at a Liam Lynch commemoration, for instance, Éamonn de Barra attacked the 'self-appointed professional historians and their supine supporters' who relied on 'doctored documents, specially prepared to produce propaganda-slanted records for the purpose of slandering our heroic dead' in order to 'rid us of militant nationalism'.[67] Sixteen years later, in his 1989 Kilmichael oration, Fr Paddy Ryan, a Tipperary priest who the British tried to extradite twice (and who, in 2019, admitted to being actively involved in several IRA bombings in Britain), advocated the re-establishment of Irish nationalism as the 'norm of political thinking on the island'. He castigated 'rent-a-pen academics', the 'paid pens of the establishment media' and the 'moral bankruptcy of the revisionists of Irish history'.[68]

Yet there were also contexts in which republicans in the 1970s and 1980s were just as inclined to explode myths as their media *bêtes noires*.[69] Cork republican Jim Lane, in 1972, described the April 1922 attacks on Protestants in West Cork as a 'pogrom every bit as vicious as any one in Belfast'.[70] In 1985, Sinn Féin's Publicity Department produced *The Good Old IRA*. Its precis of brutal 'Tan War' operations (including Kilmichael) was intended to confront 'those hypocritical revisionists who winsomely refer to the "Old IRA" whilst deriding their more effective and, arguably, less bloody successors [the Provisionals]'. The War of Independence had no clear democratic mandate, it said, and 'no struggle involves a clean fight'.[71]

A parallel but related development to the emergence of revisionism (in all its permutations) was the release in Britain and Ireland of archival collections on which most modern academic research into the 1916–23 period relies. David Fitzpatrick and Charles Townshend were among the first beneficiaries of Britain's 1967 Public Records Act.[72] In Ireland, releases of private papers gathered apace over the later 1970s and the 1980s.[73] The National Archives Act (1986) mandated the annual release of government and official papers subject to a thirty-year rule, and the establishment of a National Archives. The legislation also facilitated the reorganisation and re-establishment of the Irish Army's archives. Under Commandant Peter Young, civilians were allowed to access its collections.[74]

THE TOM BARRY STORY

In the south, while the Northern Ireland conflict was undoubtedly complicating the reception of histories of the revolutionary period, often it was still little more than a backdrop to the OIRA's long-standing allegiances, personal rivalries and disagreements. Meda Ryan's 1982 biography of Tom Barry reflected both southern nationalism's obsessive focus on the minutiae and controversies of the 1916–23 period (unrelated to contemporary politics) and the more critical 'revisionist' turn within contemporary republicanism.[75] She described her biography as an attempt to present the 'true man with all his faults'. Ryan discussed Barry's recurrent episodes of 'heart trouble', his hatred of Liam Lynch, and his contrariness and unpredictability, particularly towards the end of his life. She also made a point of noting the views of Barry's 'critics' on other issues relating to Barry's involvement in the IRA during and after the revolutionary era. There were local suspicions that Barry had been groomed as a British agent before joining the IRA in 1920 and might even have had 'other than honourable' motives, initially, for joining the insurgents.[76] The West Cork IRA's killing of the retired Vice Admiral Somerville in March 1936 was not an accident, some argued, and Barry (who ordered it) made sure he was somewhere else when it was carried out.[77]

In relation to Kilmichael, she was less beholden to *Guerilla Days* than Ewan Butler's *Barry's Flying Column* had been, correctly pointing out that, despite what Barry said, two Auxiliaries (Guthrie and Forde) had survived the ambush, although, in Guthrie's case, not for long.[78] The fact that these revelations were presented as new information reflected how dominant Barry's account had become. Flor Crowley discussed local folklore relating to Forde's survival in 1947. Forde, he said, had identified 'at least seven' members of the column. The allegations of mutilation also came from him.[79] Ryan gave a cautious, if rather confused, endorsement of the Kilmichael account in Barry's memoir but also acknowledged the Deasy–Barry dispute. Barry's critics were of the view, she noted, that he should have accepted what she referred to as the Auxiliaries' 'second surrender' because the IRA fatalities had been killed in action.[80]

She also described how Barry's attacks on Deasy's book had divided the OIRA men: 'Memory began to play tricks on many of the old men, and strangely enough I found that some of them whom I had interviewed previous to this event, who had thought Barry one of the greatest men who ever walked on Irish soil, had altered their attitudes and begun to have doubts about him after the Deasy–Barry controversy.'[81] According to her, Barry had been asked to read a draft of *Towards Ireland Free* before publication but refused. 'Barry could be arrogant,' she commented, and 'may have been annoyed that someone else had "dared" to write another book on the Third West Cork Brigade.'[82]

An Phoblacht's reviewer praised Ryan's depiction of the brutal realities of war: 'the book has it all – shooting unarmed and off-duty British soldiers and RIC constables (Catholics and Irish men), executing spies and informers, and conducting an arson campaign against civilian pro-British dwellings (Protestant without exception)'. He was critical of Ryan's supposedly excessive focus on Barry's life up to 1923. This was not an uncommon attitude among republicans. Brendan Vaughan, a member of Cork Sinn Féin who interviewed Jack O'Sullivan in the 1980s, was far less interested in O'Sullivan's criticisms of Barry's Kilmichael account than he was in the fact that RTÉ had, it seems, refused to interview O'Sullivan because he was sympathetic to Gerry Adams and Sinn Féin. *An Phoblacht*'s reviewer of Ryan's book also insisted that, despite his reservations about the modern IRA's tactics, Barry had endorsed the 'freedom struggle whole heartedly'.[83]

Correspondence following other early reviews of Ryan's book shine a rather hypocritical light on some of the accusations that would later be made against Peter Hart. Ulick O'Connor criticised Ryan for 'making serious accusations against public figures without disclosing the source of the information', referring particularly to Barry's possible pre-IRA association with British intelligence. Donal MacGiolla Phóil immediately came to Ryan's defence, confirming that what she said was well known locally.[84] Ryan herself responded by saying that although she had 'revealed information which appears unfavourable', this did not 'take from Barry's greatness; his place in history is assured'.[85]

As discussed, even in the face of other, rival Kilmichael veterans' testimony, long-time supporters of Barry like journalist Pat Lynch had continued to insist that the *Guerilla Days* account had never been challenged. Dan Nolan's reaction to Ryan's biography was indicative of the extent to which even the slightest deviation from Barry's memoir was understood by his friends and defenders to be a betrayal. Nolan's long-standing efforts to accommodate and protect Barry's reputation continued after his death. In 1983, he asked Frances Mary Blake to help him locate the 'official British account' of Kilmichael to verify whether or not two of the Auxiliaries had actually survived the ambush. He also remarked on

> the very subtle campaign of character assassination against Tom Barry being carried on from Cork. Tom, God rest him, was my friend of many years and I am quietly getting verification of what I know to be the facts behind the statements and stories that are being circulated through newspaper stories, statements to the press, radio and by the Ryan book.[86]

Ryan's original biography was a brave effort for its time and accurately reflected what a controversial figure Barry had been. Later versions of her book omitted or revised most of these critical passages.

By the 1990s, two different understandings of historical revisionism had fused in popular discourse. New interpretations and recounting of past events were automatically translated into support or opposition to political questions. Joe Lee described this well:

> The tragedy from a purely historian's point of view is ... that ... Irish historical writing in the 1960s ... was beginning to be revised anyway ... away from pure political history, then the North blows up and re-politicises everything ... what I would call historical revisionism in a purely scholarly sense was blown aside by historical revisionism which was inevitably partly the prisoner of current politics.[87]

A NEW REVOLUTIONARY HISTORY

Peter Hart, a Canadian doctoral student from Newfoundland, commenced his doctoral studies in Trinity College Dublin in October 1987 under the supervision of David Fitzpatrick.[88] It was then unusual for academic researchers to choose the 1916–23 period as their subject, never mind conduct interviews or use oral history evidence. Fitzpatrick had made little use of his own recorded interviews with Clare veterans, but neither Hart nor his contemporary, Joost Augusteijn, a Dutch graduate student based in TCD (and a friend of Hart's) had any of the prejudices against oral history common among many academic historians at the time. Both combined conventional and unorthodox source material.[89] No third-level history department in Ireland in the 1980s and 1990s had methodological protocols in place for researchers and students conducting oral history interviews. Augusteijn recorded his; Hart tended to take notes.[90] Hart's sister, Susan, was an archivist and folklorist. Anne Hart (1934–2019), their mother, was a librarian, archivist, writer, feminist and anti-Vietnam war protester who served on Newfoundland's Human Rights Council in the 1980s. She played an integral role in the establishment of Memorial University of Newfoundland Libraries' archives unit in 1982.[91]

Within a few months, Hart met Marion O'Driscoll, a mature student taking history courses at Trinity. Her husband, Jim, was a popular and well-regarded barrister from West Cork.[92] The O'Driscolls let Hart stay in their West Cork holiday home when he was carrying out fieldwork and put him in touch with local IRA veterans, including Ned Young. Hart conducted interviews in the spring and summer of 1988, and in April, May and November 1989. At least one of Hart's interviewees, who was not a Kilmichael veteran and died in 1996, spoke to him 'on the understanding that my name is not used by you in anything that may be published later on.'[93] By February 1990, Hart had also listened to excerpts from Fr Chisholm's interviews with Young and O'Sullivan.[94] His correspondence with Chisholm shows that he had hoped to identify the interviewees by name in his own work:

> There remains the question of ... use and attribution. As this is your material, this is entirely at your discretion. If you prefer, I will not use your name or your interviewees names, but I would like to give as complete an account of the source as possible. I would suggest

the following acknowledgement for footnotes and the bibliography: 'Interview with (for example) Paddy O'Brien by Dr. John Chisholm. Tape in the possession of Dr. Chisholm, Dublin.' Would this be alright?[95]

Chisholm initially agreed to this, but then changed his mind.

When Hart was researching his PhD, the Troubles were ongoing, the broadcasting ban (Section 31) was still in force and a general 'anti-republican bias'[96] existed within the media and in Southern Ireland. Yet Hart was, if anything, conspicuously broad-minded in terms of the range of organisations and individuals he approached in search of material and opinion. He wrote to Sinn Féin looking for possible interviewees. He made contact with George O'Mahony, a veteran of the 1960s Cork IRA, who allowed him to consult his recorded interviews with Tom Barry and Tom Kelleher.[97] Hart was also on friendly terms with individuals who would later be at the forefront of attacks on him, particularly Brian P. Murphy.[98] His letter to Meda Ryan, sent via her publishers, received no response.[99]

Hart also actively sought out the views of well-known republicans like Éamonn de Barra, Séan O'Mahony and Uinseann MacEoin. He sent the latter two a draft of his article on the assassination of Sir Henry Wilson.[100] MacEoin disagreed with Hart's conclusions and disapproved of his 'pejorative terminology': 'Your research is very thorough though that need not prevent you reaching wrong conclusions.'[101] Whatever about his conclusions, it is a pity that Hart did not take more account of MacEoin's remarks on his tone.

It seems to have been Kevin Myers who brought the April 1922 killings to Hart's attention.[102] Myers was on friendly terms with several TCD doctoral students, discussed Trinity Workshop publications in his column and praised Hart's work from early on.[103] David Fitzpatrick cautioned Hart at draft stage that Myers's assertions in relation to April 1922 were 'unconfirmed rumour' rather than solid evidence, and also that Hart was 'too ready to attribute sectarianism to the Republican identity in general'.[104] Hart took his advice, and his thesis chapter about these killings drew mostly on loyalist claim files and newspapers. His PhD was finished by the summer of 1992. Charles Townshend, his external examiner, described it as 'outstanding'.[105] He was particularly impressed with the chapters on Kilmichael and the April 1922 attacks.

After submitting, Hart was keen to conduct further research on the Protestant experience of the revolutionary period. He secured a two-year postdoctoral research fellowship and, over 1993 and 1994, in addition to visiting several regimental archives in Britain, interviewed twenty Cork Protestants.[106] In 1995, he also consulted further material relating to Kilmichael. In order to give a more rounded view of both Hart's general approach and the furore provoked by his research, a short digression discussing his 'Protestant' interviews is in order.

HART'S 'PROTESTANT' INTERVIEWS

Southern Protestants very rarely spoke openly or outside the family about their memories of the revolutionary period.[107] In 2017, Paul Colton, the Anglican Bishop of Cork, Cloyne and Ross, noted that, even then, some West Cork Protestants dreaded the centenary events marking the War of Independence and Civil War.[108] However, Hart obviously earned their trust. His three recorded interviews indicate that he was a very good, patient interviewer. That Protestants were frightened during the revolutionary period, and had to be especially careful what they said, was a reoccurring theme. There had not been much tension between Catholics and Protestants in most areas, they said, but Bandon and Ballineen/ Enniskeane were 'bad'.[109] One interviewee agreed that religion was a factor in determining who was targeted:

Interviewee: ... there was a couple of people there shot for very, no reason at all, they came and they shot them like that.

Hart: Because they were Protestant?

Interviewee: Because they were Protestant, yes, and they were, I suppose, helping the establishment if you think that way. I know that we were on very dangerous ground at that time.[110]

Two interviewees gave more detailed information about some of the April 1922 killings, which were still a 'bitter memory' for many local Protestants, particularly the older generation.[111] One spoke about a man he knew who witnessed one of the incidents:

> Interviewee: ... they tied Woods up to the back of the car and they dragged him right to the road.

> Hart: So he was dead?

> Interviewee: ... and a rough road. He was dead, I suppose, that was the end of him ... [name omitted by author] witnessed that, the old man, and he never told any of his family because he said he was so horrified about it. But he told his son-in-law many years afterwards about what he witnessed ... he was afraid to tell anybody he was so horrified at what he saw ... things very hot here at the time ... desperate hot ...[112]

Another interviewee named an IRA man suspected of being involved. When Rev. (now Canon) David Catterall entered the room towards the end of the interview, he was told that Hart had 'heard the whole story'. Hart promised to 'mention no names'.[113]

In April 1994, Hart sent Myers an update, remarking that he had found some 'terrific – and horrific – material'.[114] A few months later, in August, just days before the Provisional IRA announced a conditional ceasefire, Myers cited the 'pogrom of Protestants' in Dunmanway in his 'Irishman's Diary' column as one of several instances of sectarian killings by the IRA before and after the July 1921 Truce. He argued that it was directly relevant to unionists who had been excluded from the ongoing peace talks with Sinn Féin.[115] Not for the last time, Myers cited Hart's work for polemical effect, predicting that his as yet unpublished book would 'establish new standards of demythologising' the events of the revolutionary period.[116]

David Fitzpatrick encouraged Hart to enlist Myers's help in promoting his work even before his PhD was submitted, on the grounds that the 'furious responses' would improve sales of his book.[117] He was perhaps not the best judge. Fitzpatrick's own appetite for 'acerbic remarks' was legendary, and his advice to Hart suggested he was too quick to interpret offending traditionalists as evidence of a successful intervention.[118] Arguably, Hart should have taken more account of how Myers's advocacy would impact on responses to his work. The end result was that, even before the publication of *The IRA and Its Enemies*, he was associated with a more extreme and overtly polemical set of assertions about revolutionary violence and sectarianism than he actually argued for. In years to come, the fact that anti-republican journalists like Myers and Eoghan Harris were so adamantly on Hart's side, and were employing his work to discredit Irish nationalism and republicanism generally, made it easy for many to accept that Hart was part of a conspiracy.[119]

The Myers column sparked a debate that continued in *The Irish Times* letters page into February 1995. The exchanges, in many respects, prefigured the debates over Hart's work some four years later. Nationalists and republicans, such as J.P. Duggan, Brian P. Murphy, and Brendan Ó Cathaoir, either denied that the attacks on Protestants (during the War of Independence or later) had been motivated by sectarianism, or focused on the IRA leadership's efforts to protect Southern Protestants, quoting the latter's public pronouncements praising the IRA.[120] Ó Cathaoir used passages from the 'Record of the Rebellion in Ireland', noting that the IRA had executed several Protestant farmers in Bandon who were aiding the authorities.[121] Uinseann Mac Eoin emphasised atrocities committed by Crown Forces.[122] Criostóir de Baróid, another staunch republican and admirer of Tom Barry's, objected to Myers's 'denigration' of the IRA, pointing out that the British administration in Ireland was 'appallingly' sectarian.[123]

At the same time, there was no consensus on April 1922, even among those with republican sympathies. Murphy maintained that Protestants did not view IRA actions as sectarian at the time.[124] De Baróid's understanding of events was far less naive. He significantly underplayed the scale of the attacks but did acknowledge that a 'maverick' IRA group in southwest Cork had carried them out. He said Protestants had called on IRA leaders to protect them against 'vengeful elements which every armed conflict throws up'.[125] J.L.B. Deane, the 'Canon from Bandon', one of two Protestant clergymen who intervened in the debate, confirmed what de Baróid said, remarking that local Protestants were especially grateful to local IRA officer Séan Buckley for halting the attacks.[126] Quoting a passage from Archbishop Gregg's plea for government protection (see Chapter Four), Deane stated unequivocally that in April 1922, Protestants had been 'murdered because of their religion, and without any suggestion of wrongdoing on their part'.

Deane also requested that all those involved in the debate, including Myers, desist from lumping pre- and post-Treaty killings of Protestants together. He acknowledged that, although there was no firm evidence to 'prove or disprove' their guilt, those Protestants executed by the IRA before December 1921 were suspected spies. A letter from another clergyman was critical of the treatment meted out to some local Protestants before the Truce. There was no justification 'from any perspective', he said, for the treatment of the Good family from Barryshall, Timoleague.[127]

BALLINEEN AND ENNISKEAN AREA HERITAGE GROUP

In May 1995, Hart was contacted by Bernadette Whyte on behalf of the Ballineen and Enniskean Area Heritage Group, a local history society in West Cork compiling a commemorative booklet about Kilmichael veterans for the ambush's seventy-fifth anniversary.[128] They had been advised by staff in the Military Archives that Hart was 'one of the best people to talk to' about their project. At some subsequent point, Hart visited Whyte and her husband, Louis, in West Cork to consult their material. Hart's 'Ballineen/ Enniskean' folder contained notes from Jack Hennessy's witness statement, Barry's 1941 An Cosantóir article, details on various other Kilmichael veterans, and notes from an interview with Jack O'Sullivan. The name and Dublin address of Dan O'Sullivan, one of Jack's sons, is written across the top of these.[129] According to Hart, the Ballineen/Enniskean group also requested that he only quote from this interview anonymously.[130]

Hart stayed in touch with the group and sent them his Kilmichael chapter in 1996. After several members met and discussed it, Mrs Whyte drafted a response.[131] They identified a few errors and said that they had no evidence that 'HJ' (Willie Chambers) had taken part in the ambush. This was true. Chambers, who had died in April 1992, had never said he took part in the actual ambush. Mrs Whyte also described the false surrender issue as having been 'as big a question then for us as it now is for you'. One man, whom they trusted, said his father was 'rock solid' that it had occurred, but the group were making further enquiries. The committee's overall advice was, quite sensibly, that

> there seemed to be so much confusion e.g. shooting, shouting, running, firing, dying, bleeding, screaming, begging for life etc etc that different people remember different things, also darkness had come ... as you saw the ambush site yourself, you can fully understand that the men in Section 1 or 2 didn't know what the men of Section 3 were doing at that time of the combat and likewise with each section and group of men.
>
> So what we are saying is: each man had his own story to tell, from where he was positioned ...[132]

She contacted Hart again in November 1996. The group had consulted the sons of two Kilmichael veterans. Both said their fathers had never mentioned any surrenders, false or genuine: 'It could become as big a question', she said (more prophetically than she realised), 'as who shot J.F.K. or who shot Michael Collins.'[133]

9

War by Other Means

PETER HART'S *THE IRA AND Its Enemies: Violence and Community in Cork 1916–1923*, along with Joost Augusteijn's *From Public Defiance to Guerrilla Warfare* and Marie Coleman's *County Longford and the Irish Revolution, 1910–1923* all belied the 'loose consensus among historians' that a lack of sources made academic local studies of the revolutionary period impossible.[1] Augusteijn's and Coleman's complicated and less-idealised portraits of the radical nationalist campaign against British rule were, in that respect, just as 'revisionist' as Hart's.[2] Outside of academia, local historians like Michael Farry and Oliver Coogan also produced exceptionally well-researched county studies of, respectively, Sligo and Meath.[3]

Hart employed detailed statistical analysis, extensive primary research, oral history interviews and folklore to profile the Cork IRA from 1916 to the Civil War (1922–3). He analysed the growth and support for radical nationalism and the IRA's military campaign against British rule. He explored how the IRA's perception of its enemies was shaped and influenced by pre-existing social and political conditions, local and sectarian tensions, and communal traditions and habits. He also discussed how racial stereotypes informed the attitude of Crown Forces towards the Irish population in general, and how it fuelled their casual violence and an 'accelerating cycle of terror and counter terror'.[4]

Hart's book contained vivid and horrifying descriptions of the violence meted out to captured IRA men. Pat Harte and Tom Hales, two 3rd Cork Brigade officers arrested on 27 July 1920 'were stripped, tied up, and savagely beaten and pistol-whipped'. After quoting Hales's subsequent description of their ordeal, Hart described how Harte was knocked senseless when his nose was smashed by a rifle butt, and how Hales gave away nothing, despite being beaten with canes, interrogated and tortured. Most of his teeth were crushed with pliers.[5] Hart also maintained that there had been no false surrender at Kilmichael as Barry had depicted it in his memoir, which he described as 'riddled with lies and evasions'.[6] In addition, he argued that sectarianism influenced the course of the Irish independence struggle generally and was a significant factor fuelling the April 1922 attacks. The general tenor of Hart's work, and what he said in early interviews, was sometimes more emotive than was strictly necessary. Derivations of the word 'murder' appeared over seventy times in his book, 'massacre' on thirty-four occasions. Polarising expressions like 'serial killers', 'death squads' and 'ethnic cleansing' were picked up and magnified in the press.[7]

Most reviewers, within and outside academia, even when critical of some of Hart's conclusions, recognised his book as an ambitious, pioneering and exceptional piece of research.[8] Some were irritated by his tone, and felt that accusing Barry of lying was pushing beyond the evidence presented.[9] Others argued that Hart's analysis was too decontextualised, and that he should have made more effort to discuss events at the local level within the wider political context and in terms of underlying causes.[10] Joost Augusteijn contended that Hart's close focus on exceptional rather than typical events, like Kilmichael and April 1922, allowed the 'extreme to come to represent the ordinary', and that he had not sufficiently explained his reasoning for this approach.[11]

What made Hart's work especially controversial was that he made no distinction between the IRA's dubious killings and those committed by Crown Forces:

> We have less evidence from inside the RIC but there were clearly informal police death squads as well, often masquerading under titles such as 'the Anti-Sinn Féin Society'. The O'Briens on White Street, Tom Barry at Kilmichael, and Daithi O'Brien at Carrigtwohill all carried out unauthorized operations and got away with it just as did

the assassins of Tómas MacCurtain and of the victims at Clogheen and Clonmult … As time went by, these political serial killers and their methods became virtually indistinguishable.[12]

Regardless of how righteous the cause and the essential decency of most of the men and women involved in the independence struggle, he argued, idealised narratives of the IRA's actions effectively concealed the reality of what essentially became a 'civil war within and between communities', driven to a significant extent by the 'tit for tat dynamics' of violence fuelled by fear and the desire for revenge.[13] Only a minority of deaths occurred in combat, he argued, and many of those executed for informing by the IRA were innocent.

Hart's refusal to distinguish, as he put it, 'between state and insurgent violence or between killers in and out of uniform' was always going to be divisive and for some, a step too far.[14] His overarching conclusions about the corrosive impact of violence were essentially pacifist, but situating Kilmichael, Clonmult and April 1922 on the same moral plane of illegality and massacre was, for many, utterly shocking. Stathis Kalyvas's *The Logic of Violence in Civil War*, a study of the 'red terror' in 1940s Greece, which was published a few years later, was challenging for similar reasons. Kalyvas cited Hart's work, and both rejected the notion that violence could be ranked ideologically. For their critics, equating the violent acts of leftist guerrillas in Greece or the IRA during the 1916–23 with the violence of their opponents was, by definition, ideological. Kalyvas's work was characterised by left-leaning historians and anthropologists as right-wing.[15] Hart, as we shall see, was accused of being a 'neo-unionist'. Both responded by saying that their critics were threatened by the implications of the findings.[16]

The public debate over Hart's work was kickstarted in May 1998 when, once again, Kevin Myers used his 'Irishman's Diary' column to extol *The IRA and Its Enemies*. Myers focused almost exclusively on Hart's conclusions about the IRA, ignoring the fact that he had actually analysed both state and insurgent violence and refused to distinguish between them. Hart was praised for exposing the immorality of the 'folklore' and 'hagiographical culture' associated with the revolutionary period. Myers was sympathetic to the Auxiliaries, described April 1922 as a 'pogrom', and credited Hart's research with exposing Barry's Kilmichael account as a 'fiction' concocted to cover up the fact that he 'systematically slaughtered disarmed RIC Auxiliaries'.[17]

Arguably, this was another instance in which Hart could have made more of an effort to distance himself from Myers's overstated, oversimplified polemic. David Fitzpatrick, however, who thought that the furore would boost sales, congratulated him: 'you must have been delighted'.[18] Others took a different view. Jim O'Driscoll SC (d. 2009), who admired Hart's work (and had introduced him to Ned Young), felt that Myers had done his book 'an injustice'.[19] Myers demonstrated little awareness of the actual living memory of Kilmichael, which made it easier for Hart's detractors to misrepresent it themselves. His critics to this day claim to be defending the authentic, uncontested, grass-roots nationalist history.[20] In reality, the campaign mounted against Hart involved a blatant and sustained effort to silence and censor it. Brendan Bradshaw's 'purposeful unhistoricity' had come home to roost.

The correspondence between Hart, Meda Ryan, Brian P. Murphy and others following the Myers column went on for several weeks and was reproduced in a 1999 pamphlet edited by Jack Lane and Brendan Clifford of the Aubane Historical Society.[21] Lane and Clifford maintained that Barry's 1949 account had been 'generally accepted for almost eighty years'.[22] Murphy argued that the captured report was a forgery.[23] The April 1922 killings were not sectarian, said Hart's critics, rather those killed had been informers. As the controversy gathered pace, it was implied that Hart had fabricated some of his interviews in order to undermine Barry's reputation. Most infamously, it was alleged that Hart had claimed that he interviewed Ned Young six days after the latter had died.

It is important to say, from the outset, that there are people in Cork who have always known the identity of the veterans on whose testimony Hart based his conclusions, and whom he interviewed himself. If some of them had come forward, the argument that he fabricated interview evidence would have collapsed. That they did not is frustrating, but understandable. As the attacks on Hart intensified, any suggestion that he

was not a fraudulent revisionist conspirator was (and is) greeted with a
hail of polemic, vilification, public attacks and internet trolling (much of
it anonymous).

The assertions of Hart's critics from the outset hinged on ignoring
and/or misrepresenting a substantial amount of information that had long
been in the public domain. The inconsistencies and differences between
Barry's and other veterans' Kilmichael accounts were ignored. Evidence
in Ernie O'Malley's and Uinseann MacEoin's interviews relating to Barry's
unreliability as a narrator was overlooked. Flor Crowley's position on the
Deasy–Barry dispute was misrepresented.[24] The implications of Ó Dúlaing's
interviews with O'Sullivan, Young and others (available in RTÉ's archives)
were never addressed. No effort was made to acknowledge the diversity
of opinion on both Kilmichael and April 1922, or that some of even the
staunchest republicans and nationalists found a way to acknowledge, at
least implicitly, both the brutality of war and the humanity of their enemies.
Hart described Clonmult as 'Kilmichael in reverse', borrowing Flor
Crowley's phrase which had first appeared in *The Southern Star*. Erskine
Childers, Dorothy Macardle, Tim Pat Coogan, Jim Lane and Criostóir de
Baróid had all characterised the April 1922 killings as sectarian.[25]

Instead, Hart's critics homed in on discrediting or otherwise nullifying
evidence for Barry's Kilmichael account having been challenged by other
veterans. The Aubane Historical Society argued that O'Brien 'forgot' to
mention the false surrender.[26] Donal Mac Goilla Phóil, a long-standing
member of the Kilmichael commemoration committee, maintained that
he had never heard any Kilmichael Volunteers denying that there had
been one.[27] In November 2000, in a *Leargas* documentary directed by
Paul Larkin and written by Pat Butler, Peadar Ó Riada insisted that Barry
'wasn't capable of lying'.[28] Ryan's revised biography of Barry, published in
2003, differed markedly from the original. She appeared to suggest that
Fr Chisholm had rewritten Paddy O'Brien's *Towards Ireland Free* account
and that it did not represent O'Brien's real opinion. Also, according to her,
O'Brien had not been 'aware of what he was signing' when he put his name
to the veterans' letter disassociating themselves from Barry.[29] Yet Paddy
O'Brien's witness statement confirmed that he had been giving essentially

the same version of events since the 1950s. The idea that he did not realise what he was signing in 1974 was scarcely credible, but this remains Ryan's position.

The paperback edition (2005) of Ryan's biography, revised after she had consulted the Kilmichael witness statements, largely dismissed them. She maintained – without adducing any evidence apart from Barry's suspicions of the project – that BMH witnesses 'answered leading questions, but were not queried on any omissions or inaccuracies'.[30] She argued (unconvincingly) that Jack Hennessy's account supported that of Barry (see Chapter Seven).

In her first biography of Barry, Ryan had identified or cited very few of the sources she used, and the later versions relied heavily on her own interviews and Barry's inaccessible papers. Nevertheless, at the time, she seemed more convincing to many than Hart, because she named her interviewees and he did not. Hart was called on repeatedly to identify them but never did.[31] Even neutral commentators like Bill Kautt and Seámus Fox – neither of whom credited assertions that Hart had actually fabricated some of his interviews – were uncomfortable with his decision to anonymise them.[32] As discussed, Hart had wanted to identify Chisholm's interviewees but was denied permission (see Chapter Seven). Neither did he have authorisation to release the name of the Ballineen/Enniskean interviewee (Jack O'Sullivan). Several of the individuals he spoke to also requested anonymity. It was a choice between removing the names or not using these sources at all.

Ironically, one of the few historians to explicitly defend Hart on this was John Regan: 'Hart, honour bound to protect his sources, should not be prevailed upon to do anything further. Responsibility lies with Ryan to prove beyond question that there were neither IRA scouts nor riflemen available for interview in 1988 and 1989 or retract.'[33]

Hart's critics argued that Ryan's book was 'censored out of academic and media existence'.[34] They praised her work to the skies. Seán Kelleher commended her for proving 'conclusively that the false surrender called by the auxiliaries led to the killing of three members of the ambushing party'.[35] Manus O'Riordan described her book as an 'outstanding tour de force' that demolished Hart's arguments. Her research, he concluded, was an 'indispensable' weapon against revisionists.[36] Martin Mansergh was of the view that Ryan had crossed 'swords convincingly with Peter Hart' over the false surrender question.[37] The fact that no one else could consult many of the sources Ryan cited did not seem to matter.

THE CHISHOLM INTERVIEWS

Approaches were also made to Fr Chisholm in relation to his interviews which he found rather strange and, as time went on, increasingly intimidating. Chisholm had remained on very good terms with the Deasy family. In November 2007, he and two of Liam Deasy's daughters (Kathleen and Ena) met and collectively decided to give the tapes to Liam Deasy, their cousin.[38] Maureen, another sister, was invited to this meeting but refused to attend. She wrote several letters to Chisholm independently, in hopes of securing access to the tapes so that Hart's conclusions could be challenged. These varied markedly in style. It transpired, as Chisholm suspected, that although Maureen had signed the letters, several had been drafted by someone else. That person was Criostóir de Baróid.[39] In December 2007, although he no longer had the tapes, Chisholm received a five-page typed letter entitled 'Vindication of the Heroic Dead' acknowledging de Baróid's involvement: 'Many people, some of exalted status ... availed of ... skilled secretarial assistance ... I owe no explanation, apology or preliminary confession to you or anyone ... to avail of a more facile pen ... to express in writing my deeply felt sentiments ... how dare you talk down to me, from your celestial eminence.'[40]

The missive railed against 'neo-colonial (aka "revisionist") detractors and their equally guilty collaborators' and was accompanied by seven appendices of material relating to de Baróid, including correspondence concerning an approach he had made to the Deasy family in 2006, offering to help them draft a letter to Chisholm asking about his interviews. The Deasys met him, but in the end decided to approach Chisholm themselves.[41] This seems to be what upset Maureen, who had been in favour of working with de Baróid.

A further communication in March 2008 (also entitled 'Vindication of the Heroic Dead') warned Chisholm that his attitude would 'arouse suspicions that he was in collusion with Hart's vilification of the noblest dead of our race'.[42] A 'sworn affidavit', it said, would soon become available to say that Hart could not have carried out 'at least two of his interviews'. This, presumably, was a reference to an affidavit by John Young (one of Ned Young's four children), which was published a several months later (discussed below). In April, Chisholm received a short note from Maureen to say that, as he had not replied, she would 'pass the baton to others'.[43]

Within a few days, he received a letter from John Young asking if he had had an interview with his father. Chisholm told him he may well have interviewed him but did not have a recording of it.[44] This turned out not to be true. Chisholm had misplaced it. In June 2011, he rang me out of the blue to say that he had found another tape in his attic, insisting that I come at once to listen to it. On it were his interviews with Ned Young and another OIRA veteran.

Hart had put me in touch with Chisholm in February 2010, just a few months before the former's death. Chisholm and Liam Deasy (nephew) consented to the interviews being digitised and for the identity of his interviewees to be made public. Both were, rightly or wrongly, selective about whom they allowed to consult the tapes. They were especially wary of approaches from University College Cork (UCC), where de Baróid spent his career as an administrator.[45]

I was allowed to play excerpts from the O'Sullivan and Young interviews to about thirty people during a seminar I gave in TCD in October 2011 on the condition that no other recording was made without permission. Niall Meehan, one of the attendees, made an unsanctioned recording of my paper.[46] Meehan, a former press officer for the Dublin Branch of People's Democracy (PD), had entered the fray in 2004.[47] He contacted one of Hart's friends without identifying himself as a journalist and, according to Hart, without attempting to contact him directly.[48] He then posted the results of his queries online without permission, professing not to understand why anyone would object.[49] After my 2011 seminar, a recording of my talk was played in UCC (of which I only became aware when one of those in attendance congratulated me). From then on, Chisholm and Deasy (nephew) were even warier.

Fr Chisholm declined a subsequent request from John Borgonovo to listen to the tapes, and the latter then attacked Chisholm's credibility in an ill-judged review. In 2013, Chisholm became aware that another individual claiming to represent the 'Irish government' had approached Norma Deasy, who was in possession of the tapes after her husband Liam's death in late 2012, asking for the recordings. She then returned them to Chisholm, who requested that I take custody of them. He asked me to give the recordings and correspondence concerning Kilmichael to TCD Manuscripts Department when I felt the time was right.

The matter of selective access or withholding of relevant material is certainly very frustrating for researchers (myself included). Yet singling Chisholm out for criticism is unreasonable and unfair. He and Liam Deasy (nephew) gave far more access to their material than anyone else involved. Equally, while it is perfectly valid to raise the issue of 'bias' both in oral history interviews and generally, it is inconsistent and problematic to argue that Chisholm's firm belief that there was no false surrender pollutes his interviews, without noting the unwavering commitment of Ryan and others to the contrary view. This is particularly so in light of the fact that, as earlier chapters have discussed, the conclusions of Hart's critics are at odds with most of the evidence relating to Kilmichael.

It is also worth noting that although Willie Chambers's movements on that day have not been satisfactorily established, and consequently it has not yet been confirmed whether he witnessed Auxiliaries being put to death after the ambush, what he told Hart is still broadly supported by several other participant accounts:

> Hysterical – Barry had to calm them shot wounded men – Barry made them – he shot one, they shot one. Barry waved them to stop wore uniform. Others wore helmets. Ned Young only thought he shot man – got away – local informed Column – shot him. –Auxies did try false surrender: but not how Deasy etc. were killed. Then showed no mercy. No bayonetting ...[50]

The same cannot be said for several of Ryan's inaccessible interviews.

Similarly, it is important to point out that Hart had not ruled out there having been confusion over the Auxiliaries' surrender. He acknowledged that one of the veterans he spoke to (Chambers) told him a 'sort' of false surrender had occurred but, contrary to what Barry said in his memoir, it had not caused any IRA deaths. Chisholm was sceptical about this but Hart obviously felt it was important to acknowledge the alternative view.[51]

MISTAKES AND ERRORS

The attacks on Hart were relentless after the publication of his book, and much of what was said could scarcely be categorised as reasonable historical debate. His public appearances, conferences and lectures were picketed, and leaflets were handed out denouncing his work.[52] Jack Lane and others also forwarded negative comments and reviews mentioning Hart to Memorial University, where he worked.[53]

Hart's errors have been blown out of all proportion, but he did make some. In a chapter dealing with spies and informers arguing that Protestants had little information to give the authorities and had not been a major source of information, he quoted from the 'Record of the Rebellion in Ireland' without including the sentence noting that Protestant farmers executed by the IRA in Bandon in West Cork had been giving information:

> In the South the Protestants and those who supported the Government rarely gave much information because, except by chance, they had not got it to give. An exception to this rule was in the Bandon area where there were many Protestant farmers who gave information. Although the Intelligence Officer of this area was exceptionally experienced … it proved almost impossible to protect these brave men, many of whom were murdered while almost all of the remainder suffered grave material loss.[54]

This was an error of judgement on Hart's part. However, as I pointed out to John Regan in 2012, in arguing that this was an example of Hart deliberately omitting direct evidence confirming that the April 1922 killings were not sectarian, he and Hart's detractors were misreading the document. The volume in which the passage appeared had already been written and was only in the process of being typeset when the April 1922 killing occurred, so it plainly referred to killing carried out before the July 1921 Truce.[55] The Strickland papers, extant in the Imperial War Museum since 1978 (and consulted by Hart), confirmed that the volume had been completed by March 1922.[56] The accusations of Hart's critics, who continue to insist that Hart, like them, thought the 'Record' was referring to April 1922, are speculative, unproven and based on inadequate research.

Hart's overall conclusions in relation to Kilmichael – that there had been no false surrender as Barry depicted it, that other ambush veterans had objected to the version in Barry's memoir, and that some of the Auxiliaries were killed after genuinely surrendering – was in keeping with what most veterans (who went on the record) said occurred. Hart was also very far from being the first person to suggest that Barry was an unreliable narrator. However, Hart's description of Dublin Castle's notorious account published on 2 December 1920 as 'remarkably accurate', juxtaposed with Barry's 'omissions and lies' was off the mark.[57] His theory that the ambush had not been sanctioned by Barry's superiors and that he did not have permission to carry it out was, as Meda Ryan correctly pointed out early on, also entirely wrong.[58] As discussed, the attack had been initiated by IRA GHQ.

There are also minor errors in Hart's footnotes relating to the Chisholm interviews. His original notes were very truncated, and the excerpts from them in his thesis and book are not always exact transcriptions of what was said.[59] When he checked back over his notes, Hart was also unsure whether he had listened to three or two interviews about Kilmichael.[60] His thesis and book said three, but in fact he had only listened to two (Jack O'Sullivan and Ned Young).[61] For someone who has listened to all Chisholm's interviews (as I have), the difficulty is easily resolved. At the end of Hart's notes from Chisholm's Young interview there was a quote attributed to Paddy O'Brien, and he obviously thought it might have come from an actual interview with the latter.[62] As discussed, most of Chisholm's O'Brien interview had been taped over. Hart's notes referred to the point when, in Chisholm's Ned Young interview, he asked Young about Paddy O'Brien's story of the wounded Auxiliary begging for his life: 'I'm a Catholic.'

When Hart asked Chisholm about his O'Brien interview in 1990, Chisholm replied that he could not find the tape.[63] Hart sent him a draft of the Kilmichael chapter of his PhD in October 1991 and Chisholm said the quotes were fine.[64] The confusion over O'Brien was never resolved. In the spring of 2009, Hart re-established contact with Chisholm. Both he and Liam Deasy (nephew) agreed to let Hart hear the tapes again. Chisholm told Hart that Deasy understood his difficulties and that he had been attacked himself about the recordings.[65] Sadly, the planned meeting fell through and Hart died the following year.

Finally, one line from Chisholm's Jack O'Sullivan interview describing the wounded Auxiliary crying after him, and Barry ordering O'Sullivan to 'finish him', is attributed in Hart's book to a quote from the Chambers interview (the 'unarmed scout').[66] The excerpts from both interviews are cited correctly in three earlier versions of the Kilmichael chapter (1991, 1992, 1994).[67]

Over the years, more and more evidence has become available to confirm the broad thrust of Hart's conclusions in relation to Kilmichael and April 1922, while crucial documents cited by his critics have either never materialised or have been countered by other sources. The 'Dunmanway dossier' reputedly listing as informants most of those killed in April 1922, cited by Ryan, has never been located. The most recent academic assessment of these killings has also qualified Hart's wider sectarian thesis but confirmed his assertion that the April 1922 attacks were sectarian.[68] The Barry letter (in his inaccessible papers) protesting the removal of details relating to the 'false surrender' from the 1932 *Irish Press* account – which appeared at the time to be one of Ryan's strongest pieces of evidence undermining Hart's key argument that Barry had changed his story – has been superseded by another, freely available Barry letter confirming he wrote it.

Yet Hart's critics remain inordinately focused on discrediting him, Fr Chisholm and, more recently, me. Their arguments become more convoluted, speculative and hypocritical with every passing year. Some of the dissimulations have been astonishingly brazen. It was argued for years, for instance, that the *three* IRA fatalities having been fatally wounded or killed by the false surrender was central to the Kilmichael ambush story.[69] Then, between late 2009 and early 2010, Jerry O'Callaghan was allowed to listen to and take notes from Chisholm's Jack O'Sullivan interview for a documentary about Barry that was broadcast in January 2011.[70] O'Sullivan said at one point that it was 'very wrong' to say Michael McCarthy stood up after the false surrender. Denying that this was a criticism of Barry was now, it seems, a priority.

Suddenly the 'three Volunteers' version was no longer central to Barry's account. According to Niall Meehan, it never had been. In fact, Meehan and others now argued that Barry had *never* said McCarthy was killed in the false surrender, and Hart having said so was yet another of his egregious errors. As discussed, in reality Barry gave contradictory and ambiguous accounts of who stood up, and the story that all three IRA fatalities were caused by a false surrender was, and continues to be, the most well-known version of the ambush. Seán Kelleher, Meda Ryan and Meehan have all switched their position on this, however, and now say it was only two.[71]

The most notorious (and again entirely false) allegation – that Hart claimed to have interviewed a dead man – grew wings after the publication of Ryan's revised Barry biography.[72] The accusation has never gone away, despite the fact that Niall Meehan consulted Hart's PhD three times between 2006 and 2008, and noticed that Hart's interview dates for Ned Young – April and June 1988 – were over a year before Young died.[73] This discovery by one of Hart's most trenchant critics demolished the claim that Hart had interviewed a dead man, and it should really have marked the beginning of the end of the accusations. Instead of abandoning the dead man interview claim, however, another surge of attacks was initiated.

Troubled History, an Aubane Historical Society publication, included an August 2007 affidavit from Ned Young's son, John, stating Hart could not have interviewed his father because Ned was wheelchair-bound and unable to speak after suffering a stroke in 'circa late 1986'.[74] Meehan promoted John Young's allegations. Yet an individual he described as 'one of the signatories to the affidavit'[75] – Jim O'Driscoll SC – had, in fact, flatly refused to sign it precisely because he knew the allegations against Hart were not true. O'Driscoll had simply witnessed John Young's signature.[76]

In the summer of 2012, when I spoke to John Young on the telephone, he insisted that he was certain Hart had not interviewed his father because, he said, someone would have told him about it at the time. He also said, however, that his father could speak clearly and his mental faculties were not impaired. Young then publicly contradicted my account of our telephone conversation.[77] Before and after I spoke to him, other individuals had confirmed to me both that Hart *did* interview Ned Young and that the latter had not been incapacitated in 1988 in any way which would have prevented him from being interviewed. Convincing them to say so publicly remains a different matter, with one exception.

In October 2012, Jim O'Driscoll's widow, Marion, did not hesitate to confirm that Hart had indeed interviewed Ned Young and that her husband had made the introductions.[78] She also asked me to investigate why the *Irish Times*'s obituary of her husband stated that he had signed John Young's affidavit.[79] The obituary's author, the late Donal Musgrave, told me that his information came from 'the internet'.[80] In April 2013, Marion publicly entreated John Young to stop associating her late husband with his attacks on Hart.[81] He did not comply, instead writing a further cascade of letters.

However fervently John Young believed otherwise, Hart did interview his father. I sourced photographs of Ned Young taken at the Kilmichael commemorations in 1987 and 1988 (when he was supposedly wheelchair-bound and rendered speechless by a stroke), standing up and also walking around. One newspaper report quoted directly from his oration at the November 1988 commemoration and described him 'lining up' at the monument.[82] One of Hart's Protestant interviewees knew Ned Young, and during the interview Hart mentioned that he had interviewed Young about five years earlier.[83] Hart's notes for both his Young interviews are in his papers.

The Ballineen/Enniskean Jack O'Sullivan interview (conducted by his son Dan) and Jack Hennessy's witness statement are cited in Hart's book but not his thesis. According to Meehan, this indicates that Hart concocted his November 1989 interview with Willie Chambers (the 'unarmed scout'), which appears in his thesis, from Hennessy's witness statement.[84] The actual reason for the differences between Hart's book and PhD is simply that in 1992, when he submitted the latter, Hart had not yet consulted either the Ballineen/Enniskean interview with Jack O'Sullivan or Hennessy's witness statement. His first contact with the Ballineen/Enniskean Heritage Group was in May 1995. The BMH witness statements were not released to the public until 2003. Meehan's argument is, consequently, untenable, though evidently it sounds convincing to Brendan O'Leary. In 2018, O'Leary accepted Meehan's assertion that Hart's anonymous interviews could not be verified, despite the fact that by then all his interviewees had been identified and Hart's interview notes were available in his papers.[85]

NEO-UNIONIST?

Although ostensibly about sources and methodology, the most vocal of Hart's critics and defenders in the public debate effectively used the language of historical debate and the actual events under discussion as proxies to address other issues. Associating Hart's work – and anyone who defended him – with a perceived wider neo-unionist campaign to discredit nationalism and republicanism was (and remains) a key component of the attacks on him. In 1998, Hugo Flinn, the businessman and ardent nationalist, denounced Hart and other historians as 'anglicised scribes' whose 'fraudulent revision of our sad but proud history' was a 'threat to the Irish nation'.[86] The Aubane Historical Society described Hart's book as having been 'written in the frantic rhetoric of Ulster Unionism'.[87]

It was widely assumed that there was a coherent nationalist narrative of the revolutionary era to either question or deride, and that the arguments made by Hart's critics represented the authentic, uncontested local memory of events. Despite the fact that Seámus Deane and Luke Gibbons (theorists associated with the Field Day cultural and political project) challenged what they understood to be the universalist norms promoted by 'revisionist' historians, both accepted the arguments against Hart, it seems, without a backward glance.[88] In 2001, Deane questioned how Hart could be characterised as a 'non-unionist' historian.[89] Gibbons sided with Hart's critics in relation to sectarianism in West Cork.[90] In the 1990s, Gibbons had rightly criticised those who characterised Irish nationalism as 'one-dimensional' and 'immune to change'. It is a pity that he did not make more effort to apply the 'theoretical voltage of Marxism, psychoanalysis and post-structuralism' to the diverse and contradictory social memory of 1916–23.[91]

At the more extreme end of the spectrum, the accusations that Hart fabricated some of his Kilmichael interviews are a central plank of the argument that 'historical revisionism' is a plot to 'neuter' Irish history orchestrated at the highest levels. The British Foreign Office and Irish Department of Foreign Affairs, Oxbridge, and Irish universities have all been accused of being in nefarious collusion to replace 'nationalist sources' with 'British sources' in order to produce a 'narrative acceptable to Britain'.[92]

Meehan in particular devotes much energy to how Harris, Myers, Paul Bew and Roy Foster promoted and referenced Hart's research in support of characterising Hart's work as neo-unionist.[93] He suggests that Hart had been 'unconsciously' influenced by sectarian tensions in Newfoundland.[94] Barry Keane, who once described the April 1922 killings as an 'act of self-defence' and not at all sectarian has, more recently, carried this extremely dubious line of reasoning further in a piece on Hart's 'Irish unionist background'.[95] While these sorts of arguments do not deserve to be taken seriously (although they have surprising purchase in some quarters), it is common for views expressed on Hart's work to be interpreted as indicative of a person's wider political attitudes.

Characterisations of Hart as a neo-unionist are hard to substantiate in any meaningful way. Arguments that he wrote in the 'tradition of' Walter Alison Phillips, the first Lecky Chair of Modern History in TCD (1914–39), sound convincing unless you actually read what Phillips and Hart wrote.[96] The former was indeed a committed unionist who repeated several erroneous claims made by the authorities at the time.[97] In Phillips's history, he excused reprisals, said the police were fired on first at Croke Park on

Bloody Sunday, and that the IRA, not a police killing gang, assassinated Tomás MacCurtain and George Clancy. He blamed the Belfast violence on IRA Volunteers and characterised the shipyard expulsions in 1920 as justified and non-sectarian.[98] Hart, by contrast, argued that the IRA were *not* responsible for most of the violence in Belfast, gave visceral accounts of IRA Volunteers being tortured in custody, and noted that police records regularly omitted or covered up the real facts of many Crown Forces killings.[99] These are not unionist arguments.

In 2012, British-based academic David Miller published Meehan's and Young's attacks on me on his website Spinwatch.org, and initially declined to offer me a right of reply. He tagged both pieces under 'Northern Ireland, Propaganda & Collusion'.[100] After several more exchanges, in which I asked Miller how he justified categorising historians who do not comment or write about the North in this fashion, he eventually agreed to change the descriptor to 'Ireland, Propaganda, Collusion, History'. A few weeks later, speaking at a commemoration of the Crossbarry Ambush, Meehan gave what seems to be the rationale for including me on his roster of neo-unionist conspirators without any evidence whatsoever – the conflict in Northern Ireland 'silently animates' the debate over events in West Cork.[101]

John Regan accuses Hart and myself of all manner of methodological sins, including 'weak induction', the 'fallacy of negative proof' and a reliance on 'unverifiable oral sources'.[102] 'Unverifiable' sources seems to be a reference to material in private possession rather than in a public archive, and he is not the only one of Hart's critics to make the argument. This would be a reasonable (but contestable) stand to take if everyone involved was held to the same standard, but they are not. Meda Ryan is more reliant on 'unverifiable' and in some cases questionable sources than anyone else involved in the debate. Yet Regan, as well as Borgonovo, Meehan and Keane promote her arguments.[103] Regan supports several of Ryan's conclusions in relation to Kilmichael, despite the fact that they derive from sources to which no one else has access.[104] Meehan even objected to the suggestion that she make her interviews available for others to consult, but then, without a blush, reiterated that Chisholm's should be.[105]

HART IN CONTEXT

As has quite correctly been observed, if Hart's book had appeared in the 1970s or 1980s, the revelation that the OIRA could be just as ruthless as the Provisionals would have been grist to the republican mill.[106] The circumstances were very different in 1998. The public debate around republicanism was shifting. The peace process was being negotiated and arms were in the process of being decommissioned.[107] With the ending of the IRA's armed campaign, the main impetus for republican challenges to idealised narratives of the revolutionary period was gone. What lasting impact 'revisionism' in all its various permutations in the 1970s and 1980s had actually made on popular perceptions of the revolutionary period is hard to judge, but the earlier, more critical sensibilities apparent in some nationalist and republican discourse were rapidly fading away by the end of the 1990s.

In May 1998, simultaneous referendums took place on the island to approve the terms of the Good Friday Agreement (in Northern Ireland) and, in the South, to remove the Irish constitution's territorial claim on the North (Articles 2 and 3).[108] In July, Sinn Féin took its seats in the Northern Ireland Assembly and Gerry Adams declared that violence was a 'thing of the past'.[109] Pundits such as Kevin Myers and Eoghan Harris continued to attack Sinn Féin and the IRA, but the latter's most vociferous critics were now their former members who opposed the peace process.[110]

Both Stephen Howe and Ian McBride have remarked on the parochialism and insularity of the Irish revisionist debate.[111] In 2017, McBride subjected Regan's general arguments to a devastating critique, describing 'recent books' dealing with Irish historiography as 'conceptually unsophisticated', 'obscure', 'clumsy' and reluctant to situate their arguments 'within broader theoretical or comparative frameworks'.[112] He also noted the triviality and conspiratorial speculation of many of the attacks on Hart. Using examples from Britain, Australia and the United States, McBride pointed out that characterising mistakes in footnoting or note-taking as deliberate fraud or forgery is a depressingly common means of making what tend to be, in reality, deeply ideological attacks on other historians.[113] The willingness of some to attempt to destroy the credibility and, in some cases, the careers of their contemporaries does not shine a particularly positive light on the discipline.

It is also the case that, regardless of the specific political context, individual narratives and oral history by their very nature tend to undermine overarching, over-theorised or ideologically committed readings of study of the past. The response to Alistair Thomson's *Anzac Memories* is a particularly apposite comparison for the Hart debate. The 'Anzac legend' extolling the military prowess and egalitarianism of Australian soldiers in the Great War, he argued, had been 'conscripted for political use and abuse since 1915'.[114] Thomson was not at all unsympathetic to the Diggers he interviewed – quite the opposite – but their experiences and memories still complicated the mythology surrounding the Australian national character. In an aptly titled journal article, 'Memory as a Battlefield', Thomson described how his work upset some members of his own family, was attacked in the popular press, and criticised by conservative historians and commentators.[115]

There are also obvious parallels between the Hart debate and the Teddy Katz affair in Israel, although the consequences for Katz, a postgraduate student, were far more serious. In 2000, he was sued for libel by an Israeli veterans' organisation after his master's thesis concluded that Jewish soldiers had massacred Palestinians at a village called Tantura in 1948. Some members of the brigade responsible, as well as Palestinian interviewees, confirmed the event to Katz, but during the trial he was accused of fabricating his material on the basis of a very small number of misquotations (six, later reduced to four in an internal investigation by Haifa University).[116] His university then failed his revised master's thesis (which had been awarded an 'A'). Ilan Pappé and Benny Morris, two Israeli historians with opposing perspectives, listened to Katz's interviews. Both concluded (although Morris was more sceptical and critical of Katz) that he had uncovered evidence of war crimes.[117]

High-profile public efforts to censor, discourage or otherwise prevent research into controversial historical events are not unusual. Spain witnessed bitter 'history wars' in the 1990s in relation to the Civil War (1936–9).[118] Both the Polish League Against Defamation and the

Polish Law and Justice Party campaign to criminalise research into Polish complicity in the Holocaust.[119] Right-wing Israeli student groups like *Im Tirzu* accuse public universities in Israel of promoting the defamation of Zionism and Israel. They picket lectures, inspect reading lists and record the lectures of suspect academics, looking for signs of anti-Zionist bias.[120]

That said, the stormy extremes of the public debate in Ireland were not as reflective of either the academic or the wider public's response to Hart's work as is sometimes assumed. In addition to McBride and Howe, fair-minded commentary on issues raised by the debate have been made by Fergus Campbell, Seámus Fox, Fearghal McGarry, Bill Kautt, Patrick Maume, David Leeson, Richard English, Eunan O'Halpin and John Dorney.[121] David Miller's advocacy gives Niall Meehan's arguments an undeserved radical gloss, but Hart's critics have never had it all their own way, not even on the internet. The Aubane Historical Society comes in for particularly biting commentary. In July 2007, 'Starkadder' observed that the Aubanites 'would have been cheering Hart till their throats were sore' twenty or thirty years ago.[122]

From the beginning, there were individuals who ignored the rhetorical excesses on both sides and engaged reflectively with critical assessments of the Irish independence struggle. Martin D. Bates, an Irish Army officer involved in adult education, who was as dismayed as Declan Kiberd at the state's ambiguity and reluctance to commemorate the seventy-fifth anniversary of the Easter Rising, attributed the controversies over Hart's work to a surfeit of purposeful unhistoricity, rather than a lack of it:

> We were never given enough of the truth ... Any attempt to get to the heart of things was dismissed as shoneenism or whatever other pejorative epithet was currently in fashion. Nobody seems to have foreseen the consequences of having a new generation of historians quite prepared to put an end to a half century of plying sleeping dogs with tranquillisers, and revealing a lot of unpalatable items about what really had happened and who was involved.[123]

The response on the ground in Cork was not uniformly hostile either. Members of the Hales family were very positive about Hart's work.[124] Many of the local Protestants Hart interviewed were happy that he had placed their experiences on record. They and their families were upset at the attacks on his scholarship.[125] The alternative versions of Kilmichael also survive. It just depends on who you speak to. When I asked Liam Deasy (nephew) how Barry succeeded in persuading so many veterans to go along with the false surrender story, his reply was 'He didn't succeed.'[126] Dave Crowley, Sonny Dave Crowley's grandson, always had reservations about the Kilmichael account in *Guerilla Days*. He does not take a side one way or the other on the 'false surrender' question, but he considers Paddy O'Brien's version in *Towards Ireland Free* to be the more accurate account of the ambush.[127]

Others have challenged some of the assertions of Hart's critics more overtly. In August 2007, the Kilmichael History Society erected a plaque at Buttimer's house in Gortroe recounting the deaths of the three IRA Kilmichael fatalities in the same order as Flor Crowley had in 1947: 'Jim O'Sullivan died during the ambush. Michael McCarthy died on the journey here. Pat Deasy passed away at Buttimers at 10pm.'[128] Liam Deasy (nephew) attended the unveiling. In his oration, local historian Seán Crowley described the captured report as Barry's 'very first report on the ambush'.[129] The society's journal later published a Kilmichael account very similar to Crowley's and those of other veterans.[130]

In 2013, the society submitted a proposal jointly with the Kilmichael and Crossbarry Commemoration Committee to rejuvenate the ambush site. It included plans to commemorate 'both IRA Volunteers and Auxiliaries'.[131] The furore that followed ensured that the mooted skeleton Crossley tender memorial to the Auxiliaries was dropped, but the fact that it was proposed at all is yet another indication that Cork and/or nationalist opinion in relation to Kilmichael is more nuanced than is often assumed. Mick Clifford, special correspondent for *The Irish Examiner*, was obviously disappointed at the outcome of the controversy:

> So, a site of violent death is to be remembered solely in military terms and those who died won't even be acknowledged by name. This

accommodates remembering the dead Brits not as human beings but disembodied, evil, expressions of occupation ... History here is not so much being written by the victors as scrawled like graffiti over the graves of the defeated.[132]

This is not to suggest that issues raised in relation to commemorating, researching and writing about the revolutionary period are easily resolved or uncontroversial. A plurality of very strongly held views is evident. The necrology wall in Glasnevin cemetery in Dublin, which lists combatants from both sides, and civilians who died from 1916 to 1918, in chronological order, is a recent case in point. John Green, chairman of the Glasnevin Trust, said the design for their necrology wall was intended to embody 'historical fact, without judgment or hierarchy. Each will be free to take from the wall what they wish.'[133]

The wall was modelled on the Ring of Remembrance at Ablain-Saint-Nazaire in France. Inaugurated in November 2014, it lists 580,000 dead German, British and French soldiers alphabetically without stating their nationality in 'posthumous fraternity'.[134] The French monument's overt internationalist and pacifist intent was at variance with most Great War commemorative efforts, which tended to focus on 'national losses and a national narrative', but caused little controversy.[135] The Glasnevin wall, by contrast, has been vandalised twice; two 1916 relatives groups threatened legal action; and the original plan to list the names of all the dead up to 1923 is currently suspended.[136] A government-sponsored event to commemorate the RIC and Dublin Metropolitan Police (DMP) in January 2020 was also cancelled due to objections.

Community or family-led efforts at reconciliation have negotiated sensitivities more successfully.[137] In April 2016, at the commemoration of DMP Constable James O'Brien, the Easter Rising's first Dublin fatality, the great-grandniece of Seán Connolly, the Irish Citizen Army officer who shot him (and was killed himself a few hours later), laid a wreath in O'Brien's honour.[138] Similarly, the community-focused and organised centenaries of the Soloheadbeg (21 January 1919) and Clonfin (2 February 1921) ambushes were models of 'ethical remembering', honouring both the

IRA men involved in the actions and the policemen (RIC and Auxiliaries) killed.[139]

Hart did not get everything right, but if his mistakes and those of any one of his detractors were placed on a scales, the weighing pan of his critics would crash through the floor. Many of his conclusions have stood the test of time. Hart was unfortunate in some of his supporters. He did not always defend himself well. The tenor of his prose and the language he used was often more extreme and emotive than was necessary. Critiquing and taking issue with Hart's arguments, mistakes and the tone of his work was justified. Accusing him of fabricating some of his sources, relying on forged documents, misrepresenting the authentic grass-roots memory of the revolutionary era and of having a neo-unionist agenda was not. Hart's contribution to scholarship has been obscured by the tendency to cite him only on points of disagreement, although his books have been sucked dry of sources and ideas by many of those whose attack his work. The reaction to his research was out of all proportion to what he wrote and said. Both sides oversimplified or misconstrued his arguments. If the modern Kilmichael debate proves anything, it is that the revisionism/anti-revisionism binary is a toxic analytical framework, at least for those who are interested in making an honest appraisal of past events and how they are remembered.

Conclusion

Decommissioning Irish History

THE KILMICHAEL DEBATE'S 'CONSPIRATORIAL TURN' has fuelled a staggering amount of misinformation and slander. It is a cautionary tale, a reminder that progress is not inevitable, that situations regress, research ethics collapse, and bullies sometimes get their way. The tendency to either promote or deride Tom Barry's *Guerilla Days* version of events as a matter of political faith will no doubt continue *ad nauseam*, but there are alternatives to this war by other means. A return to reasoned inquiry and honest disputation is long overdue. This book, which has examined Kilmichael as both an historical and remembered event within the context of both Irish and British circumstances, is my contribution to that process.

The binaries promoted by the 'revisionist/anti-revisionist' debate are more than just unhelpful. They are actively destructive. The suggestion that Irish people are damaged by critical engagement with their history is absurdly patronising. The real living memory of Kilmichael and the Irish revolution – which is far more reflective and complex than either side in the revisionist/anti-revisionist debate allows for – is testament to that. As Gearóid Ó Tuathaigh and others have long argued, significant cohorts of the Irish population have always been at home with a complicated version of their history, although they may write a few letters to the newspapers.

Offering an often complex version of the past is an obligation rather than an option for historians. When the situation warrants it, acknowledging that the evidence clearly does support one side of an historical debate, even if saying so is unpopular, is important as well. It is impossible to write anything that does not upset someone, but orthodoxies can be challenged constructively. Overly astringent prose, arrogance and excessively negative judgements are needlessly alienating and often counterproductive. Tearing down national heroes is not an obligation. The most productive way to take account of the victims or the losers is to tell their stories too.

In the modern Kilmichael debate, Hart's critics ignored the nuance and diversity of local social memory relating both to the ambush and the revolutionary period generally. This informal silence and self-censorship – on the part of both historians and individuals on the ground – is a damaging legacy. All the combatants at Kilmichael, those who lived as well as those who died there, deserve better. Is there a Kilmichael around which all sides can rally and remember? At present, it does not seem so. What stands out for this historian are those few moments when two men, surrounded on all sides by death, looked each other in the eye and decided not to fire:

> He could have shot me and I could have shot him but I thought it was the bravest thing I could do, maybe, at the time.[1]

Appendix 1

Dublin Castle's Version
of Events

BUXTON SMITH ACCOUNT VIA H.B.C. POLLARD AND
BASIL CLARKE, ORIGINAL TELEGRAM[1]

POLLARD HAS INTERVIEWED COLONEL BUXTON Smith commanding Macroom company. His story supersedes all others most newspaper accounts proved inaccurate.

D.I. Crake took out the patrol in ordinary course of duty. They were going in search of wanted man out in Dunmanway direction and ~~had been previously~~ were working in cooperation Essex Regt at Dunmanway.

Dusk falling about 5 p.m. the patrol was proceeding along Macroom Dunmanway road and reaching point where road curves ~~slightly~~. Low stone wall flank it at this point & ~~road~~ then narrow strips tussocky bog land rising to boulder covered slopes of high ground on either side.

It ~~is surmised~~ appears ~~from examination of site and statement inquiries only survivor~~ that the murder gang who were all clad khaki, trench coats wore steel helmets had drawn their motor lorry across road and were mistaken by first car of cadets for ~~the~~ military.

The first car halted, cadets unsuspecting got out approaching murder lorry. Second car 100 yards behind now came up. ~~Something aroused suspicion of cadets who had got out of first car.~~ Shooting began. Three cadets were killed instantaneously first fire others began turn back to ~~first~~ car. Cadets in second car began run along road help their comrades.

Then from a depression in hill side behind second car came close range devastating fire. Cadets were shot down by concealed men firing from road wall and all round. Direct fire from murder lorry swept down road. ~~All were shot without a chance.~~ After many were disabled ~~Then~~ overwhelming forces enemy came ~~following~~ out forcibly disarming survivors.

Followed a brutal massacre it being policy of murder gang allow no survivors to disclose their treacherous methods. The dead and wounded were hached [*sic*] about ~~the head~~ with axes and bayonetted. Shotguns were fired into their bodies many were savagely mutilated after death.

The one wounded was axed on the head and left for dead has also two bullet wounds. May conceivably survive.

Bodies were robbed rifled even clothes taken. Ambush party who had come in lorries departed lorries but ~~terrible treachery~~ local knew something of their plan inhabitants is ~~manifested~~ indicated by fact that although many ~~all~~ people attending mass Sunday morning were diverted from that route by murder gang, no ~~word~~ warning however sent to police by local people and ambush sat there till dusk.

When ~~lorries parl~~[?] patrol failed return Macroom search parties went out that evening but no news reached Castle Macroom till 9.30 following morning when report of ambush came in.

~~Platoon went out found site of massacre.~~

~~Houses round actual site of deed were burnt but countryside is deserted. No wave of reprisal has taken place. Only one house in Macroom injured, but Macroom kept within doors no traffic no trade no anything till after funeral is over.~~

Stet for tone ~~Moral is murder gang depend on motor traffic no motor traffic must be allowed Ireland till murder gang ambushed out of existence.~~

Sending sketch diagram by courier. Examination [unintelligible word] ambush showed walls of stone heightened and loopholed and depression housing nest of gun men behind second car shielded by camouflage representing artificial rocks etc.

DUBLIN CASTLE PRESS RELEASE, 2 DEC. 1920 AS REPRODUCED IN
THE *BELFAST NEWS-LETTER*[2]

MACROOM MASSACRE.
A TERRIBLE STORY.
Dead and Wounded Savagely
Mutilated After Attack.
INHABITANTS KNEW OF AMBUSH.

Shocking details are now forthcoming regarding the ambush and murder
of sixteen Constabulary cadets near Macroom, County Cork, on Sunday
last, showing that the victims were brutally mutilated after the attack, and
that the local inhabitants, though aware of the plot, took no steps to warn
the police ... Details of the massacre are still difficult to obtain owing to
the fact that, with the exception of one man, Cadet Guthrie, who is still
missing, and another, who was wounded so severely that it is doubtful if
he will survive, the whole patrol was killed. Yesterday, however, the most
coherent account of the dreadful affair which has yet been published was
supplied through official channels. It was prepared by a senior officer of
police in the Cork neighbourhood and makes charges of horrible savagery
against the attackers. The account reads:–

'District-Inspector Crake took out a patrol in the ordinary course
of duty. They were going in search of a man wanted in the Dunmanway
direction and had been previously working in co-operation with the Essex
Regiment at Dunmanway. When dusk was falling at about 5 p.m. (on
Sunday) the patrol was proceeding along the Macroom–Dunmanway road
and reached a point where the road curves. Low stone walls flank the road
and then narrow strips of tussocky bogland, rising to boulder-covered
slopes of high ground on either side.

'It is surmised, from examination of the site, and from inquiries, that
the attackers, who were all

CLAD IN KHAKI AND TRENCH COATS

and wore steel helmets, had drawn their motor lorry across the road and
were mistaken by the first car of cadets for military. The first car halted,

and the cadets, unsuspecting, got out and approached the motor lorry. The second car, which had been travelling 100 yards behind, now came up. Something aroused the suspicion of the cadets who had got out of the first car. Shooting began and three were killed instantaneously. Others began to run back to the first car. The cadets in the second car ran along the road to the help of their comrades. Then from a depression in the hillside, behind the second car, came a devastating fire at close range. The cadets were shot down by concealed men firing from the walls and all around. A direct fire from the ambushers' lorry also swept down the road.

'After firing had been continued for some time, and many men were wounded, overwhelming forces of the ambushers came out and forcibly disarmed the survivors.

'A BRUTAL MASSACRE

'It appearing to be the policy of the murder gang to allow no survivor to disclose their methods, the dead and wounded were hacked about the head with axes, and shot guns were fired into their bodies, which were savagely mutilated. The one survivor, who was wounded, was hit about the head and left for dead. He had also two bullet wounds. The bodies were rifled and even the clothes taken. The ambushing party, which had come in lorries, departed in those vehicles.

'Terrible treachery on the part of the local inhabitants is indicated by the fact that, although many people attending mass on Sunday morning were diverted from their route by the murder gang, no word was sent to the police, and the ambush sat there until dusk.

'When the patrol failed to reach Macroom search parties were sent out, but no news reached Macroom Castle (where the cadets were stationed) until 9:30 the following (Monday) morning, when a report of the ambush came in.'

Appendix 2

The Captured Report[1]

THE COLUMN PARADED AT 3.15 a.m. on Sunday morning. It comprised 32 men armed with rifles, bayonets, five revolvers, and 100 rounds of ammunition per man. We marched for 4 hours and reached a position on the Macroom–Dunmanway road in the townland of Shanacashel. We camped in that position until 4.15 p.m., and then decided that as the enemy searches were completed, that it would be safe to return to our camp. Accordingly we started the return journey. About 5 minutes after the start we sighted two enemy lorries moving along the Macroom–Dunmanway road at a distance of about 1,900 yards from us. The country in that particular area [district] is of a hilly and rocky nature, and, although suitable to fighting, it is not at all suitable to retiring without being seen. I decided to attack the lorries. The action was carried out in the following manner: –

I divided the Column into three sections, viz.: one to attack the first lorry; this section was in a position to have ample cover, and at the same time to bring a frontal and flank fire to bear on the enemy. The second section was in a position about 120 yards from the first section and at the same side of the road. Its duty was to let the first lorry pass to No.1 section, and to attack the second lorry. The third section was occupying sniping positions along the other side of the road and also guarding both flanks. The action as carried out successfully. Sixteen of the enemy who were belonging to the Auxiliary Police from Macroom Castle being killed, one wounded and escaped, and is now missing.

The captures were as follows: –

14 rifles, bayonets, 17 revolvers, 719 rounds of .303, 136 rounds of .450,

with equipment and two lorries, which were subsequently burnt.

Our casualties were one killed, and two who have subsequently died of wounds.

O.C. Flying Column,
3rd Cork Brigade

P.S. – I attribute our casualties to the fact that these three men (who were part of No. 2 section) were too anxious to get into close quarters with the enemy. They were our best men, and did not know danger in this or any previous actions. They discarded their cover, and it was not until the finish of the action that P. Deasy was killed by a revolver bullet from one of the enemy whom we [he] thought dead.

Appendix 3

Frederick H. Forde Account[1]

A HEAVY FIRE BROKE OUT from both sides of the road. I could see little puffs of smoke from here and there amongst the rocks. I saw the first lorry slow up and then run on again and run into a ditch or trench across the road. At the same time as our lorry was pulling up, I heard cries from the other occupants and could see that most if not all of them had been more or less severely hit. However, as soon as the lorry stopped all managed to scramble out, and we took up positions at each side of the road, lying down to return the fire.

After about ten minutes I felt as though struck by a heavy blow above my eye, and all at once began to feel very sick. I believe it was about ten minutes later than this that I suddenly heard a whistle blown loudly, and a cry of cease fire. Then a large number of the attackers from both sides rushed into the road, shouting in the foulest language. They wore the uniforms of British soldiers. These men proceeded to handle us all very roughly, not excepting even those who were by this time dead. After knocking us about, they called on us all to stand up and hold our hands up.

There was no response for a time, but after about two minutes two of the party were able to stagger to their feet, and were immediately shot down again at very close range by the Shinners. Then one of the cadets quite near me, who had been lying on his back, groaned heavily and turned over. One of the civilians, who had a rifle and bayonet, immediately walked up to him and plunged the bayonet into his back as near as I could see between the shoulder blades.

I could see the others going through the clothes of the cadets, and I could see they were being treated brutally. Then one of the civilians came up to me and tried to pull a gold ring off my finger. He failed to do this, and in view of the treatment of the others I fully expected him to cut my finger to get it off. This, however, I am glad to say, he did not do. The next thing I remember is that one of them came up to me and rolled me over roughly to see, I suppose, whether I was not dead. He swung his rifle and gave me a blow with the butt end of it on the back of my head. When I woke up again it was pitch dark, and I must have been conscious and unconscious alternately throughout the night. The ambushers had retired to their previous positions, and I only remember that now and again, presumably when they saw or heard any movement amongst us, they fired a few shots. It was in the afternoon of the following day when the rescuing party arrived, and I was taken in a state of semi-consciousness to a hospital in Cork.

Appendix 4

'Kilmichael: The Fight that Roused a Nation' by Flor Crowley[1]

AT DAWN ON SUNDAY MORNING, November 28, Tom Barry gave the order "Fall in!" Though most of the Column suspected that something big was afoot, they had no certain knowledge of what that something was to be. Had Barry himself been gifted with a pre-vision of how really big that something was destined to be, of what a fateful day awaited himself and his little band, he could not have been more fired with enthusiasm or more inspired by the battle-fervour of the born fighter facing conflict.

To those men, standing proudly to attention, he spoke calmly but clearly. His words, emanating from the burning depths of his own patriotic soul, etched themselves indelibly upon the minds and hearts of his men. We read of inspiring addresses before Gettysburg, before Clontarf, before the Curhues. Barry's words, brief though they were, proved every jot as inspiring as Lincoln's noble words, or Brian Boru's exalting entreaties, or Aodh Ruadh's fiery eloquence. "Comrades", he said, "upon this day we go into action. For this day and the fight it shall bring us we have trained hard and assiduously. For many of us it is to be our first engagement with the enemy, but I have faith, I have confidence that every man here will deport himself as befits a soldier and an Irishman. Make no mistake, our fight will be a hard one. Our foes are no mean foes, but the war-toughened products of a great world war. From them we cannot expect and will not expect any quarter. But we will despise quarter, and every last one of us will fight to the last breath and to the last heart-throb.

"For us this day the words 'Retreat' and 'Surrender' do not exist. This is to be a fight to the death, and win or lose let us fight like men, and if some of us have to die, then let us look upon such a death as a privilege, as a soldier's greatest glory. Win we must, lose we cannot but if we place our Cause above and before all personal danger [next line illegible on microfilm].

"If there is any man listening to me here who feels he cannot go through with this fight, who thinks that he may not be able to stand up to the terrible strain which this day may bring, then let him fall out now, and neither I, as his officer, nor his comrades in the ranks will think the less of him for doing so".

It was the offer of a thoughtful gentleman as well as a competent leader. But there was never a murmur; the ranks remained unbroken.

Then began a rite that, even more than their commander's touching words, must have brought clearly to the minds of those youths the seriousness of the task that confronted them that day. In the grey dawn of that late autumnal morning each man in turn knelt in Confession before the Pastor of Enniskeane, Fr O'Connell, who had come to the camp to administer the sacraments to the Column. Then Holy Communion and the solemn words of General Absolution pronounced, the boys knelt in devout thanksgiving. A singular and memorable feature of that thanksgiving was that the last man to finish praying that morning was Michael McCarthy, one of the three to die that day. It is said that men on the battlefield sometimes have a prescience of impending death. Perhaps it was that Michael had that premonition that morning and that that Communion and Thanksgiving were to be his last.

It may not be out of place to put on record here that it was then, and later, the custom of the Column to recite the Rosary before returning to its precarious rest each night, with, as frequently happened, Michael Driscoll of Dunmanway, then of Snave, Bantry, giving out the Mysteries and the prayers and the entire Column responding.

With a great day so well begun, the Column moved off on its hard ten-mile trek from Ahilnane through Cahir, Teenagh, Dromfeigh and Buckaree, across Lisheenleigh bog to Shanacashel and on to the pre-selected scene of the ambush. Positions were taken up at 9 a.m., and the little band of march-weary men were glad of the respite after the trying journey from their week-end camp.

It may be of interest to note that it was originally intended to stage this attack on the Auxiliaries in Coppeen village, but the day before the fight Tom Barry decided to seek an alternative position. Accompanied by another Column officer, he travelled along the road through Gloun and Shanacashel, and his practised eye saw at once the tactical possibilities of the site at Kilmichael.

What those possibilities were, and what it was that prompted Barry to select Kilmichael instead of Coppeen, we may leave to the experts to decide, since our interest must be the human rather than the military side of the affair. Enough for us to know that events proved how absolutely correct was Barry's pre-concept of the fight, for though he might have selected a safer ambush position for his own men, he could not have picked a position which afforded less cover to the enemy. Personal danger did not enter into Barry's scheme of things that day. His ideal was to show the enemy that they could still be met and defeated, to make this day's work an example which the rest of Ireland could follow.

And how well he succeeded!

Dividing the Column into two sections, he placed Section 1 in position at Murray's Lane, and on the little hillock immediately to the North of the lane, where he posted seven men. A party of snipers occupied the low hills on the south of the road, with no man in the section more than twenty yards from the road, while Barry himself and five men took up position inside the low fence at Murray's Lane. This section, under the personal command of the Column leader, was to carry out the attack on the first lorry, and consisted of, besides Barry himself, Sonny Dave Crowley, Stephen O'Neill, "Spud" Murphy, "Flyer" Nyhan, Batty Coughlan, Tim Connell, John Donovan, Sonny Carey, Neilius Cotter, "Kilmallock" McCarthy (later killed in action at Skibbereen in 1922), Jack Aherne, Paddy O'Brien, and three or four others.

Section II, under the command of Vice-Commandant Michael McCarthy, was placed on the low range of rocks overlooking Kelly's Cross, 150 yards north of the position occupied by Section 1, and immediately behind the spot where the ambush monument now stands. Here even more than in position 1, the cover afforded the attackers was negligible, but they dug themselves in as best they could, and took what meagre cover the bare rocks and stones afforded. It was here that the three Volunteers, Michael McCarthy, Jim Sullivan and Pat Deasy, were killed in the ensuing fight, as we shall see later.

The orders to this section were to allow the first lorry to pass beyond them to position 1, and then to engage the second lorry as it ran into their position. Barry had calculated his distances well, for it had been noted that those two lorries usually travelled about 200 yards apart.

So the Column, every man in position and knowing to the letter what was expected of him that day, settled down to the enervating task of waiting for the arrival of the enemy. That long wait, lying in cramped and uncomfortable positions, must have been one of the greatest trials suffered on that arduous day by those boys of Barry's Column. From 9 a.m. to 4 p.m. they watched and waited, with the damp ground making their vigil all the more trying and uncomfortable.

Local farmers on their way to Johnstown Mass had to be turned back, for it was not known at what moment the lorries might be heard on the way from Cooldorrihy. Scouts reported frequently to the commander. The day wore on, and still there was no sign of Captain Craig and his Auxiliaries. At midday the strain of waiting was somewhat relieved when some thoughtful ladies arrived with supplies of steaming-hot tea. Refreshed, the Column again settled down to continue its wait.

In the early afternoon, John Lordan of Newcestown arrived at the ambush position, and, tried and noted fighter as he was even at that early stage of the struggle, his arrival was welcome indeed to the boys of the Column.

Shortly before 4 p.m. two traploads of reinforcements arrived from the Kealkil and Bantry Companies. The Column leader went on to the road to interview them, but at that moment the sound of the Crossleys was heard on the way from the north on the long gradient above the village at Cooldorrihy. The two trap-loads of men had no time to take up positions, and they were ordered to retreat at full speed back the old road from Kelly's Cross to Johnstown. They had barely but rounded a bend on the road and out of sight when the first of the enemy lorries came within view of the ambush position.

It is not difficult to imagine the feelings of those boys lying but poorly concealed within a few yards of the road as that lorry passed beyond them on its way. One nervous move, one careless act and all Tom Barry's carefully laid plans were gone for nothing. For most of the boys their baptism of fire was just about to begin. But not a sound, not a move escaped them. The Auxiliaries passed on, some smoking, others laughing at some joke or other, all apparently in the best of humour. The first lorry rounded the bend 100 yards above Murphy's Lane. Still no shot rang out. Within twenty yards of the lane it passed a small white stone on the southern side of the road. That inconspicuous stone was the dead-line, placed there by Barry, with the order that when the lorry passed that stone Section 1 was to go into action.

The bonnet of the tender covered the stone. Barry's whistle sent out its piercing blast. The Battle of Kilmichael was on.

Specially selected marksmen had been told off to fire on the driver of the lorry. The success or failure of the fight depended upon their success. But with the very first volley the driver slumped behind that wheel. Out of control, the lorry zig-zagged from side to side and lodged in the southern ditch 10 yards from Barry's position in the Lane.

At the first shots of the attack the Auxiliaries leaped from the lorry and took what cover they could on the roadsides and under the lorry. At a range of less than a dozen yards that fight was fought out to its finish, sharp and short and decisive. Barry's grenades, the concentrated fire from both sides of the road, the deadly marksmanship of the chosen snipers soon accounted for the greater number of the Auxiliaries. But let it not be forgotten that they fought a daring fight, that they were not easily overcome, that Barry and his little section had to exert all their courage and nerve to cope with them. For ten minutes they fought like demons, fought with the bravery of despair.

Only five were left. That five put up their hands in token of surrender. It was but a ruse, however, a ruse to lure their attackers from the little cover they enjoyed, for those five Auxiliaries immediately opened fire again, in hopes of catching some members of the Column by surprise.

Then rang out Barry's cry to close in upon them. From the north, from the Lane, from the scattered rocks to the south, the boys began to close in, and the first lorry and its occupants were no more. Section 1 of the column had deported itself well. Barry's training and stinging precepts had not been wasted. That section of the little Column had annihilated its foes without a scratch to itself.

Meanwhile things were not going so well with the boys in Position II.

For once those lorries had broken routine on this afternoon. Instead of travelling less than 200 yards apart, as was their usual custom, at least 400 yards divided them today. But even that contingency had been foreseen by Tom Barry; foreseen and guarded against, for he placed two reliable and trustworthy members of the Column in good rear positions from which they could cover the advance line of the attackers in the event of the second lorry attempting a surprise rearguard action. But that strategy was not undertaken by the members of the second lorry.

With the sound of the first shots of the fight they accelerated speed in the hope of assisting their friends in the first lorry. They were, therefore, on the alert as they approached the ambush scene, and, strictly speaking, they were not ambushed at all. Apparently, however, they felt that all the attacking force was concentrated upon the lorry already in action, and they did not consider the possibility of a second ambush section awaiting themselves. They could not, of course, see the actual fighting at Murray's Lane until they had made the bend below Kelly's Cross.

They never made that bend. Alert though they were, they had run into the fire of Michael McCarthy and his section before they were well beyond the cross. A withering first volley accounted for some of them. The remainder tumbled or leaped out of the lorry on to the road, and returned a deadly fire. Even though wounded through the arm, the driver of that lorry reversed and tried to turn at Kelly's Cross. He almost succeeded in doing so when he was killed by a well-aimed bullet. The other Auxiliaries of that lorry proved themselves clever fighters. There was but one suggestion of cover that offered any protection to them – the outer edge of the very rocks from which they were being attacked. Some of them crawled along the dyke to those rocks, and having gained that comparative cover, they fought doggedly back.

The range was less than five yards, and the firing was intense and murderous. Yet it was difficult for the members of the Column to dislodge the few remaining enemy without exposing themselves to a deadly cross-fire. It was something of a stalemate.

But not for long. Having finally disposed of the occupants of the first lorry, Barry and four of his section went on the double to the assistance of the other section. Running along the road with complete disregard for their own safety, they rounded the bend and, catching the Auxiliaries upon the exposed flank, they finished the fight. One volley and Kilmichael was over. Over and won! ... For those of them that are dead – Michael McCarthy, Jim Sullivan, Pat Deasy, and later John Lordan, "Flyer" Nyhan and Jer McCarthy, we can only pray ... But the great victory of Kilmichael was not a bloodless one for the men of the Column. The price of that victory was the lives of three grand youths – Michael McCarthy of Dunmanway, son of that grand old Fenian and Nationalist, Dan McCarthy of East Green; Jim Sullivan of Knockawaddra, Rossmore, and Patrick Deasy of Bandon, younger brother of the well-known Liam Deasy, Brigade Adjutant.

All three were killed in the attack upon the second lorry. It is believed that Michael McCarthy left his original position to get a better sight upon the Auxiliaries who had taken cover under the outer rim of the rocks. In moving he exposed himself momentarily to the fire of three of the Auxiliaries who had crept further down towards the bend, one of whom shot him through the head, the bullet entering behind his left ear and lodging in his head. One would have expected so terrible a wound to be followed by instantaneous death, but Michael, fatally wounded though he was, struggled manfully with the Grim Reaper, and survived for almost an hour after being hit. It was not until he was being taken in a horse-cart to the appointed billet for the dead and welcomed at the house of Neilus Buttimer, of Gortroe, that he finally breathed his last, though he never regained consciousness. Jim Sullivan was, it is almost certain, killed in the first blast of retaliatory fire from the second lorry. The bullet hit his left hand, blew the bolt off his rifle, and passed through his lower jaw. In his case death was instantaneous.

Pat Deasy, lying within a few feet of Michael McCarthy's position, and almost shoulder to shoulder with Mick Driscoll, of Dunmanway, was hit near the left hip, the bullet passing through his stomach and out at the groin. This young lad, only just over 16 years, never murmured, and though hideously wounded, he lived on until 10 p.m. that night. He was attended by Fr Gould of Kilmichael and by Dr Nyhan, of Johnstown, who pronounced him beyond human aid. He passed away peacefully after having been given the last rites of the Church ... Three of the men of Kilmichael were dead. But the miracle of that great day was that many more than three did not have to pay the supreme sacrifice. The fight was fought at point-blank range, and how it was that Craig and his men, experienced fighters that they were, did not take a heavier toll of Barry's men, is one of the mysteries of Kilmichael.

For one of those men it was indeed a lucky day. That man was Jack Hennessy, of Ballineen. Occupying a position a little to the left of Michael McCarthy, in the disused sand-pit, he wore a trench helmet. That tin hat was hit at least five times. Any one of those five bullets would have made Jack a fourth martyr of Kilmichael. But it was not to be his fate.

One other had as close an escape as Jack, and he neither a member of the attackers or of the attacked. An hour before the fight began a tramp walked into the ambush position from the south. Doubting the wisdom of allowing him to pass on to the North, on the way by which the lorries were expected to come, the Column leader ordered him to lie low in the old sand pit until the evening's work was over. No sooner had the firing on the first lorry started than this unwilling spectator decided to take peep out of his bolt-hole. He had scarcely lifted his head when an Auxiliary bullet hit his hat off. So, apparently, he too was not destined to be a victim of Kilmichael.

But what of the other side? The two lorries had contained seventeen men, nine in the first lorry and eight in the second. The entire complement of the first lorry was accounted for in the fight, though it has been claimed that Forde, the driver of the lorry, though shot high up in the forehead, was only wounded, and survived the terrible night of the 28th on that rain-swept road. It was said that he was still alive when his comrades from Macroom arrived on the following morning, that he was later sent back to England and operated upon, and that he lived in hospital for some time. Our only authority for this claim is the word of the Black and Tans at Dunmanway, who showed a photograph of a man in hospital, propped up in bed with his head swathed in bandages. They declared that Forde, if he were Forde, could identify at least seven of the men who took part in Kilmichael, and quoted him as the author of the fables which they spread regarding the atrocities and mutilations which the Column were supposed to have committed upon the bodies of the dead Auxiliaries after the fight. If their claims that Forde survived the ambush is no more true than their libels about atrocities and mutilations that never existed, then Forde, too, died at Kilmichael.

Of the eight men killed in the second lorry, seven were killed in the fight. The eighth man, Gatrie [*sic*], made his escape through a bunch of cattle near the roadside and got clear away from the ambush. He tried to make his way back to Macroom, but was captured later in the evening at Dromcara by two local Volunteers, Jack Mahony and his brother. It was decided that he, too, should be shot, for had Gatrie arrived in Macroom that evening with word of the ambush it is almost certain that reinforcements would have been rushed to the scene and the surrounding countryside thoroughly searched for traces of the Column. Had that occurred there was grave danger that the bodies of the three dead Volunteers might have been discovered, and that those Volunteers whose duty it was to guard them, might have been captured. There seemed then no alternative but that Gatrie must die since it was not a question that he could be held prisoner. So it was that the last shots of the Kilmichael ambush were fired at Dromcara.

But to return to the scene of the ambush. At 4 p.m. the first shots of the attack rang out. By 4.20 p.m., victory was complete. In those twenty tense and dramatic minutes the Alamein, the Stalingrad, of our history had been enacted. There remained but the task of removing the three dead and dying comrades, and the important duty of collecting that precious booty of rifles, revolvers and ammunition, which had belonged to the Auxiliaries. The lorries were sprinkled with petrol and set afire and –

The flames of their lorries gave signal that the boys of Kilmichael had won.

Appendix 5

Paddy O'Brien, Kilmichael Ambush, as told to Liam Deasy[1]

ON SUNDAY 21ST NOVEMBER 1920 a Bde meeting was held at Nelius Kelly's, Glaun, Dunmanway. Its business was to collect the Arms fund and organise a Flying Column for the Bde.

Liam Deasy will describe how members of the 1st Battalion and Bde staff were captured at Coppeen. Then, as arranged, the Column would meet at Togher. Tim Farrell's, Clogher, was Head Quarters. There was also a disused cottage nearby, so we arrived there Sunday night, (21st Nov [handwritten note])

It was then decided to get some bedding in a local gentleman's house at Coolkelure near Dunmanway. Jim Burke and Tim Hurley with some of their men raided, and delivered the goods consisting of about 20 blankets and sheets; of course it was easy to get the under mattresses which consisted of a few pikes of straw. That is how the Column Hotel started.

Dunmanway men were first installed – M. (Mick [handwritten note]) McCarthy, Ned Young, Battie Coughlan and Sonny Carey. Four men arrived earlier on Sunday from the 7th Batt. but failed to get in touch and returned home. The Bde were insistent on men on the run only to form the column. On Monday Tom Barry started training – the usual routine –, there were then about 12 men. On Wednesday evening Tom Barry decided to go near Ballineen; so we moved to Jack Sullivan's unused farm house at Ahilnane.

We were only landed when our big news came, that 7 carbines (captured at Schull [handwritten note]) were coming after us from S (Shaun in charge of

VIIth Batt. [hand-written note]). Lehane with Paddy McCarthy (Kilmallock) (password & nickname [hand-written note]) in charge. The rifles came by the West Cork Bottling Co. lorry c/o Griffin. There was an awful scramble for the rifles.

Now the official Q.M. Mick Dwyr [*sic*] of the 3rd Batt., took over the catering – plenty of everything but very poor cooking. Now training by Tom Barry was the routine and action was what he was looking for; Of course he had the previous Sunday's raid by the Macroom Auxiliaries and he made up his mind they would come again. So on Friday T. Barry, Ml McCarthy, Sonny Dave Crowley set off for a suitable position. I was left to mind the house so I was in a position to know each one in the Column and to form a comradeship that has lasted to the present day.

When T. Barry, M. McCarthy and Sonny Dave Crowley came back we had a chat but T. Barry was not satisfied and decided that the 3 of them would try again on Saturday. They went on Saturday and returned fairly satisfied. Then I told T.B. that we had only 28 men and that I would go to Ballinacarriga and bring a few men. I knew previously that the Dunmanway R.D.C.[2] was meeting at Behaug School. So off I went and informed Tom Donovan what was on as we had arranged to come to Granure and to have his area scouted.

So I went along to Girlough and sent Jack Hourihane for Pat Donovan Inchafune. Dan Hourihane was then sent up for Michael C. Driscoll and John Aherne. They got 4 double barrel guns from Jack Riordan and ammunition; so we returned to Ahilinane. We now had 33 men.

I was only back when T. Barry ordered me to get 2 armed men as two Tommies were seen in the locality that evening – why he waited I do not know –. We went in their direction, and with our local scout, Dan Coakley, we went to Bill Howes house. He got up and denied seeing any one around. Then we made a thorough search of the Hay Shed and found our two boys buried in a corner of hay. We brought them to H.Q.

Fr. O'Connell was sent for T. Barry explained that the Column wanted confessions as they would probably be going into action in the morning. Fr O'Connell then blessed the men and they retired. Some of them were not feeling well.

At about 5 a.m. we got ready and eat [ate] breakfast. We started about 7 a.m. for Kilmichael. The morning was dull and wet, so we paddled on and really it was so dark you would not know who was next to you. Anyway when we arrived near Glaun Cross people were going to Mass, so T. Barry ordered them home for one Sunday. Day was dawning so it was daylight when we arrived at the positions selected the previous day. T. Barry then divided the Column, half to Ml McCarthy and the rest to himself. I was on the loose end so I went first to help Michael McCarthy and we built the stone single fence and camouflaged it with furze bushes. Ned Young was placed west of the road. M.C. Driscoll was placed at the most northern – in fact it was he who gave the signal 'they are coming'. I then went back to the first position inside the fence. At the lane was T. Barry, next was Sonny Dave Crowley, then Jim Spud Murphy, Mick Herlihy, John Nyhan & Flyer. In Murrays field were John Ahern and Battie Coughlin; on the rock overlooking were Tim Connell, Jer Cotter, Mick Donovan, etc.

I then went south of the road. There I met Stephen O'Neill and Jack Hegarty straight across from the first position. Then I went on and met Paddy McCarthy, Kilmallock; and on the last point over the second position was Jack O'Sullivan, Carmounteen.

Tim Sullivan, the official scout (Jack Kelly, Johnstown, was the other official scout), was living close by. He and his brother, Jer, made provision to feed to the boys. Bread and buckets tea were coming on the horison [sic]

Everything was now in readiness, faces were getting lonesome; mist all the time; everything damp but spirits still high.

At about time to retreat the alarm sounded (about 4:10pm [handwritten note]), and with that four men in horse & trap drove into the position – it is easy to be correct afterwards –, they got orders to drive on instead of sending them back in the direction they came from. For a few minutes it could have upset the whole plan. As I was on the loose end all day I ran across the 30 yds and took up [a] position with S. O'Neill and Jack Hegarty.

In a few minutes the first lorry drove into the position. It was met with a terrific fusillade and stopped immediately. T. Barry then threw a hand-grenade; it landed in the lorry; all was over. T. Barry then came on the road and ran up to the second lorry. I jumped on the road immediately and followed him. When I heard all the calling – there was an auxiliary after coming out from under the lorry – I turned back. When I went back to the lorry Flyer was out, also Spud and Stephen. Flyer ordered them not to burn the lorry as he was going to drive it back to Clonakilty. After taking down the driver, who was dead, and placing him on the southern bank, Flyer got on the lorry, but there was not stir. There were two dead in the lorry so we decided to put them on the bank south [sic] also; I went into the lorry; Spud and Stephen took the bodies and laid them down. I can say definitely they were killed by the hand grenade. All were on the road by now and relieving the dead of their arms and gathering up all the paraphernalia they had.

I then went up to the second lorry. I did not know till then that we had three of our men shot. When I arrived there Michael Con and Ned Young were following one auxiliary who had escaped – and he did escape to Annahala bog.

Michael McCarthy was shot through the head (dead); Jim Sullivan was shot in the jaw (dead); Pat Deasy was shot through the body – we did not think he was serious at the time. Jack Hennessy and John Lordan had slight wounds and plenty blood. The fight over we now make the long march to Granure; we were short 10 men, 3 dead, 3 local men, the 2 scouts, John Lordan (1st Batt came that morning [handwritten note]) and Jerimiah [sic] O'Mahony (not member of column, simply came for [the] fight [handwritten note]).

(one was wounded & brought to hospital lived for 12 months afterwards – [?] became conscious & gave an a/c of the fight. The one who escaped to Anahala [sic] bog was captured on his way to Macroom & was shot. Win lose or draw t'was arranged to come back to Granure [handwritten note]).

We started off just as darkness was setting in, each man had 2 rifles, hand grenades and ammunition. We went down to Glaun, over to Ahakeera, on to Thomes (Behaugh). Denis Cronin, Kealkil, got sick there so we had to get him fixed up. Then we went on to Behaugh and on to Manch Bridge which we crossed about 9.30; from that on to Granure; We had to rest several times. At last we arrived about 11 o'clock and everyone was dying to lie down. The Ballinacarriga Coy were all there to take over.

Nean Driscoll, Cissie Cronin and Molly Riordan provided supper. We then sent for a stimulant (drop of whiskey [handwritten note]) and gave each a good glass. Then nearly all were sound asleep and had forgotten all their ordeal.

On Monday morning [29 Nov.] the Clon trio were ordered to check all the rifles, revolvers and ammunition; so they had a busy few hours.

When were arrived T. Barry sent immediately for C. (Charlie [handwritten note]). Con Driscoll was dispatched; we went on to Mick Dineens (Knockea); he had information that he was at Kilbree; he was brought to the camp.

T. Barry, C. Hurley and myself went to Con Driscoll's house. They both discussed the day's work there. Charlie Hurley decided to go to Ahakeera. I think Con Driscoll drove him there – but I am not sure. We went back to the camp; all were dead asleep. T. Barry saw a bit of room by the fireplace and he lay down to sleep – but no sleep. I am sure you will find all about C. Hurley in the Aultagh Coy report, in one of the little ledger books.

Monday. [29 Nov.]
T. Barry had a long interview with the 2 Tommies and sent a letter, signed by one of the Tommies to be delivered to his brother. Katty O'Driscoll was sent with it to O'Donoghues of Shannon St., Bandon. Timmie Warren, Ballineen, joins the Column.

Tuesday. [30 Nov.]
As arranged the previous Saturday evening at the R.D. (Rural District [handwritten note]) Council meeting I was selected to go on a deputation to Skib. along with Jim Burke, his sister, Kit, and Tom O'Donovan. Henry Smith was the driver; we arrived at Clancy Dreeney Bridge and had a drink – 4 wines and one bottle of stout. They informed us that 12 lorries were after passing up the Dreeney road; so we made for Skib. to meet John Collins (he was in charge of the Skib. Work House) and to get him to think as we did about abolishing the British Local Government. On our way back Henry Smith's car stalled on the top of Dreeney Bridge. In less than a minute the lorries were back; we were caught red-handed; we were all as cool as

possible. Henry Smith opened the bonnet. He asked the officer in charge for a mechanic. As the car was stuck the officer obliged and then interviewed us; we passed our examination, but I was taken out and passed again. Henry Smith was told to sit in, and were told to come out and shove. Four I.R.A. at one side and 4 Tommies at the other side got the car moving. We got into the car again and, I can tell you, we said no more until we landed at Ballinacarriga forge. H. Smith boasted and challenged any one in Ireland to have both armies pushing his car.

Wednesday [1 Dec.]
The Column left for Lyre Coy area. All spare arms were dumped by the Ballinacarriga Coy.

Sunday [5 Dec.]
We took out the arms for a day's training at Edencurra. We had Ballinacarriga Coy and part of the Clubhouse. At about 2 p.m. Mick Dineen arrived and stated that Charlie Hurley had given orders to me to go to Ahiohill and take charge of Tom Barry. We arrived as fast as possible. He was at John McCarthy's, Kilmoyerane; he did not look too bad. We chatted about every item of the previous week. I slept there that night. On Monday [6 Dec.] about 4 p.m. he passed out so we lost no time in getting Dr. Fehily. The Dr arrived shortly afterwards and gave him 2 injections; the patient recovered immediately. The Dr came again on Tuesday [7 Dec.] evening; he was much improved.

Wednesday [8 Dec.]
On Wednesday evening the Dr sent word that what Barry wanted now was nursing. We decided to move him as there was too much traffic around the place. Séan Buckley had arranged to let him know how he was, and that he would be in Newcestown. We sent him word that we would go to O'Neill's, Shanavagh for a few days as Mary O'Neill, the nurse, was there. We were not long left when John Lordan and Séan Buckley got up to us. After landing at O'Neills, John Lordan said that he would take him to his aunt's place at Granure. It was now midnight, and after landing a Granure they decided

to take T. Barry back to Newcestown; back we came to O'Neills again. We sent a scout to call Enniskeane Co Capt. and immediately scout Murragh Cross. T. Barry, Séan Buckley, and John Lordan left for their destination. I did not see T. Barry again until New Year's Day at O'Neill's, Shanavagh. [1 Jan. 1921]

I must apologise for using 'I' so often, but I am only giving a personal version.

   Paddy O'Brien, Girlough, Ballinacarrige [*sic*], Dunmanway'

Endnotes

INTRODUCTION

1   'O' is used inconsistently in both Irish place names and surnames. Jim O'Sullivan, for instance, was often called 'Jim Sullivan' at the time. The rule of thumb adopted in this book is to omit the 'O' as appropriate in direct quotations but to use it in the text if that is the current usage.

2   Tom Barry, *Guerilla Days in Ireland* (Dublin, 1981 [org. 1949]), pp. 23–35.

3   Liam Deasy, *Towards Ireland Free: The West Cork Brigade in the War of Independence, 1917–1921* (Dublin and Cork, 1987 [org. 1973]) pp. 170–2.

4   Peter Hart, *The IRA and Its Enemies: Violence and Community in Cork, 1916–1923* (Oxford, 1998).

5   Jack Lane and Brendan Clifford (eds), *Kilmichael: The False Surrender, a Discussion by Peter Hart, Padraig O'Cuanachain, D.R. O'Connor Lysaght, Dr. Brian Murphy and Meda Ryan* (Millstreet, Nov. 1999).

6   Jack Lane, 'Biographers at loggerheads – Ryan versus Hart – both books launched this week', 11 Oct. 2005 (www.indymedia.ie/article/72403?search_text=Kilmichael, accessed 17 Dec. 2021).

7   *The Southern Star*, 5 July 2008.

8   Eve Morrison, 'Kilmichael revisited: Tom Barry and the "False Surrender"', in David Fitzpatrick (ed.), *Terror in Ireland: 1916–1923* (Dublin, 2012), pp. 158–80; *The Southern Star*, 11 June 2017.

9   John Borgonovo, 'Review Article: Revolutionary Violence and Irish Historiography' in *Irish Historical Studies* [*IHS*], vol. 38, iss. 150 (Nov. 2012), pp. 325–31; *IHS* editors, 'Apology' [to Eve Morrison], *IHS*, vol. 38, iss. 153 (May 2014), p. 177.

10 Brendan O'Leary, *A Treatise on Northern Ireland, Volume 2: Control, the Second Protestant Ascendancy and the Irish State* (Oxford, 2019), pp. 92–8; *The Irish Times*, 16 Nov. 2016.

11 Seanad Éireann debate, Thursday, 30 Apr. 2015, vol. 239, no. 13.

12 Guy Beiner, *Remembering the Year of the French: Irish Folk History and Social Memory* (London, 2007), pp. 28–32.

13 M.A.G. Ó Tuathaigh, 'Irish Historical Revisionism' in Ciaran Brady (ed.), *Interpreting Irish History: The Debate on Historical Revisionism* (Dublin, 1994; 2nd ed., 1999), p. 322.

14 Ibid., p. 324.

15 Cormac Ó Gráda, *Black '47 and Beyond: The Great Irish Famine in History, Economy, and Memory* (Princeton, N.J., 1999); Alistair Thomson, *Anzac Memories: Living With the Legend* (Melbourne & Oxford, 1994); Alessandro Portelli, 'Oral History in Italy' in D.K. Dunaway and W.K. Baum, *Oral History: An Interdisciplinary Anthology* (Walnut Creek, Ca., 1996); Paul Thompson, *The Voice of the Past: Oral History* (Oxford, 2000).

16 Alistair Thomson, 'Memory as a Battlefield: Personal and Political Investments in the National Military Past' in *Oral History Review*, 22/2 (Winter 1995), pp. 55–73, see p. 65.

17 Thomson, 'Memory as a Battlefield', p. 61.

18 Ibid., p. 72.

19 Ibid., p. 70.

20 Efrat Ben-Ze'ev, 'Imposed silences and self-censorship: Palmach soldiers remember 1948' in Efrat Ben-Ze'ev, Ruth Ginio and J.M. Winter (eds), *Shadows of War: A Social History of Silence in the Twentieth Century* (Cambridge, 2010), p. 182.

21 Guy Beiner, *Forgetful Remembrance: Social Forgetting and Vernacular Historiography of a Rebellion in Ulster* (Oxford, 2018), p. 13.

22 Ben-Ze'ev, 'Imposed silences and self-censorship', p. 183.

23 In the early 1980s, Jack O'Sullivan told Brendan Vaughan that he had been interviewed twice by his sons. (www.youtube.com/watch?v=qGiZ9STi-1o, accessed 17 Dec. 2021), [hereafter O'Sullivan/Vaughan, *c.* 1980s]; Notes from 'Taped interview with Jack Sullivan, Kealkil', n.d. (Archives and Special Collections, Queen Elizabeth II Library Memorial University [hereafter ASC/QEII/MUN], Peter Hart [hereafter PH], Coll–455–1.02.017) [hereafter Sullivan, Kealkil/PH].

24 Telephone conversations with Meda Ryan, 7 July 2012, and David Willis, 11 Oct. 2013.

25 Quoted in David Leeson, *The Black and Tans: British Police and Auxiliaries in the Irish War of Independence, 1920–1921* (Oxford, 2011), p. 155.

CHAPTER 1. KILMICHAEL IN CONTEXT

1   Martin Pugh, *The Tories and the People, 1880–1935* (Oxford, 1985), p. 98; Daniel M. Jackson, *Popular Opposition to Irish Home Rule in Edwardian Britain* (Liverpool, 2009), pp. 13–14; Jeremy Smith, *The Tories and Ireland 1910–1914: Conservative Party Politics and the Home Rule Crisis* (Dublin, 2000), pp. 2–8.

2   Jackson, *Popular Opposition*, pp. 1, 6, 37, 48.

3   Carson was a member of the Ulster Unionist Council, while Craig was a leading member of the Irish Unionist Alliance. T.P. Daly, 'James Craig and Orangeism, 1903–10', *IHS*, vol. 34, iss. 136 (Nov. 2005), pp. 431–48, see p. 443; P.J. Buckland 'Southern Irish Unionists, the Irish Question, and British Politics 1906–14', *IHS*, vol. 15, iss. 59 (Mar. 1967), pp. 228–55, see pp. 232–40.

4   Ian F. W. Beckett, *The Army and the Curragh Incident 1914* (London, 1986).

5   David Fitzpatrick, 'Militarism in Ireland, 1900–1922' in Tom Bartlett and Keith Jeffery (eds), *A Military History of Ireland* (Cambridge, 1996), p. 383.

6   David Fitzpatrick, 'Irish Consequences of the Great War', *IHS*, vol. 38, iss. 156 (Nov. 2015), pp. 643–58, see pp. 656–7; G.R. Searle, *A New England? Peace and War, 1886–1918* (Oxford, 2004), p. 141.

7   Fitzpatrick, 'Militarism in Ireland', pp. 385–6.

8   Charles Townshend, *Easter 1916: The Irish Rebellion* (London, 2015, 2nd ed.); Fearghal McGarry, *The Rising: Ireland, Easter 1916* (Oxford, 2010).

9   Michael Laffan, *The Resurrection of Ireland: the Sinn Fein Party, 1916–1923* (Cambridge, 2004), p. 60.

10 Laffan, *Resurrection*, pp. 75–101.

11 Ibid.

12 Padraig Yeates, 'Have you in Ireland All Gone Mad – the 1918 General Strike Against Conscription', *Saothar* 43 (Apr. 2018), p. 10.

13 D.G. Boyce, *Englishmen and Irish Troubles: British Public Opinion & the Making of Irish Policy, 1918–22* (London, 1972), p. 42.

14 The most recent study of this subject is Elaine Callinan, *Electioneering and Propaganda in Ireland, 1917–1921: Votes, Violence and Victory* (Dublin, 2020).

15 Donal Ó Drisceoil, 'Keeping disloyalty within bounds? British media control in Ireland, 1914–19', *IHS*, vol. 38, iss. 149 (May 2012), pp. 53–69, see pp. 67–8.

16 'K Company' Auxiliary Notebook, Jan.–Mar. 1920 (Bureau of Military History [hereafter BMH], Flor Begley, CD 31).

17 *The American Commission on Conditions in Ireland: Interim Report* (1921), p. 128.

18 Donal Ó Drisceoil, '"Sledge-hammers and blue pencils": censorship, suppression and the Irish regional press, 1916–23' in Ian Kenneally and James T. O'Donnell (eds), *The Irish Regional Press, 1892–2018* (Dublin, 2018), pp. 149–50.

19 Dublin Castle, alleged acts of reprisals by police and soldiers, Sept. 1920 and memo on Thomas Hales and Patrick Harte, Oct. 1920 (The National Archives United Kingdom (Kew) [hereafter TNAUK], Colonial Office [hereafter CO] 904/168).

20 'Department of Publicity', Kathleen McKenna Napoli, June 1920 (National Library of Ireland [hereafter NLI], Kathleen McKenna Napoli Papers, ms 22,783).

21 Maurice Walsh, *The News from Ireland: Foreign Correspondents and the Irish Revolution* (London, 2008), pp. 109–16; Ian Kenneally, '"A Tainted Source"? The *Irish Bulletin*, 1919–1920' in Mark O'Brien and Felix Larkin (eds), *Periodicals and Journalism in Twentieth-Century Ireland* (Dublin, 2014), pp. 92–8.

22 Report of Propaganda Department, 25 June 1920 (National Archives of Ireland [hereafter NAI], DE, 4/1/3); Walsh, *The News from Ireland*, p. 17; Arthur Mitchell, *Revolutionary Government in Ireland: Dáil Éireann, 1919–22* (Dublin, 1995), pp. 99–105.

23 Laurence Nugent, 2 Nov. 1953 (Military Archives of Ireland [hereafter MAI], BMH, witness statement [hereafter WS] 907), pp. 204, 174–5, 203–4; Larry Nugent interview (University College Dublin Archives [hereafter UCDA], Ernie O'Malley notebooks [hereafter EOMNbks], p. 70.

24 10 Apr. 1919, *Dáil Éireann: Minutes of Proceedings of the first parliament of the Republic of Ireland, 1919–1921: Official Record* (Dublin, 1994), p. 67.

25   W.J. Lowe and E.L. Malcolm, 'The Domestication of the Royal Irish Constabulary, 1836–
      1922', *Irish Economic and Social History*, XIX (1992), pp. 29–31, 35–6; Brian Hughes,
      Defying the IRA? Intimidation, Coercion, and Communities During the Irish Revolution
      (Liverpool, 2016), p. 21; W.J. Lowe, 'The War against the RIC, 1919–21', *Éire-Ireland*, vol.
      37, nos 3&4 (Fall/Winter 2002), p. 80.

26   Clare, Cork, Donegal, Galway, Kerry, Limerick, Longford, Mayo, Roscommon, Sligo, and
      Tipperary. Lowe, 'The War against the RIC', pp. 89, 90, 94; James Scannell, 'DMP Casualties
      During the War of Independence', *Dublin Historical Record*, vol. 61, no. 1 (Spring 2008), pp.
      5–19.

27   IRA Weekly Memorandum no. 4, 16 Oct. 1920 (UCDA, EOMNbks, P17b/127). A section
      of this notebook contains transcriptions of IRA correspondence from 1920, much of which
      is not otherwise in the public domain. Leeson, *Black & Tans*, p. 22; Lowe, 'The War against
      the RIC', p. 106.

28   A.E. Percival, 'Guerilla Warfare – Ireland 1920–21, pt. 1' (Imperial War Museum [hereafter
      IWM], A.E. Percival Papers [hereafter AEPP], P18/4/1); Charles Townshend, *The British
      Campaign in Ireland, 1919–1921: The Development of Political and Military Policies* (Oxford,
      1978), p. 55.

29   Peter Rigney, *The Irish Munitions Embargo of 1920: How Railwaymen and Dockers Defied
      an Empire* (Dublin, 2021).

30   Patrick Doyle, *Civilising Rural Ireland: The Co-operative Movement, Development and the
      Nation-State, 1889–1939* (Manchester, 2019), p. 123.

31   Terence M. Dunne, 'Emergence from the Embers: The Meath and Kildare Farm Labour
      Strike of 1919', *Saothar* 44 (2019), pp. 59–68, see p. 66. The classic accounts of the labour
      movement in this period are: Arthur Mitchell, *Labour in Irish Politics, 1890–1930: The Irish
      Labour Movement in an Age of Revolution* (New York, 1974); Emmet O'Connor, *Syndicalism
      in Ireland, 1917–1923* (Cork, 1988) and *A Labour History of Ireland, 1824–2000* (Dublin,
      2011), pp. 74–127.

32   The agitation commenced after the Irish branch of the new agricultural wages boards fixed
      a minimum wage for both male and female agricultural labourers in September 1917.
      Increased levels of violence and disruption in the first six months of 1921 made union
      organisation more difficult but strikes and agitation continued. Catriona Lisa Curtis, 'The
      agricultural labourer and the state in independent Ireland, 1922–26' (unpublished PhD,
      NUI Maynooth, June 2007), pp. 70–128; Dan Bradley, *Farm Labourers: Irish Struggle,
      1900–1976* (Belfast, 1988), pp. 43–73.

33   *The Skibbereen Eagle*, 4 Dec. 1920.

34   Leeson, *Black & Tans*, p. 24.

35   Ibid.

36   Townshend, *British Campaign*, pp. 110–11. Auxiliary companies in place by the end
      of November: Depot (Beggar's Bush Barracks, Dublin); A (Inistioge, Kilkenny); B
      (Newcastlewest, Limerick); C (Macroom, Cork); D (Galway); E (Sligo/Roscommon);
      F (Dublin); G (Killaloe, Clare); H (Tralee, Kerry); I (Mohill, Leitrim); J (Thomastown,
      Kilkenny). Another ten companies (L–S, Z) were created between late December 1920 and

May 1921 (https://theauxiliaries.com/companies/auxiliary-companies.html, accessed 27 Feb. 2020). This exceptionally well-researched website is the creation of David Grant. See also his https://www.cairogang.com/, accessed 30 Dec. 2021.

37   Charles Townshend, *The Republic: The Fight for Irish Independence, 1918–1923* (London, 2004), p. 151.

38   Tom Garvin, *1922: The Birth of Irish Democracy* (Dublin, 1996), pp. 67–8.

39   Townshend, *Republic*, pp. 151, 303.

40   Fisher to Austen Chamberlain, Bonar Law and Lloyd George, 15 May 1920 quoted in Eunan O'Halpin, *Head of the Civil Service: A Study of Sir Warren Fisher* (London and New York, 1989), pp. 84, 87, 88. Anderson was appointed joint under-secretary with James MacMahon, the most senior Roman Catholic in Dublin Castle. A.W. Cope and Mark Sturgis became assistant under-secretaries. Eunan O'Halpin, *The Decline of the Union: British Government in Ireland, 1892–1920* (Dublin, 1987), p. 208.

41   Townshend, *British Campaign*, p. 78.

42   These figures have been compiled from Irish Situation Cabinet Committee reports for 1920 (TNAUK, CAB 27/108). See also Townshend, *British Campaign*, p. 214.

43   Diary, 7 July 1920. See also 1, 10, 12 July; 12, 24 Sept. 1920 (IWM, Henry Wilson Papers [hereafter HWP], HHW 1/35/6 and 1/35/9); Townshend, *Republic*, pp. 154–7.

44   Townshend, *Republic*, pp. 154–72. The British Army were also carrying out reprisals.

45   For the text of this document see David Leeson, 'Select document: the Prescott-Decie letter', *IHS*, vol. 38, iss. 151 (May 2013), pp. 511–22, see p. 522. The relevant passages in Wilson's diaries have been in the public domain since 1927 and were cited by Charles Townshend in 1975. I am grateful for his advice on this issue. C.E. Callwell, *Field-Marshal Sir Henry Wilson, his Life and Diaries, Vol. II* (London, 1927), pp. 247, 251–2; Townshend, *British Campaign*, pp. 100–3. Keith Jeffery, 'Field Marshal Sir Henry Wilson: Myths and the Man', *Journal of the Society for Army Historical Research*, vol. 86, no. 345 (Spring 2008), pp. 57–82.

46   Townshend, *British Campaign*, p. 100; J.M. McEwen (ed.), *The Riddell Diaries, 1908–1923* (London, 1986), p. 314.

47   Tomás MacCurtain (Cork, 20 Mar. 1920), and George Clancy and Michael O'Callaghan (Limerick, 7 Mar. 1921).

48   Diary, 1 Oct. 1920. See also 1, 7, 10, 12 July; 12, 21, 23, 24, 29 Sept. 1920 (IWM, HWP, HHW 1/35/6 and 1/35/9).

49   House of Commons debate [hereafter HC] 20 October 1920, vol. 133, c.929.

50   *Report of the Labour Commission to Ireland* (London, 1921).

51   HC 11 November 1920, vol. 134, cc.1345–46.

52   This figure is taken from the 'Dead of the Irish Revolution' database.

53   The division was also in charge of two Leinster counties, Kilkenny and Wexford.

54   General Staff, 6th Division, 'The Rebellion in Ireland: Important Episodes, Outrages, Operations, and Encounters between Crown Forces and Rebels in the 6th Divisional Area, April 1920 to July 11th 1921' (IWM, Strickland Papers [hereafter SP], P362).

55   *The Skibbereen Eagle*, 26 June 1920.

56   Weekly Intelligence Summary, 6th Division, 19 July 1920 (IWM, SP, P363).

57 Unless otherwise stated, details of the 1st Battalion's experiences are drawn from July to November 1920 entries in their War Diary. Record of Service, 1st Bn, Manchester Regiment (Thameside Local Studies and Archives Centre [hereafter TLSAC], MR 1/1/2/5).

58 22 Sept. 1920, 1st Bn. Manchester Regiment (TLSAC, MR 1/1/2/5).

59 Auxiliary Division Register (TNAUK, Home Office [hereafter HO] 184/50).

60 8–12 Sep. 1920, 1st Bn, Manchester Regiment (TLSAC, MR 1/1/2/5).

61 *The Southern Star*, 18 and 25 Sep. 1920; *The Cork Examiner*, 25 Sep. 1920.

62 Eunan O'Halpin and Daithí Ó Corráin, *The Dead of the Irish Revolution* (London, 2020) [hereafter *DOIR*], p. 194.

63 Cafferata's account is confusing on several points, and he misidentifies Lehane as 'Lynch'. Raymond Cafferata memoir, n.d. (St Antony's College Oxford Middle Eastern Archive [hereafter OMEA], Cafferata Papers, 6B165-0044/LA 1 no.9); *DOIR*, p. 194.

64 *The Cork Examiner*, 11 Nov. 1920; *DOIR*, p. 215.

65 William Munro, 'The Auxiliary's Story', n.d. reproduced in James Gleeson, *Bloody Sunday* (London, 1962), p. 72. Summary of police reports Nov. 1920 (TNAUK CO 904/143). My thanks to Alison Campbell for information about Munro. For a different account of how the Auxiliaries responded to the incident see Donal Cronin, 'Ballingeary Volunteers 1920', *Ballingeary & Inchigeela Historical Society Journal*, 1997 (https://ballingearyhs.com/legacy/journal1997/ballingearyvolunteers1920.html, accessed 17 Dec. 2021).

66 Munro, 'The Auxiliary's Story', p. 72.

67 Ibid., p. 73; A.E. Percival, 'Guerilla warfare – Ireland 1920–21, pt. 2 (IWM, AEPP, P18/4/1); *DOIR*, p. 215.

68 Special Deasy Note, n.d. (UCDA, Mulcahy Papers [hereafter MP], P7/D/45); Basil Clarke to CJC Street, 29 Nov. 1920 (TNAUK, CO 904/26).

69 Special Deasy note, n.d. (UCDA, MP, P7/D/45).

70 O'Sullivan, BMH, WS 1478, p. 26; Con Flynn, 24 May 1957 (MAI, BMH, WS 1621), p. 13; Jeremiah Deasy, 6 June 1958 (MAI, BMH, WS 1738), p. 18.

71 Brigade Activities file, 5th (Kinsale) Bn (MAI, Military Service Pensions Collection [hereafter MSPC]/A/3(5)).

72 Seán Murphy, 20 June 1956 (MAI, BMH WS 1445), p. 9; Brigade Activities file, 5th (Kinsale) Bn (MAI, MSPC/A/3(5)).

73 Mossie Donegan, 28 Jan. 1952 (MAI, BMH, WS 639), p. 2.

74 Seán O'Driscoll, 20 Oct. 1956 (MAI, BMH, WS 1518), pp. 9–10.

75 Ted Sullivan interview, 10 Dec. 1950 (UCDA, EOMNbks, P17b/108), p. 8; Special Deasy note, n.d. (UCDA, MP, P7/D/45); Ted O'Sullivan, 24 Aug. 1956 (MAI, BMH, WS 1478) [hereafter O'Sullivan BMH, WS 1478], pp. 22–4.

76 Meda Ryan, *Tom Barry: Irish Freedom Fighter* (Cork, 2012), pp. 39–41.

CHAPTER 2. LIFE AND DEATH AT A BEND IN THE ROAD

1 DI Macroom to Under Secretary, Dublin Castle, 29. Nov. 1920 (TNAUK, CO 904/126).

2 *Irish Independent*, 1 Dec. 1920.

3   Townland names were anglicisations of Irish place names. The literal translations from Irish of the four townlands are (respectively) hillock of the hare, back of the cradle, sunny field and old stone fort. Kilmichael is likewise an anglicisation of *Cill mhichil*, Church of Saint Michael. Bruno O'Donoghue, *Parish Histories and Place Names of West Cork* (Bandon, 1983), pp. 249–52.

4   Lewis to 'Mother', 17 Dec. 1920 (Royal Aviation Museum of Western Canada (RAMWC), Alexander Lewis Papers (ALP)). My thanks to Head Archivist/Librarian Pam McKenzie for sending me a scanned copy of the original letter. For a full account of Lewis's life see Pam McKenzie, *The Lewis Letters: The Exploits of a 20th Century Aviator and Adventurer* (Victoria, Ca., 2017).

5   Michael Eyre, Chris Heaps and Alan Townsin, *Crossley* (Hersham, 2002), pp. 64, 80.

6   Peter Leslie, 'Armour in Ireland 1916–1923' in *Military Modelling* (June 1980), p. 513.

7   For British Pathé footage of Auxiliaries see www.britishpathe.com/video/staged-bridge-assault-1920, accessed 17 Dec. 2021; HC, 30 Nov. 1920, vol. 135, cc.1097–8.

8   British Rainfall Association, *British Rainfall*, 1920, vol. 60 (HMSO, London, 1921).

9   Munro, 'The Auxiliary's story', pp. 74–5; Raymond O. Cafferata memoir, n.d. (OMEA, Cafferata Papers, 6B165-0044/ LA1, no. 9).

10   Court of Inquiry on Kilmichael, 28 Nov. 1920 (TNAUK, WO 35/152). Unless otherwise cited, details of injuries, etc., are from this file.

11   Munro, 'The Auxiliary's story', pp. 74–5.

12   Kilmichael Ambush map, 25 Jan. 1921 (Bodleian Library, Francis Hemming Deposit, Box 19, ms CCC 536, QD.2.42, Irish Papers). Unless otherwise cited, the locations of the bodies are based on this map. Hemming was Hamar Greenwood's private secretary.

13   Court of Inquiry on Kilmichael, 28 Nov. 1920 (TNAUK, WO 35/152); *DOIR*, p. 207.

14   Conor Mulvagh, *The Irish Parliamentary Party at Westminster, 1900–18* (Manchester, 2016), pp. 112–14, 138–9; Michael Bentley, *The Liberal Mind 1914–1929* (Cambridge, 1977), pp. 151–2; Ivan Gibbons, *The British Labour Party and the Establishment of the Irish Free State, 1918–1924* (London, 2015), pp. 12–13.

15   HC 29 November 1920, vol. 135, cc.1070–3, 1077–8. Paul Seaward and Paul Silk, 'The House of Commons' in Vernon Bogdanor (ed.), *The British Constitution in the Twentieth Century* (Oxford, 2004), p. 148.

16   HC 29 November 1920, vol. 135, cc.1078, 1083–4.

17   McKee and Clancy were, respectively, O/C and vice O/C of the IRA's Dublin Brigade. Clune was a civilian. See Michael Foy, *Michael Collins's Intelligence War: The Struggle between the British and the IRA 1919–1921* (Chalford, 2008); Jane Leonard '"English Dogs" or "Poor Devils"? The Dead of Bloody Sunday Morning', and Eunan O'Halpin, 'Counting Terror: Bloody Sunday and The Dead of the Irish Revolution' in Fitzpatrick (ed.), *Terror in Ireland*, pp. 102–40, 141–57.

18   HC 22 November 1920, vol. 135, cc.34–43; *The Hull Daily Mail*, 23 Nov. 1920. Greenwood also denied Crown Force involvement in the death of Fr Michael Griffin in Galway, whose funeral had taken place earlier that day. It was (and is) widely believed that Griffin was killed by the police. *DOIR*, pp. 217–18.

19   Diary, 10 and 16 Nov. 1920 (IWM, HWP, HHW 1/35/11). Ronan Fanning, *Fatal Path: British Government and the Irish Revolution, 1910–1923* (London, 2013), pp. 241–2.

20   Townshend, *British Campaign*, p. 100; Peter Rowland, *Lloyd George* (London, 1975), p. 547; HC 20 October 1920, vol. 133 c.954.

21   A.J.S. Brady, *The Briar of Life* (Dublin, 2010), pp. 182–3; Charlie Browne, *The Story of the 7th: A Concise History of the 7th Battalion, Cork No.1 Brigade, Irish Republican Army from 1915 to 1921* (Ballydehob, 2007), p. 40.

22   *Evening Echo*, 13 Jan. 1921; Charles Browne, 19 June 1953 (MAI, BMH, WS 873) [hereafter Browne, BMH, WS 873], p. 30.

23   1 Dec. 1920, Manchester Regiment Record of Service (TLSAC, MR 1/2/4).

24   Patrick Dromey interview, 'The Boys of Kilmichael', 25 Oct. 1970 (RTÉ Radio Centre [RTERC], Donncha Ó Dúlaing (radio broadcast) [hereafter Ó Dúlaing], AR0020655/LA 000559).

25   I.O. [C.J.C. Street], *The Administration of Ireland, 1920* (London, 1921), pp. 157–60; Nevil Macready, *Annals of an Active Life*, vol. 2 (London., 1923). pp. 512–13.

26   *Belfast News-Letter*, 2 Dec. 1920. See Appendix 1 for a transcription of Pollard's original account edited by Basil Clarke and the full report as it appeared in the *Belfast News-Letter*.

27   The British did not recognise the IRA as a legitimate force or that the conflict in Ireland was a war. Therefore, Kilmichael could be classed as an atrocity, but not a war crime. As far as the IRA was concerned, however, they were an army fighting a war. Seán A. Murphy, *Kilmichael: A Battlefield Study* (Skibbereen, 2014), p. 163.

28   *Irish Bulletin*, 23 Dec. 1920; 'Erskine Childers Tells the Story of the War of Independence', *Catholic Press*, 22 Dec. 1921.

29   *Daily Dispatch*, 1 Dec. 1920. At least four different accounts of finding the bodies were published. See *The Freeman's Journal*, 1 Dec. 1920; *Daily Dispatch*, 2 Dec. 1920; *The Leicester Daily Post*, 3 Dec. 1920; *The Western Morning News*, 6 Dec. 1920; *The Teignmouth Post* and *The Scotsman*, 10 Dec. 1920.

30   For a catalogue of arrests, raids, attacks, shootings in Cork in Jan. 1921 and a summary of cases tried before the military courts in Cork between 10 Dec. 1920 and the Truce of 11 July 1921 see UCDA, Desmond and Mabel Fitzgerald Papers, P80/104 and P80/105.

31   Lewis to 'Mother', 17 Dec. 1920 (RAMWC, ALP).

32   Ibid.

33   Raymond O. Cafferata, 'The Kilmichael Ambush', n.d. (OMECA, Cafferata Papers, 6B165-0044/ LA1, no 7).

34   It was reproduced in the Irish Labour Party & Trade Union Congress pamphlet, *Who Burnt Cork City* (Dublin, Jan. 1921), pp. 18, 58–9. A copy of the letter is in the Mary Alden 'Molly' Childers Papers (MAI, BMH, CD 6/9/16/E). For a discussion of the letter see Gerry White, *The Burning of Cork* (Dublin and Cork, 2006), pp. 187–9.

35   Quoted in Hopkinson, *The Irish War of Independence*, p. 83.

36   General Staff, 6th Division, 'The Rebellion in Ireland' (IWM, SP, P362).

37   Diary, 1 Jan. 1921 (IWM, SP, P363).

38   *DOIR.*

39   Fr Dominic to Adjutant Cork No.1 Brigade, 15 Dec. 1920 [copy] (Cork Public Museum,
      Jim Hurley Papers, 2006.28.1). Lawrence William White, 'Father Dominic O'Connor' in
      Dictionary of Irish Biography [hereafter *DIB*] (https://www.dib.ie/biography/oconnor-
      father-dominic-a9752, accessed 17 Dec. 2021). The books of Maccabees were in the
      Vulgate Bible, which was the standard version until the Reformation.

40   Two members of K Company, Andrew K. Watson and Edwin S. Radford were arrested
      and charged with murder. For an account of Prendergast's death see the statement re the
      conduct of Crown Forces in Fermoy, 1 Dec. 1920 (UCDA, Desmond and Mabel Fitzgerald
      Papers, P80/93/1–4); *DOIR*, p. 247.

41   *DOIR*, pp. 248–9.

42   Operations report, 2nd Bn. Hampshire Regiment (TNAUK, WO 35/88b); Tom O'Neill, *The
      Battle of Clonmult: The I.R.A.'s Worst Defeat* (Dublin, 2006); *DOIR*, p. 307.

43   Diary entry, 4 Apr. 1921 (IWM, SP, P363).

44   Lionel Curtis, 'Ireland' in *The Round Table*, vol. 11, no. 43 (June 1921), pp. 499–500; Paul
      Canning, *British Policy Towards Ireland 1921–1941* (Oxford, 1985), p. 14.

45   Curtis, 'June 1921', p. 499.

46   Clarke to Street (Buxton Smith account), 1 Dec. 1920 (TNAUK, telegram and phone
      messages, CO 904/127).

47   'The Irish Republican Army (from captured documents only)' [hereafter IRACD]
      (TNAUK, WO 141/40). See also 6th Division GHQ, 17th Infantry Brigade, *Summary of
      Important Instructions*, June 1921 (IWM, SP, P363).

48   Paul McMahon, 'British intelligence and the Anglo-Irish Truce, July–December 1921', *IHS*,
      vol. 35, iss. 140 (Nov. 2007), pp. 520–2, 525; Townshend, *British Campaign*, p. 125.

49   'O' [Ormond Winter], A report on the Intelligence branch of the Chief of Police (TNAUK,
      CO 904/156/b).

50   Memo, MP, 19 Nov. 1920 (TNAUK CO 904/168); Clarke to Street, 29 Nov. 1920 (TNAUK,
      CO 904/26). Michael Hopkinson (ed.), *The Last Days of Dublin Castle: The Mark Sturgis
      Diaries* (Dublin, 1999), p. 250. It is also worth pointing out that even IRA veterans knew
      that captured documents published in the press by both the British and the 'Staters' during
      the Civil War (1922–3) were, for the most part, genuine. See Frank Aiken memoir, *c.* 1925
      (MAI, Mollie Childers Papers, BMH CD 6/36/22–23); Lynch to O'Malley, 28 Sep. 1922,
      O'Malley, Cormac and Anne Dolan (eds), *No Surrender Here! The Civil War Papers of Ernie
      O'Malley 1922–1924* (Dublin, 2008) [hereafter *No Surrender Here*], pp. 232–3; Florence
      O'Donoghue, *No Other Law* (Dublin: Anvil Books, 1986 [1st ed. 1954]), p. 299; Moss
      Twomey, April 1950 (UCDA, EOM, P17b/107), pp. 38–9. For another instance in which
      Ryan assumes that captured documents are forgeries, see Meda Ryan, *Liam Lynch: The Real
      Chief* (Dublin and Cork, 1986), pp. 146–7.

51   Various indexes and epitomes (Liddel Hart Centre for Military Archives, Charles Foulkes
      Papers, Foulkes, 7/24).

52   Instructions for compiling the order of battle of the IRA, n.d., and 'Blacklist no. 2 *c*. June
      1921 (IWM, Jarvis Papers, 98/11/1); Percival, Guerilla warfare – Ireland 1920–21, II (IWM,
      EP, P18/4/1); 'O' [Ormond Winter], A report on the Intelligence branch of the Chief of
      Police (TNAUK, CO 904/156/b); Irish Command, 'Record of the Rebellion in Ireland
      in 1920–21 and the part played by the Army in dealing with it' [hereafter RORI], vol. II
      (TNAUK, WO 141 93).

53   IRACD, printed June 1921 (TNAUK, WO 141/40). It was an addendum to an earlier pamphlet,
      'Sinn Féin and the Irish Volunteers' published in 1919. It was completed by June 1921 but does
      not seem to have been printed until October. RORI, vol. II (TNAUK, WO 141 93); Notes, Sept.
      1922 (TNAUK, WO 141/94); Brind to Strickland, 1 Mar. 1922 (IWM, SP, P363).

54   RORI, vol. IV, 6th Division [Jan/Feb. 1922] (TNAUK WO 141/93); IRACD (TNAUK, WO
      141/40).

55   RORI, vol. II.

56   For the forgery arguments see Brian P. Murphy, *The Origins & Organisation of British
      Propaganda in Ireland 1920* (Millstreet, 2006), pp. 62–74; Ryan, *Tom Barry: IRA Freedom
      Fighter* (Cork, 2012), pp. 73–81. For the reasons why it is almost certainly genuine see
      Townshend, *Republic*, p. 215; William Kautt, *Ambushes and Armour: The Irish Rebellion
      1919–1921* (Dublin and Portland, 2010), pp. 109–14.

57   IRACD (TNAUK, WO 141/40).

58   *The Southern Star*, 3 Dec. 1921.

59   *The Cork Examiner*, 29 Nov. and 1 Dec. 1921; *The Southern Star*, 3 Dec 1921.

60   November 1921 newspaper articles relating to the Essex Regimental Museum, Essex
      Regiment Collection (ERCB, 6,7).

61   RORI, vol. IV (TNAUK, WO 141/93).

62   Service records of Thomas B. Barry (TNAUK, WO 363).

63   *The Southern Star*, 22 Jan. 1916. Thanks to Gerry White for this reference.

64   Thomas Barry, disability pension card (Western Front Association, PRC Ledgers/562/13/
      MB/690); Ryan, *Tom Barry* (2012), p. 152.

65   IRA membership was not considered grounds for stopping an award. Paul Taylor, *Heroes
      or Traitors? Experiences of Southern Irish Soldiers Returning from the Great War 1919–1939*
      (Liverpool, 2015), pp. 127–8; Michael Robinson '"Nobody's children?": the Ministry of
      Pensions and the treatment of disabled Great War Veterans in the Irish Free State, 1921–
      1939', *Irish Studies Review*, 25:3 (2017), p. 318.

66   Edgar Jones and Simon Wessely, *Shell Shock to PTSD: Military Psychiatry from 1900 to the
      Gulf War* (Hove and New York, 2005), pp. 35, 51, 204–5; Joel D. Howell, "Soldier's Heart":
      the Redefinition of Heart Disease and Speciality Formation in Early Twentieth Century
      Great Britain', *Medical History*, supplement no. 5 (1985), pp. 34–52, see p. 44.

67   The National Federation of Discharged and Demobilised Sailors and Soldiers barred
      commissioned officers from membership and lobbied for veterans' pensions to be made
      a statutory right. Niall Barr, *The Lion and the Poppy: British Veterans, Politics, and Society,
      1921–1939* (Westport, Conn; London, 3005), p. 12.

68 'Candidates who failed to pass the Examination, Ireland Division, Male Clerk Reconstruction Scheme', Dec. 1919 (TNAUK, Min of Labour, CSC 10/4505). Gerry White, 'From Gunner to Guerrilla – Tom Barry's Road to Rebellion', *The Irish Times*, 3 June 2020; Hart, *The IRA & Its Enemies*, pp. 30–2.

69 Ted O'Sullivan, 10 Dec. 1950 (UCDA, EOMNbks, P17b/108), p. 8.

70 Ryan, *The Tom Barry Story* (1982), pp. 17, 20.

71 K Company Auxiliary Notebook, Jan.–Mar. 1921 (BMH, Flor Begley, CD 31). I am grateful to Jerry O'Callaghan for digital images of the cover pages and fly leaves not copied by the BMH. Ernie O'Malley and Seán Hales, the Cork TD, were both named in contemporary press reports as having led the ambush. The authorities maintained that some of the slain Auxiliaries' personal items were found in the house where O'Malley was captured on 9 December 1920 just outside Inistioge, Kilkenny. 'O' [Ormond Winter], A Report on the Intelligence Branch of the Chief of Police (TNAUK, CO 904/156/b) p. 58; Macready, *Annals of an Active Life, Vol. II*, p. 512; *The Hull Daily Mail*, 6 Nov. 1922; *Belfast News-Letter*, 13 Dec. 1922; *The Londonderry Sentinel*, 14 Dec. 1922.

72 Chambre Baldwin (72947), a former lieutenant in the Royal West African Frontier Force and the Gloucester Regiment, was K Company intelligence officer from 28 Nov. 1920 to 19 Mar. 1921 (TNAUK, HO 184/37), p. 193 (http://theauxiliaries.com/men-alphabetical/men-b/baldwin-c/baldwin.html, accessed 21 Dec. 2021).

73 Patrick O'Brien, 5 Mar. 1951 (MAI, BMH, WS 812) [hereafter O'Brien, BMH, WS 812], p. 19.

74 Tim Keating, a member of Caheragh Company, 5th (Bantry) Battalion, was arrested on 14 January 1921. The anonymous source 'from Bandon' is probably Patrick Coakley, a Volunteer from Crosspound Company 1st (Bandon) Battalion who was arrested after the Upton Ambush (15 February). Flor Begley interview, 18 Oct. 1950 (UCDA, EOMNbks, P17b/111); H/Crosspound Company nominal roll (MAI, MSPC/RO/47); G/Caheragh Company nominal roll (MAI, MSPC/RO/53); *The Southern Star*, 27 Nov. 1971.

75 *DOIR*, p. 314. I am indebted to local historian Don Wood for additional information regarding William Howe and Richard Cox. He is of the view that neither man informed on the IRA in relation to who killed Cotter.

76 Blacklist, *c.* autumn 1920 (ERM, ER, ERCB/6). Several names also appear on a list covering all counties in the martial law area compiled *c.* June 1921. 'Blacklist No.2', *c.* June 1921 (IWM, Jarvis Papers, 98/11/1).

77 Jack Hennessy, 23 Aug. 1955 (MAI, BMH, WS 1234) [hereafter Hennessy, BMH, WS 1234], p. 8.

78 'Ireland', *The British Medical Journal* [hereafter *TBMJ*], vol. 1, no. 3139 (26 Feb. 1921), p. 319; 'Ireland', *TBMJ*, vol. 1, no. 3143 (26 Mar. 1921), p. 477.

79 Barry, *Guerilla Days*, p. 56.

80 Jack Hennessy's 1925 wound pension application mentions both men as having treated him at Granure after the ambush. John 'Jack' Hennessy, application for a wound pension, 1 Mar. 1925; medical report, 13 May 1925 (MAI, MSPC, DP4354).

81 *The Cork Examiner*, 3 Apr. 1967.

82   Denis Lordan, 18 Dec. 1950 (MAI, BMH WS 470), p. 20; *1921 Guy's Cork Almanac* (Cork, 1921), p. 20; *1925 Guy's Cork Almanac* (Cork, 1925), p.132.

83   William Desmond, 19 Apr. 1953 (BMH, WS 832), pp. 36–7. Desmond was attached to Newcestown Company, 1st (Bandon) Battalion. This passage is currently redacted, one of some fifty-seven witness statements that were censored by the Military Archives before the release of the collection in March 2003. The redacted sections of all but one of these statements can now be consulted in the archive. Ballineen Company, 3rd (Dunmanway) Brigade Activities (MAI, MSPC/A/3/4).

84   Barry's successor, one of the men who had attempted to assassinate Strickland in September 1920, was hardly less provocative. Townshend, *Republic*, pp. 311–12; 18 July 1921, Diary (IWM, SP, P363).

85   Diary, 16 July 1921 (IWM, SP, P363); *Belfast News-Letter* and *The Cork Examiner*, 19 July 1921.

86   Lynch to Mulcahy, 4 Oct. 1921 (UCDA, MP, P7/A/26).

87   *The Londonderry Sentinel*, 10 Sep. 1921. Before joining the RIC in May 1920, Prescott-Decie had been a Royal Artillery officer attached to the Irish Command's General Staff, Army Headquarters (TNAUK, WO 35/215); Circulars, Inspector General, 17 May 1920 (TNAUK, HO 184/119), p. 263.

88   The MPs were Captain Charles Foxcroft, Secretary of the Society for the Relief of Distressed Southern Irish Loyalists and Colonel Martin Archer-Shee. *The Freeman's Journal*, 28 Oct. 1921.

89   *The Southern Star*, 1 Oct. 1921.

90   18 July, 29 Aug. 1921, diary entries (IWM, SP); Barry to Adj. Gen. IRA, 15 July 1921 (Digital Repository of Ireland [hereafter DRI], Dáil Éireann [hereafter DE] 2/255 via DRI (https://repository.dri.ie/catalog/t148v311v, accessed 17 Dec. 2021); *An t-Óglách*, vol. III, no. 22, 19 Aug. 1921.

91   Thomas Bernard Barry (TNAUK, WO 35/206/5).

92   MacMahon, *British Intelligence*, p. 526; Charles Townshend, 'The Irish War of Independence: context and meaning' in Pat Brennan (ed.), *Guide to the Military Service Pensions Collection (1916–1923)*, pp. 110–16, see p. 116.

93   Collins to de Valera, 20 July 1921 (DRI, DE 2/244).

94   O/C 1st Southern Division [hereafter 1SD] to CS, 4 Oct. 1921 (UCDA, MP, P7/A/26/88); CS to O/C 1SD, 7 Oct. 1921 (UCDA, MP, P7/A/26/85); [CS] to A Liam a Loagh [Loach] [Liam the hero], 7 Oct. 1921 (UCDA, MP, P7/A/26/87); *An t-Óglách*, vol. III, no. 22, 19 Aug. 1921; *Éire: The Irish Nation*, 5 Jan. 1924.

95   Wyse Power to Sighle Humphreys, 21 Nov. 1921 (UCDA, SH, P106/732).

96   D/Eng to CS, 19 July 1921 (UCDA, MP, P7/A/22/144); Barry to CS, 21 July 1921 (UCDA, MP, P7/A/22/180–183 & 218–219); CS to O/C 1SD, 22 July 1921(UCDA, MP, P7/A/22/223); Barry to CS and 'all brigades in the martial law area', 23 July 1921 (UCDA, MP, P7/A/22/200); CS to O/C 1SD, 10 Oct. 1921 (UCDA, MP, P7/A/26/81–82).

97   Barry to D/Org., 27 Sep 1921 (UCDA, P7/A/26/89); O/C 1SD to CS, 4 Oct. 1921 (P7/A/26/88).

98   [CS] to A Liam a Loagh [Loach] [Liam the hero], 7 Oct. 1921 (UCDA, MP, P7/A/
     26/87).

99   Fintan Murphy to CS, 8 Oct. 1921 (UCDA, MP, P7/A/26/88); CS to O/C 1SD, 10 Oct.
     1921 (UCDA, MP, P7/A/26/81–2). William Murphy, *Political Imprisonment & the Irish,
     1912–1921* (Oxford, 2014), pp. 224–30.

100 O/C 1SD to CS, 13 Oct. 1921 (UCDA, MP, P7/A/26/84).

101 Liaison officers to CS, 19 Oct. 1921 (UCDA, MP, P7/A/26/256–257).

102 Ryan misattributes this quote to Barry. Ryan, *Tom Barry* (2012), p. 203; O/C 1SD to CS,
     27 Oct. 1921 (UCDA, MP, P7/A/26/32). *The Freeman's Journal*, 13 Oct. 1921; Barry to O/C
     Cork I Brigade, 25 Oct. 1921 (UCDA, MP, P7/A/26/79); O/C 1SD to CS, 31 Oct. 1921
     (UCDA, MP, P7/A/26/31); Liaison officers to CS, 19 Oct. 1921 (UCDA, MP, P7/A/26/256–
     257); Barry to D/Org, 27 Sep 1921(UCDA, MP, P7/A/26/89); Barry to Collins, 29 Sep.
     1921; Collins to Barry, 5 Oct. 1921 (NABS/DRI, DE/2/255).

103 Wyse Power to Sighle Humphreys, 7 Feb. 1922 (UCDA, Sighle Humphreys Papers,
     P106/743/1).

CHAPTER 3. *RUSE DE GUERRE* OR ATROCITY?

1   *La Vanguardia* (Buenos Aires), 1 and 3 Dec. 1920; *Le Temps* (Paris), 1 Dec. 1920. The
     analysis that follows draws on the post-ambush news coverage of Kilmichael and its
     aftermath in just over 250 Irish, British and international newspapers.

2   *Evening Echo* (Cork), *Evening Herald* (Dublin), *Waterford Evening News, The Glasgow
     Citizen, Liverpool Echo, The Manchester Evening News, The Midland Daily Telegraph,
     Yorkshire Telegraph and Star, The Evening News (Portsmouth)*, 29 Nov. 1920. Daniel R.
     Headrick, *The Invisible Weapon: Telecommunications and International Politics, 1851–1945*
     (Oxford, 1991), pp. 46, 98–111; Simon J. Potter, 'Empire and the English Press, *c.* 1857–
     1914' in Simon J. Potter (ed.), *Newspapers and Empire in Ireland and Britain: Reporting the
     British Empire, c. 1857–1921* (Dublin and Portland, 2004), p. 41; Peter Puntis, 'International
     News Agencies, News-Flow, and the USA–Australia Relationship from the 1920s till the
     End of the Second World War', *Media History*, 18:3–4 (2012), pp. 424–5.

3   Walsh, *The News from Ireland*, p. 19.

4   Stephen Kern, *The Culture of Time & Space, 1880–1918* (Cambridge, Mass., 2003), pp.
     34–9.

5   Rachel Matthews, *The History of the Provincial Press in England* (London, 2017), p. 90.

6   Adrian Bingham, '"An Organ of Uplift?": the Popular Press and Political Culture in Interwar
     Britain' in Sarah Newman and Matt Houlbrook (eds), *The Press and Popular Culture in
     Interwar Europe* (Abington, 2014), p. 13.

7   *The Newspaper Press Directory* (London, 1917), p. 3.

8   Matthews, *History of the Provincial Press*, pp. 114–16, 142–4.

9   Christopher Doughan, *Voice of the Provinces* (Liverpool, 2020), p. 15; Morash, *A History of
     the Media in Ireland* (Cambridge, 2010), p. 116.

10   Adrian Bingham and Martin Conboy, *Tabloid Century: The Popular Press in Britain, 1896 to the Present* (Oxford, 2015), p. 64.

11   Walsh, *The News from Ireland*, pp. 72–3.

12   *The Times*, 30 June 1920; *The Londonderry Sentinel*, 30 Nov. 1920; Adrian Gregory, 'A clash of cultures: The British press and the opening of the Great War' in Troy R.E. Paddock (ed.), *A Call to Arms: Propaganda, Public Opinion and Newspapers in the Great War* (Westport, Conn., 2004), p. 18; J.M. McEwen, 'Northcliffe and Lloyd George at War, 1914–1918', *Historical Journal*, vol. 24, no. 3 (Sept 1981), pp. 651–72.

13   Walsh, *The News from Ireland*, pp. 95–8; Henry Wickham Steed, *Through Thirty Years, 1892–1922: A Personal Narrative*, vol. II (London, 1924), p. 352. Ben Novick, *Conceiving Revolution: Irish Nationalist Propaganda during the First World War* (Dublin, 2001), p. 167.

14   Boyce, *Englishmen and Irish Troubles*, pp. 57–60; Walsh, *The News from Ireland*, pp. 72–5, 118–19; David Ayerst, *Guardian. Biography of a Newspaper* (London, 1971), p. 419.

15   *The Daily News*, 23 Nov. 1920.

16   Walsh, *The News from Ireland*, pp. 25–6, 198; J.M. McEwen, 'George's Acquisition of the *Daily Chronicle* in 1918', *Journal of British Studies*, vol. 22, no. 1 (Autumn 1982), pp. 127–44; Philipp Gibbs, *The Pageant of the Years* (London and Toronto, 1946), pp. 266–7.

17   Richard Evans, *From the Frontline: The Extraordinary Life of Sir Basil Clarke* (Stroud, 2013), ebook, pl. 3343.

18   Major Hugh Bertie Campbell Pollard (1888–1966) and Sir William Young Darling (1885–1962) were, respectively, press officer and secretary of the Information Section of the Police Authority. Hugh Pollard (TNAUK, Special Operations Executive Personnel File, HS 9/1200/5); *Irish Independent*, 27 Nov. 1920; Memo, Battle of Tralee, 13 Nov. 1920 (TNAUK, CO 904/168); *Report of the Labour Commission on Ireland* (London, 1921), pp. 43–51; *The Illustrated London News*, 27 Nov. and 11 Dec. 1920 (for their apology).

19   Evans, *From the Frontline*, ebook, pl. 3601; Ian Kenneally, *The Paper Wall: Newspapers and Propaganda in Ireland, 1919–1921* (Cork, 2008), pp. 39–40.

20   Ireland: *Belfast Evening Telegraph, Belfast News-Letter, The Freeman's Journal, Irish Independent, The Irish Times*, 2 Dec. 1920. Britain: *The Aberdeen Daily Journal, Daily Chronicle, Daily Dispatch, Daily Express, Daily Herald, The Daily Mail, Daily Sketch, The Daily Telegraph, The Devon and Exeter Gazette, The Evening News (Glasgow), Dundee Evening Telegraph, The Glasgow Citizen, The Hull Daily Mail, The Lancashire Daily Post, The Leicester Daily Post, Lincolnshire Echo, The Liverpool Courier, The Manchester Guardian, The Morning Post, The Newcastle Daily Chronicle, The Newcastle Daily Journal, The Scotsman, Sheffield Daily Telegraph, The Shields Daily News, The Times, Western Daily Press, Western Evening Herald, Western Mail, The Yorkshire Herald, Yorkshire Post*, 2 Dec. 1920. See also *The Western Gazette*, 3 Dec. 1920; *The Fifeshire Advertiser, Kent Messenger, Liverpool Weekly Courier, Liverpool Weekly Post, The Wiltshire Telegraph*, 4 Dec. 1920. *The Orkney Herald*, 8 Dec. 1920, *The Scotsman*, 10 Dec. 1920; *The Army and Navy Gazette*, 11 Dec. 1920. Australia: *The Daily Examiner* (Grafton, NSW), *The Maitland Daily Mercury*

(NSW), 3 Dec. 1920. India: *Amrita Bazar Patrika*, 5 Dec. 1920; *The Times of India*, 6 Dec. 1920. USA: *The New York Herald, The New York Times*, 2 Dec. 1920.

21   *Evening Echo*, 29 Nov. 1920; *Evening Herald, The Freeman's Journal, The Irish News*, 30 Nov. 1920; *Daily Chronicle*, 30 Nov. 1920; *Belfast News-Letter*, 1 Dec. 1920; *The Pall Mall Gazette*, 30 Nov. 1920; *The Evening Telegraph (Dundee)*, 2 Dec. 1920; *The Daily Colonist*, 30 Nov. and 1 Dec. 1920; *Greymouth Evening Star*, 2 Dec. 1920; *Santa Ana Register*, 1 Dec. 1920.

22   The Irish Office in London was a branch of the British civil service that liaised between the Dublin Castle administration and Whitehall. Its main function was to support the Chief Secretary for Ireland in his cabinet and parliamentary work. Pollard thought that some of the Auxiliaries who died had appeared in a film clip of the discovery of an illicit still (which had been staged). I am grateful to Martin Dwan for his help in sourcing the footage (www. britishpathe.com/video/staged-bridge-assault-1920, accessed 17 Dec. 2021).

23   *Evening Herald* and *Waterford Evening News*, 29 Nov. 1920.

24   *The Freeman's Journal*, 30 Nov. 1920.

25   *Evening Echo*, 29 Nov. 1920.

26   On 30 November 1920, *The Cork Examiner* published the first Press Association telegrams, the *Evening Echo* report and another report from Macroom stating that fourteen Auxiliaries had been killed.

27   *Irish Bulletin*, 2 Dec. 1920.

28   *The Globe, The Pall Mall Gazette, The Westminster Gazette*, 30 Nov. 1920.

29   Dublin Castle statement, 30 Nov. 1920 (TNAUK, CO 904/68/203). Not all newspapers mentioned the hatchets. See *Evening Herald, Dublin Evening Telegraph*, 30 Nov. 1920.

30   *Daily Chronicle, Daily Dispatch, The Lancashire Daily Post*, 30 Nov. 1920.

31   *Daily Chronicle, The Shields Daily News, The New York Times, Evening World* (New York), *Telegraph* (Brisbane), 30 Nov. 1920; *Irish Independent, The Yorkshire Herald, Glasgow Citizen, Warwick Daily News, Queensland Times, Darling Downs Gazette, Sidney Morning Herald*, 1 Dec. 1920; *The Liberator* (Tralee), *The Nenagh Guardian, The Kerryman, Donegal News, The Sligo Champion, Fermanagh Herald, Leader* (India), 4 Dec. 1920.

32   *Evening Echo*, 30 Nov. 1920.

33   Ireland and Britain: *The Cork Examiner, Evening Echo, Daily Chronicle, The Devon and Exeter Gazette*, 30 Nov. 1920; *Aberdeen Daily Journal, Belfast News-Letter, Daily Dispatch, The Daily Mail, The Daily Telegraph, The Derry Journal, The Devon and Exeter Gazette, The Evening Chronicle, Edinburgh Evening News, The Freeman's Journal, The Glasgow Citizen, Glasgow Evening News, Illustrated Chronicle, The Irish Times, The Irish News, The Leeds Mercury, The Leicester Daily Post, The Liverpool Courier, The Morning Post, The Newcastle Daily Journal, Sheffield Independent, The Shields Daily News, Sunderland Daily Echo, The Times, Western Evening Herald, Western Mail, The Yorkshire Herald, Yorkshire Post*, 1 Dec. 1920; USA: *The New York Times*; 1 Dec. 1920; New South Wales, Australia: *The Daily Examiner, Riverine Herald, The Daily Observer, The Sun, The Newcastle Sun*, 2 Dec. 1920.

34   Irish and British journalists representing different press agencies and newspapers often joined forces on the ground. *The Freeman's Journal* worked closely with *The Manchester*

Guardian. The Cork Examiner was a founding member of the Press Association. George Scott, *Reporter Anonymous: The Story of the Press Association* (London, 1968), p. 19; Ayerst, *Guardian*, p. 419.

35   Munro, 'The Auxiliary's Story', p. 77; *The Irish Times*, 1 Dec. 1920.

36   *The Freeman's Journal*, 1 Dec. 1920; *Daily Dispatch, Daily Sketch, The Irish Times*, 2 Dec 1920.

37   *Belfast News-Letter, The Cork Examiner, Cork Echo, The Londonderry Sentinel, The Evening News (London)*, 1 Dec. 1920; *The Daily Mirror*, 2 Dec. 1920.

38   *The Irish Times, Belfast News-Letter, Yorkshire Post, Daily Dispatch, Sheffield Independent, The Times, The Evening Chronicle, Nottingham Evening Post, The Morning Post, Daily Sketch, The Newcastle Daily Chronicle, Daily Chronicle* (London), *The Dundee Courier, The New York Times*, 1 Dec. 1920. The Central News Agency, founded in 1871, supplied copy to the London papers but was considered less reliable than other agencies. Two of its journalists are widely suspected of having authored the infamous 1888 Jack the Ripper letters. L. Perry Curtis Jr, *Jack the Ripper and the London Press* (New Haven, 2001), pp. 59, 292, 316.

39   *Daily Sketch*, 1 and 2 Dec. 1920; *The Daily Mirror*, 1 and 3 Dec. 1920.

40   *The Freeman's Journal*, 1 Dec. 1920.

41   *The Cork Examiner*, 1 Dec. 1920. The Gneeve's Cross account also appeared on the same day in the *Belfast News-Letter, Evening Echo, The Freeman's Journal, Irish Independent, The Irish News, The Derry Journal, The Daily News* (London), *Devon and Exeter Gazette, The Edinburgh Evening News, The Evening News* (London), *The Glasgow Citizen, The Manchester Guardian, Western Daily Press, The Western Morning News, Yorkshire Post*.

42   *The Manchester Guardian*, 1 Dec. 1920. The report also stated that a new '"official" account' claimed the patrol was fired on by men marching in the road. The *Guardian* reports were most likely written by either Alfred Powell Wandsworth or Charles R. Green, who had both been in Ireland since 24 November. Reporters' Diary, 1 Jan.–31 Dec. 1920 (John Rylands Library, *The Manchester Guardian* Archive, GDN/53).

43   *The Edinburgh Evening News*, 1 Dec. 1920.

44   Ned Young, 17/04/1956 (MAI, BMH, WS 1402) [hereafter Young, BMH, WS 1402]. I am not suggesting that Young was the source for the newspaper report.

45   See Appendix 1 for transcriptions of Pollard's telegram and the 'official' version based on it, which appeared in the press on 2 Dec. 1920. The *Irish Independent's* published version of Forde's account is given in Appendix 3.

46   See Appendix 1. Major Buxton Smith (1877–1922), a native of Beccles, Suffolk, and son of a corn merchant, was a maltster and former officer in the RFA. He served in France and Egypt during the Great War, joining the Auxiliaries in July 1920. He resigned at the end of February 1921 and committed suicide in London in 1922. Auxiliary Division–Journal No. 1 (TNAUK, Royal Irish Constabulary Service Records, HO 184/52).

47   Ryan Linkof, *Public Images: Celebrity, Photojournalism, and the Making of the Tabloid Press* (London, 2018), ebook, para. 8.10. para. 8.32, para. 10.12.

48 *Daily Sketch, Daily Dispatch, The Daily Mirror, The Leeds Mercury, The Liverpool Courier, Nottingham Evening Post, Sheffield Independent,* 3 Dec. 1920; *The Cork Examiner, The Freeman's Journal, The Sphere* (London), 4 Dec. 1920; *The Illustrated London News, Le Monde Illustré,* 11 Dec. 1920. British press photographers working for the dailies continued to use large-format plate cameras until the 1950s. Peter Twaites, 'Circles of Confusion and Sharp Vision: British News Photography, 1919–39' in Peter Catterall, Colin Seymour-Ure, Adrian Smith (eds), *Northcliffe's Legacy: Aspects of the British Popular Press, 1896–1996* (London, 2000), p. 110.

49 James Jarché, *People I Have Shot* (London, 1934), p. 217; 'Obituary' Hannen Swaffer, *The Stage and Television Today,* 28 Jan. 1962.

50 *The Illustrated Chronicle,* 1 Dec. 1920. Crake's father-in-law worked for the paper.

51 The two clergymen were Rev. Alfred Ellis Farrow and Rev. Richard M. Marsh-Dunn. *The Newcastle Daily Journal, Sheffield Independent, The Yorkshire Herald, Yorkshire Post,* 6 Dec. 1920; *Teignmouth Post,* 10 Dec. 1920.

52 For popular support garnered in northern England and lowland Scotland by the Ulster Unionist campaign against home rule, see Jackson, *Popular Opposition,* pp. 1–28. A not insignificant cohort of the Irish diaspora, radical Liberals, British Labourites (despite the caginess of the party leadership) and the (much smaller) anarchist, socialist and communist left supported Irish self-determination. Mo Moulton, *Ireland and the Irish in Interwar England* (Cambridge, 2014), p. 59.

53 *The Morning Post,* 30 Nov. 1920.

54 *The Liverpool Courier,* 1 Dec. 1920.

55 A *ruse de guerre* is a war stratagem, a legitimate act of war. Ambushes are classed as *ruses de guerre* unless there is some kind of perfidy or treachery involved.

56 *Evening News* (Glasgow), 30 Nov. 1920.

57 *The Communist,* 2 Dec. 1920.

58 Ross McKibbin, *The Ideologies of Class: Social Relations in Britain, 1880–1950* (Oxford, 1990), pp. 21–3.

59 *The Croydon Advertiser & Surrey County Reporter,* 4, 12 and 18 Dec. 1920; *The Sentinel* (Southgate), 10 Dec. 1920.

60 *The Croydon Advertiser & Surrey County Reporter,* 4 Dec. 1920.

61 *Daily Herald,* 4 Dec. 1920.

62 *Birmingham Gazette, Liverpool Echo,* 4 Dec. 1920.

63 *The Sunday Post* (Glasgow), 5 Dec. 1920; *Daily Dispatch, Evening News* (Glasgow), 6 Dec. 1920. Moulton, *Ireland and the Irish,* pp. 52–4, 73.

64 Moulton, *Ireland and the Irish,* p. 81.

65 Simon (1873–1954) was a lawyer and then an Independent Liberal MP. He later became a cabinet minister in the Baldwin and Chamberlain Conservative governments. Memoirs of Captain George Berkeley (NLI, GFH Berkeley Papers, mss 10,924–8).

66 *The Illustrated Chronicle,* 4 Dec. 1920; Simon to Childers, 30 Jan. 1921; Simon to Childers, 20 Jan. 1921 (NLI, Erskine Childers Papers, ms 48,056/2); *Daily Dispatch,* 22 Nov. 1920.

67 Gibbons, *British Labour Party*, p. 72.

68 Ibid., p. 70.

69 *The Cork Examiner*, 12 Dec. 1920.

70 *Belfast News-Letter*, 12 Jan. 1921.

71 D.R. Miers, 'Compensating Policemen for Criminal Injuries', *Irish Jurist*, new series, vol. 7, no. 2 (Winter 1972), pp. 241–2; Albert D. Bolton, *The Criminal Injuries (Ireland) Acts* (Dublin, 1922).

72 *Evening Echo*, 12 and 13 Jan. 1921; *The Freeman's Journal* and *The Irish Times*, 17 Jan. 1921; *The Freeman's Journal*, 7 Apr. 1921; *The Cork Examiner*, 13 June 1921; Note 14, *c.* 1925, Frederick H. Forde (TNAUK, WO 339, 43241).

73 I am indebted to Alan Guthrie for access to his papers relating to the death of his uncle.

74 An Garda Síochána to Dep. Justice, 12 Aug. 1925 and 3 Dec. 1926 (NAI, Jus/2019/58/5); Kevin Corcoran, *Saving Eden: The Gearagh and Irish Nature* (Co. Cork, 2021), pp. 100–1; Browne, BMH, WS 873, p. 29.

75 They were awarded £70. *Evening Echo*, 13 Jan. 1921.

76 *The Irish Times*, 13 Jan. 1921; Appendix D, *American Commission*, pp. 129–31; HC 21 Feb. 1921, vol. 38, cc.625–723.

77 *Evening Echo*, 12 Jan. 1921; *The Cork Examiner*, 9 Apr. 1921 and 21 Oct. 1926.

78 *The Skibbereen Eagle*, 23 Apr. 1921. Establishing when claimants actually received payment is harder to determine. O'Brien received £300 and £22 14s in 1924, *Iris Oifigiuil*, 1 Jan. 1924; D.R. Miers, 'Paying for Malicious Injuries Claims', *Irish Jurist*, New Series, vol. 5, no. 1 (Summer 1970), pp. 57–8.

79 *DOIR*, p. 544.

80 *The Northern Whig*, 25 Mar. and 3 Apr. 1922; *Belfast Weekly Telegraph*, 15 Apr. 1922; *Belfast Telegraph*, 25 Mar. 1924; *Ballymena Weekly Telegraph & Larne Times*, 15 Apr., 26 Aug. and 2 Sep. 1922, 29 Mar. 1924; Tim Wilson, '"The most terrible assassination that has yet stained the name of Belfast": The McMahon murders in context', *IHS*, vol. 37, iss. 145 (May 2010), pp. 83–6.

81 Deirdre Nuttall, *Different and the Same: A Folk History of the Protestants of Independent Ireland* (Dublin, 2020), pp. 57–75; J. Morrow to J.R.W. Goulden, 22 Jan. 1956 (Trinity College Dublin Manuscripts [hereafter TCDM], J.R.W. Goulden Papers [hereafter JRWGP], Folder 7382a/19-36); Brian Hughes and Conor Morrissey, *Southern Irish Loyalism, 1912–1949* (Liverpool, 2020), pp. 1–24.

CHAPTER 4. BARRY VERSUS DEASY

1 Cormac Moore, *The GAA v Douglas Hyde: The Removal of Ireland's First President as GAA Patron* (Dublin, 2012); Paul Rouse, *Sport and Ireland: A History* (Oxford, 2015), pp. 273–9.

2 *The Cork Examiner*, 31 Dec. 1921.

3 Cumann na mBan GHG to May Conlon, 4 Apr. 1922 (CPM, May Conlon Collection, 2007: 38: 259). A rail strike prevented many Cork and Kerry delegates from attending

the February 1922 Cumann na mBan Convention. Its vote against the Treaty represented about half the membership. Mary McAuliffe, 'An idea has gone abroad that all women were against the Treaty: Cumann na Saoirse and pro-Treaty women, 1922–3' in Liam Weeks and Mícheál Ó Fathartaigh (eds), *The Treaty: Debating and Establishing the Irish State* (Newbridge, 2018), p. 168.

4   *Irish Independent*, 18 Apr. 1938; *The Irish Press*, 21 Feb. 1952, 2 Feb. 1965, 8 Apr. 1971; *The Southern Star*, 29 Mar. 1952, 8 Dec. 1952, 24 Aug. 1963, 7 May 1966, 17 Apr. and 25 May 1971; O'Malley to Mairghread Murphy, 9 Sep. 1953, *No Surrender Here*, p. 309.

5   *The Cork Examiner*, 11 Sep. 1961.

6   *The Southern Star*, 27 Aug. 1921.

7   Louis Whyte, *The Wild Heather Glen: The Kilmichael Story of Grief and Glory* (Ballincollig, 1995), p. 163.

8   *The Southern Star*, 25 Feb. 1922 and 28 Nov. 1925.

9   C Company memorial service, 28 Nov. 1921, brochure (scan in author's possession).

10   *The Northern Whig*, 22 Apr. 1924. The tablet is now in the Cork County Museum. I am indebted to the late Billy Good for tracking down its whereabouts.

11   Mike Cronin, *The Blueshirts and Irish Politics* (Dublin: Four Courts Press, 1997), pp. 17–25; Mike Cronin, 'The Blueshirt Movement, 1932–5: Ireland's Fascists?', *Journal of Contemporary History*, vol. 30, no. 2 (Apr. 1995), pp. 311–32, see pp. 326–7.

12   Mel Farrell, *Party Politics in a New Democracy: The Irish Free State, 1922–37* (London, 2017).

13   Bill Kissane, *Explaining Irish Democracy* (Dublin, 2002), p. 99; 'Pro-Treatyite' here encompasses Cumann na nGaedheal, Fine Gael, Farmers' Party, Clann na Talmhann, National Centre Party, and the National League. This calculation has been made by combing the electoral results of the various Cork constituencies, which are taken from Michael Gallagher, *Irish Election Results 1922–44: Results and Analysis* (Limerick, 1993).

14   Fearghal McGarry, 'Ireland and the Spanish Civil War', *History Ireland*, iss. 3, vol. 9 (Autumn 2001).

15   Brian Hanley, *The IRA, 1926–1936* (Dublin, 2002), pp. 113–44.

16   The 1924 MSP applied only to pro-Treaty (National Army) Civil War veterans with pre-Truce (1916–21) service from 1923 onwards various Army Pension Acts created pensions for disabled veterans, allowances and gratuities for the dependents of veterans killed on active service. Marie Coleman, 'Military Service Pensions for Veterans of the Irish Revolution, 1916–1923', *War in History*, 20(2), (2013), pp. 201–21.

17   Uinseann MacEoin, *The IRA in the Twilight Years, 1923–1948* (Dublin, 1997), p. 274.

18   Flor Begley, 18 Oct. 1950 (UCDA, EOMNbks, P17b/111), p. 45; O'Malley to Seámus O'Donovan, 7 Apr. 1923, *No Surrender Here*, p. 367; O'Malley statement on Barry, 19 Apr. 1940 (MAI, MSPC, MSP34/57456).

19   Evidence of Senator William Quirke on behalf of Tom Barry [2 Nov. 1939] (MAI, MSPC, MSP34REF57456).

20   Michael Hopkinson, *Green Against Green: The Irish Civil War* (Dublin, 1988), p. 209.

21   Adj. 1SD, Notes on the 26 Mar. 1922 Army Convention, 29 Mar. 1922 (UCDA, FA, P104/1234/1–7). Adj. 1SD, Notes on the 26 Mar. 1922 Army Convention, 29 Mar. 1922 (UCDA, FA, P104/1234/1–7).

22   From March 1921, he was brigade O/C. By July, he was vice O/C of the 1SD and divisional O/C from the end of June 1922. Hopkinson, *Green Against Green*, p. 162; Cork no. 3 Bge, lists of elected Bn. Staff, Aug. 1919 (DRI, DE/4/3/1) Jeremiah Deasy, 6 July 1958 (MAI, BMH, WS 1738).

23   Liam Deasy, *c.* 1944–1945 (UCDA, EOM, P17b/34).

24   Hopkinson, *Green Against Green*, p. 101.

25   Ibid., p. 115; Flor Begley, 18 Oct. 1950 (UCDA, EOM, P17b/111), p. 53. Begley said the same of Séamus Robinson, O/C of the 3rd (South) Tipperary Brigade.

26   O'Donoghue, *No Other Law*, p. 244. *Plain People*, 7 May 1922. Barry was on the temporary executive in place on 26 March but not the permanent one elected on 9 Apr. 1922 although he and O'Malley were put in joint charge of planning operations 'against England'. Handwritten notes by O'Malley on the Army Conventions, *c.* June 1922, *No Surrender Here*, p. 29; Executive and Army Council, 26 Mar. 1922, Executives, 9 Apr. 1 and 28 June 1922 (UCDA, MT, P69/179/141–142); Joseph O'Connor, 28 June 1951 (MAI, BMH, WS 544), p. 4; John Dorney, *The Civil War in Dublin: The Fight for the Irish Capital 1922–24* (Dublin, 2017), pp. 86, 291.

27   Meda Ryan misdates this incident as occurring in May. Ryan, *Tom Barry* (2012), pp. 230–1. Report for Min. of Defence (Richard Mulcahy), 18 June 1922, *No Surrender Here*, p. 24. Excerpts from diary captured on Seán MacBride, July 1922 (copy) [original in NAI, D/T S1233] (New York University Tamiment Library [hereafter NYU/TL], EOMP, AIA.060/Box 25/Folder 8).

28   Hopkinson, *Green Against Green*, pp. 14–15.

29   Northern Catholics, particularly in Belfast, bore the brunt of the violence although a significant number of Protestants suffered as well. For a grim overview see Robert Lynch, *The Partition of Ireland: 1818–1925* (Cambridge, 2019), pp. 100–13; Alan F. Parkinson, *Belfast's Unholy War: The Troubles of the 1920s* (Dublin, 2004); Bill Kissane, *The Politics of the Irish Civil War* (Oxford, 2005), p. 69; Robert Lynch, *The Partition of Ireland: 1918–1925* (Cambridge, 2019), p. 11.

30   Conor Morrissey, *Protestant Nationalists in Ireland, 1900–1923* (Cambridge, 2019), pp. 198–200; Andy Bielenberg, John Borgonovo, James S. Donnelly Jr, '"Something of the Nature of a Massacre": The Bandon Valley Killings Revised', *Éire-Ireland*, vol. 46, issues 3 & 4 (Fall/Winter 2014), p. 36.

31   Barry Keane, *Massacre in West Cork: The Dunmanway and Ballygroman Killings* (Cork, 2014), pp. 204–6; Bielenberg, Borgonovo, Donnelly, '"Something of the Nature of a Massacre"', pp. 7–59.

32   *The Skibbereen Eagle*, 6 May 1922; *The Southern Star*, 29 Apr. 1922. Bielenberg, Borgonovo, Donnelly, '"Something of the Nature of a Massacre"', p. 36; Keane, *Massacre in West Cork*, pp. 204–6; Don Wood, unpublished notes, 27 Feb. 2014.

33   Morrissey, *Protestant Nationalists*, p. 199.

34   *Church of Ireland Gazette*, 5 May 1922.

35   Ibid.

36   Quoted in Morrissey, *Protestant Nationalists*, p. 199.

37   Quoted in Bielenberg, Borgonovo, Donnelly, '"Something of the Nature of a Massacre"', p. 38.

38   C/S to O/Cs all divisions and independent brigades, Special Memorandum no.2, 6 May 1922 (UCDA, EOM, P17a/6).

39   Bielenberg, Borgonovo, Donnelly, '"Something of the Nature of a Massacre"', p. 39.

40   Confidential Police Reports, 28 Feb. to 30 June 1924 (NLI, DT S 3435).

41   Alan Parkinson, *A Difficult Birth: The Early Years of Northern Ireland 1920–25* (Dublin, 2020).

42   Statement, IRA Executive, 28 June 1922 (UCDA, FA, P104/1235); IRA Executive, 29 June 1922 (UCDA, MT, P69/179/142); O'Donoghue, *No Other Law*, p. 285.

43   Lynch to O'Malley, 7 and 12 Sep. 1922, O'Malley to Seámus O'Donovan, 7 Apr. 1923, Minutes, IRA Executive, 16 Oct. 1922, *No Surrender Here*, pp. 162, 174, 336–7, 367; Report of Divisional Meeting, 1SD, 26 Feb 1923 (NLI, EOM, ms 10,973/7/42). The anti-Treaty forces were divided into three commands (Southern, Northern and Western) in October 1922.

44   Ryan, *Tom Barry* (2012), pp. 247, 253. Hopkinson, *Green Against Green*, p. 209; O'Donoghue, *No Other Law*, p. 280; O'Malley (Director of Operations) to Robert Brennan, 28 Oct. 1922, *No Surrender Here*, pp. 250, 308; IRA Executive and Substitutes, 26 Nov. 1922 (UCDA, MT, P69/179/150–1); Divisional Dir of Operations to OCs, 19 Dec. 1922 (UCDA, MT, P69/25/71–3); Activity Report, 1SD, 3 Oct. 1922 (UCDA, MT, P69/25/181); Barry to Adjutant General, 15 Dec. 1922 (UCDA, MT, P69/25/84); Adjutant, 1SD to C/S, 7 Jan. 1923 (UCDA, MT, P69/25/29); Stephen O'Neill, 19 Sep. 1951 (UCDA, EOM, P17b/112), p.105; O'Malley to Lynch, 2 Oct. 1922 and Seán Daly, 10 Oct. 1950 (UCDA, EOM, P17b/112), p. 118.

45   The term 'National Army' refers to the pro-government forces during the Civil War only.

46   Mossy Donegan, Sep.–Oct. 1950 (UCDA, EOM, P17b/108), p. 78; Adjutant 1SD to C/S, 7 Jan. 1923 (UCDA, MT, P69/25/29); Hopkinson, *Green Against Green*, p. 228.

47   O'Donoghue to Deasy, 12 Jan. 1923 (NLI, Florence O'Donoghue Papers [hereafter FOD], ms 31261/1); Tom Crofts to Deasy, 16 Jan. 1923; Mary MacSwiney to Lynch, 7 Feb. 1923 (UCDA, Éamon de Valera Papers [hereafter deV], P150/1697).

48   Prout to Adj Gen, 24 Jan. 1923; C-in-C to Prout, Prout to C-in-C, 26. Jan. 1923 (TCDM, MJC, IE TCD ms 11504).

49   Deasy to Lynch, 29 Jan. 1923 (UCDA, deV, P150/1697). Copies of Deasy's appeal and the various responses are in de Valera's papers. It was sent to several members of the IRA GHQ, provisional IRA officers and members of the Republican government (UCDA, deV, P150/1697).

50   Bill Quirke, 31 August 1948 (UCDA, EOM P17b/86), p. 67.

51 Barrett to Deasy [public], Barrett to Deasy [private], 5 Feb. 1923 and Lynch to All Ranks of the Army, 9 Feb. 1923 (UCDA, deV, P150/1697); C/S to O/C 1SD, 11 Feb. 1924 (UCDA, MT, P69/27/128); MacSwiney to Deasy [public] and 'personal note', 5 Feb. 1923; Frank Carty to Deasy, 6 Feb. 1923 (TCDM, MJC, IE TCD ms 11504); Donal O'Callaghan to CS, 4 Feb. 1923 (UCDA, deV, P150/1697); O'Malley to Sighle Humphreys, 9 Feb. 1923, *No Surrender Here*, p.359; Mutt [Madge Clifford] to O'Malley, 27 June 1923 (UCDA, EOM, P17a/289); *Southern Star*, 13 Mar. 1923; *The Cork Examiner*, 19 Feb. 1923; Hopkinson, *Green Against Green*, p. 239; Daniel Murray, 'The Self-Deceit of Honour: Liam Lynch and the Civil War, 1922 (Part IV)' (Éireann Ascendant, https://erinascendantwordpress. wordpress.com, accessed 21 Dec. 2021).

52 Report of Divisional meeting, 1SD, 26 Feb. 1923 (NLI, EOM, ms 10,973/7/42).

53 Liam Tobin, 1 May 1949 (UCDA, EOM, P17b/96), pp. 31–2; Frank McKenna to O'Malley, 12 Sep. 1922, *No Surrender Here*, p. 174; Deasy, *Brother Against Brother* (Dublin & Cork, 1994), p. 74.

54 Lynch to MacSwiney, 8 Feb. 1923; O'Donoghue Diary, 1, 6, 12 Mar. 1923 (NLI, FOD, ms 31,189); Eithne [Annie] MacSwiney to de Valera, 25, 26 and 30 Apr. 1923 (UCDA, deV, P150/665); Barry to Mary MacSwiney, 9 May 1923 (Cork City & County Archives [hereafter CC&CA] St Ita's/MacSwiney Collection, U329-4); Stephen O'Neill 19 Sep. 1951 (UCDA, EOM, P17b/112), p. 105; Moss Twomey, April 1950 (UCDA, EOM, P17b/107), p. 38; Mossy Donegan, Sep.–Oct. 1950 (UCDA, EOM, P17b/108), p. 78.

55 EOM to Sighle Humphreys (Mountjoy Prison), 7 Apr. 1923, *No Surrender Here*, p. 369; Máire MacSwiney to A/P (copy to C/S, D/I), 29 July 1924 (UCDA, MT, P69/17/3); Handwritten notes, Seán MacBride, 11 Apr. 1923 (NYU/TL, EOMP, AIA.060/Box 25/ Folder 8); Moss Twomey, April 1950 (UCDA, EOM, P17b/107), p. 38.

56 Intelligence Report re Tom Barry, 16 Jan. 1924 (UCDA, MP, P7/B/140/ 189-190). Michael Hopkinson misdates this report as January 1923. Hopkinson, *Green Against Green*, p. 231; O/C ISD to CS, 25 Aug. 1924; C/S to O/C 1SD, 1 Sep. 1924 (UCDA, MT, P69/27/85).

57 Ted Sullivan, 10 Dec. 1950 (UCDA, EOMNbks, P17b/108), p. 24; Charles Browne, 13 Nov. 1950 (UCDA, EOM, P17b/112), p. 25.

58 Mary MacSwiney to de Valera, 7 Feb. 1923 (UCDA, deV, P150/1697); Mary MacSwiney to de Valera, 1 Mar. 1923 (NLI, EOM, ms 10,973/7/36); O'Callaghan to de Valera, 21 Feb. and 4 May 1923 (UCDA, deV, P150/1712); de Valera to Frank Aiken, 5 May 1923 and Aiken to de Valera, 7 May 1923. (UCDA, deV, P150/1752); Barry to de Valera, 7 May 1923 and Barry to de Valera, 9 May 1923 (UCDA, deV, P150/1752).

59 Report, Metropolitan Police Office, Dublin Castle, May 1923 (NAI, DT, S 3435).

60 Lt Gen Seán O'Murthile testimony, 15 May 1924 (MAI, Army Inquiry Committee, AMTY-03-43); Dáil Proceedings, 26 June 1924 (www.oireachtas.ie/en/debates/debate/ dail/1924-06-26/30/?highlight%5B0%5D, accessed 17 Dec. 2021); Daniel Murray, 'Career Conspirators: The (Mis)Adventures of Seán Ó Muirthile and the Irish Republican Brotherhood in the Free State Army, 1923–4', 29 June 2015 (www.theirishstory. com/2015/06/29/career-conspirators-the-misadventures-of-sean-o-muirthile-and-the-

irish-republican-brotherhood-in-the-free-state-army-1923-4/#.YbyC8MnP3IU, accessed 17 Dec. 2021).

61 O'Donoghue Diary, 19 Feb. 1923 (NLI, FOD, ms 31,189).

62 GO/C Cork to C in C, 21 Feb. 1923 (TCDM, MJC, IE TCD ms 11504); Diary, 18 Feb. 1923 (NLI, FOD, ms 31,189); O'Callaghan to de Valera, 21 Feb 1923 (UCDA, deV, P150/1712).

63 1SD Council minutes, 26 Feb. 1923 (NLI, EOM, ms 10,973/7/42); Tom Crofts to AG, 11 Feb. 1925 (NLI, EOM, ms 10,973/7/52); Dr Padraic O'Sullivan, 12 Nov. 1950 (UCDA, EOMNbks, P17b/111), p. 97.

64 O'Donoghue Diary, 25 Feb. 1923 (UCD, FOD, ms 31,189).

65 Seán McLoughlin (Limerick prisoner) to Brennan, 21 Feb. 1923 (NLI, EOM, ms 10,973/7/39); McLoughlin to Deasy, 9 Feb. 1923 (NLI, EOM, ms 10,973/7/29).

66 O'Donoghue Diary, 1, 6, 9 March 1923 (NLI, FOD, ms 31,189).

67 Irish Independent, 8 Mar. 1923; Eithne [Annie] MacSwiney to de Valera, 26 Apr. 1923 (UCDA, deV, P150/665).

68 Irish Independent, 9 Apr. 1923; O'Donoghue, No Other Law, pp. 299–301; 1SD Council minutes, 26 Feb. 1923 (NLI, EOM, ms 10,973/7/42).

69 Moss Twomey, April 1950 (UCDA, EOM, P17b/107), p. 39; Twomey to O'Donoghue, 11 Feb. 1953 (NLI, FOD, ms 31,421/12/77).

70 Handwritten notes, Seán MacBride, 11 Apr. 1923 (NYU/TL, EOMP, AIA.060/Box 25/ Folder 8); Moloney [from Limerick Jail] to Kathy Barry, 11 Apr. 1923 (UCDA, KMB, P94/71).

71 De Valera to Comdt T, 9 Mar. 1923 (UCDA, deV, P150/1749); de Valera to Aiken, 9 May 1923 (UCDA, deV, P150/1752).

72 Barry to de Valera, 8 June 1923 (UCDA, deV, P150/1752).

73 Aiken to Barry and Aiken to de Valera, 13 June 1923, de Valera to Barry, 14 June 1923 (UCDA, deV, P150/1752); IRA Executive Minutes, 11/12 July 1923 and Barry to Army Executive IRA, 11 July 1923 (UCDA, FA, P104/1264); IRA C/S Report, 9 Aug. 1924 (UCDA, EOMP, P17a/12).

74 Brian Hanley to Editor, History Ireland, iss. 2, vol. 12 (Summer 2004); McGarry, Frank Ryan, p. 53. Meda Ryan's assertions that Barry remained in the IRA between 1923 and 1932 derive in part from misattributing correspondence from a different Tom Barry (the former O/C of Castletownroche Battalion, Cork II Brigade) to him. Correspondence between the IRA CS and both men in 1924 are grouped together in a single archival folder. The 'other' Barry joined the Garda Síochána in 1936. Barry to Aiken, c. 5 Oct. 1924 (UCDA, MT, P69/27/52); Tomás de Barra to CS, 24 Nov. 1924 (UCDA, MT, P69/27/58); Tomás de Barra to Sec. Mil. Pensions, 4 June 1936 (MAI, MSPC/RO/39); Ryan, Tom Barry (2012), p. 270.

75 Limerick Leader, 7 Mar. 1925.

76 The Cork Examiner, 22 Oct. and 8 Nov. 1923; Daily Sheet (Sinn Féin), 20 Nov. 1923; Hopkinson, Green Against Green, pp. 268–71.

77 Barry to Aiken, 19 Oct. 1923 (UCDA, MT, P69/43/167-168); Aiken to Barry, 2 Nov. 1923 and Barry to Aiken, 21 Nov. 1923 (UCDA, MT, P69/43/153-6); Barry to Aiken,

c. 5 Oct. 1924 (UCDA, MT, P69/27/52); Intelligence Note, 2 Dec. 1924 (MAI, MSPC, MSP34REF4067-W2_21085).

78   *The Cork Examiner*, 21 Dec. 1923; Telegrams, Cork Command to Mulcahy and Mulcahy to Seán Prior, 20 Dec. 1923 (MAI, A-Series, DOD.A.06842-1610).

79   Crofts to Aiken, 31 Dec. 1923 (UCDA, MT, P69/27/134); Intelligence Report, IO Cork to GHQ, 7 Jan. 1924 (UCDA, MP, P7/b/140/101).

80   Deasy said the same. Deasy, *Brother Against Brother*, p. 113. Pa Murray, 10 Sep. 1948 (UCDA, EOM, P17b/88), p. 43; Tom Crofts, 11 Oct. and Dec. 1950 (UCDA, EOM P17b/108), p. 31; Liam Deasy, *c.* 1944–1945 (UCDA, EOM, P17b/34), pp. 37, 39; Florry Begley, 18 Oct. 1950 (UCDA, EOM, P17b/111), p. 53; Mossy Donegan, Sep.–Oct. 1950 (UCDA, EOM, P17b/108), p. 78; Mick Leahy, 14/10/1950 (UCDA, EOMNbks, P17b/108), pp. 98–9; Mick O'Sullivan, 13/10/1950 (UCDA, EOMNbks, P17b/108), p. 112; Frank Busteed, 19 Nov. 1950 (UCDA, EOMNbks, P17b/112), pp. 81–2; Hopkinson, *Green Against Green*, pp. 146–53.

81   Uinseann MacEoin, *Survivors*, 2nd ed. (Dublin, 1987), pp. 230, 291.

82   Pax Ó Faoláin, Dec. 1978 (MAI, UMcE, UMCE-S-A-16); MacEoin, *Survivors*, p. 621; Bill Quirke, 31 August 1948 (UCDA, EOM P17b/86), p. 59.

83   Archie Doyle, Nov./Dec. 1949 (UCDA, EOM, P17b/105), p. 90. Doyle was one of those who assassinated Kevin O'Higgins in 1927. Uinseann MacEoin, *Harry: The Story of Harry White* (Dublin, 1986), p. 106.

84   Seán Cooney, 1 Dec. 1949 (UCDA, EOMNbks, P17b/103), pp. 44–5; Tom Crofts, 11 Oct. and Dec. 1950 (UCDA, EOM, P17b/108), pp. 32, 60; Todd Andrews, *Dublin Made Me* (Cork and Dublin, 1979), pp. 280, 255; Ted O'Sullivan, 10 Dec. 1950 (UCDA, EOMNbks, P17b/108) p. 27.

85   Seán Cronin and Jim Savage interview, 1992, Cork (MAI, Uinseann MacEoin Interviews [hereafter UMacE], UMCE-T-A-16); MacEoin, *Twilight Years*, p. 810.

86   Eugene 'Nudge' Callanan interview, *c.* April 1969 (TCDM, Chisholm Papers/Recordings [hereafter CP], uncatalogued).

87   *Irish Independent*, 17 July 1924.

88   MacSwiney to AP, CS, DI, 29 July 1924 (UCDA, MT, P69/17/3).

89   O/C 1SD to CS, 3 Sep. (UCDA, MT, P69/27/138); Minutes, Executive Council, 30 Nov. 1923; Memo from Min of Home Affairs, 12 Feb. 1924, 15 Feb. 1924.

90   I am grateful to Tom Lyons for his advice on Deasy's involvement in the GAA. See also *The Southern Star*, 5 Feb. 1927; *The Cork Examiner*, 15 Feb. 1927; www.carberygaa.ie/contentPage/10058797/, accessed 17 Dec. 2021.

91   Eugene 'Nudge' Callanan [2nd interview], *c.* Apr. 1969 (TCDM, CP, uncatalogued).

92   Deasy, *Brother Against Brother*, pp. 8–9.

93   Liam Deasy claim file (MAI, MSPC, MSP34REF2087).

94   There were several different veterans' organisations, including Old Cumann na mBan.

95   Minutes, 18 Feb. 1934 and 25 July 1936 (CC&CA, Old IRA Men's Association Minute Book, IE CCCA/U342/1); *The Irish Press*, 14 Sep. 1936; *Labour News*, 27 Mar. 1937.

96   Eugene 'Nudge' Callanan [2nd interview], *c.* Apr. 1969 (TCDM, CP, uncatalogued).

97   Batt Murphy interview, *c.* Apr. 1969 (TCDM, CP, uncatalogued).

98   *The Cork Examiner*, 28 Dec. 1923 and 4 Oct. 1924; *Limerick Leader*, 30 Jan. 1924. David Lee, 'The Munster Soviets and the Fall of the House of Cleeve' in David Lee and Debbie Jacobs (eds), *Made in Limerick, Vol. 1, History of Industries, Trade and Commerce* (Limerick Civic Trust, 2003), p. 305.

99   *The Cork Examiner*, 8 Dec. 1927.

100 *Voice of Labour*, 20 Mar. 1926.

101 For more on the CPA, Barry's contacts see Tate to Brennan, 2 June 1935 (UCDA, FA, 2 June 1935); Intelligence Report on Cork Progressive Association, 6 Nov. 1923 (UCDA, MP, P7/b/140/52); Timothy Cadogan and Jeremiah Falvey (eds), *A Biographical Dictionary of Cork* (Dublin, 2006), pp. 70, 87–8, 270–1.

102 *The Cork Examiner*, 20 Dec. 1927.

103 Mossy Twomey confirmed that Barry did not rejoin the IRA until 1932. MacEoin, *Twilight Years*, p. 837. Twomey inspected all the Cork IRA units in 1924 and 1925. See Report on First Southern Division, 7 July 1924 (UCDA, MT, P69/27/97); Frank Aiken, Report to Executive Meeting, 10 Aug. 1924 (UCDA, FA, P104/1266); Barry to Twomey, 13 May 1932 (UCDA, MT, P69/52/63); Thomas Barry (MAI, BMH WS 430), p. 20. See also Sworn evidence of Frank Aiken, 15 May 1940 (MAI, MSPC, MSP34/57456); Hanley, *The IRA*, pp. 127, 191.

104 TB to MT, 20 and 24 July 1932 (UCDA, MT, P69/52/47) MT to O/C Cork no.1 Bge, 19 July 1932 (UCDA, MT, P69/52/54); Hanley, *The IRA*, p. 186; *Evening Echo*, 16 May 1979.

105 Hanley, *The IRA*, p. 111.

106 Minutes, 6 Dec. 1935 (CC&CA, Old IRA Men's Association Minute Book, IE CCCA/ U342/1). For O'Donoghue's links with Barry in this period see Hanley, *The IRA*, p. 111.

107 IRA statement quoted in *The Cork Examiner*, 2 Apr. 1934; Report of Gen Army Convention, 17 Mar. 1933 (UCDA, MT, P69/187/50–116); Hanley, *The IRA*, p. 144; Brian Hanley, 'The IRA and Trade Unionism, 1922–72' in Francis Devine, Fintan Lane and Niamh Puirséuil (eds), *Essays in Labour History: A Festschrift for Elizabeth and John W. Boyle* (Dublin and Portland, 2008), pp. 157–77, see pp. 160–1; Fearghal McGarry, *Frank Ryan* (Dublin, 2010), pp. 28–9.

108 Quoted in Hanley, *The IRA*, p. 178, pp. 195–6.

109 Murphy TD to Army Pensions Dept, 22 Oct. 1924, Kingston to AG, 30 May 1924, Murphy to Defence, 22 Nov. and 6 Dec. 1933 (MAI, MSPC, MSP34REF19353/ 1P295); Sec. Pres. to Sec. Army Pensions, 10 Oct. 1924, Murphy to Sec. Army Pensions 18 Oct. 1924 and 2 Nov. 1924 (MAI, MSPC, 1D295).

110 Twomey to O/C West Cork Battalion, 7 Oct. 1932 (UCDA, MT, P69/54/111); Hanley, *The IRA*, p. 25.

111 *The Southern Star*, 24 Dec. 1932 and 14 Jan. 1933.

112 *The Southern Star*, 14 Jan. 1933.

113 *The Cork Examiner*, 22 Dec. 1932. Barry's threats to finish Murphy's 'career as a public representative' had no appreciable impact. Murphy ran in nine elections between 1923 and

1949. He was elected on the first count five times, topping the poll on three occasions. Gallagher, *Irish Elections 1922–44*, pp. 29, 59, 99, 129, 161, 221, 250, 283; Cadogan & Falvey, *A Biographical Dictionary of Cork*, p. 215. Murphy died in 1949, shortly after becoming minister for local government.

114 Barry to Twomey, 23 Dec. 1932 (UCDA, MT, P69/155/3).

115 *The Southern Star*, 5 Nov. 1932.

116 Mike Cronin, 'The Blueshirt Movement, 1932–5: Ireland's Fascists?', *Journal of Contemporary History*, vol. 30, no. 2 (Apr. 1995), pp. 311–32, see p. 312; McGarry, *Frank Ryan*, p. 28.

117 *An Phoblacht*, 3 Dec. 1932.

118 Barry to Twomey, 28 Nov. 1932; [?] to Seán Martin, 6 Dec. 1932 (UCDA, MT, P69/54/52); Michael Richard Heffernan, Farmer's Party TD, is registered at living at the address on the letter, 28 Elgin Road, Ballsbridge, Dublin. *Thom's Directory* (1932).

119 *The Cork Examiner*, 24 Jan. 1933.

120 In March 1934, 9,955 out of 37,937 members were in Cork. In August of the following year, the ratio was 10,530 out of 47,923. The rest of the membership was spread over twenty-five counties. Mike Cronin, *The Blueshirts and Irish Politics* (Dublin, 1997), p. 115.

121 *Evening Herald*, 30 Oct. 1933; *The Cork Examiner*, 29 Dec. 1933 and 5 Jan. 1934; *Evening Echo*, 29 Dec. 1933; *Irish Independent*, 30 Dec. 1933; Joe Collins, in the Dunmanway IRA, maintained that the organisation had no part in Daly's death, and that Daly had fallen over drunk and cracked his skull. Seán McConville, *Irish Political Prisoners, 1920–1962: Pilgrimage of Desolation* (London and New York, 2014), pp. 290, 317, ft 80.

122 Tim Pat Coogan, *A Memoir* (London, 2008), pp. 33–4.

123 Hanley, *The IRA*, p. 87; Report of Gen Army Convention, 17–19 Mar. 1933 (UCDA, MT, P69/187/114).

124 *Evening Herald* and *The Cork Examiner*, 26 Apr. 1935; *The Irish Press*, 27 Mar. 1935; Special Powers Tribunal, charge sheet, 18 Apr. 1935 (NLI, Seán O'Mahony Papers, ms 44,097/1).

125 The '77' referred to the executions carried out by the Free State government during the Civil War. *Evening Echo*, 13 May 1935; *Irish Independent*, *The Irish Press*, *The Cork Examiner*, *Belfast News-Letter*, 14 May 1935.

126 For a painstaking overview of these exchanges see Daniel Murray, 'An Unclean Scab: The Public Feud between Tom Barry and Frank Aiken, 1935' (https://erinascendantwordpress.wordpress.com/2016/05/13/an-unclean-scab-the-public-feud-between-tom-barry-and-frank-aiken-1935/comment-page-1/, accessed 22 Dec. 2021).

127 *The Liberator*, 4 June 1935; *Irish Independent*, 8 Mar. 1923.

128 *The Irish Press*, 7 June 1935; *Evening Echo*, 14 June 1935.

129 Moss Twomey, April 1950 (UCDA, EOM, P17b/107), p. 38; MacEoin, *Twilight Years*, p. 837.

130 Moss Twomey, April 1950 (UCDA, EOM, P17b/107), p. 38.

131 Twomey to O'Donoghue, 17 July 1952 (NLI, FOD, ms 31,421/12/53–54).

132 *Irish Independent*, 20 May 1935; *Evening Echo*, 11 June 1935.

133 *Evening Echo*, 11 June 1935.

134 *The Irish Press* and *Irish Independent*, 20 May 1935; *Cork Echo*, 1 June 1935; Tom Crofts to AG, 11 Feb. 1925 (NLI, EOMP, ms 10,973/7/52).

135 McGarry, *Frank Ryan*, p. 53.

136 Notes on German IRA and related contacts, n.d. [*c.* Nov. 1941], Southern Command HQ to C/S Officer i/c G2, Dep. Of Defence, 27 Nov. 1941, Barry to Dr Hempel, 27 Apr. 1942 (MAI, G2 Records, G2/3020); Florrie O'Donoghue, Memo on conversation with Tom Barry in June 1940, 23 Nov. 1943 (MAI, G2 Records, G2/0333/F); Eunan O'Halpin, *Defending Ireland: The Irish State and its Enemies since 1922* (Oxford, 1999) pp. 126–8; Hanley, *The IRA*, p. 20; Brian Hanley to Editor, *History Ireland*, iss. 2, vol. 12 (Summer 2004); Emmet O'Connor, *Reds and the Green: Ireland, Russia and the Communist Internationals, 1919–43* (Dublin, 2004), pp. 222–3.

137 Interview with Jack Lynch (Dunmanway, West Cork, brother of Tadgh Lynch), *c.* 1983 (MAI, UMacE, 'Harry' Interviews).

138 *The Irish Press*, 17 June 1938; Letter to Editor and response, *Saoirse Eireann–Wolfe Tone Weekly*, 6 June 1938.

139 MacEoin, *Survivors*, pp. 363–9; Mai Dálaigh interview, April 1979 (MAI, UMacE, UMCE-S-A-39). MacEoin did not include her comments in the published version of this interview. Newspaper reports of the funeral record Barry as sending a message of sympathy but not as an attendee. *The Irish Press*, 23 and 24 Aug. 1939.

140 Barry, Sworn Statement before the Advisory Committee, 4 Jan. 1938 [1939]; Barry to Military Service Registration Board [hereafter MSRB], 29 Jan. 1940 (MAI, MSPC, MSP34REF57456).

141 Barry, Sworn Statement before the Advisory Committee, 4 Jan. 1938 [1939] (MAI, MSPC, MSP34REF57456).

142 Ted O'Sullivan, 10 Dec. 1950 (UCDA, EOMNbks, P17b/108) p. 24.

143 Barry to MSRB, 29 Dec. 1938; Barry to Advisory Committee, 4 Jan. 1939; 29 Mar. 1940 (MAI, MSPC, MSP34REF57456).

144 Aiken to O'Malley, 4 Feb. 1935 (NYU/TL EOMP, AIA 060 Box 3, Folder 20); Richard English, *Ernie O'Malley: IRA Intellectual* (Oxford, 2002, 2nd ed.), pp. 6–7.

145 English, *Ernie O'Malley*, pp. 6–9.

146 Issues relating to how the pensioning process was organised and structured, and the involvement of local veterans' committees are discussed further in Chapter Five.

147 Barry and Tom Hales, interview before Referee and Advisory Committee, 10 June 1941 (NAI, DT S/9243); Barry to Military Service Registration Board, 29 Jan. 1940 (MAI, MSPC, MSP34REF57456).

148 Begley to Cremin, 17 June 1941 (NAI, DT, S 9243); Ted Sullivan, 10 Dec. 1950 (UCDA, EOMNbks, P17b/108), p. 24

149 HQ Curragh to GW Branch, Dept. of Defence, 11 July [1940] (MAI, G2 Records, G2/3020).

150 *Irish Independent*, 7 June 1946; *The Cork Examiner*, 8 and 14 June 1946; *The Irish Press*, 11 June 1946; Micheál O'Riordan review of *Seán Moylan: Soldier, Politician and Independent Spirit* in *Irish Democrat*, July 2005 (https://archive.irishdemocrat.co.uk/features/sean-moylan-soldier-politician-and-independent/, accessed 22 Dec. 2021).

151 Various amounts, all extraordinarily large, are given in newspapers and in other sources. Some Irish reports say £30,000,000, others £35,000,000. According to one USA newspaper Barry said $100,000,000. *Pittsburg Post-Gazette*, 21 Nov. 1949; *The Irish Times*, 19, 21, 26 Nov. and 1, 3, 12 Dec. 1949; *Pittsburg Press*, 18 Nov. 1949; *Boston Globe*, 30 Nov. 1949; Dáil Éireann debate, vol. 118, no. 11, 30 Nov. 1949; Seámus McCall, Report on the North, Nov. 1949 (UCDA, FA, P104/4583); Christopher Norton, *The Politics of Constitutional Nationalism in Northern Ireland,1932–1970: Between Grievance and Reconciliation* (Manchester, 2014), pp. 89–90; Stephen Kelly, 'A Policy of Futility: Eamon de Valera's Anti-Partition Campaign, 1948–1951', *Études Irlandaises*, 36–2 (2011) (https://doi.org/10.4000/etudesirlandaises.2348, accessed 17 Dec. 2021).

152 *The Irish Times*, 12 Dec. 1949.

153 Mac Eoin, *Survivors*, pp. 368, 621, 657.

154 MacEoin, *Survivors*, p. 329; Tony Woods, July 1979 (MAI, UMacE, UMCE-S-A-34).

155 O'Donoghue, *No Other Law*, pp. 298–9.

156 Twomey to O'Donoghue, 8 Nov. 1952 (NLI, FOD, ms 31,421/12/68).

CHAPTER 5. ISSUES AND PARTICIPANTS

1 A 'telling' is the initial outing of a personal narrative. A 'retelling' is a personal account that (inevitably) becomes more structured with the passage of time. Samuel Schrager, 'What is social in oral history?' in Robert Perks and Alistair Thomson (eds), *The Oral History Reader* (London 1998), pp. 284–99, see p. 284.

2 Memoirs and books that were serialised in part or in full include: Piaras Béaslaí, *Michael Collins* (*The Cork Examiner*, 3 July–20 Nov. 1926); Frank Pakenham, *Peace by Ordeal* (*Irish Independent*, 14 June–19 Aug. 1935); Ernie O'Malley, *On Another Man's Wound* (*The Irish Press*, 16 Oct. 1936–24 Dec. 1937); W.J. Maloney, *The Forged Casement Diaries* (*The Irish Press*, 13 Jan.–6 Feb. 1937); Tom Barry, *Guerilla Days in Ireland* (*The Irish Press*, 10 May–3 July 1948) and *The Reality of the Anglo-Irish war 1920–21 in West Cork* (*The Southern Star*, 4 Jan.–15 Feb. 1975). Excerpts from Florence O'Donoghue, *No Other Law: The Story of Liam Lynch* appeared in *The Sunday Press* in 1952.

3 One recent study has concluded both that episodic details of memories declined with age and, over time, the accuracy of what was recalled remained very high. The authors further argued that academics studying memory have been overly pessimistic about the reliability of memories of 'real-world experiences'. Nicholas B. Diamond, Michael K. Armson and Brian Levine, 'The Truth Is Out There: Accuracy in Recall of Verifiable Real-World Events', *Psychological Science*, 2020, vol. 31 (12), pp. 1544–56. For a survey of the conclusions across several disciplines relating to combatants' personal memories and factors influencing their recollections see Azharul Island, Elizabeth Sheppard, Martin A. Conway, Shamsul Haque, 'Autobiographical memory of war veterans: A mixed-studies systematic review', *Memory Studies* (2019), pp. 1–26. For an overview of the debates and approaches to studying autobiographical memory see Gillian Cohen and Martin A. Conway (eds), *Memory in the Real World* (Hove, 2008).

4   Author interview, Gearóid Ó Tuathaigh, 29 Nov. 2012.

5   Dick Humphries to Caulfield, 14 Apr. 1964 (copy) (UCDA, deV, P150/1661). Caulfield tried, without success, to secure an interview with de Valera. M. Ó Slataraigh to Caulfield, Nov. 1961 (UCDA, deV, P150/1661).

6   *Evening Press*, 6 Apr. 1964.

7   Tim Pat Coogan, *De Valera: Long Fellow, Long Shadow* (London, 1993), pp. 70–1.

8   Simon Donnelly interview, Max Caulfield *c.* 1959–61 (Max Caulfield Interviews, CD 3, private collection); Caulfield to Humphries, 18 Apr. 1964 (copy) (UCDA, deV, P150/1661); *The Sunday Press*, 12 Apr. 1964.

9   Simon Donnelly, 'Thou shall not pass – Ireland's Challenge to the British Forces at Mount Street Bridge, Easter 1916' (BMH CD 62/3/7); Simon Donnelly, 21 Apr. 1948 (MAI, BMH, WS 113); Charles Townshend, *Easter 1916*, pp. 200–1.

10   Irish Distress Committee and Irish Grants Committee (TNAUK, CO 762); Royal Irish Constabulary Collection (TCDM, JRWGP, TCD mss 7376–7382).

11   Dept. of Defence, *Guide to the Military Service (1916–1923) Pensions Collection* (Dublin, 2012).

12   Dáil Debates, 14 February 1945, vol. 96, c.64.

13   To the delegates, Fianna Fáil ard fheis [1935] (NLI, FOD, ms 31,270/1); 'Military Service Pensions Act, 1934' (www.irishstatutebook.ie/eli/1934/act/43/enacted/en/html, accessed 17 Dec. 2021).

14   The statements have been freely available online since August 2012. Eve Morrison, 'The Bureau of Military History' in *The Atlas of the Irish Revolution* (Cork, 2017), pp. 876–80; Eve Morrison 'Witnessing the Republic: The Ernie O'Malley notebook interview and the Bureau of Military History Compared' in Cormac K.H. O'Malley (ed.), *Modern Ireland and Revolution: Ernie O'Malley in Context* (Dublin: Irish Academic Press, 2016).

15   Barry requested that his 1958 letter refusing to contribute to the BMH be submitted as his statement (MAI, BMH, 1743).

16   Barry to McDunphy, 4 July 1948 (MAI, BMH, WSO 26); Barry to P.J. Brennan, 21 Oct. 1958 (MAI, BMH, S 894).

17   Barry, *Guerilla Days*, p. 94; Barry, *Reality*, p. 9; Ryan, *Tom Barry* (2012), pp. 13, 323, 325, 373.

18   Barry to McDunphy, 4 July 1948 (MAI, BMH, WSO 26).

19   Buro Staire Míleata [BMH], 1913–1921: Chronology Part III Section 2, The Year 1920, p. 274.

20   McDunphy note of conversation with Seán Collins, 11 May 1949 (MAI, BMH, S 1355). McDunphy did not mention names.

21   Young, BMH, WS 1402; O'Brien, BMH, WS 812; Hennessy, BMH, WS 1234; Timothy Keohane, 28 Nov. 1955 (MAI, BMH, WS 1295) [hereafter Keohane, BMH, WS 1295]; Michael O'Driscoll, 25 Nov. 1955 (MAI, BMH, WS 1297) [hereafter O'Driscoll, BMH, WS 1297]; Murphy, BMH, WS 1684.

22   This information is taken from the investigator's notes originally attached to each BMH witness statement. These were removed before the collection was released in 2003. They

are now available for consultation in the MAI and will eventually be re-attached to the statements.

23   Investigator's notes, 11 Mar. 1951 for Paddy O'Brien, 5 Mar. 1951 (MAI, BMH, WS 812).

24   Con Kelleher, 19 July 1957 (MAI, BMH, WS 1654), pp. 9–10. See also (among others) Peter Kearney, 6 Nov. 1950 (MAI, BMH, WS 444), p. 15; Thomas Duggan, 2 July 1951 (MAI, BMH, WS 551), p. 3; Browne, BMH, WS 873, pp. 29–30; Ted Sullivan, 24 Aug. 1956 (MAI, BMH, WS 1478), pp. 22–6.

25   Morrison, 'Witnessing the Rebublic', pp. 124–40.

26   Donal Hales, 16 Sep. 1949 (MAI, BMH, WS 292), p. 5.

27   Seán O'Driscoll, 20 Oct. 1956 (MAI, BMH, WS 401), pp. 12–13.

28   Eamon Broy, 17 Nov. 1955 (MAI, BMH, WS 1285), p. 27.

29   Extract, Charles Saurin to Secretary, 16 May 1951 (MAI, BMH, S 1781); Notes of conversation with Liam Deasy, 10 Aug. 1973 (John O'Beirne Ranelagh Papers, privately held). I am indebted to O'Beirne Ranelagh for providing me with scanned copies of several documents from his personal papers.

30   Deasy to O'Donoghue, 27 Apr. 1950 (NLI, FOD, ms 31,421/10).

31   This includes dependents' claims made by relatives of deceased Kilmichael veterans.

32   As of November 2021, files relating to the claims of twenty-six women involved in these activities have been released (http://mspcsearch.militaryarchives.ie/brief.aspx, accessed 28 Nov. 2021).

33   Catherine Griffin *née* Kattie O'Driscoll, 19 Jan. 1939 (MAI, MSPC, MSP34REF28773).

34   Both Meda Ryan and Brian P. Murphy make this argument. *The Irish Times*, 10 Aug. 1998; Ryan, *Tom Barry* (2012), p. 76.

35   Interviews with Ned Young, Jack O'Sullivan, Nell Kelly, Josie Coughlan and others in 'The Boys of Kilmichael', 25 Oct. 1970 (RTERC, Ó Dúlaing, AR0020655/LA 000559) [hereafter Young/Ó Dúlaing (1970); O'Sullivan/Ó Dúlaing (1970); Kelly/Ó Dúlaing (1970); Coughlan/Ó Dúlaing (1970)].

36   Paddy O'Brien account, *c.* 1969 (NLI, LD, ms 43,554/13) [hereafter O'Brien/LD (1969)]; Ned Young interview, *c.* Apr. 1969 (TCD, JC, uncatalogued) [hereafter Young/JC (1969)]; Jack O'Sullivan interview, *c.* Apr. 1969 (TCD, JC, uncatalogued) [hereafter O'Sullivan/JC (1969)]; The O'Brien and Aherne interviews were recorded over. Kilmichael is not mentioned in the fragments that survive on Chisholm's tapes.

37   Sullivan, Kealkil/PH; O'Sullivan/Vaughan, *c.* 1980s.

38   See also interview notes John L. O'Sullivan 2 Apr. 1988 (ASC/QEII/MUN, PH, Coll–455–17.03.002); Ned Young interviews (notes), 3 Apr. and 25 June 1988 (ASC/QEII/MUN, PH, Coll–455–17.03.002 and ASC/QEII/MUN, PH, Coll–455–17.03.007) [hereafter Young/PH (3 Apr. 1988) and/or Young/PH (25 June 1988)]; Mary O'Sullivan to Hart, 1 Jan. 1988 (ASC/QEII/MUN, PH, Coll–455–27.01.028). Hart also interviewed a few relatives or close associates of OIRA men.

39   Young/PH (3 Apr. 1988 and 25 June 1988). Hart also interviewed the following in 1988: Seán O'Driscoll [*c.* Apr. 1988], Donal O'Donovan (nephew of Dan O'Donovan) (6 Nov. 1988) (ASC/QEII/MUN, PH, Coll–455–17.03.002).

40 Recorded interview, 21 Apr. 1993 [name withheld at request of archive] (ASC/QEII/MUN, PH, Coll–455–17.04.001); Hart's notes from same interview (ASC/QEII/MUN, PH, Coll–455–17.03.003).

41 Willie Chambers interview (notes), 19 Nov. 1989 (ASC/QEII/MUN, PH, Coll–455–1.02.017) [hereafter Chambers/PH (19 Nov. 1989); Interview notes; Jerry Murphy 27 Apr. 1989, Cormac McCarthy, 28 Apr. 1989, Eamonn de Barra, 9 May 1989, Dan Cahalane, 19 Nov. 1989 (ASC/QEII/MUN, PH, Coll–455–17.03.002).

42 Young/PH (3 Apr. 1988 and 25 June 1988). Hart to Chisholm, c. 1990 (TCDM, CP, uncatalogued); Chambers/PH (19 Nov. 1989); Author interview (telephone) Liam Chambers, 17 Aug. 2013; Chambers to Author (email), 22 Aug. 2020. Originally, Mr Chambers was of the view that his father said he was at the Enniskeane Bridge. He now believes it was the Manch Bridge, further west.

43 Author interview, Donncha Ó Dúlaing, 13 Feb. 2014.

44 The folklore relating to Cadet Frederick Forde (the Auxiliary who survived) in Flor Crowley's 1947 account (discussed in the next chapter) is one example.

45 IRACD (TNAUK, WO 141/40); Murphy, BMH, WS 1684, pp. 5–6; Hennessy, BMH, WS 1234, p. 5; Young, BMH, WS 1402; Young/JC (1969); O'Brien, BMH, WS 812; O'Brien/LD (1969).

46 O'Neill to Sec., 3 June 1939, Tom Barry to Sec., 23 June 1939 (MAI, MSPC, MSP34REF2822).

47 Whyte, The Wild Heather Glen; The Southern Star, 18 Nov. 1995. A chapter profiling the Auxiliaries and their Great War service originally intended for this book will be published elsewhere.

48 See the profiles of Denis Cronin, Jack McCarthy, Denis O'Brien, Michael O'Donovan (Leap), and Michael O'Driscoll in The Wild Heather Glen.

49 DOIR; Patrick 'Kilmallock McCarthy, d. 4 July 1922 (MAI, MSPC, DP7700); John 'Jack' Hourihan, d. 30 Aug. 1922 (MAI, MSPC, 2D178); Whyte, The Wild Heather Glen, p. 63.

50 Whyte, The Wild Heather Glen.

51 The Southern Star, 25 Aug. 1923. Barry was also present at this event. For a general discussion of post-Civil War emigration see Gavin Foster, The Irish Civil War and Society (Houndsmills, 2015), pp. 203–21.

52 Babie to Ellie and Tadg, 29 [Nov. 1926] (Dave Crowley Papers, private collection); Whyte, The Wild Heather Glen, pp. 61–4.

53 Sonnie [sic] to Ellie and Tadg [c. 1927] (Dave Crowley Papers, private collection).

54 See The Kerryman, 3 Dec. 1938 for a now famous group photograph of Kilmichael veterans taken on the day.

55 The Cork Examiner, 28 Nov. and 1 Dec. 1938. O'Sullivan spent periods living outside of Ireland. See Whyte, The Wild Heather Glen, pp. 119–21.

56 O'Brien lived in San Francisco and died in a car accident in 1968. His participation in Kilmichael is also mentioned in witness statements. The Southern Star, 3 and 10 Dec. 1938, 29 Nov. 1941, 28 Aug. 1948, 3 July 1965, 30 Mar. 1968, 6 Nov. 1971, 27 Oct. 1973; The Kerryman, 17 Apr. 1948; IRA Nominal rolls, L (Lisheen) Company, 7th Battalion, Cork 3 Brigade and 1st Battalion, Cork 5 Brigade (MAI, MSPC, RO 56 and RO 65); Stephen

O'Brien, 30 Oct. 1951 (MAI, BMH, WS 603), p. 2; Patrick O'Sullivan, 23 Aug. 1956 (MAI, BMH, WS 1481), p. 7; William Crowley, 27 Sep. 1956 (MAI, BMH, WS 1502), p. 8.

57   *The Kerryman*, 17 Apr. and 18 Dec. 1948, 1 Jan. 1949.

58   *The Southern Star*, 20 Oct. Denis O'Neill was included on earlier lists so it is not clear why he had to be re-inserted.

59   *Irish Independent*, 12 Mar. 1946. Cronin (1897–1946) was a leader of the Blueshirts and Fine Gael member. A man named Thomas Healy was also described as a Kilmichael veteran. I can find no evidence for his involvement, but I am happy to be proved wrong. *The Irish Press*, 18 Jan. 1958.

60   For example, see Labhras Joye and Brenda Malone, 'The Roll of Honour of 1916', *History Ireland*, iss. 2, vol. 14 (Mar./Apr. 2006), pp. 10–11.

61   Author interview (video), David Crowley, 14 Feb. 2013.

62   Young, BMH, WS 1402, p. 14; Young/JC (1969); O'Brien, BMH, WS 812, p. 15; O'Brien/LD (1969); *The Kerryman*, 13 Dec. 1947.

63   Thomas O'Driscoll's obituary described him as a Kilmichael participant. *The Southern Star*, 15 Jan. 1972; For his rank and IRA unit see C Coy, 1st Bn 5th Cork Brigade nominal roll (pre-Truce company attached to 7th Bn. 3rd Cork Bge) (MAI, MSPC, RO 65 and RO 56); Author interview with Brother John O'Driscoll (O'Driscoll's son), 23 July 2020.

64   *Ireland's Own*, 20 Dec. 1985.

65   See Dónall Mac Amhlaigh's 'The Irish Abroad' column over several issues of *Ireland's Own*, Brother John O'Driscoll, 28 June and 25 Oct. 1985; Anonymous, 9 Aug. 1985; Meda Ryan, 23 Aug. and 20 Dec. 1985; Louis Whyte/Kilmichael Commemoration Committee, 20 Sep. 1985; Seán de Búrca, 1 Nov. 1985; *The Southern Star*, 17 Aug. 1985.

66   William W. Allen to John O'Driscoll, 1 Apr. 1986, scanned copy in author's possession. I am very grateful to Brother O'Driscoll who, in addition to spending well over an hour on the telephone with me, sent scanned copies of his father's medals and other material.

67   *The Southern Star*, 10 Dec. 1983 and 25 Nov. 1995; *Ireland's Own*, 20 Dec. 1985. None of the witness statements mentioning the side car incident identify O'Driscoll as one of the men in the car.

68   John Condon (MAI, MSPC, DP3798); Farnivane Company roll (MAI, MSPC, RO 47), pp. 24, 111.

69   Peter Kearney, 6 Nov. 1950 (MAI, BMH, WS 444), p. 15; Seán Murphy, 20 June 1956 (MAI, BMH, WS 1445), p. 61; Paddy O'Brien (adj.) and Dan Hourihane (quartermaster after Dwyer) were also replaced in July, but this seems to have been because the battalion was divided; *The Southern Star*, 27 Nov. 2010 and 1 Jan. 2011; Barry, *Reality of the Anglo-Irish War*, p. 14. It should be noted that whatever problems Mick O'Dwyer might have had after Kilmichael, he seems to have recovered. He fought on the anti-Treaty side in the Civil War. He was arrested in March 1921 and interned until at least the summer of 1924 (www.oireachtas.ie/en/debates/debate/dail/1924-06-26/10/?highlight%5B0%5D=co, accessed 29 Nov. 2021).

70   Ballineen Company membership rolls for 11 July 1921 and 1 July 1922 (MAI, MSPC, RO/49 and RO/52).

71   Ballineen Company, 3rd Battalion activity lists (MAI, MSPC, A/3/4).

72   But not as a suspected Kilmichael participant. K Coy Auxiliary Diary, *c.* Nov. 1920–Apr. 1921 (MAI, BMH CD 31).

73   Ballineen Company, 3rd Battalion activity lists (MAI, MSPC, A/3/4).

74   Colum Cronin, a distant relative of Curlus, discovered in recent years that he settled in England.

75   Coppeen Company, 3rd (Dunmanway) Bn, 3rd Cork Brigade nominal roll (MAI, MSPC, RO 49).

76   *The Southern Star*, 23, 27 Oct. and 6, 13, 20, 27 Nov. 1971.

77   Keohane, BMH, WS 1295, pp. 5–7; Timoleague Coy activities, 2nd Bn, 3rd Cork Bge (MAI, MSPC, A/3/2), p. 55; *Irish Independent*, 10 Aug. 1970; *The Southern Star*, 20 Oct. 1973. There are no robust grounds for refusing Keohane although some still do. Ryan, *Tom Barry* (2012), pp. 59, 63.

78   My list is compiled mainly from *The Wild Heather Glen*, MSP records, BMH witness statements, newspapers and the K Company Auxiliary diary (see Chapter Two). I divided participants into four categories: 'ambush', 'logistics', 'more information needed' and 'other'.

79   O'Neill was also interviewed by Ernie O'Malley but sadly only discussed his arrest afterwards rather than the ambush itself. O'Neill, 19 Sep. 1951 (UCDA, EOMNbks, P17b/112), pp. 103–8.

80   Damian Shiels quoted in Pádraig Óg Ó Ruairc, 'Another controversy at Kilmichael' in *History Ireland*, iss. 6, vol. 22 (Nov./Dec. 2014).

81   Special Roads Committee, minutes 13 March 1951, Cork County Council Minute Book (CC&CA, IE CCCA/CC/CO/M/022); Special Roads Committee, minutes 20 Feb. 1953 meeting, Cork County Council Minute Book (CC&CA, IE CCCA/CC/CO/M/023), *The Southern Star*, 31 Oct. 1953.

82   *Daily Dispatch*, 3 Dec. 1920; *The Kerryman*, 13 Dec. 1947.

83   *The Southern Star*, 13 June 1953. It also important to note that the Auxiliaries did not wear helmets.

84   The original Fleming map is in the Bodleian Library in Oxford. The Coppeen Archaeological Historical Society holds a copy of it that was annotated by Barry. *Daily Sketch* and *Daily Dispatch*, 3 Dec. 1920.

85   Contact sheet, Kilmichael Commemoration, 1970, *Irish Examiner* library. Thanks to Tim Ellard and Anne Kearney for making these and other contacts sheets available to me.

CHAPTER 6. TELLINGS AND RETELLINGS 1921–80

1   Meda Ryan, 'Controversy rages on over "false surrender"', *The Southern Star*, 21 Nov. 2020; John Borgonovo, 'The War Escalates: Bloody Sunday, Kilmichael and November 1920', *The Cork Examiner*, 2 Jan. 2021; interview with Meda Ryan, *The Clare Champion*, 8 Dec. 2011.

2   Acting Command Adj., HQ Southern Command Cork to Adj. Gen. GHQ, Dublin, 3 June 1924 (MAI, MSPP, 1D295); DAAG Cork Command to Adjutant General, 22 Feb. 1924

(MAI, MSPP, 1D117); Army Pensions Act, 1923. Both claims were initially refused but reconsidered after interventions on the claimants' behalf. TD Timothy J. Murphy (Labour, Dunmanway) raised the issue in the Dáil in November 1924. Dáil Éireann Debate, 26 Nov. 1924, vol. 9, no. 16.

3   Piaras S. Béaslaí, *Michael Collins and the Making of a New Ireland* (London, 1926), p. 97.

4   *The Cork Examiner*, 13 Sep. 1926.

5   *The Cork Examiner*, 3 and 5 Apr. 1924. An unarmed British soldier was shot dead in Cobh on 24 March, and others wounded, when fired on by an IRA party using a Lewis gun mounted on a stolen motor car as they disembarked from a ferry. Afterwards, Cork Sinn Féin publicly stated that Republican soldiers 'never at any time did, or would ... turn their guns on unarmed and defenceless men'.

6   Frank Percy Crozier, *Ireland Forever* (London, 1932), pp. 127–8. A slightly different version was published in *The Kerryman*, 12 Mar. 1938.

7   *The Irish Press*, 26 Nov. 1932; *The Southern Star*, 3 Dec. 1932; Souvenir Programme of the Manchester Martyrs and Kilmichael Anniversary, 25 Nov. 1934 (NLI, FOD, ms 31,446). Barry delivered the oration at the event. *The Cork Examiner* and *The Southern Star*, 24 Nov. 1934.

8   *The Irish Press*, 26 Nov. 1932; Queries form, Tom Barry, 4 Jan. 1935 and *The Irish Press* cutting, 26 Nov. 1932 (MAI, MSPC, DP87/2RB1048).

9   *The Kerryman*, 11 Dec. 1937.

10 Ibid. O'Neill's account was reproduced in the first edition of *Rebel Cork's Fighting Story, Told by the Men Who Made It* in early 1947. Subsequent editions used Barry's account in *Guerilla Days in Ireland*.

11 'Eyewitness' [Tom Barry], 'Kilmichael', Pt. 2, *An Cosantóir*, vol. 2, no. 21 (16 May 1941), p. 649. The O'Neill, Barry 1932 and 1941 accounts are in, respectively, the following pensions files: Tom Barry (MAI, MSPC, MSP34REF57456); Patrick Deasy (MAI, MSPC, DP87/2RB1048); 3rd Cork Brigade activities, correspondence file (MAI, MSPC, A/3(6)).

12 Ryan, *Tom Barry* (2012), p. 317.

13 Ibid., pp. 87, 104.

14 F.C. [Flor Crowley], *The Kerryman*, 13 Dec. 1947; 11 Dec. 1948, 1 Jan. and 10 Dec. 1949; *The Southern Star*, 7 Nov. 1959, 29 Apr. 1978 and 2 Aug. 1980. Crowley was paid for three history articles in June/July 1947. Creditor's Ledger, 1944–1950 and Invoice Book, Jan. 1944–June 1949 (Kerry County Library, *The Kerryman* financial records, uncatalogued).

15 *The Kerryman*, 5 Feb. 1965; *The Southern Star*, 3 July 1965; Fintan Lane, *Long Bullets: A History of Road Bowling in Ireland* (Ardfield, 2005), p .69; 'Out for a day with the Ferret in Dunmanway, West Cork, Long Ago' (https://durrushistory.com/2014/08/18/out-for-a-day-with-the-ferret-in-dunmanway-west-cork-long-ago/, accessed 23 Dec. 2021).

16 *The Southern Star*, 29 Apr. 1978.

17 See Flor Crowley, *In West Cork Long Ago* (Dublin and Cork, 1979), pp. 17–25.

18 *The Kerryman*, 13 Dec. 1947. The identities of the scouts and the tramp are given in Whyte, *The Wild Heather Glen*, pp. 75, 108.

19 Barry, *Guerilla Days*, p. ix.

20 Bureau Journal entry, 23 [May 1947] (NLI, FOD, ms 31,355/1); Ryan, *Tom Barry* (2012), p. 327; Deasy and Chisholm recorded conversation, *c.* Apr. 1969 (TCD, JC, uncatalogued) [hereafter Deasy/JC (1969)].

21 Ryan, *Tom Barry* (2012), pp. 326–7.

22 Bureau Journal entry, 15, 24 and 25 Sep. 1947 (NLI, FOD, ms 31,355/1).

23 Deasy/JC (1969).

24 O'Donoghue, 'Clonbannin, Kilmichael, Dromkeen and some other actions of the Anglo-Irish War in the South', *c.* 1950s (NLI, FOD, ms 31,301/1).

25 Bureau Journal entry, 28 Apr. 1948 (NLI, FOD, ms 31,355/2).

26 Bureau Journal entry, 1 May 1948 (NLI, FOD, ms 31,355/2).

27 Barry, *Guerilla Days*, pp. 44–5.

28 Spud Murphy says that he, Barry, Nyhan, O'Herlihy, Denis O'Brien, Newcestown, and 'one other' were in the Command Post. James 'Spud' Murphy, 4 Oct. 1957 (MAI, BMH, WS 1684) [hereafter Murphy, BMH, WS 1684], p. 5.

29 Tom Barry, *The Reality of the Anglo–Irish War: Refutations, Corrections, and Comments on Liam Deasy's Towards Ireland Free* (Tralee and Dublin, 1974), p. 15.

30 Barry, *Guerilla Days*, pp. 44–5.

31 Tom Barry interview, n.d. [1969?] (RTERC, Nollaig Ó Gadhra, AR0021152/LA 000502) [hereafter Barry/Ó Gadhra (1969)]; Barry interview, 'The Boys of Kilmichael', 25 Oct. 1970 (RTERC, Ó Dúlaing, AR0020655/LA 000559) [hereafter Barry/Ó Dúlaing (1970)]; Ó Dúlaing included further excerpts from this interview in 'General Tom Barry on the occasion of his death', 2 July 1980 (RTERC, Ó Dúlaing, (radio broadcast), AA3472 02071980) [hereafter Barry/Ó Dúlaing (1980)]; Tom Barry, *c.* 1973 (RTERC, Kenneth Griffith/Curious Journey interviews, Tape AA2792) [hereafter Barry/Griffith (*c.* 1973)]; Tom Barry interview, 17 May 1979 (IWM Sound & Video Archive [IWMS&VA], 'The Troubles', LO/C 446) [hereafter Barry/Troubles (1979)].

32 Two sections of the same interview (B&W) filmed on 1 Nov. 1966 are preserved on separate tapes. Seámus Kelly (1919–1969) wrote 'An Irishman's Diary' in *The Irish Times* under the pen name 'Quidnunc'. Tom Barry interview, 1 Nov. 1966 (RTÉ Television Archive [RTETA], Seámus Kelly, TY0097761) [hereafter Barry/Kelly (1966)]; Tom Barry interview, 1 Jan. 1968 (RTETA, Survivors, TY0105141) [hereafter Barry/Survivors (1968)]; *The Irish Times*, 11 June 1979.

33 Barry/Ó Gadhra (1969).

34 Ryan, *Tom Barry* (2012), pp. 65, 429.

35 Barry/Ó Dúlaing (1970).

36 Barry, *Reality of the Anglo-Irish War*, p. 17.

37 *The Kerryman*, 10 Dec. 1949; O'Donoghue, 'Clonbannin, Kilmichael, Dromkeen and some other actions of the Anglo Irish War in the South', *c.* 1950s (NLI, FOD, ms 31,301/1); Eamon Broy, 17 Nov. 1955 (MAI, BMH, WS 1285); Kilmichael Ambush, 1 Nov. 1966 (RTÉ Archives, Séamus Kelly, TY0097761); Padraig Ó Maidin in *The Cork Examiner*,

28 Nov. 1969; Ewan Butler, *Barry's Flying Column* (London, 1972), p. 70; 'Kilmichael' in James Cooney, *Macroom People & Places* (Macroom, 1976), pp. 28–30; *The Southern Star*, 8 Jan. and 17 June 1978, 6 Dec. 1980; 'Anonymous' to Donall MacAmhlaigh 'The Irish Abroad', *Ireland's Own*, 9 Aug. 1985; Whyte, *The Wild Heather Glen*, p. 80: A.J.S. Brady, *The Briar of Life* (Dublin, 2010), p. 181; May Twomey to John A. Murphy, 30 Nov. 2000 (in author's possession). Thanks to John A. Murphy for sending me this letter; 'Kilmichael', 28 Nov. 2000 (RTÉ Archives, Léargas, IH27219); Seán Kelleher in *The Southern Star*, 3 Apr. 2004; Meda Ryan speech, Kilmichael Commemoration, 28 Nov. 2004 (www.indymedia.ie/article/67691?search_text= kilmichael+cork, accessed 7 May 2021); Niall Meehan, 'John Bruton looks into his own "Hart"', 12 Oct. 2004 (www. indymedia.ie/article/66994?userlanguage=ga&save _prefs=true, accessed 7 May 2021); *The Southern Star*, 8 July 2006; Domhnall Mac Giolla Phóil [Donie Powell] interview by Harry McGee, *Luiochán Chill Mhichíl*, broadcast TG4, June 3 2011 (www.youtube. com/watch?v=IIIveJreejA, accessed 7 May 2021); Ryan, *Tom Barry* (2012), p. 70; Seán Kelleher to Editor, *History Ireland*, iss. 5, vol. 20 (Sep./Oct. 2012) (www.historyireland. com/20th-century-contemporary-history/kilmichael-ambush/, accessed 17 Dec. 2021); Speeches, Kilmichael Commemoration, 28 Nov. 2014 (sound recording, courtesy of Colum Cronin). Explanatory plaques old and new at the ambush site (photographed by me in 2011 and 2015) state that three Volunteers stood up and were shot by the Auxiliaries. *An Phoblacht*, 28 Nov. 2015 and 27 Nov. 2020.

38   *The Kerryman*, 10 Dec. 1949. Another possibility is that Crowley's text was altered by the newspaper.

39   *The Southern Star*, 7 Nov. 1959.

40   *The Irish Press*, 29 Nov. 1956.

41   Begley to Deasy, 22 May 1948 (NLI, Liam Deasy Papers [hereafter LDP], ms 43,554/23); *The Irish Press*, 17–20 May 1948.

42   Ryan, *Tom Barry* (2012), pp. 327–34, 461–2.

43   Deasy, *Towards Ireland Free*, p. 131.

44   Note on Liam Deasy at Lissinfield, 18 Oct. 1962 (UCDA, MP, P7/D/45); Special Deasy note, n.d. (UCDA, MP, P7/D/45). Richard Mulcahy was IRA C/S 1919–22, Minister of Defence during the Civil War and later a Fine Gael TD.

45   O'Donoghue Diary, 27 Jan. 1947 (NLI, FOD, ms 31,355/1); O'Malley to Deasy, 3 Nov. 1950 (NLI, LD, ms 43,556/1–3).

46   Twomey to Brother Lynch, 21 Apr. and 27 Apr. 1950 (private collection). I am indebted to Brian Hanley for copies of this and other correspondence. Correspondence from Deasy, Twomey and Power relating to the book is in O'Donoghue's papers (NLI, FOD, ms 31,421/10–12); O'Donoghue, *No Other Law*.

47   *The Irish Press*, 25 Oct. 1955.

48   Deasy to de Valera, 20 Sep. 1964; de Valera to Deasy, 16 Oct. 1964 (UCDA, deV, P150/1639); Liam Deasy, 'The Schull Peninsula in the War of Independence', *Éire–Ireland*, 1:2 (1966), 5–8; Liam Deasy, 'The Beara Peninsula Campaign', *Éire–Ireland*, 1:3 (1966), pp. 63–81.

49 Deasy to O'Donoghue, 17 Jan., 3, 10, 20, 25 Mar., 7 and 13 Apr., 7 May, 20 and 29 Oct., 13 Nov., 1 Dec. 1962; Deasy to O'Donoghue, 12 Mar. 1964; 18 May, 1 Jun., 10, 21 and 27 July, 28 Aug. 1965 (NLI, FOD, ms 31,301/7/1–19).

50 Father Lyne was based in Ballinakill College in Laois from 1958 until his death in 1977. He also edited *Brother Against Brother*, Deasy's posthumous Civil War memoir. *Nationalist and Leinster Times*, 11 Feb. 1977; *The Irish Times*, 2018; Deasy, *Brother Against Brother*.

51 Author interview, Fr John Chisholm, 15 Mar. 2010.

52 The Spiritans founded and ran several prestigious fee-paying schools including Blackrock, St Michael's, St Mary's and Templeogue Colleges in Dublin, and Rockwell College in Tipperary. Father Chisholm lectured in UCD from 1966 to the late 1980s. Unless otherwise specified, his biographical details come from Brian O'Toole, 'John Chisholm and the Arab World' in *Glowing Embers: Spiritan Mission Resource and Heritage Centre* (June 2016) and his obituary (by Caroline Mullen) in the *Blackrock College Annual* (2015), p. 418. Thanks to Clare Foley, Blackrock College Archive for sending me this and other material about Fr Chisholm.

53 Chisholm to 'Mum', 12 Mar. 1983 (Kimmage Manor Archives [KMA], CP, Box 1, Folder P/C 75/1/1/4). He was vice chairman of the Arab-Irish Society (AIS) (established in 1969 by Seán T. Ryan) to promote links between Ireland and the Arab world, an organisation that actively supported the establishment of a Palestinian state governed by the Palestine Liberation Organisation. Ryan was a Dublin businessman who had been interned in the 1950s for IRA activities. It was rumoured that the IRA established links with Libya through the AIS. Marie-Violaine Louvet, 'Light on the Arab World: The "Irish–Arab News", 1975–85' in *Irish Studies in International Affairs*, vol. 23 (2012), pp. 191–203, see pp. 191, 200; Yasser Arafat to Chisholm, 8 May 1981 (KMA, CP, Box 4).

54 Author interview, Kathleen McCaul *née* Deasy, 15 Jan. 2015.

55 Deasy/JC (1969).

56 Author interview (video) with Liam Deasy (nephew), 27 July 2012; John E. Chisholm tapes (TCDM, JC, uncatalogued).

57 Author interview (video) with Liam Deasy (nephew), 27 July 2012.

58 Ibid.; O'Brien/LD is transcribed in full in Appendix 5. Deasy (nephew) told me what O'Brien said but would not give details during his recorded interview. For this reason, I have not included them.

59 Chisholm to Hart, 22 Feb. 1990 (ASC/QEII/MUN, PH, Coll–455–27.01.007).

60 Young/JC (1969).

61 Liam Deasy, *Towards Ireland Free*, pp. 171–2.

62 See Appendix 5 for full transcription of O'Brien's original account.

63 Note, n.d. (NLI, LDP, ms 43,554/14).

64 Robert Dudley Edwards, notes on 'Irish Guerillas versus British Might', unpublished mss ed. J.E. Chisholm, n.d. [1971] (John O'Beirne Ranelagh Papers, private collection).

65 Nolan to Deasy, 4 Aug. 1971 (NLI, LD, ms 43,554/22).

66   Lynch to Chisholm [Oct. 1971] and Chisholm to Lynch, Oct. 1971 (NLI, LD, ms 43,554/22); Nolan to Florrie O'Donoghue, 4 Oct. 1961 (NLI, FOD, ms 31,306/1/41).

67   Pat Lynch, notes on 'Irish Guerillas versus British Might' [Oct. 1971] (NLI, LD, ms 43,554/22).

68   Ibid.

69   Nolan, Rena Dardis and Seamus McConville jointly founded Anvil Press in 1962.

70   For Pat Lynch's involvement in the second edition of the Cork volume see the correspondence between Nolan and O'Donoghue (NLI, FOD, ms 31,306/1); Nolan to O'Donoghue, 10 Oct 1961 (NLI, FOD, ms 31,306/1/43).

71   Nolan to O'Donoghue, 28 June 1961 (NLI, FOD, ms 31,306/1/3); *The Kerryman, Rebel Cork's Fighting Story 1916–21: Told by the Men Who Made It, with a Unique Pictorial Record of the Period* (Tralee, 1947); *The Kerryman, Rebel Cork's Fighting Story: From 1916 to the Truce with Britain* (Tralee, 1961).

72   Deasy to Nolan [Oct. 1971] (NLI, LD, ms 43,554/22); statements by Tim O'Connell and Spud Murphy are listed in *Towards Ireland Free*'s bibliography.

73   Nolan to Deasy, 22 Feb. 1972 (NLI, LD, ms 43,554/22).

74   Quoted in Brennan to Deasy, 22 July 1972 (NLI, LD, ms 43,554/22). Nolan said much the same to Chisholm around the same time. Nolan to Chisholm, 10 Apr. 1972 (NLI, LD, ms 43,554/22). See also Helen O'Brien to Máire Comerford, 16 Oct. 1973 (UCDA, MC, LA 18/46/62–65).

75   Barry to Nolan, 4 May 1977 (UCDA, Frances Mary Blake [hereafter FMB], P244/16).

76   Nolan to Barry, 9 May 1977 and Nolan to Blake, 31 May 1977 (UCDA, FMB, P244/16). When Barry realised Nolan had accepted the manuscript for publication, he asked Nolan to 'destroy my damn letter' and suggested they find a method of dealing with 'O'Malley's illusions'. Barry to Nolan (UCDA, FMB, P244/16). O'Malley's son Cormac later re-inserted most of the names removed from the initial publication. The Nolan/Blake letters suggest many other details and passages of O'Malley's memoir were also edited and revised.

77   Deasy to Chisholm, 2 Nov. 1972 (KMA, CP, P/C75/1/1/1).

78   *The Cork Examiner*, 25 Sep. 1973.

79   Barry to Editor, 1 Oct. 1973 (CC&CA, TB, U16/1/1); *The Cork Examiner*, 4 Oct. 1973 and 10 Apr. 1974; *The Southern Star*, 6 Oct. 1973.

80   *The Southern Star*, 20, 27 Oct. and 3 Nov. 1973.

81   Crowley used several pen names, including 'Raymond', *The Southern Star*, 20 Oct. 1973.

82   *The Southern Star*, 27 Oct. 1973.

83   *The Southern Star*, 3 Nov. 1973.

84   Tom O'Neill, *The Battle of Clonmult: The IRA's Worst Defeat*, 2nd ed. (Cheltenham, 2019); *DOIR*, pp. 306–9; 2nd Battalion notes, *Hampshire Regimental Journal*, vol. XVI, no. 3 (Mar. 1921), p. 37.

85   Deasy notes on revisions to *TIF*, n.d. [*c.* 1974] (NLI, LD, ms 43,554/20).

86   Some of Barry's nastier remarks about O'Brien were omitted from the published version. Barry, handwritten draft 'Refutations, Corrections and Comments', book no. 1 (CC&CA, TB, U16/1/1); *The Southern Star*, 11 Jan.–15 Feb. 1975.

87 Lyne to Chisholm, 29 Nov. 1974 (TCDM, CP, uncatalogued).

88 *The Irish Times*, 12 Dec. 1974. Flor Begley kept the original letters and statement. Diarmuid, his son, has his father's papers and intends to give the collection to the Cork City and County Archives.

89 *The Southern Star*, 11 Jan.–15 Feb. 1975.

90 Chisholm to Lyne, 28 July 1976 and 29 Nov. 1976 and Mary Feehan to Chisholm, 5 Aug. 1976 (TCDM, CP, uncatalogued). Deasy, *Towards Ireland Free* (1977). It was not included in subsequent editions, perhaps to avoid reigniting the controversy.

91 *An Cosantóir*, Aug. 1975.

92 *The Southern Star*, 29 Apr. 1978.

93 *The Southern Star*, 17 June 1978.

94 *The Cork Examiner, The Irish Press* and *Irish Independent*, 3 July 1980.

95 *The Southern Star*, 2 Aug. 1980; *The Cork Examiner*, 8 Aug. 1980.

CHAPTER 7. 28 NOVEMBER 1920

1   Seán O'Faolain, *Vive Moi: An Autobiography* (London, 1965), p. 144.

2   Barry/Kelly (1966); O'Sullivan/Ó Dúlaing (1970); Young, BMH, WS 1402; Young/JC (1969).

3   Josie Coughlan/Ó Dúlaing (1970). Johnstown is a nearby townland from where she came.

4   *The Southern Star*, 31 July 1976.

5   Young, BMH, WS 1402; Young/JC (1969); O'Brien/LD (1969); Murphy, BMH, WS 1684.

6   Barry, *Guerilla Days*, p. 43.

7   Young/JC (1969).

8   O'Brien does not mention the sidecar in his witness statement.

9   This is despite Young contradicting Chisholm on this point in the interview, Young/JC (1969). *The Southern Star*, 27 Oct. 1973.

10 Deasy, *Towards Ireland Free*, p. 171. Hennessy, BMH, WS 1234; Keohane, BMH, WS 1295; O'Driscoll, BMH, WS 1297, all in Section Two, do not mention the sidecar.

11 Barry/Kelly (1966). See also Barry/Ó Dúlaing (1970).

12 Whyte to Hart, 20 Oct. 1996 (ASC/QEII/MUN, PH, Coll–455–27.01.013); Ryan, *Tom Barry* (2012), p. 66.

13 Sworn statement of Mrs Marjorie Mooney (*née* Cahalane), 15 Mar. 1940 (MAI, MSPC, MSP34REF46237).

14 O'Brien, BMH, WS 812, p. 12. Kautt, *Ambushes and Armour: The Irish Rebellion 1919–1921* (Dublin, 2010), p. 106.

15 Murphy, BMH, WS 1684, pp. 12–13. Barry, Liam Deasy, Murphy and Peter Monahan (a Scottish deserter) all seem to have taken some part in Bradfield's execution. *DOIR*, pp. 279–80; Anna Hurley O'Mahony, 20 June 1951 (MAI, BMH, WS 540), p. 4.

16 The interviewee also said that, in conversation, Barry told people he killed eight Catholics and six Protestants but 'never lost a night's sleep over it'. The 'Cotter' referred to could be either Alfred (d. 25 Feb. 1921) or Thomas Cotter of Curraclogh (d. 1 Mar. 1921). Recorded

interview, 18 Apr. 1993 [name withheld at request of archive] (ASC/QEII/MUN, PH, Coll–455-17.04.001); Hart's notes from same interview (ASC/QEII/MUN, PH, Coll–455-17.03.003).

17   For a discussion of this issue and more general discussions of the recognised rules of war at the time, see Kautt, *Ambushes and Armour*, pp. 104, 106, 236; Seán A. Murphy, *Kilmichael: A Battlefield Study* (Skibbereen, 2014), pp. 151–64.

18   Barry, *Guerilla Days*, p. 43.

19   Murphy, BMH, WS 1684; Hennessy BMH, WS 1234; Murphy, BMH, WS 1684; Keohane, BMH, WS 1295; O'Brien, BMH, WS 812; O'Brien/LD (1969); O'Driscoll, BMH, WS 1297. Sonny Dave Crowley maintained that he shot the driver. Author interview (video), David Crowley, 14 Feb. 2013.

20   O'Sullivan/JC (1969).

21   O'Sullivan/Ó Dúlaing (1970).

22   Murphy, *Kilmichael*, pp. 139–42, 144–5.

23   Nathan Watanabe, 'Hand Grenade', 29 Aug. 2016 (*1914–1918-online*; DOI:10.15463/ie1418.10952).

24   Young/JC (1969).

25   Murphy, *Kilmichael*, pp. 75–7.

26   Young, BMH, WS 1402, p. 15.

27   This is a bit confusing, because both Young and O'Brien say they were south of the road. From where Young said he was, O'Brien would have been on Young's right. Other members of Section One were north of the road though, so Young could be referring to them.

28   O'Brien, BMH, WS 812.

29   O'Brien/LD (1969).

30   Deasy, *Towards Ireland Free*, p. 171.

31   Young/JC (1969).

32   Young/Ó Dúlaing (1970).

33   Author interview (video), David Crowley, 14 Feb. 2013.

34   Annotated print-out Mealy's Fine Art & Rare Books Auctioneers webpage, 6 Dec. 2004 (ASC/QEII/MUN, PH, Coll–455-21.03.002).

35   *An Phoblacht*, 2 Dec. 2004.

36   Notes, 'The Truth about Kilmichael', 2004 (ASC/QEII/MUN, PH, Coll–455-21.03.002); Annotated print-out Mealy's Fine Art & Rare Books Auctioneers webpage, 6 Dec. 2004 (ASC/QEII/MUN, PH, Coll–455-21.03.002). Thanks to Fonsie Mealy's Brigid Coady for her advice in relation to the auction.

37   Annotated print-out of Mealy's Fine Art & Rare Books Auctioneers webpage, 6 Dec. 2004 (ASC/QEII/MUN, PH, Coll–455-21.03.002).

38   For examples of 'pro-Barry' maps see Whyte, *The Wild Heather Glen*, p. 37; *The Irish Press*, 18 May 1948 and 29 Nov. 1956. Another map placing the second lorry in the wrong place is in John Crowley, Donal Ó Drisceoil, Mike Murphy and John Borgonovo (eds), *Atlas of the Irish Revolution* (Cork, 2017), p. 410.

39 Barry, *Guerilla Days*, p. 43.

40 Hennessy, BMH, WS 1234; Keohane, BMH, WS 1295; O'Driscoll, BMH, WS 1297; O'Brien, BMH, WS 812; O'Sullivan/JC (1969); O'Sullivan/Ó Dúlaing (1970); Young, BMH, WS 1402; Young/JC (1969), Young/Ó Dúlaing (1970).

41 Nell Kelly interview, 'The Boys of Kilmichael', 25 Oct. 1970 (RTERC, Ó Dúlaing, AR0020655/LA 000559).

42 *Daily Dispatch* and *Daily Sketch*, 3 Dec. 1920.

43 I am indebted to Don Wood for bringing this small monument to my attention.

44 Young/JC (1969); O'Brien, BMH, WS 812; O'Brien/LD (1969).

45 Young, BMH, WS 1402.

46 Murphy, BMH, WS 1684.

47 *The Kerryman*, 11 Dec. 1937.

48 Murphy, BMH, WS 1684; O'Brien, BMH, WS 812; O'Brien/LD (1969); Young, BMH, WS 1402; Young/JC (1969); O'Driscoll, BMH, WS 1297; Hennessy, BMH, WS 1234; Keohane, BMH, WS 1295; Timothy O'Connell, note on activities, *c.* June/July 1935 (MAI, MSPC, MSP34REF2175). Hennessy only mentions McCarthy, whom he fought alongside. O'Sullivan and Deasy were above them, so it is unlikely that Hennessy could have seen them.

49 O'Driscoll, BMH, WS 1297.

50 O'Sullivan/Ó Dúlaing (1970).

51 He also told Chisholm that Jim O'Sullivan 'hadn't a hope' because 'he was up high'.

52 Young/JC (1969).

53 Ibid.

54 O'Brien, BMH, WS 812, p. 16; Timothy O'Connell, note on activities, *c.* June/July 1935 (MAI, MSPC, MSP34REF2175). O'Connell told Flor Crowley that McCarthy lived for an hour.

55 O'Brien, BMH, WS 812, p. 16.

56 Young/JC (1969).

57 Ryan, *Tom Barry* (2012), p. 79.

58 Ibid., p. 428.

59 Ibid., pp. 55, 67.

60 *The Kerryman*, 13 Dec. 1947; Young, BMH, WS 1402; O'Brien/LD (1969).

61 Ryan, *Tom Barry* (2012), p. 59.

62 Hourihan to Defence, 8 Dec. 1937, Memo, 25 Mar. 1941, Note on Hourihan testimony 'Kilmichael 24 miles', 21 Oct. 1942. Defence to Finance, 8 Jan. 1943 and Hourihan to Sec. Min. Defence, 30 Mar. 1943 (MAI, MSPC, MSP34REF1936/ 34D11). His pension was actually decreased after he tried unsuccessfully to appeal the ruling. He marched to the Kilmichael ambush site with the column and left under orders. It seems rather harsh that the board refused to award him 'key man' status. I am indebted to Dr Marie Coleman and Cecile Gordon, head archivist of the MSPC project, for clarifying that separate criteria applied for assessing service in 1916 and War of Independence. Barry Keane's

understanding of how claims were assessed is wrong. See *The Southern Star*, 3 and 26 Aug. 2017.

63 Whyte, *The Wild Heather Glen*, pp. 73–4; Deasy, *Towards Ireland Free*, p. 172; Murphy, BMH, WS 1684, p. 7.

64 Ryan, *Tom Barry* (2012), pp. 67, 430.

65 Ibid., p. 60.

66 Ibid., pp. 70–2.

67 Young/Ó Dúlaing (1970).

68 Young/JC (1969).

69 Keohane, BMH WS 1295.

70 Hennessy, BMH, WS 1234.

71 Meda Ryan in *The Cork Examiner*, 28 Nov. 2020.

72 P. Hodges. '"They don't like it up 'em!": Bayonet fetishization in the British Army during the First World War', *Journal of War and Culture Studies*, vol. 1, iss. 2 (2008), pp. 123–38; US Infantry Association, *Bayonet Training Manual used by British Forces* (New York, 1917), pp. 1, 35.

73 Young/JC (1969).

74 Hennessy, BMH, WS 1234.

75 *Irish Independent*, 17 Jan. 1921. For the full account see Appendix 3.

76 Tim O'Connell, *c.* June/July 1935 (MAI, MSPC, MSP34REF2175).

77 O'Driscoll, BMH, WS 1297.

78 Young, BMH, WS 1402.

79 Young/JC (1969).

80 Young/JC (1969).

81 O'Sullivan/Ó Dúlaing (1970); O'Sullivan/Vaughan (*c.* 1983).

82 O'Sullivan/JC (1969).

83 Young/JC (1969).

84 Hart's notes from the interview alternate between direct quotations and paraphrasing. The above excerpts are all marked in Hart's notes as direct quotes. Notes from taped interview with Jack Sullivan, Kealkil, n.d. (ASC/QEII/MUN, PH, Coll–455–455–1.02.017). He said something similar to Brendan Vaughan, but it is a bit more confusing. O'Sullivan/Vaughan, *c.* 1980s.

85 O'Sullivan/JC (1969).

86 Ian Beckett, Timothy Bowman and Mark Connelly, *The British Army and the First World War* (Cambridge, 2017), p. 159.

87 Morrison 'Kilmichael Revisited', p. 171; Murphy, *Kilmichael*, pp. 144–5.

88 O'Sullivan/JC (1969).

89 Author interview, Deasy (nephew), 27 July 2013.

90 *Abhainn*, the Bandon River, RTÉ, broadcast 14 Oct. 2013.

91 Kattie Daly *née* O'Neill, *c.* 29 July 1938 (MAI, MSPC, MSP34REF29224); Margaret Deasy (MAI, MSPC, MSP34REF29350); Nora O'Leary *née* Farrell (MAI, MSPC, MSP34REF45215).

92   Notes from taped interview with Jack Sullivan, Kealkil, n.d. (ASC/QEII/MUN, PH, Coll–455–455–1.02.017).

93   O'Brien/LD (1969); Whyte, *The Wild Heather Glen*, p. 61.

94   Tim Keohane and Tim O'Connell were both armed with shotguns.

95   Barry/Survivors (1968).

96   Court of Inquiry on Kilmichael, 28 Nov. 1920 (TNAUK, WO 35/152).

97   Young/JC (1969).

98   *The Southern Star*, 29 Apr. 1978.

99   *Meath Chronicle*, 11 Mar. 2006.

CHAPTER 8. THEY WERE ALL REVISIONISTS THEN

1   The three fatalities were David Wilson, Harold Browne and Victor Cunningham. Michael Ciarnes, 'The massacre at Darkley – and the nature of certainty' in Deric Henderson and Ivan Little (eds), *Reporting the Troubles: Journalists tell their stories of the Northern Ireland conflict* (Newtownards, 2018) [ebook], 221.0/521–228.0/521; David McKittrick, Seámus Kelters, Brian Feeney and Chris Thornton, *Lost Lives: The Stories of the Men, Women and Children Who Died as a Result of the Northern Ireland Troubles* (Edinburgh and London, 2001), pp. 963–4; David Bell, *Fire on the Mountain: The True Story of the Darkley Church in Northern Ireland* (Belfast, 2013), pp. 93–112.

2   McKittrick et al., *Lost Lives*, p. 964.

3   Ibid.

4   *The Irish Times*, 24 Nov. 2018.

5   *The Cork Examiner* and *Irish Independent*, 25 Nov. 1983.

6   *Irish Independent*, 17 Nov. 1983.

7   *Irish Independent*, 25 Nov. 1983.

8   *An Phoblacht*, 17 Nov. 1983.

9   *Irish Independent*, 17 Nov. 1983.

10   *Irish Independent*, 18 Nov. 1983.

11   *The Southern Star*, 15 Aug. 1970.

12   *Irish Independent*, 27 Sep. 1973.

13   Brian Hanley, *The Impact of the Northern Troubles: Boiling Volcano? 1968–1979* (Manchester, 2018), p. 182.

14   Ibid., pp. 177–8.

15   *An Phoblacht*, 20 Nov. 2008.

16   In the aftermath of the 1980–1 hunger strikes, Sinn Féin became more focused on becoming a serious electoral force, although the party insisted that no electoral mandate was required for the IRA's armed struggle, which would continue. C.J. Woods, *Bodenstown Revisited: The Grave of Theobald Wolfe Tone, Its Monuments and Its Pilgrimages* (Dublin, 2018), p. 194; Hanley, *The IRA*, p. 194.

17   *An Phoblacht*, 1 Dec. 1983.

18   *An Phoblacht*, 1 Dec. 1983 reported that 'several thousand' attended.

19   *The Irish Press*, 6 Dec. 1983.

20   HC 8 December 1983, vol. 50 cc517–59, 517.

21   *The Southern Star*, 31 Dec. 1983.

22   *The Cork Examiner*, 28 Nov. 1960, 7 Dec. 1962, 25 Nov. 1963, 27 Nov. 1964, 29 Nov. 1965, 28 Nov. 1966, 27 Nov.1967; *The Southern Star*, 28 Nov. 1964, 5 Dec. 1964, 3 Dec. 1966, 9 Dec. 1967, 30 Nov. 1968, 6 Dec. 1969.

23   *The Cork Examiner*, 28 Nov. 1956, 27 Oct. 1965; *The Southern Star*, 3 Dec. 1966.

24   *The Southern Star*, 28 Nov. 1964; *The Cork Examiner*, 27 Nov. 1957, 15 Dec. 1958, 2 Dec. 1967.

25   *The Southern Star*, 3 July 1965.

26   *The Cork Examiner*, 12 July 1966.

27   *The Cork Examiner*, 11 July 1966.

28   *The Cork Examiner*, 8 and 10 Dec. 1975; *The Southern Star*, 13 Dec. 1975. The Balcombe Street Gang admitted responsibility for bombings in Woolwich and the Guildford pub bombings.

29   Woods, *Bodenstown*, pp. 166–88.

30   Brian Hanley, '"But Then They Started all this Killing": Attitudes to the I.R.A. in the Irish Republic since 1969', *IHS*, vol. 38, iss. 151 (2013), pp. 439–56, see p. 440.

31   *Irish Independent*, 23 Aug. 1971.

32   Eve Morrison, 'Tea, Sandbags and Cathal Brugha: Kathy Barry's Civil Wars' in Oona Frawley (ed.), *Women in the Decade of Commemorations* (Indiana, 2021), pp. 198–9; *The Southern Star*, 18 Nov. 1972.

33   Margaret O'Callaghan, 'The Past Never Stands Still: Commemorating the Easter Rising in 1966 and 1976' in Jim Smyth (ed.), *Remembering the Troubles: Contesting the Recent Past in Northern Ireland* (Notre Dame, 2017), pp. 116, 128.

34   *Evening Echo*, 5 Dec. 1979, 5 Jan. 1980. For a report on the 1979 commemoration see *The Irish Press*, 26 Nov. 1979.

35   *The Southern Star*, 8 and 23 May 1981.

36   Alex White, 'Section 31: Ministerial Orders and Court Challenges' in Mary P. Corcoran & Mark O'Brien (eds), *Political Censorship and the Democratic State: The Irish Broadcasting Ban* (Dublin, 2005), pp. 34–47, see p. 34; Woods, *Bodenstown*, p. 199; Gerry Kelly 'Guerilla Days in 1972', *An Phoblacht*, iss. 1 (2021), pp. 41–3.

37   Invited speakers 1994–1997: Mitchel McLoughlin (1994), Martin McGuinness (1995), Lucilita Breathnach (1996), Gerry Adams (1997). For a list of the invited speakers 1978–94 see Whyte, *The Wild Heather Glen*, pp. 165–6.

38   *The Southern Star*, 11 Dec. 1995.

39   *The Southern Star*, 12 Dec. 1997.

40   *The Anglo-Celt*, 1 Aug. 1969; www.irish-showbands.com/Bands/victors.htm, accessed 3 July 2021.

41   Seán Ó Riain, *Provos. Patriots or Terrorsts?* (Dublin, 1974), p. 32.

42   Hanley, *The Impact of the Northern Troubles*, p. 188.

43   Ibid., p. 189.

44   Hanley, *The Impact of the Northern Troubles*, p. 209; Conor Cruise O'Brien, *States of Ireland* (London, 1972); Ruth Dudley Edwards, *Padraig Pearse, the Triumph of Failure* (London, 1979).

45   Michael Laffan, 'Easter Week and the Historians' in Mary Daly and Miriam O'Callaghan (eds), *1916 in 1966: Commemorating the Easter Rising* (Dublin, 2007), p. 338; Brian Hanley and Scott Millar, *The Lost Revolution: The Story of the Official IRA and the Workers' Party* (Dublin, 2009), pp. 484–5.

46   *The Irish Times*, 19 Dec. 1989, 17, 25, 26 July 1990.

47   Hanley, *The Impact of the Northern Troubles*, pp. 195–9.

48   Ibid., p. 205. The Irish Communist Organisation was founded in 1965 and renamed the British & Irish Communist Organisation in the early 1970s.

49   Lane, *On the Old IRA Belfast Brigade Area*, p. 2.

50   Nolan to Blake, 25 Jan. 1977 (UCDA, FMB, P244/16).

51   Nolan to Blake, 18 Apr. 1977 (UCDA, FMB, P244/16).

52   Tom Dunne, 'Beyond "Revisionism"', *The Irish Review*, No. 12 (Spring/Summer 1992), p. 6.

53   Robert Perry 'Revising Irish History: The Northern Ireland Conflict and the War of Ideas', *Journal of European Studies*, 40 (4), pp. 332–3, 334. For examples of this sort of analysis see Peter Beresford Ellis, *Revisionism in Irish Historical Writing: The New Anti-Nationalist School of Historians* (London, 1989); Desmond Fennell, 'Against Revisionism', *Irish Review* 4, pp. 20–6; Brian P. Murphy, 'Past Events and Present Politics: Roy Foster's 'Modern Ireland' in Daltún O'Ceallaigh (ed.), *Reconsiderations of Irish History and Culture: Selected Papers from the Desmond Greaves Summer School 1989–93* (Dublin, 1994), pp. 72–93; Kevin Whelan, 'The Revisionist Debate in Ireland', *Boundary 2* (Spring 2004), pp. 179–205.

54   Brendan Bradshaw, 'Nationalism and Historical Scholarship in Modern Ireland', *IHS*, vol. 26, iss. 104 (Nov. 1989), pp. 336, 342, 347, 349. For a discussion of Bradshaw and Fennell see Stephen Howe, 'The Politics of Historical "Revisionism": Comparing Ireland and Israel/ Palestine', *Past and Present*, No. 168 (Aug. 2000), pp. 244–5.

55   When I interviewed Bradshaw, he told me his original paper had been inspired by Kenneth O. Morgan, who characterised Welsh nationalism as an overwhelming positive and re-invigorating force. Bradshaw appealed to Irish historians to follow Morgan's lead. Author interview, Brendan Bradshaw, 9 Oct. 2012. It is worth noting that Morgan did not equate Irish and Welsh nationalisms because the latter was primarily cultural and social. It did not challenge British rule. He also described Irish nationalism as 'insular'. Kenneth O. Morgan, *Rebirth of a Nation: Wales 1880–1980* (Oxford, 1981), pp. 119–20, 377, 408, 418–19.

56   Seámus Deane, 'The Position of the Irish Intellectual', *Cambridge Review*, 18 May 1973, p. 134.

57   Deane, 'The Position of the Irish Intellectual', p. 136; Seámus Deane, 'Wherever Green is Read' in Mairín Ní Dhonnchadha and Theo Dorgan (eds), *Revising the Rising* (Derry, 1991), p. 102.

58 R.F. Foster, *Paddy and Mr. Punch: Connections in Irish and English History* (London, 1995; 2011), p. 17; Ronan Fanning 'The British Dimension', *The Crane Bag*, vol. 8, no. 1, p. 49.

59 Ronan Fanning, Desmond Fennell, Arthur Green and Stefan Collini, 'Nationalist Perspectives on the Past: A Symposium', *The Irish Review* (Cork), no. 4 (Spring 1988), pp. 15–39, see p. 16; Fanning, 'The Great Enchantment', p. 156; Cormac Ó Gráda quoted in Dunne, 'New Histories: Beyond "Revisionism"', p. 11.

60 F.S.L. Lyons quoted in Ronan Fanning, 'The Great Enchantment: Uses and Abuses of Modern Irish History' in Brady, Ciaran (ed.), *Interpreting Irish History: The Debate on Historical Revisionism* (Dublin, 1994, 2nd ed., 1999), p. 146; Ciaran Brady, '"Constructive and Instrumental": The dilemma of Ireland's first "new historians"' in Brady (ed.), *Interpreting Irish History*, p. 13; T.W. Moody, 'Irish History and Irish Mythology', *Hermathena*, no. 124 (Summer 1978), pp. 6–24.

61 Moody, 'Irish History and Irish Mythology', p. 23.

62 David Fitzpatrick, 'The Geography of Irish Nationalism 1910–1921', *Past & Present*, 78 (1978), p. 137.

63 Roy Foster, 'We are all Revisionists Now' in *The Irish Review (Cork)*, no. 1 (1986), pp. 1–5, see p. 2; Michael Laffan, 'Insular Attitudes: The Revisionists and Their Critics' in Máirín Ní Dhonnchadha and Theo Dorgan (eds), *Revising the Rising* (Derry, 1991), p. 119; Hugh Kearney 'The Irish and their History', *History Workshop Journal*, vol. 31, iss. 1 (Spring 1991), p. 151.

64 D.W. Hayton, 'The Laboratory for 'Scientific History': T.W. Moody and R.D. Edwards at the Institute of Historical Research', *IHS*, vol. 41, iss. 159 (2017), pp. 41–57, 42, 159.

65 Hanley, *The Impact of the Northern Troubles*, pp. 155, 243; Ed Moloney, 'Censorship and "The Troubles"' in Corcoran and O'Brien, *Political Censorship*, p. 101.

66 Patrick O'Farrell, 'The Canon of Irish Cultural History. A Reply to Brian Murphy', *Studies: An Irish Quarterly Review*, vol. 82, no. 328 (Winter 1993), pp. 487–98, see p. 487.

67 *The Irish Press*, 10 Sep. 1973; Eamonn de Barra interview notes, 9 May 1989 (ASC/QEII/MUN, PH, Coll–455–17–03–002); DE BARRA, Éamonn (1902–1996) (www.ainm.ie/Bio.aspx?ID=1533, accessed 16 Dec. 2021).

68 *The Southern Star*, 2 Dec. 1989; BBC News report, 24 Sep. 2019 (www.bbc.com/news/uk-northern-ireland-49797327, accessed 17 Dec. 2021).

69 Brian Hanley, 'Terror in Twentieth-Century Ireland' in Fitzpatrick (ed.), *Terror in Ireland*, p.15; Hanley, *Impact*, p. 202.

70 Lane, *On the IRA*, pp. 2, 6.

71 Sinn Féin Publicity Department, *The Good Old IRA: Tan War Operations* (Dublin, 1985), p. 1.

72 Their bibliographies are a useful guide to what was available in the late 1960s and early 1970s. Charles Townshend, *British Campaign*; David Fitzpatrick, *Politics and Irish Life 1913–1921: Provincial Experience of War and Revolution* (Dublin, 1977).

73 Two of the most significant Irish repositories for private papers are the NLI and UCDA. Important collections consulted for this book include NLI: Liam Deasy (donated Dec.

1981; released 1999); Florence O'Donoghue (donated 1967 and 1968; intermittently available in 1980s and 1990s, the final tranches of the collection were released by 2005); Seán O'Mahony (2004; 2008); Ernie O'Malley Papers (donated 1960; released c. late 1960s). UCDA: Richard Mulcahy (deposited Dec. 1970; released in tranches P7/a: 1977, P7/b: 1984; P7/c: 1985); Ernie O'Malley Papers and interviews (Gilbert Library c. 1963 to 1974. UCDA 1974; 1979); Mary MacSwiney (1979; June 1982); Moss Twomey (Aug. 1984; 1992); Desmond and Mabel Fitzgerald (May 1987; 1993); Frank Aiken (9 July 1991; June 1999); Éamon de Valera (Franciscans 1975; 1987/UCDA 1997; 2001); Máire Comerford (Feb. 1974 and March 1981; 2002); Kathy Barry Moloney (Feb. 1990; 2007); Con Moloney (Nov. 1972 and Apr. 1990; 2010); Frances Mary Blake (2010; 2018).

74   Peter Young, 'Military Archives in the Defence Forces', *An Cosantóir* (Sep. 1977), pp. 274–5; Peter Young, 'Military Archives – the First Year', *An Cosantóir* (Oct. 1983), p. 337.

75   Ryan, *Tom Barry Story* (1982), p. 9.

76   Ryan, *Tom Barry* (1982), p. 20. See also Ted Sullivan, 10 Dec. 1950 (UCDA, EOMNbks, P17b/108), p. 24.

77   Ryan, *Tom Barry* (1982), p. 145. Barry told Ryan that killing Somerville was an accident but gave a rather different story to Tim Pat Coogan. See Coogan, *A Memoir*, pp. 33–4.

78   Ryan, *Tom Barry* (1982), pp. 72, 124, 181–3; Barry, *Guerilla Days*, p. 51; Ewan Butler, *Barry's Flying Column: The Story of the IRA's Cork No.3 Brigade, 1919–21* (London, 1971), p. 78. Butler argued that the authorities had deliberately falsified the numbers (i.e., sixteen dead) to 'excuse their defeat'.

79   *The Kerryman*, 13 Dec. 1947.

80   Ryan, *Tom Barry* (1982), p. 34.

81   Ibid., pp. 180–1.

82   Ibid., p. 178. The late Fr Chisholm told me this was not true. He met Barry only once, in April 1969, before the manuscript was written. Perhaps someone else might have asked Barry to read it.

83   *An Phoblacht*, 30 Sep. 1983.

84   *Sunday Independent*, 5, 12, 26 Sep. 1982.

85   Ibid.

86   Nolan to Blake, 1 Jan. 1983 (UCDA, FMB, P244/95).

87   'Miriam Meets', interview with Joe Lee and Gearóid Ó Tuathaigh, RTÉ Radio 1, 22 Aug. 2010 (www.rte.ie/radio1/miriam-meets/programmes/2010/0822/347636-220810/, accessed 22 July 2016).

88   Graduate Studies Dept, TCD to Hart, 27 May 1987 (ASC/QEII/MUN, PH, Coll–455–27.01.004).

89   Joost Augusteijn, *From Public Defiance to Guerilla Warfare: The Experience of Ordinary Volunteers in the Irish War of Independence 1916–1921* (London and Portland, 1996), pp. 370–1.

90   Hart recorded three of his interviews 17, 18 and 21 Apr. 1993 [names withheld at request of archive] (ASC/QEII/MUN, PH, Coll–455–27.04.00). He approached oral testimony

relating to the Irish Revolution as folklore. See his discussion of archetypes and myths in 'Conspiracies of Memory: Recalling the Irish Revolution', Conference Keynote address, 21 June 2007 Canadian Association of Irish Studies Conference [CCAIS] (ASC/QEII/MUN, PH, Coll–455–9.01.026).

91 Obituary of Anne Hart, 22 Oct. 2019 (www.mccallgardens.com/obituaries/margaret-eleanor-anne-hart-hill?print, accessed 17 Dec. 2021).

92 Author interview (telephone) Marion O'Driscoll, 3 Oct. 2012.

93 11 Nov. 1989 [Name withheld at request of archive] (ASC/QEII/MUN, PH, Coll–455–27.01.032).

94 Chisholm to Hart, 22 Feb. 1990 (ASC/QEII/MUN, PH, Coll–455–27.01.007).

95 Hart to Chisholm [c. 1990] (TCDM, CP); Chisholm to Hart, draft reply [c. 1990].

96 Brian Hanley, 'Change and Continuity: Republican Thought since 1922', The Republic, iss. 2 (Spring/Summer 2001) (www.theirelandinstitute.com/wp/change-and-continuity-republican-thought-since-1922/, accessed 17 Dec. 2021).

97 John Hedges (Sinn Féin) to Hart, 12 Apr. 1988 (ASC/QEII/MUN, PH, Coll–455–27.01.005); Notes from George O'Mahony interviews (ASC/QEII/MUN, PH, Coll–455–10.04.003); O'Mahony to Hart, c. 1990 (ASC/QEII/MUN, PH, Coll–455–27.01.028).

98 Jack Lane (Aubane Historical Society) to Hart, 3 June and 16 Aug. 1989 (ASC/QEII/MUN, PH, Coll–455–27.01.006); Brian P. Murphy to Hart, 20 Mar. and 26 June 1994 (ASC/QEII/MUN, PH, Coll–27.01.011); Murphy to Hart, 15 Aug. and 11 Sep. 1996 (ASC/QEII/MUN, PH, Coll–27.01.013).

99 He told me this in conversation.

100 Hart to O'Mahony and Hart to MacEoin, 1991 (NLI, Seán O'Mahony Papers, ms 44,058/3). Hart also wrote to MacEoin in 1988 enquiring about possible interviewees, although MacEoin did not reply until March 1999. MacEoin to Hart, 22 Mar. 1999 (ASC/QEII/MUN, PH, Coll–455–27.01.016).

101 MacEoin to Hart, 11 Nov. 1991 (ASC/QEII/MUN, PH, Coll–455–27.01.008); Peter Hart, 'Michael Collins and the Assassination of Sir Henry Wilson', IHS, vol. 28, iss. 110 (Nov. 1992), pp. 150–70.

102 Hart to Myers (fax), 15 Apr. 1992 (ASC/QEII/MUN, PH, Coll–455–27.01.011).

103 Joost Augusteijn to Hart, n.d. [May 1990] (ASC/QEII/MUN, PH, Coll–455–27.01.028); The Irish Times, 23 May 1990.

104 Fitzpatrick to Hart, 2 Sep. 1991 (ASC/QEII/MUN, PH, Coll–455–27.01.008). See Peter Hart, 'The Irish Republican Army and its Enemies: Violence and Community in County Cork, 1917–1923' (TCD, unpublished dissertation, 1992), nt 46, p. 377.

105 Charles Townshend report, Dec. 1992 (ASC/QEII/MUN, PH, Coll–455–27.01.011); Fitzpatrick to Hart, 23 and 28 July, 17 Aug. 1992 (ASC/QEII/MUN, PH, Coll–455–27.01.009).

106 Progress Report, 9 Feb. 1993 (ASC/QEII/MUN, PH, Coll–455–27.01.010); Application for Leland Lyons travelling scholarship, n.d. (ASC/QEII/MUN, PH, Coll–455–27.01.028); Research Activities, 7 Sep.–23 Dec. 1993; Hart to Kevin Myers, 10 Apr. 1994 (ASC/QEII/

MUN, PH, Coll–455–27.01.011); Hart to Kevin Myers, 10 Apr. 1994 (ASC/QEII/MUN, PH, Coll–455–27.01.011).

107   Nuttall, *Different and the Same*, p. 58; Ian d'Alton and Ida Milne (eds), *Protestant and Irish: The Minority's Search for a Place in Independent Ireland* (Cork, 2019), pp. 13–16; Don Wood, 'Protestant Population Decline in Southern Ireland, 1911–1926' in Hughes and Morrissey (eds), *Southern Irish Loyalism, 1912–1949*, pp. 27–48.

108   *The Irish Times*, 11 Sep. 2017; Paul McFadden, 'Commemorating Historic Centenaries – a Journey Being Made', 5 July 2021 (https://journeyinselfbelief.org/2021/07/commemorating-historic-centenaries-a-journey-being-made/, accessed 27 Dec. 2021).

109   Recorded interviews, 17 Apr. 1993 and 18 Apr. 1993 [names withheld at request of archive] (ASC/QEII/MUN, PH, Coll–455–17.04.001); Hart's notes from same interviews (ASC/QEII/MUN, PH, Coll–455–17.03.003); Bielenberg, Borgonovo, Donnelly, '"Something of the Nature of a Massacre"', pp. 7–59. The remainder of his interviews were taken down as notes.

110   Recorded interview, 18 Apr. 1993 [name withheld at request of archive] (ASC/QEII/MUN, PH, Coll–455–17.04.001); Hart's notes from same interview (ASC/QEII/MUN, PH, Coll–455–17.03.003). The interview does not say when or who was killed.

111   Joseph Ruane, 'Pluralism and Silence: Protestants and Catholics in the Republic of Ireland' in Diarmuid Ó Giolláin (ed.), *Irish Ethnologies* (Notre Dame, 2017), p. 99.

112   Recorded interview, 18 Apr. 1993 [name withheld at request of archive] (ASC/QEII/MUN, PH, Coll–455–17.04.001); Hart's notes from same interview (ASC/QEII/MUN, PH, Coll–455–17.03.003).

113   Recorded interview, 21 Apr. 1993 [name withheld at request of archive] (ASC/QEII/MUN, PH, Coll–455–17.04.001); Hart's notes from same interview (ASC/QEII/MUN, PH, Coll–455–17.03.003). Thanks to Canon Catterall for consenting to be identified.

114   Hart to Myers, 10 Apr. 1994 (ASC/QEII/MUN, PH, Coll–455–27.01.011).

115   *The Irish Times*, 27 Aug. 1994. Peace talks between John Hume and Gerry Adams culminated in a joint statement in April 1993 in which they voiced their commitment to securing a peace that would be supported by the different traditions on the island. The British and Irish governments issued the Downing Street Declaration in December. The broadcasting ban on Sinn Féin was lifted in January 1994 in Ireland. Britain lifted its broadcasting ban in September, and the Loyalist paramilitaries declared a ceasefire in October.

116   *The Irish Times*, 12 Jan. 1995.

117   Fitzpatrick to Hart, 3 June 1991 (ASC/QEII/MUN, PH, Coll–455–27.01.008).

118   Patrick Maume, 'The Search for Truth and the Revision of Irish History', *History Ireland*, iss. 2, vol. 29, (Mar./Apr. 2021) (www.historyireland.com/volume-29/understanding-our-own-ignorance/Understanding our own ignorance, accessed 17 Dec. 2021).

119   *The Irish Times*, 7 July 1998.

120   *The Irish Times*, 8 and 27 Sep., 24 Oct., 3 Nov. 1994, 24 Feb. 1995.

121   *The Irish Times*, 24 Feb. 1995. For a discussion of the 'Record' see Chapter Two.

122   *The Irish Times*, 11 Oct. 1994.

123 *The Irish Times*, 3 Nov. 1994.

124 *The Irish Times*, 24 Oct. 1994.

125 *The Irish Times*, 3 Nov. 1994.

126 *The Irish Times*, 10 Nov. 1994, 5 May 2012 (obituary).

127 *The Irish Times*, 19 Sep. 1994. John Good was killed by the IRA on 10 March 1921, and his son William was killed two weeks later. The family's cattle and property were confiscated, and his wife and daughter were forced to leave a few months later. *DOIR*, pp. 330, 361.

128 Bernadette Whyte to Hart, 17 May 1995 (ASC/QEII/MUN, PH, Coll–455–27.01.012); *The Southern Star*, 8 Apr. 1995.

129 Hart's papers (released in 2016) were disaggregated and reorganised thematically as per standard North American archival practice. Before giving the material to the archive, Robin Whitaker photographed as many of Hart's interviews notes as she could locate (in their folders and as he had left them) and sent them to me. The description of what Hart consulted is derived from her photographs of Hart's files. Sullivan, Kealkil/PH; Whitaker photographs, February 2013, in author's possession.

130 Notes, 'The Truth about Kilmichael', 2004 (ASC/QEII/MUN, PH, Coll–455–21.03.002).

131 Bernadette Whyte to Hart, 20 Oct. 1996 (ASC/QEII/MUN, PH, Coll–455–27.01.013).

132 Ibid.

133 Bernadette Whyte to Hart, 9 Nov. 1996 (ASC/QEII/MUN, PH, Coll–455–27.01.028)

CHAPTER 9. WAR BY OTHER MEANS

1 Margaret O'Callaghan, 'Propaganda Wars: Contexts for Understanding the Debate on the Meaning of the Irish War of Independence', *Journal of the Old Athlone Society*, no. 9 (2013), pp. 367–72, see pp. 369–70; Augusteijn, *From Public Defiance to Guerrilla Warfare*; Marie Coleman, *County Longford and the Irish Revolution, 1910–1923* (Dublin, 2003). Peter Hart, *The IRA and Its Enemies*. Hart wrote or edited three further books: Peter Hart (ed.), *British Intelligence in Ireland, 1920–21: The Final Reports* (Cork, 2002); Peter Hart, *The IRA at War, 1916–1923* (Oxford, 2003); Peter Hart, *Mick: The Real Michael Collins* (London, 2005).

2 Charles Townshend, 'Reviewed Works: *From Public Defiance to Guerrilla Warfare: The Experience of Ordinary Volunteers in the Irish War of Independence, 1916–1921* by Joost Augusteijn and *The IRA in the Twilight Years, 1923–1948* by Uinseann MacEoin', *Saothar* 22 (1997), p. 107.

3 Oliver Coogan, *Politics and War in Meath, 1913–1923* (Dublin, 1983); Michael Farry, *Sligo 1914–1921: A Chronicle of Conflict* (Trim, 1992). Both have been revised and re-issued. Oliver Coogan, *Politics and War in Meath, 1919–1923* (Navan, 2012); See also Michael Farry, *The Aftermath of Revolution: Sligo, 1921–23* (Dublin, 2000) and Michael Farry, *Sligo: The Irish Revolution, 1912–23* (Dublin, 2012).

4 Hart, *The IRA and Its Enemies*, p. 83.

5   Ibid., p. 196.

6   Ibid., p. 36.

7   *The Sunday Times*, 19 Apr. 1998; Geoffrey Wheatcroft review, *New Statesman*, 10 July 1998.

8   *The Times*, 21 May 1998; *Times Literary Supplement*, 6 Nov. 1998; Adrian Gregory, 'Review Article: The Boys of Kilmichael', *Journal of Contemporary History*, vol. 34 (3) (1999), pp. 489–96; Arthur Mitchel review, *History Ireland*, vol. 7, no. 2 (Summer 1999), pp. 48–50; Ben Novick review, *History*, vol. 84, no. 275 (July 1999), p. 556; David W. Miller review, *The American Historical Review*, vol. 104, no. 5 (Dec. 1999), p. 1762.

9   Pauric Travers review, *IHS*, vol. 31, iss. 122 (Nov. 1998), pp. 292–5, see p. 294; *The Cork Examiner*, 7 July and 1 Aug. 1998.

10 Pauric Travers review, *IHS*, p. 294; *The Cork Examiner*, 1 Aug. 1998, 15 Dec. 2000; Senia Pašeta, review, *English Historical Review*, vol. 115, no. 464 (Nov. 2000), p. 246.

11 Joost Agusteijn review, *Saothar* 23 (1998), p. 76.

12 Hart, *The IRA and Its Enemies*, p. 100.

13 Ibid., p. 314.

14 Brian Hanley and Peter Hart, 'Hart to Heart', *History Ireland*, iss. 2, vol. 13 (Mar./Apr. 2005) (www.historyireland.com/volume-13/hart-to-heart/, accessed 17 Dec. 2021).

15 Neni Panourgiá, *Dangerous Citizens: The Greek Left and the Terror of the State* (2009), pp. 118–22; Evi Gkoksaridis, 'What is Behind the Concept: Fragmentation and Internal Critique in the Revisionist Debates of Greece and Ireland', *Ricerche Storiche*, vol. XLI, N. 1 (Mar./Apr. 2011), pp. 87–110.

16 Giorgos Antoniou, 'The Lost Atlantis of Objectivity: The Revisionist Struggles Between the Academic and Public Spheres', *History and Theory*, Theme Issue 46 (December 2007), p. 101; Hanley and Hart, 'Hart to Heart'.

17 *The Irish Times*, 29 May 1998.

18 Fitzpatrick to Hart, 30 June 1998 (ASC/QEII/MUN, PH, Coll–455–27.01.015).

19 Marion & Jim to Hart, Dec. 1998 (ASC/QEII/MUN, PH, Coll–455–27.01.015).

20 Jack Lane, 'What is Revisionism?', n.d. (https://aubanehistoricalsociety.org/ahs40.pdf, accessed 27 Dec. 2021).

21 Jack Lane and Brendan Clifford (eds), *Kilmichael: The False Surrender, a Discussion by Peter Hart, Padraig O'Cuanachain, D.R. O'Connor Lysaght, Dr. Brian Murphy and Meda Ryan* (Millstreet, Nov. 1999).

22 Ibid.

23 Murphy, *The Origins & Organisation of British Propaganda*, p. 73.

24 Ryan, *Tom Barry* (2012), pp. 56, 61, 92, 209–10.

25 Bielenberg, Borgonovo, Donnelly, '"Something in the Nature of a Massacre"', p. 57.

26 Lane and Clifford (eds), *Kilmichael: The False Surrender*, p. 30.

27 Leargas: Kilmichael 28 Nov 2000 (RTÉ Archives, IH27219).

28 Ibid. See also *The Southern Star*, 25 Nov. 2000 and *The Sunday Times*, 26 Nov. 2000.

29 Ryan, *Tom Barry* (2003 ed.), pp. 42–5; Ryan, *Tom Barry* (2012 ed.), pp. 54–7.

30 Ryan, *Tom Barry* (2012), pp. 59, 323–5. This is not the case. For a discussion of the BMH's methodology see Morrison, 'Witnessing the Republic', pp. 124–40; Morrison 'Case Study: The Bureau of Military History', pp. 876–80.

31 *The Cork Examiner*, 29 Nov. 2004.

32 Seámus Fox, 'The Kilmichael Ambush – A Review of Background, Controversies and Effects' (Sep. 2005) (http://irishhistory1919-1923chronology.ie/Kilmichael%20(seamus)%20Ver%204%20-%20Sept%2005.pdf, accessed 30 Dec. 2021); Bill Kautt, *Ambushed and Armour: The Irish Rebellion 1919–1921* (Dublin and Portland, 2010), p. 109.

33 John Regan review of Ryan, *Tom Barry* (2003), *History*, vol. 91, no. 1 (301) (Jan. 2006), pp. 163–4, see p. 164.

34 Liam Ó Ruairc, 'Kilmichael Controversy Continues', 5 Dec. 2004, *The Blanket* (http://indiamond6.ulib.iupui.edu:81/lor05121g.html, accessed 27 Dec. 2021); Niall Meehan, 'The War of Independence 1919–2004: What Is The Dispute About Kilmichael And Dunmanway Really About?', 3 Dec. 2004 (www.indymedia.ie/article/67769, accessed 17 Dec. 2021); *The Cork Examiner*, 8 Dec. 2004; *The Southern Star*, 11 Dec. 2004;

35 *The Southern Star*, 3 Apr. 2004.

36 *Irish Literary Supplement*, vol. 24, No. 1 (Fall 2004).

37 *Irish Independent*, 8 Jan. 2004.

38 Chisholm to Liam Deasy (nephew), 5 Nov. 2007 and Ena Bates to Chisholm, 15 Nov. 2007 (TCDM, CP, uncatalogued); Liam Deasy (nephew) 12 Nov. 2007.

39 Chisholm to Maureen, 19 Oct. 2007 (TCDM, CP, uncatalogued); Chisholm, note of telephone conversation Maureen Deasy, 22 Oct. 2007 (TCDM, CP, uncatalogued); Maureen Deasy to Chisholm, 12 Oct. 2007. See also Maureen Deasy to Chisholm, 20 and 28 Sep. and 31 Oct. 2007 (TCDM, CP, uncatalogued).

40 Maureen Deasy/de Baróid to Chisholm, 18 Dec. 2007 (TCDM, CP, uncatalogued).

41 Author interview, Kathleen McCaul *née* Deasy, 15 Jan. 2015; Draft letter Ena Bates, Maureen Deasy and Kathleen McCaul to Chisholm (unsigned), 5 Nov. 2006; de Baróid to Michael Deasy, 2 Oct. 2006; de Baróid to Kathleen McCaul, 20 Oct. 2006; de Baróid to Liam Deasy (nephew), 20 Oct. 2006; Maureen Deasy/de Baróid to Chisholm, 18 Dec. 2007 (TCDM, CP, uncatalogued).

42 Maureen Deasy/de Baróid to Chisholm, 7 Mar. 2008 (TCDM, CP, uncatalogued).

43 Maureen Deasy to Chisholm, 4 Apr. 2008 (TCDM, CP, uncatalogued).

44 Young to Chisholm, 10 Apr. 2008; Chisholm to Young, 12 Apr. 2008 (TCD, CP, uncatalogued).

45 Maureen Deasy to Chisholm, 3 and 29 June 2009 (TCDM, CP, uncatalogued).

46 Meehan acknowledged this. Meehan to Morrison, 9 Jan. 2012 (email). Normally, I would have no objections to a recording being made.

47 Meehan actively campaigned against state censorship of republicans in the 1980s and 1990s. *The Irish Press*, 1 Feb. 1982, 9 Jan. and 17 May 1987, 16 June 1987, 24 Apr. 1988, 18 May 1988, 7 Aug. and 9 Oct. 1992, 21 June 1993; *The Kilkenny People*, 10 Dec. 1993, 12 Jan. 1994. Paul Arthur, *The People's Democracy 1968–73* (Belfast, 1974) (https://cain.ulster.

ac.uk/events/pdmarch/arthur74.htm, accessed 30 Dec. 2021); Michael Farrell, 'Reflections on the Northern Ireland Civil Rights Movement Fifty Years On', 12 Dec. 1918 (www.qub. ac.uk/Research/GRI/mitchell-institute/FileStore/Filetoupload,864825,en.pdf, accessed 17 Dec. 2021). The PDs split in 1986, with several members joining Sinn Féin. Others founded Social Democracy in 1996.

48 Special thanks to Tim Marshall (the friend of Hart's that Meehan contacted for information) relating to this incident. Hart, 'My Correct Views on Everything' (unpublished draft), c. 2005 (ASC/QEII/MUN, PH, Coll–455–7.01.006) (http://web.archive.org/web/20041127190537/ http://www.ucs.mun.ca/~tmarshal/, accessed 17 Dec. 2021).

49 Meehan, 'John Bruton looks into his own "Hart"'.

50 Chambers/PH (19 Nov. 1989).

51 Chisholm to Hart, draft reply [c. 1990] (TCD, CP, uncatalogued).

52 Hart, Draft, 'Kilmichael book 2', last saved 23 July 2009. I am grateful to Robin Whitaker for making this available to me.

53 My thanks to Robin Whitaker for forwarding some of these emails to me.

54 Original draft of RORI, vol. II, 31 Mar. [1922] (TNAUK, WO 141/94).

55 Eve Morrison, 'Reply to John Regan', Oct. 2012, Dublin Review of Books (https://drb.ie/ articles/reply-to-john-regan/, accessed 28 Dec. 2021).

56 Brind to Strickland, 1 Mar. 1922 (IWM, SP, P363).

57 The Irish Times, 14 Sep. 1998.

58 The Irish Times, 10 Nov. 1998.

59 Hart, IRA and Its Enemies, p. 34; Peter Hart, 'The Irish Republican Army and its Enemies: Violence and Community in County Cork, 1917–1923' (TCD, unpublished dissertation, 1992), p. 48.

60 Hart notes, 'The Truth about Kilmichael', 2004 (ASC/QEII/MUN, PH, Coll–455– 21.03.002); Flyer Maynooth Research Seminar, Hart 'The Truth about Kilmichael', 9 Dec. 2004 (ASC/QEII/MUN, PH, Coll–455–9.01.018).

61 Peter Hart, 'The Irish Republican Army and its Enemies: Violence and Community in County Cork, 1917–1923' (TCD, unpublished dissertation, 1992), nt 50, p. 46; Hart, IRA and Its Enemies, p. 33.

62 John E. Chisholm tapes (ASC/QEII/MUN, PH, Coll–455–21.03.002).

63 Chisholm to Hart, 22 Feb. 1990 (ASC/QEII/MUN, PH, Coll–455–27.01.007).

64 Hart to Chisholm, 18 Nov. 1991 (ASC/QEII/MUN, PH, Coll–455–27.01.007); Hart to Chisholm, 22 Oct. 1991; Draft chapter on Kilmichael Ambush [Oct. 1991] (TCD, CP, uncatalogued).

65 Hart to Luka Hrstic (on behalf of Chisholm) and Luka Hrstic (on behalf of Chisholm) to Hart, 21 Apr. 2009, emails (printouts) (TCDM, JC, uncatalogued). Chisholm was using a neighbour's computer because his was broken. Chisholm to Hart, 29 Apr. 2009 (TCDM, CP, uncatalogued).

66 Hart, The IRA and Its Enemies, p. 35. The error is also in the 1997 galley proofs. Hart part 1, 25 Nov. 1997 (ASC/QEII/MUN, PH, Coll–455–1.01.030); Kilmichael chapter draft c. 1997

(ASC/QEII/MUN, PH, Coll–455–1.02.012); see comments in Ryan, *Tom Barry* (2012), pp. 69–70.

67 Draft chapter on Kilmichael Ambush [Oct. 1991] (TCD, CP, uncatalogued); Peter Hart, 'The Irish Republican Army and its Enemies: Violence and Community in County Cork, 1917–1923' (TCD, unpublished dissertation, 1992), nt 56, p. 50; draft chapter on Kilmichael Ambush (ASC/QEII/MUN, PH, Coll–455–1.02.015).

68 Bielenberg, Borgonovo, Donnelly, '"Something of the Nature of a Massacre"'.

69 Meehan, 'John Bruton looks into his own "Hart"'; Meda Ryan speech, Kilmichael Commemoration, 28 Nov. 2004 (www.indymedia.ie/article/67691?search_text=kilmichael+cork, accessed 7 May 2021); *The Irish Times*, 10 Nov. 1998; *An Phoblacht*, 30 Nov. 2000.

70 Author interview with Chisholm and Liam Deasy (nephew), 20 Apr. 2010.

71 See Seán Kelleher to Editor, *History Ireland*, iss. 5, vol. 20 (Sep./Oct. 2012) versus Seán Kelleher to Editor, Letters Extra, 2013 (www.historyireland.com/letters-extra/peter-hart-etc/, accessed 17 Dec. 2021]); Seán Kelleher in *The Southern Star*, 3 Apr. 2004. See also Niall Meehan to Editor, 2013, Letters Extra, *History Ireland* (www.historyireland.com/letters-extra/peter-hart-etc/, accessed 17 Dec. 2021).

72 Flyer for a book signing by Ryan, 14 Oct. [2005].

73 Until theses were made available online, individuals consulting PhDs in TCD had to sign and date a 'Reader's Declaration' pasted on the inside cover. Meehan consulted Hart's PhD on 3 June 2006, 1 June 2007 and 1 May 2008. He said he 'deduced' that Young was one of Hart's interviewees. *Irish Political* Review, Mar. 2008. See also *The Southern Star*, 5 July 2008.

74 Brian P. Murphy and Niall Meehan, *Troubled History: A 10th Anniversary Critique of Peter Hart's The IRA and Its Enemies* (Millstreet, 2008). John Young died in November 2015.

75 *The Southern Star*, 5 July 2008.

76 Interview, Marion O'Driscoll, 3 Oct. 2012; Response from Eve Morrison and Marion O'Driscoll, 9 Apr. 2013, *History Ireland*, Letters Extra (www.historyireland.com/letters-extra/peter-hart-etc/, accessed 17 Dec. 2021).

77 *The Sunday Times* (Irish edition), 26 Aug. 2012. I did not misrepresent anything Mr Young said, but no doubt I was naive in not foreseeing this outcome.

78 Interview, Marion O'Driscoll, 3 Oct. 2012.

79 Author interview (telephone) with Marion O'Driscoll, 3 Oct. 2012; *The Irish Times*, 21 Mar. 2009.

80 Author interview (telephone) with Donal Musgrave, 20 Mar. 2014. This was clearly an innocent error on Musgrave's part.

81 Response from Eve Morrison and Marion O'Driscoll, 9 Apr. 2013.

82 *The Cork Examiner*, 30 Nov. 1987 and 28 Nov. 1988; *The Southern Star*, 3 Dec. 1988; Interview (telephone), Eddie Cassidy, 2 Apr. 2013; photographic contact sheets for Kilmichael commemorations in 1987 and 1988 from the *Irish Examiner* archives.

83 Recorded interview, 21 Apr. 1993 [name withheld at request of archive] (ASC/QEII/MUN, PH, Coll–455–17.04.001); Hart's notes from same interview (ASC/QEII/MUN, PH, Coll–455–17.03.003).

84 Niall Meehan, 'Troubles in Irish History' in Brian P. Murphy and Niall Meehan, *Troubled History: A 10th Anniversary Critique of Peter Hart's The IRA and Its Enemies* (Millstreet, 2008), pp. 21–8; Niall Meehan, 'Examining Peter Hart', *Field Day Review* (Oct. 2014), p. 110; Niall Meehan, 'The Kilmichael Ambush, Why it Matters Today', 28 Nov. 2020 (www. academia.edu/44592922/Kilmichael_Ambush_Centenary_talk_transcript_28_Nov_2020_ Niall_Meehan, accessed 17 Dec. 2021). He does not accept that Chambers was the 'unarmed scout' either. *The Southern Star*, 6 Aug. 2017. His (and Regan's) attempts to link the killing of three British officers in Macroom with the April 1922 attacks are even more speculative and unconvincing as is their argument that Hart was somehow disingenuous in not seeing the two incidents as related.

85 O'Leary, *A Treatise on Northern Ireland*, vol. 2, pp. 97–8. For more informed discussions of Hart's sectarianism thesis, including the April 1922 killings, see Hanley, 'Terror in Twentieth Century Ireland', pp. 12–13; Bielenberg, Borgonovo, Donnelly Jr, '"Something of the Nature of a Massacre"', p. 59. For an interesting challenge to O'Leary's consociationalism theories see Robin Whitaker, 'Writing as a Citizen? Some Thoughts on the Uses of Dilemmas' in *Critique of Anthropology*, vol. 28 (3), pp. 321–38, see pp. 321–2. For subtler political analyses of radical nationalist ideology, colonialism and the Irish independence struggle generally see Kissane, *The Politics of the Irish Civil War* and Kissane, *Explaining Irish Democracy*.

86 *The Southern Star*, 12 Dec. 1998 (www.dib.ie/biography/flinn-hugo-hugh-a9817, accessed 17 Dec. 2021).

87 Lane and Clifford, *Kilmichael: The False Surrender*, p. 2.

88 Their general arguments, though specific to Ireland, were similar to those being made by postmodernists and historians of race and gender in Europe and the USA. For a discussion on Field Day and those associated with it see Joe Cleary, 'Introduction: Ireland and modernity' in J. Cleary and C. Connolly (eds), *The Cambridge Companion to Modern Irish Culture* (Cambridge, 2005), p. 17; Ben Novick, *That Noble Dream: The 'Objectivity Question' and the American Historical Profession* (Cambridge, 1998), pp. 494, 469; Patrick Joyce, 'The Return of History: Postmodernism and the Politics of Academic History in Britain' in *Past & Present*, no. 158 (Feb. 1998), pp. 207–35.

89 *The Guardian*, 6 Jan. 2001.

90 *The Irish Times*, 17 June 2006.

91 Luke Gibbons, 'Challenging the Canon: Revisionism and Cultural Criticism' in Seámus Deane (ed.), *The Field Day Anthology of Irish Writing*, vol. III (Derry, 1991), p. 568.

92 Dave Alvey/Irish Political Review Group Leaflet, 'Defend 1916, defend Irish History!' (https://irishelectionliterature.com/2016/04/14/defend-1916-defend-irish-history-leaflet-from-the-irish-political-review-group/, accessed 28 Dec. 2021).

93 Niall Meehan, 'Distorting Irish History, the Stubborn Facts of Kilmichael: Peter Hart and Irish Historiography', 24 Oct 2010 (www.academia.edu/357237/Distorting_Irish_History_ One_the_stubborn_facts_of_Kilmichael_Peter_Hart_and_Irish_Historiography, accessed 30 Dec. 2021). The Spinwatch website has been taken down. The original posting of

Meehan's article can be accessed via Wayback Machine capture on 1 Dec. 2010 (https://web.archive.org/web/*/https://spinwatch.org/, accessed 30 Dec. 2021).

94 In fact, Newfoundland was more successful in overcoming sectarian divides than many other parts of the British Empire. Robert Chr. Thomen, 'Democracy, Sectarianism and Denomi(-)nationalism: The Irish in Newfoundland', *Nordic Irish Studies*, vol. 4 (2005), pp. 13–27, see p. 19.

95 Barry Keane, 'Another Small Point ... Peter Hart and his Ancestors' (www.academia.edu/34521711/Peter_Hart_and_his_ancestors, accessed 17 Dec. 2021); Barry Keane, 'Killings were Self Defence', @dunmanway*times*, vol. 1, iss. 12 (4 Sep. 2012). Hart's sister Susan, to whom I sent Keane's piece, was baffled. She said that they had not known about their 'unionist roots'. On the question of sectarianism, she said they were brought up to respect but avoid religion. In a draft introductory chapter in an unfinished book on the Kilmichael controversy, Peter Hart said the grandfather they knew best, a former British Army NCO born in England and later an Anglican minister, was a Liberal and convinced Irish home ruler. Kilmichael book, 2009 (ASC/QEII/MUN, PH, Coll–455–3.02.054).

96 Meehan, 'The Kilmichael Ambush, Why it Matters Today'.

97 W. Alison Phillips, *The Revolution in Ireland, 1906–1923* (2nd ed., London, 1926, 1st ed., 1923); *DIB*.

98 Phillips, *The Revolution in Ireland*, pp. 175, 263, 265, 268, 313–17.

99 Hart, *The IRA and Its Enemies*, pp. 50–1, 196–7, 322–3.

100 Email Miller to Morrison, 29 Aug. 2012.

101 Quoted in *The Southern Star*, 5 Apr. 2014. The actual *Spinwatch* page tag to the articles mentioning me remained 'Northern Ireland'. The website has been taken down, but an example of the original web link appears in a comment by 'Gary Oldman', 31 Aug. 2012 (www.indymedia.ie/article/102322?search_text=Old&userlanguage=ga&save_prefs=true, accessed 31 Dec. 2021).

102 John Regan, *Myth and the Irish State* (Newbridge, 2013), p. 216; John Regan, 'The Kilmichael ambush and the outer limits of Irish historical revisionism', *History Ireland*, iss. 6, vol. 28 (Nov./Dec. 2020) (www.historyireland.com/volume-28/the-kilmichael-ambush-and-the-outer-limits-of-irish-historical-revisionism/, accessed 17 Dec. 2021).

103 John Borgonovo, 'Review Article: Revolutionary Violence and Irish Historiography' in *IHS*, vol. 38, iss. 150 (Nov. 2012), pp. 325–31; *IHS* editors, 'Apology' [to Eve Morrison], *IHS*, vol. 38, no. 153 (May 2014), p. 177.

104 Regan, 'The Kilmichael Ambush and the outer limits'; John Regan, '"All the Nightmare Images of Ethnic Conflict in the Twentieth Century are Here": Erroneous Statistical Proofs and the Search for Ethnic Violence in Revolutionary Ireland, 1917–1923', *Nations and Nationalism* (2021), p. 11.

105 *The Southern Star*, 6 Aug. 2017.

106 Hanley, 'Terror in Twentieth Century Ireland', p. 15.

107 Ian McBride, 'The Peter Hart Affair in Perspective: History, Ideology, and the Irish Revolution' in *The Historical Journal*, vol. 61, iss. 1 (March 2018), p. 20.

108 Richard English, *Armed Struggle: The History of the IRA* (London, 2003), pp. 285–337. An overwhelming 94 per cent of the southern electorate voted in favour of the proposal, and 71 per cent in Northern Ireland approved the agreement. In 2005, the IRA announced the formal end of their armed campaign.

109 Quoted in Robert Perry, 'Revisionism: The Provisional Republican Movement', *Journal of Politics and Law*, vol. 1, no. 1 (Mar. 2008), p. 50.

110 McBride, 'The Shadow of the Gunman: Irish Historians and the IRA', pp. 706–7, 709.

111 McBride, 'The Peter Hart Affair', p. 5; Howe, 'The Politics of Historical "Revisionism"', p. 244.

112 McBride, 'The Peter Hart Affair', p. 6.

113 Ibid., p. 253.

114 Thomson, *Anzac Memories*, p. 315.

115 Alistair Thomson, 'Memory as a Battlefield'.

116 Ilan Pappe, *Out of the Frame: The Struggle for Academic Freedom in Israel* (London, 2010), pp. 71–86; Benny Morris 'The Tantura "Massacre" Affair', *The Jerusalem Report*, 4 Feb. 2004, pp. 18–22.

117 Pappe, *Out of the Frame*, p.79; Morris 'The Tantura "Massacre"', pp. 19, 21, 22.

118 Carolyn P. Boyd, 'The Politics of History and Memory in Democratic Spain', *Annals of the American Academy of Political and Social Science*, vol. 617 (May 2008), pp. 140–1.

119 *The Guardian*, 3 Feb. and 16 Aug. 2021; Jörg Hackmann, 'Defending the "Good Name" of the Polish Nation: Politics of History as a Battlefield in Poland, 2015–2018', *Journal of Genocide Research*, vol. 20, no. 4 (2018), pp. 587–606.

120 Guy Beiner, 'Sifting and Winnowing. Review of *Out of the Frame: The Struggle for Academic Freedom in Israel* by Ilan Pappe', *Dublin Review of Books* (https://drb.ie/articles/sifting-and-winnowing/, accessed 17 Dec. 2021).

121 McBride, 'The Peter Hart Affair', pp. 249–71; Seámus Fox, 'The Kilmichael Ambush'; Eunan O'Halpin, review of *The IRA and Its Enemies*, *Times Literary Supplement*, 6 Nov. 1998, p. 32; Richard English, review of Ryan, *Tom Barry* (2004 ed.) and Hart, *The IRA at War, 1916–1923* in *The Irish Times*, 17 Jan. 2004; Fearghal McGarry, 'Peter Hart (1963–2010)', 3 Aug. 2010 (https://puesoccurrences.wordpress.com/2010/08/03/peter-hart-1963-2010/, accessed: 19 Dec. 2021; John Dorney, 'Peter Hart-A Legacy' (www.theirishstory.com/2010/08/09/peter-hart-a-legacy/#.Yb9smsnP1hE, accessed 19 Dec. 2010); Fergus Campbell, 'Land and Revolution Revisited' in Fergus Campbell and Tony Varley (eds), *Land Questions in Modern Ireland* (Manchester, 2015), p. 162; Stephen Howe, 'Killing in Cork and the Historians', *History Workshop Journal*, iss. 77 (Spring 2014), pp. 160–86; Leeson, *The Black and Tans*, pp. 152–6.

122 Comment by 'Starkadder', 21 July 2007. See also 12 May 2007 (www.indymedia.ie/article/72403?, accessed 28 Dec. 2021); 'British and Irish Communist Organisation ... The Irish Communist from 1973', 9 Aug. 2007 (https://cedarlounge.wordpress.com/2007/08/09/, accessed 28 Dec. 2021). It is a pity Starkadder uses a pseudonym.

123 Martin D. Bates, 'They Were the Boys', *Books Ireland*, no. 226 (Nov. 1999), pp. 319–20; *The Irish Times*, 19 Nov. 2001 (appreciation of Bates).

124 Seán Hales to Hart, 21 May 2003 (ASC/QEII/MUN, PH, Coll–455–27.01.020).

125 Ruane, 'Pluralism and Silence, pp. 100–1.

126 Author interview with Liam Deasy (nephew), 20 Apr. 2010.

127 Author interview Dave Crowley (video), 14 Feb. 2013.

128 *The Cork Examiner*, 4 Aug. 1998; *The Corkman*, 21 Aug. 2007; *The Irish Times*, 7 Sep. and 10 Nov. 1998.

129 Seán Crowley to Author, 23 Nov. 2012; 'Gortroe, Kilmichael, 6:30pm, Sunday August 12th 2007' [text of oration]. I am indebted to Mr Crowley for supplying me with a signed copy of his oration.

130 Anonymous, 'Kilmichael Ambush 28th November 1920' in *Kimichael Through the Ages* (2010), pp. 107–16.

131 Introduction and application Drawings L201, L210A, L210B and L210C, 26 Apr. 2013 Kilmichael Ambush Site Planning Application 13307 (http://planning.corkcoco.ie/ePlan/AppFileRefDetails/13307/0, accessed May 2015); *An Phoblacht*, 13 Nov. 2013; *The Southern Star*, 7 and 8 Aug. 2013, 14 June 2014.

132 *Irish Examiner*, 24 Aug. 2013. See also 9 Sep. 2013 and 19 Jan. 2019.

133 Quoted in *The Irish Times*, 6 Feb. 2020.

134 Philippe Prost, the architect who designed the monument, quoted in Sabina Tanović, *Designing Memory: The Architecture of Commemoration in Europe, 1914 to the Present* (Cambridge, 2019), pp. 205–8.

135 Tanović, *Designing Memory*, p. 205; *The Guardian*, 2 Nov. 2014.

136 *Irish Examiner*, 22 Mar. 2016; *The Irish Times*, 6 Feb. 2020.

137 *The Irish Times*, 10 Jan. 2020.

138 *The Irish Times*, 25 Apr. 2016; *Irish Examiner*, 28 Dec. 2016; *DOIR*, pp. 26, 33.

139 *The Irish Times*, 20 Jan. 2019 and 24 Feb. 2021.

CONCLUSION

1 Young/JC (1969).

APPENDIX 1

1 Clarke to Street, 1 Dec. 1920 (TNAUK, CO 904/127). The text in hyperscript indicates later annotations and revisions pencilled into the original text.

2 *Belfast News-Letter*, 2 Dec. 1920. One paragraph concerning funeral arrangements has been omitted.

APPENDIX 2

1 IRACD (TNA UK, WO 141/40); RORI, vol. IV, 6th Division [Jan/Feb. 1922] (TNAUK WO 141/93). It should be noted that the wording in the 'Record' was altered slightly. The changes made in the latter have been inserted within hard brackets in the text.

APPENDIX 3

1   *Irish Independent*, 17 Jan. 1921. Another, slightly different version was reproduced in *The Dundee Courier* on the same date. It said that 'Eighteen of us in two lorries ... left Macroom on the afternoon of Nov. 28, and had been on patrol for about an hour when we came to a point along the road with high ground on both sides, particularly favourable for an ambush.'

APPENDIX 4

1   The *Kerryman*, 13 Dec. 1947. The full article is over 6,000 words long. Passages not dealing directly with the ambush have been omitted.

APPENDIX 5

1   O'Brien/LD (1969).
2   R.D.C. = Rural District Council – County Council [handwritten, bottom of page].

Bibliography

ARCHIVES, REPOSITORIES AND PAPERS IN PRIVATE HANDS

Ireland

Cork City and County Archives (CC&CA)
Tom Barry papers
Cork County Council minute books
Minute book Old IRA Mens' Association (Cork County)
Scoil Íte papers

Cork Public Museum
May Conlon Collection
Jim Hurley papers
Michael Leahy papers

Irish Railway Records Society (IRRS)
Great Southern and Western Railway records

Local History & Archives Department, Kerry Library (LH&AKL)
Kerryman administrative records

Kimmage Manor Archives
John Chisholm papers

Met Éireann Library
Daily and monthly rainfall registers

Military Archives of Ireland (MAI)
A-Series
Bureau of Military History witness statements and papers (BMH)
G2 Collection

Military Service Pensions Collection (MSPC)
Uinseann MacEoin Interviews (UmacE)

National Archives of Ireland (NAI)
Dáil Eireann papers, DE2 and DE4 (accessible via Digital Repository of Ireland)
Department of Justice
Department of the Taoiseach

National Library of Ireland (NLI)
George Berkeley papers
Erskine Childers papers
Liam Deasy papers
Kathleen McKenna Napoli papers
Florence O'Donoghue papers
Ernie O'Malley papers
Seán O'Mahony papers

Oxford University Press Archives
Peter Hart file

RTÉ Television Archives
Kilmichael Ambush, Seámus Kelly, 1 Nov. 1966, TY0097761
Survivors, 1 Jan. 1968, TY0105141
Tom Barry interview, Nollaig Ó Gadhra, n.d. [1969?] AR0021152/LA 000502
Leargas: Kilmichael 28 Nov. 2000, IH27219

RTÉ Radio Centre
Kenneth Griffith/Curious Journey interviews, Tape AA2792
'The Boys of Kilmichael', 25 Oct. 1970, Donncha Ó Dúlaing, AR0020655/LA 000559
'General Tom Barry on the occasion of his death', 2 July 1980, Donncha Ó Dúlaing, AA3472
    02071980

Trinity College Dublin Manuscripts & Archives (TCDM)
Father John Chisholm papers and recordings
General M.J. Costello papers
J.R.W. Goulden papers
Michael McDunphy papers
Royal Irish Constabulary Collection

University College Dublin Archives (UCDA)
Frank Aiken papers
Frances Mary Blake papers

Máire Comerford papers
Desmond and Mabel Fitzgerald papers
Sighle Humphreys papers
Con Moloney papers
Kathleen Barry Moloney papers
General Richard Mulcahy papers
Ernie O'Malley papers and notebooks
Maurice Twomey papers
Éamon de Valera papers

Papers in private hands
Max Caulfield papers and recordings
Dave Crowley papers
Cecil Guthrie family papers
John O'Beirne Ranelagh papers
Interview with Peter Hart in 'The Road to Freedom: *Guerilla Days in Ireland*', Black Rock
    Pictures (broadcast 2011)

United Kingdom

Bodleian Library, Oxford
Francis Hemming deposit

Cheltenham College Archives
Admission applications, 1910

Hampshire Regiment Museum
Hampshire Regiment Record of Service

Imperial War Museum
A.E. Percival papers
Peter Strickland papers
Henry Wilson papers

Imperial War Museum Sound & Video Archive (IWMS&VA)
The Troubles series

Manchester University John Rylands Library
The Manchester Guardian archive

Meteorological Office, London
Air Ministry, Daily Weather Reports

National Archives, London
CAB 27
CO 762, CO 904, CO 905
CSC 10
HO 184
HS 9
WO 35, WO 95, WO 100, WO 141, WO 146, WO 339, WO 363, WO 364, WO 372, WO 374, WO 399

Oxford University Press Archives
Peter Hart file

St Antony's College, Oxford Middle East Centre Archive
Raymond Cafferata papers

Tameside Local Studies and Archives Centre
1st Battalion, Manchester Regiment Record of Service

United States and Canada

Archives and Special Collections, Queen Elizabeth II Library Memorial University, Newfoundland (ASC/QEII/MUN)
Peter Hart Collection

New York University Tamiment Library (NYU/TL)
Ernie O'Malley papers

Royal Aviation Museum of Western Canada
Alexander Lewis papers

Official Publications

Ireland

Dáil Eireann, Minutes of Proceedings of the first Parliament of the Republic of Ireland 1919–1921: official record (Dublin, 1994)
Oireachtas.ie

United Kingdom

Hansard (Parliamentary Debates)
ProQuest UK Parliamentary Papers

Newspapers (selected)

Anglo-Celt

Ballymena Weekly Telegraph & Larne Times

Belfast Evening Telegraph

Belfast News-Letter

Belfast Telegraph

Birmingham Gazette

The Clare Champion

Communist

The Cork Examiner

Croydon Advertiser

Daily British Colonist

The Daily Chronicle

Daily Despatch

Daily Herald

The Daily Mirror

The Daily News

Daily Sketch

Darling Downs Gazette

Donegal News

Dublin Evening Telegraph

Dundee Courier

Edinburgh Evening News

Evening Echo

Evening Herald

Evening News

Evening Telegraph

Fermanagh Herald

The Freeman's Journal

Glasgow Citizen

Gravesend & Dartford Reporter

Greymouth Evening Star

Hull Daily Mail

Illustrated Chronicle

Illustrated Sporting and Dramatic News

Irish Independent

The Irish News

The Irish Press

The Irish Times

The Kerryman

Lancashire Daily Post

Leader

Liberator

Liverpool Echo

Londonderry Sentinel

The Midland Daily Telegraph

The Manchester Evening News

The Manchester Guardian

La Vanguardia

Le Monde Illustré

Le Temps

The Morning Post

Nenagh Guardian

The New York Times

The Newcastle Daily Chronicle

The Newcastle Daily Journal

Northern Whig and Belfast Post

Nottingham Evening News

The Pall Mall Gazette

The Evening News (Portsmouth)

Queensland Times

Santa Ana Register

The Shields Daily News

Sheffield Independent

Sidney Morning Herald

Skibbereen Eagle

Sligo Champion

The Southern Star

Sphere

St James's Gazette

Sunday Independent

Teignmouth Post

The Times

Warwick Daily News

Yorkshire Gazette

Yorkshire Herald

Yorkshire Telegraph and Star

Books, Chapters and Articles

Adams, Robin, 'Tides of change and changing sides: The collection of rates in the Irish War of Independence', in D. Kanter and P. Walsh (eds), *Taxation, Politics and Protest in Ireland* (London, 2019), pp. 253–75

The American Commission on Conditions in Ireland: Interim Report (1921)

Andrews, C.S., *Dublin Made Me: An Autobiography* (Dublin, 1979)

Antoniou, Giorgos, 'The Lost Atlantis of Objectivity: The Revisionist Struggles Between the Academic and Public Spheres', *History and Theory*, Theme Issue 46 (December 2007), pp. 92–112

Arthur, Paul, *The People's Democracy 1968–73* (Belfast, 1974)

Augusteijn, Joost, *From Public Defiance to Guerilla Warfare: The Experience of Ordinary Volunteers in the Irish War of Independence 1916–1921* (Dublin, 1996)

— Review, *Saothar*, vol. 23 (1998), p. 76

Ayerst, David, *The Guardian: Biography of a Newspaper* (London, 1971)

Barr, Niall, *The Lion and the Poppy: British Veterans, Politics, and Society, 1921–1939* (Westport, 2005)

Barry, Tom, 'Eyewitness' [Tom Barry], 'Kilmichael', Pt. 2, *An Cosantóir*, vol. 2, no. 21 (16 May 1941)

— *Guerrilla Days in Ireland* (Dublin, 1989; 1st ed., 1949)

— *The Reality of the Anglo-Irish War in West Cork, 1920–1921* (Cork, 1974)

Bartlett, Tom and K. Jeffery (eds), *A Military History of Ireland* (Cambridge, 1996)

Bates, Martin D., 'They Were the Boys', *Books Ireland*, no. 226 (Nov. 1999), pp. 319–20

Beaslaí, Piaras, *Michael Collins and the Making of a New Ireland* (London, 1926)

Beckett, Ian, *The Army and the Curragh Incident 1914* (London, 1986)

— *Britain's Part-time Soldiers: The Amateur Military Tradition, 1558–1945* (Barnsley, 2011)

Beckett, Ian, Timothy Bowman and Mark Connelly (eds), *The British Army and the First World War* (Cambridge, 2017)

Beckett, Ian and Keith Simpson (eds), *A Nation in Arms: The British Army in the First World War* (Barnsley, 2014)

Beiner, Guy, *Remembering the Year of the French: Irish Folk History and Social Memory* (London, 2007)

— 'Sifting and Winnowing. Review of *Out of the Frame: The Struggle for Academic Freedom in Israel* by Ilan Pappé', *Dublin Review of Books* (Dec. 2011) (https://drb.ie/articles/sifting-and-winnowing/, accessed 17 Dec. 2021)

— *Forgetful Remembrance: Social Forgetting and Vernacular Historiography of a Rebellion in Ulster* (Oxford, 2018)

Bell, David, *Fire on the Mountain: The True Story of the Darkley Church in Northern Ireland* (Belfast, 2013)

Ben-Ze'ev, Efrat, 'Imposed silences and self-censorship: Palmach soldiers remember 1948', in Ben-Ze'ev et al., *Shadows of War: A Social History of Silence in the Twentieth Century* (Cambridge, 2010), pp. 181–96

Ben-Ze'ev, Efrat, Ruth, Ginio, and Jay Winter, *Shadows of War: A Social History of Silence in the Twentieth Century* (Cambridge, 2010)

Bentley, Michael, *The Liberal Mind 1914–1929* (Cambridge, 1977)

Biagini, Eugenio, *British Democracy and Irish Nationalism, 1876–1906* (Cambridge, 2007)

Bielenberg, Andy, John Borgonovo and James S. Donnelly, '"Something of the nature of a massacre": The Bandon Valley killings revisited', *Éire-Ireland*, vol. 46, 3 & 4 (Fall/Winter 2014), pp. 7–59

Bingham, Adrian, 'An organ of uplift?' in Newman and Houlbrook (eds), *The Press and Popular Culture in Interwar Europe* (London, 2017), pp. 651–62

Bingham, Adrian and M. Conboy, *Tabloid Century: The Popular Press in Britain, 1896 to the Present* (Oxford, 2015)

Bolton, Albert, *The Criminal Injuries (Ireland) Acts* (Dublin, 1922)

Borgonovo, John, 'Review Article: Revolutionary Violence and Irish Historiography', *IHS*, vol. 37, iss. 150 (Nov. 2012) [see also 'Apology' below]

Bowman, Timothy, *The Edwardian Army: Recruitment, Training and Deploying the British Army, 1902–1914* (Oxford, 2012)

Boyce, D.G., *Englishmen and Irish Troubles: British Public Opinion & the Making of Irish Policy, 1918–1922* (London, 1972)

Boyd, Carolyn P., 'The Politics of History and Memory in Democratic Spain' in *Annals of the American Academy of Political and Social Science*, vol. 617 (May 2008), pp. 133–48

Bradley, Dan, *Farm Labourers: Irish Struggle, 1900–1976* (Belfast, 1988)

Bradshaw, Brendan, 'Nationalism and Historical Scholarship in Modern Ireland', *IHS*, vol. 26, iss. 104 (Nov. 1989), pp. 329–51

Brady, A.J.S., *The Briar of Life* (Dublin, 2010)

Brady, Ciaran, '"Constructive and Instrumental": The dilemma of Ireland's first "new historians"', in Ciaran Brady (ed.), *Interpreting Irish History: The Debate on Historical Revisionism* (Dublin, 1994, 2nd ed., 1999), pp. 3–31

Brady, Ciaran (ed.), *Interpreting Irish History: The Debate on Historical Revisionism* (Dublin, 1994, 2nd ed., 1999) Brennan, Patrick and C. Crowe (eds), *Guide to the Military Service (1916–1923) Pensions Collection* (Dublin, 2012)

Browne, Charlie, *The Story of the 7th: A Concise History of the 7th Battalion, Cork No. 1 Brigade Irish Republican Army from 1915 to 1921* (Ballydehob, 2007)

Buckland, Patrick, 'Southern Irish Unionists, the Irish Question, and British Politics, 1906–14', *IHS*, vol. 15, iss. 59 (Mar. 1967), pp. 228–55

Butler, Ewan, *Barry's Flying Column: The Story of the IRA's Cork No. 3 Brigade, 1919–21* (London, 1971)

Cain, P.J. and A.G. Hopkins, *British Imperialism 1688–2015* (London, 2016)

Cairns, Michael, 'The Massacre at Darkley – and the Nature of Certainty', in D. Henderson and I. Little (eds), *Reporting the Troubles: Journalists Tell Their Stories of the Northern Ireland Conflict* (Newtownards, 2018), pp. 221–8

Callinan, Elaine, *Electioneering and Propaganda in Ireland, 1917–1921: Votes, Violence and Victory* (Dublin, 2020)

Callwell, C.E., *Field-Marshal Sir Henry Wilson, His Life and Diaries*, vol. II (London, 1927)

Campbell, Fergus, 'Land and Revolution Revisited' in Fergus Campbell and Tony Varley (eds), *Land Questions in Modern Ireland* (Manchester, 2015), pp. 149–72

Canning, Paul, *British Policy towards Ireland, 1921–1941* (Oxford, 1985)

Catterall, Peter, C. Seymour-Ure and A. Smith (eds), *Northcliffe's Legacy: Aspects of the British Popular Press* (London, 2000)

Cleary, Joe, 'Introduction: Ireland and modernity' in J. Cleary and C. Connolly (eds), *The Cambridge Companion to Modern Irish Culture* (Cambridge, 2005)

Coleman, Marie, *County Longford and the Irish Revolution, 1910 –1923* (Dublin, 2003)

— 'Military Service Pensions for Veterans of the Irish Revolution, 1916–1923', *War in History* 20(2) (2013), pp. 201–21

Cohen, Gillian and M. Conway (eds), *Memory in the Real World* (Hove, 2008)

Collins, Jude (ed.), *Whose Past Is It Anyway? The Ulster Covenant, the Easter Rising & the Battle of the Somme* (Dublin, 2012)

Coogan, Oliver, *Politics and War in Meath, 1913–1923* (Dublin, 1983)

— *Politics and War in Meath, 1919–1923* (Navan, 2012)

Coogan, Tim Pat, *De Valera: Long Fellow, Long Shadow* (London, 1993)

— *A Memoir* (London, 2008)

Cooney, James, *Macroom People & Places* (Macroom, 1976)

Corcoran, Kevin, *Saving Eden: The Gearagh and Irish Nature* (Co. Cork, 2021)

Corcoran, Mary and Mark O'Brien (eds), *Political Censorship and the Democratic State: The Irish Broadcasting Ban* (Dublin, 2005)

Corporaal, Margaret *et al.*, *Irish Studies and the Dynamics of Memory: Transitions and Transformations* (Berne, 2016)

Costello, Francis, 'Labour, Irish republicanism, and the social order during the Anglo-Irish War', *The Canadian Journal of Irish Studies*, vol. 17, no. 2 (Dec. 1991), pp. 1–22

Cronin, Donal, 'Ballingeary Volunteers 1920', *Ballingeary & Inchigeela Historical Society Journal* (1997) (https://ballingearyhs.com/legacy/journal1997/ballingearyvolunteers1920.html, accessed 20 Apr. 2021)

Cronin, Mike, 'The Blueshirt Movement, 1932–5: Ireland's Fascists?', *Journal of Contemporary History*, vol. 30, no. 2 (Apr. 1995), pp. 311–32

— *The Blueshirts and Irish Politics* (Dublin, 1997)

Crowley, Flor, *In West Cork Long Ago* (Cork, 1979)

Crowley, John, D. Ó Drisceoil and M. Murphy (eds) *Atlas of the Irish Revolution* (Cork, 2017)

Crozier, F.P., *Ireland Forever* (London, 1932)

Cullinane, Liam, '"A Happy Blend"? Irish Republicanism, Political Violence and Social Agitation, 1962–69', *Saothar* 35 (2010), pp. 49–65

Curtis, L. Perry, *Jack the Ripper and the London Press* (New Haven, 2001)

Curtis, Lionel, 'Ireland', *The Round Table*, no. 43 (June 1921), pp. 499–500

D'Alton, Ian and Ida Milne, 'Introduction', in I. D'Alton and I. Milne (eds), *Protestant and Irish: The Minority's Search for a Place in Independent Ireland* (Cork, 2019), pp. 1–18

D'Alton, Ian and Ida Milne (eds), *Protestant and Irish: The Minority's Search for a Place in Independent Ireland* (Cork, 2019)

Daly, Mary, and Margaret O'Callaghan (eds), *1916 in 1966: Commemorating the Easter Rising* (Dublin, 2007)

Daly, T.P., 'James Craig and Orangeism, 1903–10', *IHS*, vol. 34, iss. 136 (Nov. 2005), pp. 431–48

Daunton, Martin, *Wealth and Welfare: An Economic and Social History of Britain 1851–1951* (Oxford, 2007)

Deane, Seámus, 'Wherever Green is Read', in M. Ní Dhonnchadha and T. Dorgan (eds), *Revising the Rising* (Derry, 1991), pp. 91–105

— 'The Position of the Irish Intellectual', *Cambridge Review*, 18 May 1973, pp. 134–8

Deane, Seámus (ed.), *The Field Day Anthology of Irish Writing*, vol. III (Derry, 1991)

Deasy, Liam, *Towards Ireland Free: The West Cork Brigade in the War of Independence, 1917–1921* (Dublin & Cork, 1987; 1st ed., 1973)

— *Brother Against Brother* (Dublin & Cork, 1994)

— 'The Schull Peninsula in the War of Independence', *Éire-Ireland* 1:2 (1966), pp. 5–8

— 'The Beara Peninsula Campaign', *Éire-Ireland* 1:3 (1966), pp. 63–81

Dening, B.C., 'Modern problems of guerrilla warfare', *The Army Quarterly*, Oct. 1926–Jan. 1927, vol. XIII, pp. 247–354

Devine, Francis, Fintan Lane and Niamh Puirséuil (eds), *Essays in Labour History: A Festschrift for Elizabeth and John W. Boyle* (Dublin, 2008)

Diamond, Nicholas, 'The truth is out there: Accuracy in recall of M.K. Armson & B. Levine, verifiable real-world events', *Psychological Science*, vol. 31 (12) (2020), pp. 1544–6

Dolan, Anne, *Commemorating the Irish Civil War: History and Memory, 1923–2000* (Cambridge, 2005)

Dorney, John, *The Civil War in Dublin: The Fight for the Irish Capital, 1922–1924* (Dublin, 2017)

— 'Peter Hart-A Legacy' (https://www.theirishstory.com/2010/08/09/peter-hart-a-legacy/#. Yb9smsnP1hE, accessed 19 Dec. 2010)

Doughan, Christopher, *The Voice of the Provinces: The Regional Press in Revolutionary Ireland, 1914–1921* (Liverpool, 2019)

Doyle, Patrick, *Civilising Rural Ireland: The Co-operative Movement, Development and the Nation-state, 1889–1939* (Manchester, 2019)

Dunaway D. K. and W. K. Baum, *Oral History: An Interdisciplinary Anthology* (Walnut Creek, Ca., 1996)

Dunne, Terence, 'Emergence from the Embers: The Meath and Kildare farm labour strike of 1919', *Saothar* 44 (2019), pp. 59–68

Dunne, Tom, 'Beyond "Revisionism"', *The Irish Review*, no. 12 (Spring/Summer 1992), pp. 1–12

Edwards, Ruth Dudley, *Patrick Pearse: The Triumph of Failure* (London, 1979)

English, Richard, *Armed Struggle: The history of the IRA* (London, 2004)

— Review of Ryan, *Tom Barry* (2004 ed.) and Hart, *The IRA at War, 1916–1923* in *The Irish Times*, 17 Jan. 2004

— *Ernie O'Malley: IRA Intellectual* (Oxford, 2002, 2nd ed.)

Evans, Richard, *From the Frontline: The Extraordinary Life of Sir Basil Clarke* (Stroud, 2013)

Evans, Richard J., *In Defence of History* (London, 2000)

Eyre, Michael, Chris Heaps and A. Townsin, *Crossley* (Hersham, 2006)

Fanning, Ronan, *Fatal Path: British Government and the Irish Revolution, 1910–1923* (London, 2013)

— 'The Great Enchantment' in C. Brady (ed.), *Interpreting Irish History: The Debate on Historical Revisionism* (Dublin, 1994, 2nd ed., 1999), pp. 146–60

— 'The British Dimension', *The Crane Bag*, vol. 8, no. 1 (1984), pp. 41–52

Fanning, Ronan, Desmond Fennell, Arthur Green and Stefan Collini, 'Nationalist Perspectives on the Past: A Symposium', *The Irish Review* (Cork), no. 4 (Spring 1988), pp. 15–39

Farrell, Mel, *Party Politics in a New Democracy: The Irish Free State, 1922–37* (London, 2017)

Farrell, Michael, 'Reflections on the Northern Ireland Civil Rights Movement Fifty Years On', 12 Dec. 1918 (https://www.qub.ac.uk/Research/GRI/mitchell-institute/FileStore/Filetoupload,864825,en.pdf, accessed 17 Dec. 2021)

Farry, Michael, *Sligo: The Irish Revolution, 1912–23* (Dublin, 2012)

— *The Aftermath of Revolution: Sligo, 1921–23* (Dublin, 2000)

— *Sligo 1914–1921: A Chronicle of Conflict* (Trim, 1992)

Finn, Michael, 'Local heroes: War News and the Construction of "Community" in Britain, 1914–18', *Historical Research*, vol. 83, no. 221 (August 2010), pp. 520–38

Fitzpatrick, David, *Politics and Irish Life 1913–1921: Provincial Experience of War and Revolution* (Dublin, 1977)

— 'The Geography of Irish Nationalism, 1910–1921', *Past and Present*, no. 78 (Feb. 1978), pp. 113–44

— 'Militarism in Ireland, 1900–1922', in Bartlett & Jeffery (eds), *A Military History of Ireland*, pp. 379–406

— 'Irish consequences of the Great War', *IHS*, vol. 38, iss. 156 (Nov. 2015), pp. 643–58

Fitzpatrick, David (ed.), *Terror in Ireland, 1916–1923* (Dublin, 2012)

Foster, Gavin, *The Irish Civil War and Society* (Houndsmills, 2015)

Foster, R.F., *Paddy and Mr. Punch: Connections in Irish and English History* (London, 1995; 2011)

— 'We are all Revisionists Now' in *The Irish Review (Cork)*, no. 1 (1986), pp. 1–5

Fox, Seámus, 'The Kilmichael Ambush – A Review of Background, Controversies and Effects' (Sep. 2005) (http://irishhistory1919-1923chronology.ie/Kilmichael%20(seamus)%20Ver%20 4%20-%20Sept%2005.pdf, accessed 30 Dec. 2021)

Foxton, David, *Revolutionary Lawyers: Sinn Féin and Crown Courts in Ireland and Britain, 1916–23* (Dublin, 2008)

Foy, Michael, *Michael Collins's Intelligence War: The Struggle Between the British and the IRA 1919–1921* (Chalford, 2008)

Fraser, T.G., 'Ireland and India', in K. Jeffery (ed.), *'An Irish Empire?': Aspects of Ireland and the British Empire* (Manchester, 1996), pp. 77–93

Frawley, Una (ed.), *Women and the Decade of Commemorations* (Bloomington, 2021)

Gallagher, Michael, 'The Pact General Election of 1922', *IHS*, vol. 22, iss. 84 (Sept. 1979), pp. 404–21

— *Irish Elections, 1922–1944: Results and Analysis* (Limerick, 1993)

Garvin, Tom, *1922: The Birth of Irish Democracy* (Dublin, 1996)

Gibbons, Ivan, *The British Labour Party and the Establishment of the Irish Free State, 1918–1924* (London, 2015)

Gibbons, Luke, 'Challenging the Canon: Revisionism and Cultural Criticism' in Seámus Deane (ed.) *The Field Day Anthology of Irish Writing*, vol. III (Derry, 1991), pp. 561–8

Gibbs, Philip, *The Pageant of the Years* (London, 1946)

Gilbert, Steve, 'England', in S. Gilbert (ed.), *Tattoo History: A Source Book* (New York, 2000), pp. 103–11

Gilbert, Steve (ed.), *Tattoo History: A Source Book* (New York, 2000)

Gkoksaridis, Evi, 'What is Behind the Concept: Fragmentation and Internal Critique in the Revisionist Debates of Greece and Ireland', *Ricerche Storiche*, vol. XLI, no. 1 (Mar./Apr., 2011), pp. 87–110

Gleeson, James, *Bloody Sunday* (London, 1962)

Grayson, Richard, *Dublin's Great Wars: The First World War, the Easter Rising and the Irish Revolution* (Cambridge, 2018)

Gregory, Adrian, 'A Clash of Cultures: The British Press and the Opening of the Great War', in T. Paddock (ed.), *A Call to Arms: Propaganda, Public Opinion and Newspapers in the Great War* (Westport, 2004), pp. 15–50

— 'Review Article: The Boys of Kilmichael', *Journal of Contemporary History*, vol. 34 (3) (1999), pp. 489–96

Hackmann, Jörg, 'Defending the "Good Name" of the Polish Nation: Politics of History as a Battlefield in Poland, 2015–2018', *Journal of Genocide Research*, vol. 20, no. 4 (2018), pp. 587–606

Hanley, Brian, 'Change and Continuity: Republican Thought since 1922', *The Republic*, iss. 2 (Spring/Summer 2001) (www.theirelandinstitute.com/wp/change-and-continuity-republican-thought-since-1922/, accessed 17 Dec. 2021)

— *The IRA, 1926–1936* (Dublin, 2002)

— 'The IRA and Trade Unionism, 1922–72' in Francis Devine, Fintan Lane and Niamh Puirséuil (eds), *Essays in Labour History: A Festschrift for Elizabeth and John W. Boyle* (Dublin, 2008), pp. 157–77

— *The IRA: A Documentary History, 1916–2005* (Dublin, 2010)

— 'Terror in Twentieth-Century Ireland', in David Fitzpatrick (ed.), *Terror in Ireland, 1916–1923* (Dublin, 2012), pp. 10–15

— '"But Then They Started All this Killing": Attitudes to the IRA in the Irish Republic since 1969', *IHS*, vol. 38, iss. 151 (2013), pp. 439–56

— *The Impact of the Northern Ireland Troubles, 1968–1979. Boiling Volcano* (Manchester, 2018)

Hanley, Brian and Scott Millar, *The Lost Revolution: The Story of the Official IRA and the Workers' Party* (Dublin, 2009)

Hanley, Brian and Peter Hart, 'Hart to Heart', *History Ireland*, iss. 2, vol. 13 (Mar./Apr. 2005) (https://www.historyireland.com/volume-13/hart-to-heart/, accessed 17 Dec. 2021)

Hart, Peter, *Mick: The Real Michael Collins* (London, 2005)

— *The IRA at War, 1916–1923* (Oxford, 2003)

— *British Intelligence in Ireland, 1920–21: The Final Reports* (Cork, 2002)

— *The IRA and Its Enemies: Violence and Community in Cork, 1919–1923* (Oxford, 1998)

— 'Michael Collins and the Assassination of Sir Henry Wilson', *IHS*, vol. 28, iss. 110 (Nov. 1992), pp. 150–70

— *The Somme* (London, 2005)

Hayton, D.W., 'The Laboratory for "Scientific History": T.W. Moody and R.D. Edwards at the Institute of Historical Research', *IHS*, vol. 41, iss. 159 (2017), pp. 41–57

Headrick, Daniel, *The Invisible Weapon: Telecommunications and International Politics, 1851–1945* (Oxford, 1991)

Henderson, Deric and Ivan Little (eds), *Reporting the Troubles: Journalists Tell Their Stories of the Northern Ireland Conflict* (Newtownards, 2018)

Hirsch, Steven and Lucien Van Der Walt (eds), *Anarchism and Syndicalism in the Colonial and Postcolonial World, 1870–1940: The Praxis of National Liberation, Internationalism, and Social Revolution* (Leiden, 2010)

Hodges, P., '"They don't like it up 'em!": Bayonet fetishization in the British Army during the First World War', *Journal of War and Culture Studies*, vol. 1, iss. 2 (2008), pp. 123–38

Hopkinson, Michael, *Green Against Green: The Irish Civil War* (Dublin, 1988)

— *The War of Independence* (Dublin, 2002)

— (ed.), *The Last Days of Dublin Castle: The Mark Sturgis Diaries* (Dublin, 1999)

Howe, Stephen, 'Killing in Cork and the Historians', *History Workshop Journal*, iss. 77 (Spring 2014), pp. 160–86

— 'The Politics of Historical "Revisionism": Comparing Ireland and Israel/Palestine', *Past and Present*, no. 168 (Aug. 2000), pp. 227–53

Howell, Joel, '"Soldier's Heart": The Redefinition of Heart Disease and Speciality Formation in Early Twentieth Century Great Britain', *Medical History*, supplement no. 5 (1985), pp. 34–52

Hughes, Brian, *Defying the IRA? Intimidation, Coercion and Communities During the Irish Revolution* (Liverpool, 2016)

Hughes, Brian and Conor Morrissey (eds), *Southern Irish Loyalism, 1912–1949* (Liverpool, 2020)

'IO' [C.J.C. Street], *The Administration of Ireland 1920* (London, 1921)

Irish Congress of Trade Unions, *Who Burned Cork?* (Dublin, 1921)

Irish Historical Studies, 'Apology' [to Eve Morrison], *IHS*, vol. 38, iss. 153 (May 2014), p. 177

Island, Azharul and S. Haque, 'Autobiographical memory of war veterans: A mixed-studies systematic review', *Memory Studies*, 2019, pp. 1–26

Jackson, Daniel, *Popular Opposition to Irish Home Rule in Edwardian Britain* (Liverpool, 2009)

Jarché, James, *People I Have Shot* (London, 1934)

Jeffery, Keith, 'Field Marshal Sir Henry Wilson: Myths and the man', *Journal of the Society for Army Historical Research*, vol. 86, no. 345 (Spring 2008), pp. 57–82

Jeffery, Keith (ed.), *'An Irish Empire?': Aspects of Ireland and the British Empire* (Manchester, 1996)

Jeremy, David, *Capitalists and Christians: Business Leaders and the Churches in Britain, 1900–1960* (Oxford, 1990)

Jones, Edgar and Simon Wessely, *Shell Shock to PTSD: Military Psychiatry from 1900 to the Gulf War* (Hove, 2005)

Joy, Labhrás and Brenda Malone, 'The roll of honour of 1916', *History Ireland*, iss. 2, vol. 14 (Mar./Apr. 2006), pp. 10–11

Joyce, Patrick, 'The Return of History: Postmodernism and the Politics of Academic History in Britain', *Past & Present*, no. 158 (Feb. 1998), pp. 207–35

Kanter, Douglas and Patrick Walsh (eds), *Taxation, Politics and Protest in Ireland, 1662–2016* (London, 2019)

Kautt, William, *Ambushes and Armour: The Irish Rebellion 1919–1921* (Dublin, 2010)

Keane, Barry, *Massacre in West Cork: The Dunmanway and Ballygroman Killings* (Cork, 2014)

— 'Another Small Point … Peter Hart and his Ancestors', n.d. (www.academia.edu/34521711/ Peter_Hart_and_his_ancestors, accessed 17 Dec. 2021)

Kearney, Hugh, 'The Irish and their History', *History Workshop Journal*, vol. 31, iss. 1 (Spring 1991), pp. 149–55

Kearney, Richard, 'Faith and Fatherland' *The Crane Bag*, vol. 8, no. 1, (1984), pp. 55–66

Kelly, Stephen, 'A policy of futility: Eamon de Valera's Anti-Partition campaign, 1948–1951', *Études Irlandais* 36:2 (2011) (https://journals.openedition.org/etudesirlandaises/2348, accessed 30 Dec. 2021)

Kenneally, Ian, *The Paper Wall: Newspapers and Propaganda in Ireland, 1919–1921* (Cork, 2008)

— '"A tainted source": The *Irish Bulletin*, 1919–20', in M. O'Brien and F.M. Larkin (eds), *Periodicals and Journalism in Twentieth Century Ireland* (Dublin, 2014), pp. 89–101

Kenneally, Ian and James O'Donnell (eds), *The Irish Regional Press, 1892–2018* (Dublin 2018)

Kern, Stephen, *The Culture of Time and Space, 1880–1918* (Cambridge, Mass., 2003)

The Kerryman, Rebel Cork's Fighting Story, 1916–21: Told by the Men Who Made It (Tralee, 1947)

— *Rebel Cork's Fighting Story: From 1916 to the Truce with Britain* (Tralee, [1961])

Kilmichael Historical Society, *Kilmichael Ambush 28th November 1920* (Skibbereen, 2010)

Kissane, Bill, *Explaining Irish Democracy* (Dublin, 2002)

— *The Politics of the Irish Civil War* (Oxford, 2005)

Knirck, Jason, *Aftermath of the Revolution: Cumann na nGaedheal and Irish Politics, 1922–1932* (Madison, 2014)

Labour Party, *Report of the Labour Commission to Ireland* (London, 1921)

Laffan, Michael, *The Resurrection of Ireland: The Sinn Féin Party, 1916–1923* (Cambridge, 1999)

— 'Easter Week and the Historians', in M. Daly and M. O'Callaghan (eds), *1916 in 1966: Commemorating the Easter Rising* (Dublin, 2007), pp. 327–47

— 'Insular Attitudes: The Revisionists and Their Critics' in M. Ní Dhonnchadha and T. Dorgan (eds), *Revising the Rising* (Derry, 1991), pp. 106–21

Lane, Fintan, *Long Bullets: A History of Road Bowling in Ireland* (Cork, 2005)

Lane, Jack and B. Clifford (eds), *Kilmichael: The False Surrender – A Discussion by Peter Hart, Padraig O'Cuanachain, D.R. O'Connor-Lysaght, Dr Brian Murphy and Meda Ryan* (Millstreet, 1999)

Lane, Jim, *On the IRA: Belfast Brigade Area* (Cork, 1972)

Larkin, Felix, '"A great daily organ": The *Freeman's Journal*, 1763–1924', *History Ireland*, iss. 3, vol. 14 (May/June 2006)

Lee, David, 'The Munster Soviets and the Fall of the House of Cleeve' in David Lee and Debbie Jacobs (eds), *Made in Limerick, vol. 1, History of Industries, Trade and Commerce* (Limerick, 2003), pp. 286–306

Lee, J.J., 'Peace in Northern Ireland', in A.H. Wyndham (ed.), *Re-imagining Ireland* (Charlottesville, 2006), pp. 219–22

Leeson, David, *The Black & Tans: British Police and Auxiliaries in the Irish War of Independence* (Oxford, 2011)

— 'Select Document: The Prescott-Decie letter', *IHS*, vol. 38, iss. 151 (May 2013), pp. 511–22

Leonard, Jane, '"English Dogs" or "Poor Devils"? The Dead of Bloody Sunday Morning', in D. Fitzpatrick (ed.), *Terror in Ireland, 1916–1923* (Dublin, 2012), pp. 102–40

Leslie, Peter, 'Armour in Ireland, 1916–1923', *Military Modelling*, June 1980, p. 513

Linkoff, Ryan, *Public Images: Celebrity, Photojournalism and the Making of the Tabloid Press* (London, 2018)

Louvet, Marie-Violaine, 'Light on the Arab World: The "Irish-Arab News", 1975–85', *Irish Studies in International Affairs*, vol. 23 (2012), pp. 191–203

Lowe, W.J., 'The War against the RIC, 1919–21', *Eire-Ireland*, vol. 37, nos 3–4 (Fall/Winter 2002), pp. 79–117

Lowe, W.J. and Malcolm, E.L. 'The domestication of the Royal Irish Constabulary, 1836–1922', *Irish Economic and Social History* XIX (1992), pp. 27–48

Lynch, Robert, *The Partition of Ireland: 1918–1925* (Cambridge, 2019)

MacEoin, Uinseann, *The IRA in the Twilight Years, 1923–1948* (Dublin, 1997)

— *Survivors*, 2nd ed. (Dublin, 1987)

— *Harry: The Story of Harry White* (Dublin, 1986)

Mackenzie, J.M., *Propaganda and Empire: The Manipulation of British Public opinion, 1880–1960* (Manchester, 1984)

Mackenzie, Pam, *The Lewis Letters: The Exploits of a 20th Century Aviator and Adventurer* (Victoria, 2017)

Macleod, Jenny, *Gallipoli: Great Battles* (Oxford, 2015)

Macready, Nevil, *Annals of an Active Life*, vol. 2 (London, 1923)

Maloney, W.J., *The Forged Casement Diaries* (Dublin, 1936)

Matthews, Rachel, *The History of the Provincial Press in England* (London, 2017)

Maude, Alan, *The History of the 47th (London) Division, 1914–1919* (London, 1922)

Maume, Patrick, 'The Search for Truth and the Revision of Irish History', *History Ireland*, iss. 2, vol. 29 (April 2021) (https://www.historyireland.com/volume-29/understanding-our-own-ignorance/, accessed 17 Dec. 2021)

McBride, Ian, 'The Peter Hart Affair in Perspective: History, Ideology, and the Irish Revolution', *The Historical Journal*, vol. 61, iss. 1 (March 2018), pp. 249–71

— 'The Shadow of the Gunman: Irish Historians and the IRA', *Journal of Contemporary History*, vol. 46, no. 3 (July 2011), pp. 686–710

McConville, Séan, *Irish Political Prisoners, 1920–1962: Pilgrimage of Desolation* (London, 2014)

McEwen, J.M., 'Northcliffe and Lloyd George at war, 1914–1918', *Historical Journal*, vol. 24, no. 3 (Sept. 1981), pp. 651–72

— 'Lloyd George's acquisition of the *Daily Chronicle* in 1918', *Journal of British Studies*, vol. 21, no. 1 (Autumn 1982), pp. 127–44

McEwen, J.M. (ed.), *The Riddell Diaries, 1908–1923* (London, 1986)

McFadden, Paul, 'Commemorating Historic Centenaries – a Journey Being Made', 5 July 2021 (https://journeyinselfbelief.org/2021/07/commemorating-historic-centenaries-a-journey-being-made/, accessed 17 Dec. 2021)

McGarry, Fearghal, 'Ireland and the Spanish Civil War', *History Ireland*, iss. 3, vol. 9 (Autumn 2001) (https://www.historyireland.com/20th-century-contemporary-history/ireland-and-the-spanish-civil-war/, accessed 17 Dec. 2021)

— *The Rising: Ireland, Easter 1916* (Oxford, 2010)

— *Frank Ryan* (Dublin, 2010)

— 'Peter Hart (1963–2010)', 3 Aug. 2010 (https://puesoccurrences.wordpress.com/2010/08/03/peter-hart-1963-2010/, accessed 19 Dec. 2021)

McIntye, Anthony, 'The IRA disappeared of the 1920s: Gerry Adams vs. Niall Meehan', *The Pensive Quill.com*, 9 Nov. 2014 (https://www.thepensivequill.com/2014/11/the-ira-disappeared-of-1920s-gerry.html, accessed 17 Dec. 2021)

McKenzie, John, *Propaganda and Empire: The Manipulation of British Public Opinion, 1880–1960* (Manchester, 1984)

McKenzie, Susan, *The Lewis Letters: The Exploits of a 20th Century Aviator and Adventurer* (Victoria, 2017)

McKibbin, Ross, *The Ideologies of Class: Social Relations in Britain, 1880–1950* (Oxford, 1990)

McKittrick, David, Seámus Kelters, Brian Feeney and Chris Thornton, *Lost Lives: The Stories of the Men, Women and Children who Died as a Result of the Northern Ireland Troubles* (Edinburgh, 2001)

McMahon, Paul, 'British intelligence and the Anglo-Irish Truce, July-December 1921', *IHS* vol. 35, iss. 140 (Nov. 2007), pp. 519–40

McNamara, Conor, *Liam Mellows: Soldier of the Irish Republic – Selected Writings 1914–1924* (Newbridge, 2018)

Meehan, Niall, 'The Kilmichael Ambush, Why it Matters Today', 28 Nov. 2020 (www.academia. edu/44592922/Kilmichael_Ambush_Centenary_talk_transcript_28_Nov_2020_Niall_ Meehan, accessed 17 Dec. 2021)

— 'Examining Peter Hart', *Field Day Review* (Oct. 2014), pp. 103–48

— 'Distorting Irish History, the Stubborn Facts of Kilmichael: Peter Hart and Irish Historiography', 24 Oct. 2010 (https://www.academia.edu/357237/Distorting_Irish_ History_One_the_stubborn_facts_of_Kilmichael_Peter_Hart_and_Irish_Historiography, accessed 30 Dec. 2021. Original link (no longer functional) https://spinwatch.org/index. php/issues/northern-ireland/item/296)

— 'Troubles in Irish History' in Brian P. Murphy and Niall Meehan, *Troubled History: A 10th Anniversary Critique of Peter Hart's The IRA and Its Enemies* (Millstreet, 2008)

— 'The War of Independence 1919–2004: What is the Dispute About Kilmichael and Dunmanway Really About?', 3 Dec. 2004 (http://www.indymedia.ie/article/67769, accessed 17 Dec. 2021)

— 'John Bruton looks into his own "Hart" – to see what the Irish people should be thinking', 2004 (www.indymedia.ie/article/66994, accessed 7 May 2021)

Middlemas, Keith (ed.), *Thomas Jones' Whitehall Diaries: Vol III Ireland 1916–1923* (London, 1971)

Miers, D.R., 'Paying for malicious injuries claims', *Irish Jurist* (new series), vol. 5, no. 1 (Summer 1970), pp. 50–69

— 'Compensating policemen for criminal injuries', *Irish Jurist* (new series), vol. 7, no. 2 (Winter 1972), pp. 241–63

Mitchell, Arthur, *Labour in Irish Politics, 1890–1930: The Irish Labour Movement in an Age of Revolution* (New York, 1974)

— *Revolutionary Government in Ireland: Dáil Eireann, 1919–22* (Dublin, 1995)

Moloney, Ed, 'Censorship and "The Troubles"', M. Corcoran and M. O'Brien (eds), *Political Censorship and the Democratic State: The Irish Broadcasting Ban* (Dublin, 2005),pp. 99–112

Montgomery, B.L., *The Memoirs of Field Marshal the Viscount Montgomery of Alamein* (Cleveland, 1958)

Moody, T.W., 'Irish History and Irish Mythology', *Hermathena*, no. 124 (Summer 1978), pp. 6–24

Moore, Cormac, *The GAA vs Douglas Hyde: The Removal of Ireland's First President as GAA Patron* (Dublin, 2012)

Moorhouse, Geoffrey, *Hell's Foundation: A Town, its Myths and Gallipoli* (London, 2008)

Morash, Christopher, *A History of the Media in Ireland* (Cambridge, 2010)

Morgan, Kenneth O., *Rebirth of a Nation: Wales 1880–1980* (Oxford, 1981)

Morris, Benny, 'The Tantura "Massacre" Affair', *The Jerusalem Report*, 4 Feb. 2004, pp. 18–22

Morrison, Eve, 'Kilmichael revisited: Tom Barry and the "False Surrender"', in D. Fitzpatrick, (ed.), *Terror in Ireland, 1916–1923* (Dublin, 2012), pp. 158–80

— Eve Morrison, 'Reply to John Regan', Oct. 2012, *Dublin Review of Books* (https://drb.ie/articles/reply-to-john-regan/, accessed 30 Dec. 2021)

— 'Hauntings of the Irish Revolution: Veterans and Memories of the Independence Struggle and Civil War', in Corporaal *et al.* (eds), *Irish Studies and the Dynamics of Memory*, pp. 84–109

— 'Witnessing the Republic: The Ernie O'Malley Notebook Interviews and the Bureau of Military History Compared', in C.K. O'Malley (ed.), *Modern Ireland and Revolution* (Newbridge, 2016), pp. 124–40

— 'The Bureau of Military History', in Crowley *et al.* (eds), *Atlas of the Irish Revolution* (Cork, 2017), pp. 876–80

— 'Tea, Sandbags and Cathal Brugha: Kathy Barry's Civil War', in Frawley (ed.), *Women in the Decade of Commemorations* (Bloomington, 2021), pp. 189–204

Moulton, Mo, *Ireland and the Irish in Interwar England* (Cambridge, 2014)

Mulvagh, Conor, *The Irish Parliamentary Party at Westminster, 1900–18* (Manchester, 2016)

Murphy, Brian P., *The Origins & Organisation of British Propaganda in Ireland 1920* (Millstreet, 2006)

Murphy, Brian P. and Niall Meehan, *Troubled History: A 10th Anniversary Critique of Peter Hart's The IRA and Its Enemies* (Millstreet, 2008)

Murphy, Séan A., *Kilmichael: A Battlefield Study* (Skibbereen, 2014)

Murphy, William, *Political Imprisonment and the Irish, 1919–21* (Oxford, 2014)

Murray, Bruce, 'The "People's Budget" a century on', *Journal of Liberal History* 64 (Autumn 2009), pp. 4–13

Murray, Daniel, 'The Self-Deceit of Honour: Liam Lynch and the Civil War, 1922 (Parts I–VII), 2018. 'Éireann Ascendant'. An Irish History Blog (http://erinascendantwordpress.wordpress.com, accessed 12 Dec. 2020)

— 'An Unclean Scab: The Public Feud between Tom Barry and Frank Aiken, 1935', 2016. An Irish History Blog (http://erinascendantwordpress.wordpress.com, accessed 12 Dec. 2020)

Newman, Sarah and Matt Houlbrook (eds), *The Press and Popular Culture in Interwar Europe* (Abingdon, 2014)

Ní Dhonnachadha, Maire and Theo Dorgan (eds.), *Revising the Rising* (Derry, 1991)

Norton, Christopher, *The Politics of Constitutional Nationalism in Northern Ireland 1932–1970: Between Grievance and Reconciliation* (Manchester, 2014)

Novick, Ben, *That Noble Dream: The 'Objectivity Question' and the American Historical Profession* (Cambridge, 1998)

Nuttall, Deirdre, *Different and the Same: A Folk History of the Protestants of Independent Ireland* (Dublin, 2020)

Novick, Ben, *Conceiving Revolution: Irish Nationalist Propaganda During the First World War* (Dublin, 2001)

O'Brien, Conor Cruise, *States of Ireland* (London, 1972)

O'Brien, Mark and Felix M. Larkin (eds), *Periodicals and Journalism in Twentieth Century Ireland* (Dublin, 2014)

O'Callaghan, Margaret, 'The Past Never Stands Still: Commemorating the Easter Rising in 1966 and 1976', in Jim Smyth (ed.) *Remembering the Troubles: Contesting the Recent Past in Northern Ireland* (Notre Dame, 2017), pp. 115–41

— 'Propaganda Wars: Contexts for Understanding the Debate on the Meaning of the Irish War of Independence', *Journal of the Old Athlone Society*, no. 9 (2013), pp. 367–72

O'Connor, Emmet, *Syndicalism in Ireland, 1917–1923* (Cork, 1988)

— 'Syndicalism, industrial unionism, and nationalism in Ireland', in Hirsch and Walt (eds), *Anarchism and Syndicalism in the Colonial and Postcolonial World, 1870–1940: The Praxis of National Liberation, Internationalism, and Social Revolution* (Leiden, 2010), pp. 193–224

— *A Labour History of Ireland 1824–2000* (Dublin, 2011)

— *Reds and the Green: Ireland, Russia and the Communist Internationals, 1919–43* (Dublin, 2004)

O'Donoghue, Bruno, *Parish Histories and Place-names of West Cork* (Bandon, 1983)

O'Donoghue, Florence, *No Other Law: The Story of Liam Lynch and the Irish Republican Army, 1916–1923* (Dublin, 1986; 1st ed., 1954)

Ó Drisceoil, Donal, '"Keeping disloyalty within bounds": British media control in Ireland, 1914–19', *IHS* 38, no. 149 (May 2012), pp. 53–69

— '"Sledge-hammers and blue pencils": Censorship, suppression and the Irish regional press, 1916–23', in I. Kenneally and J.T. O'Donnell (eds), *The Irish Regional Press, 1892–2018* (Dublin, 2018), pp. 141–56

O'Faolain, Seán, *Vive Moi: An Autobiography* (London, 1965)

O'Farrell, Patrick, 'The Canon of Irish Cultural History. A Reply to Brian Murphy', *Studies: An Irish Quarterly Review*, vol. 82, no. 328 (Winter 1993), pp. 487–98

Ó Gráda, Cormac, *Black '47 and Beyond: The Great Irish Famine in History, Economy, and Memory* (Princeton, N.J., 1999)

O'Halpin, Eunan, *The Decline of the Union: British Government in Ireland, 1892–1920* (Dublin, 1987)

— *Head of the Civil Service: A Study of Sir Warren Fisher* (London, 1989)

— *Defending Ireland: The Irish State and its Enemies since 1922* (Oxford, 1999)

— 'Counting Terror: The dead of the Irish revolution', in D. Fitzpatrick (ed.), *Terror in Ireland, 1916–1923* (Dublin, 2012), pp. 141–57

— Review of *The IRA and Its Enemies*, *Times Literary Supplement*, 6 Nov. 1998, p. 32

O'Halpin, Eunan and Daithí Ó Corráin, *The Dead of the Irish Revolution* (London, 2020)

O'Leary Brendan, *A Treatise on Northern Ireland, vol. 2: Control, the Second Protestant Ascendancy and the Irish State* (Oxford, 2019)

O'Malley, Cormac K.H. (ed.), *Modern Ireland and Revolution: Ernie O'Malley in Context* (Newbridge, 2016)

O'Malley, Cormac K.H. and Anne Dolan (eds), *No Surrender Here! The Civil War Papers of Ernie O'Malley 1922–1924* (Dublin, 2008)

O'Neill, Tom, *The Battle of Clonmult – the IRA's Worst Defeat* (Dublin, 2006)

Ó Riain, Seán, *Provos. Patriots or Terrorists?* (Dublin, 1974)

O'Riordan, Micheál, Review of *Seán Moylan: Soldier, Politician and Independent Spirit, Irish Democrat*, July 2005

Ó Ruairc, Liam, 'Kilmichael Controversy Continues', 5 Dec. 2004, *The Blanket* (http://indiamond6.ulib.iupui.edu:81/lor05121g.html, accessed 30 Dec. 2021)

O'Toole, Brian, 'John Chisholm and the Arab World', *Glowing Embers: Spiritan Mission Resource and Heritage Centre* (June 2016), p. 9

Ó Tuathaigh, M.A.G., 'Irish Historical Revisionism' in Ciaran Brady (ed.), *Interpreting Irish History: The Debate on Historical Revisionism* (Dublin, 1994, 2nd ed., 1999), pp. 306–26

Paddock, Troy (ed.), *A Call to Arms: Propaganda, Public Opinion and Newspapers in the Great War* (Westport, 2004)

Panourgiá, Neni, *Dangerous Citizens: The Greek Left and the Terror of the State* (New York, 2009)

Pappe, Ilan, *Out of the Frame: The Struggle for Academic Freedom in Israel* (London, 2010)

Parkinson, Alan, *Belfast's Unholy War: The Troubles of the 1920s* (Dublin, 2004)

— *A Difficult Birth: The Early Years of Northern Ireland 1920–25* (Dublin, 2020)

Pašeta, Senia (ed.), *Uncertain Futures: Essays about the Irish Past for Roy Foster* (Oxford, 2016)

Perks, Robert and Alistair Thomson (eds), *The Oral History Reader* (London, 1998)

Perry, Robert, 'Revising Irish History: The Northern Ireland Conflict and the War of Ideas', *Journal of European Studies* 40 (4) (2010), pp. 329–54

— 'Revisionism: The Provisional Republican Movement', *Journal of Politics and Law*, vol. 1, no. 1 (Mar. 2008), pp. 43–53

Petter, Martin, '"Temporary gentlemen" in the aftermath of the Great War: Rank, status and the ex-officer problem', *Historical Journal*, vol. 37, no. 1 (Mar. 1994), pp. 127–52

Phillips, W. Alison, *The Revolution in Ireland, 1906–1923*, 2nd ed. (London, 1926; 1st ed., 1923)

Portelli, Alessandro, 'Oral History in Italy' in D.K. Dunaway and W.K. Baum (eds), *Oral History: An Interdisciplinary Anthology* (Walnut Creek, Ca., 1996)

Potter, Simon, 'Empire and the English Press, c. 1857–1914', in Simon Potter (ed.), *Newspapers and Empire in Ireland and Britain: Reporting the British Empire, c. 1857–1921* (Dublin, 2004), pp. 39–61

Potter, Simon (ed.), *Newspapers and Empire in Ireland and Britain: Reporting the British Empire, c. 1857–1921* (Dublin, 2004)

Pugh, James, *The Royal Flying Corps, the Western Front and Control of the Air, 1914–1918* (Abingdon, 2017)

Pugh, Martin, *The Tories and the People, 1880–1935* (Oxford, 1985)

— *We Danced All Night: A Social History of England Between the Wars* (London, 2009)

Puntis, Peter, 'International news agencies, news-flow, and the USA-Australia relationship from the 1920s until the end of the Second World War', *Media History* 18:3–4 (2012), pp. 423–41.

Raugh, H.E., *The Victorians at War, 1815–1914: An Encyclopedia of British Military History* (Santa Barbara, 2004)

Regan, J.M., "'All the Nightmare Images of Ethnic Conflict in the Twentieth Century are Here":
    Erroneous Statistical Proofs and the Search for Ethnic Violence in Revolutionary Ireland,
    1917–1923', *Nations and Nationalism* (2021), pp. 1–19

— 'The Kilmichael Ambush and the Outer Limits of Irish Historical Revisionism', *History Ireland*,
    iss. 6, vol. 28 (Nov./Dec. 2020) (https://www.historyireland.com/volume-28/the-kilmichael-
    ambush-and-the-outer-limits-of-irish-historical-revisionism/, accessed 17 Dec. 2021)

— *Myth and the Irish State: Historical Problems and Other Essays* (Sallins, 2013)

— *The Irish Counter-Revolution 1921–1936* (Dublin, 1999)

Rigney, Peter, *The Irish Munitions Embargo of 1920: How Railwaymen and Dockers Defied an
    Empire* (Dublin, 2021)

Robinson, Michael, "'Nobody's children?": The Ministry of Pensions and the treatment of
    disabled Great War veterans in the Irish Free State, 1921–1939', *Irish Studies Review* 25:3
    (2017), pp. 316–35

Rouse, Paul, *Sport and Ireland: A History* (Oxford, 2015)

Rowland, Peter, *Lloyd George* (London, 1975)

Ruane, Joseph, 'Pluralism and Silence: Protestants and Catholics in the Republic of Ireland' in
    Diarmuid Ó Giolláin (ed.), *Irish Ethnologies* (Notre Dame, 2017), pp. 90–110

Ryan, Meda, *The Tom Barry Story* (Cork, 1982)

— *Liam Lynch: The Real Chief* (Cork, 1986)

— *Tom Barry, IRA Freedom Fighter* (Cork, 2003; pbk, 2005; 2nd ed., 2012)

— 'The Kilmichael Ambush, 1920: Exploring the "Provocative Chapters"', *History*, vol. 92, no. 2
    (306) (Apr. 2007), pp. 235–49

Scannell, James, 'DMP casualties during the War of Independence', *Dublin Historical Record* vol.
    61, no. 1 (Spring 2008), pp. 5–19

Schrager, Samuel, 'What is social in oral history?', in R. Perks and A. Thomson (eds), *The Oral
    History Reader* (London 1998),, pp. 284–99

Scott, George, *Reporter Anonymous: The Story of the Press Association* (London, 1968)

Searle, G.R., *A New England? Peace and War 1886–1918* (Oxford, 2004)

Seward, Paul and Paul Silk, 'The House of Commons', in Vernon Bogdanor (ed.), *The British
    Constitution in the Twentieth Century* (Oxford, 2014), pp. 139–87

Silberstein-Loeb, Jonathan, *The International Distribution of News: The Associated Press, Press
    Association, and Reuters, 1848–1947* (Cambridge, 2014)

Simkins, Peter, G. Jukes and M. Hickey, *The First World War: The War to End All Wars* (Oxford,
    2003)

Sinn Féin Publicity Department, *The Good Old IRA* (Dublin, 1985)

Smith, Jeremy, *The Tories and Ireland: Conservative Party politics and the Home Rule Crisis,
    1910–1914* (Dublin, 2000)

Smyth, Jim (ed.), *Remembering the Troubles: Contesting the Recent Past in Northern Ireland*
    (Notre Dame, 2017)

Spiers, Edward M., 'The Regular Army', in I. Beckett and K. Simpson (eds), *A Nation in Arms:
    The British Army in the First World War* (Barnsley, 2014), pp. 44–6

Spiritan Mission Resources and Heritage Centre, *Glowing Embers* (Dublin, 2016)

Stanton, Helen, *For Peace and for Good: A History of the European Province of the Community of St Francis* (London, 2017)

Street, O. [C.J.C.], *The Administration of Ireland, 1920* (London, 1921)

Tanović, Sabina, *Designing Memory: The Architecture of Commemoration in Europe, 1914 to the Present* (Cambridge, 2019)

Taylor, Paul, *Heroes or Traitors? Experiences of Southern Irish Soldiers Returning from the Great War 1919–1939* (Liverpool, 2015)

Thompson, Paul, *The Voice of the Past: Oral History* (Oxford, 2000)

Thomson, Alastair, *Anzac Memories: Living with the Legend* (Melbourne; Oxford, 1994)

— 'Memory as a battlefield: Personal and political investments in the national military past', *Oral History Review* 22/2 (Winter 1995), pp. 55–73

Thwaites, Peter, 'Circles of confusion and sharp vision: British news photography, 1919–39', in P. Catterall, C. Seymour-Ure and A. Smith (eds), *Northcliffe's Legacy: Aspects of the British Popular Press, 1896–1996* (London, 2000), pp. 97–120

Townshend, Charles, *The British Campaign in Ireland, 1919–1921: The Development of Political and Military Policies* (Oxford, 1975)

— 'Reviewed Works: *From Public Defiance to Guerrilla Warfare: The Experience of Ordinary Volunteers in the Irish War of Independence, 1916–1921* by Joost Augusteijn and *The IRA in the Twilight Years, 1923–1948* by Uinseann MacEoin', *Saothar* 22 (1997), p. 107

— *Easter 1916: The Irish Rebellion* (London, 2005)

— 'Force, law, and the Irish revolution', in Senia Pašeta (ed.), *Uncertain Futures: Essays about the Irish Past for Roy Foster* (Oxford, 2016), pp. 161–73

— *The Republic: The Fight for Irish Independence 1918–1923* (London, 2013)

— *The Partition: Ireland Divided, 1885–1925* (London, 2021)

Travers, Pauric, 'Review', *IHS*, vol. 31, iss. 122 (Nov. 1998), pp. 292–5

Twomey, Carrie, 'Nameless, Faceless, an apology to our readers', 2 June 2003 (http://indiamond6.ulib.iupui.edu:81/otooledeception.html, accessed 17 Dec. 2021)

US Infantry Association, *Bayonet Training Manual used by British Forces* (New York, 1917)

Unqoed-Thomas, Jasper, *Jasper Wolfe of Skibbereen* (Cork, 2008)

Urquhart, Diane, '"An articulate and definite cry for political freedom": The Ulster suffrage movement', *Women's History Review* 11:2 (2002), pp. 273–92

Walsh, Maurice, *The News from Ireland: Foreign Correspondents and the Irish Revolution* (London, 2008)

Weeks, Liam and Micheál Ó Fathartaigh (eds), *The Treaty: Debating and Establishing the Irish State* (Dublin, 2018)

Whitaker, Robin, 'Writing as a Citizen? Some thoughts on the use of dilemmas', *Critique of Anthropology*, vol. 28 (3), pp. 321–38

White, Alex, 'Section 31: Ministerial Orders and Court Challenges', in M. Corcoran and M. O'Brien (eds), *Political Censorship and the Democratic State: The Irish Broadcasting Ban* (Dublin, 2005), pp. 34–47

White, Gerry, *The Burning of Cork* (Dublin and Cork, 2006)

White, Timothy J. (ed.), *Lessons from the Northern Ireland Peace Process* (Madison, 2013)

Whyte, Louis, *The Wild Heather Glen: The Kilmichael Story of Grief and Glory* (Ballincollig, 1995)

Wickham Steed, Henry, *Through Thirty Years, 1892–1922: A Personal Narrative: Vol II* (London, 1924)

Woods, Christopher, *Bodenstown Revisited: The Grave of Theobold Wolfe Tone* (Dublin, 2018)

Wood, Don, 'Protestant Population Decline in Southern Ireland, 1911–1926', in Brian Hughes and Conor Morrissey (eds), *Southern Irish Loyalism, 1912–1949* (Liverpool, 2020), pp. 27–48

Worley, Matthew, *Labour Inside the Gate: A History of the British Labour Party Between the Wars* (London, 2005)

Wyndham, A.H. (ed.), *Re-imagining Ireland* (Charlottesville, 2006)

Yeates, Padraig, '"Have you in Ireland all gone mad" – the 1918 general strike against conscription' (www.academia.edu/40145125/HAVE_YOU_IN_IRELAND_ALL_GONE_MAD, accessed 21 Apr. 2021)

Young, Peter, 'Military Archives in the Defence Forces', *An Cosantóir* (Sept. 1977), pp. 274–5

— 'Military Archives – the first year', *An Cosantóir* (Oct. 1983), p. 337

Theses

Curtis, Catriona Lisa, 'The Agricultural Labourer and the State in Independent Ireland, 1922–26' (PhD thesis, NUI Maynooth, 2007)

Hart, Peter, 'The Irish Republican Army and its Enemies: Violence and Community in County Cork, 1917–1923' (PhD thesis, Trinity College Dublin, 1992)

Journals, Magazines and Gazettes

An Cosantóir

An t-Óglacht

An Phoblacht

Blackrock College Annual 2015

British Medical Journal

Catholic Press

Dublin Review of Books

Éire Ireland

Études Irlandais

Field Day Review

Guy's Cork Almanac

The Hampshire Regiment Journal

Hart's Army List

History Ireland

Historical Journal
Illustrated London News
Iris Oifigúil
Irish Bulletin
Irish Economic and Social History
Irish Historical Studies (IHS)
Irish Jurist
Ireland's Own
Journal of the Old Athlone Society
Newspaper Press Directory
The Round Table
The Stage and Television Today
Thom's Directory
Wolfe Tone Weekly

Online Sources

archives.history.ac.uk
http://centenaries-ituc.nationalarchives.ie/annual-reports/
http://maps.nls.uk
https://repository.dri.ie/catalog/t148v311v (Dáil Éireann records)
http://spinwatch.org [no longer available]
http://theirishrevolution.ie/cork-fatality-register
independentleft.ie
www.1914-1918-online.net/
www.ancestry.com
www.bac-lac.gc.ca/eng/Pages/home.aspx
www.britishpathe.com
www.cairogang.com
www.cwgc.org
www.indymedia.ie
www.irishstatutebook.ie
www.orwellfoundation.com
www.princevellar.co.uk
www.rollingstone.com
www.royalirishconstabulary.com
www.scotlandspeople.gov.uk
www.sluggerotoole.com
www.theauxiliaries.com
www.thegazette.co.uk [London Gazette]
www.westernfrontassociation.com/ancestry-pension-records
www.youtube.com

Author Interviews and Communications

Brendan Bradshaw, 9 Oct. 2012

Eddie Cassidy, 2 Apr. 2013

Liam Chambers, 17 Aug. 2013

Dave Crowley, 14 Feb. 2013

Liam Deasy (nephew), 27 July 2012

John McAnulty, 1 Mar. 2020

Kathleen McCaul (*née* Deasy), 15 Jan. 2015

David Miller, 29 Aug. 2012

Marion O'Driscoll, 3 Oct. 2012

Gearóid Ó Tuathaigh, 29 Nov. 2012

Don Wood, unpublished notes, 27 Feb. 2014

Index